PROPOSITION player

♠ ♦ ♣ ♡ ♠ ♦ ♣ ♡ Bill Willingham **Writer**   Paul Guinan & Bill Willingham **Pencillers**

♣ ♡ Ron Randall & Bill Willingham **Inkers**   James Sinclair **Colorist**

♥ John Costanza **Letterer**   John Bolton **Original Series Cover Painter**

♥ ♣ ♦ ♣ ♡ PROPOSITION PLAYER created by Bill Willingham

PROPOSITION PLAYER Published by DC Comics. Cover, introduction,
and compilation copyright © 2003 DC Comics. All Rights Reserved.
Originally published in single magazine form as PROPOSITION PLAYER
1-6. Copyright © 1999, 2000 Bill Willingham. All Rights Reserved. All
characters, their distinctive likenesses and related indicia featured
in this publication are trademarks of Bill Willingham. VERTIGO is a
trademark of DC Comics. The stories, characters and incidents
featured in this publication are entirely fictional. DC Comics does not
read or accept unsolicited submissions of ideas, stories or artwork.
DC Comics, 1700 Broadway, New York, NY 10019
A Warner Bros. Entertainment Company
Printed in Canada. First Printing.
ISBN: 1-56389-808-X
Cover illustration by Bill Willingham.
Cover color by James Sinclair.
Publication design by Louis Prandi.

This one is dedicated to Las Vegas
poker dealer Brad Thomte, who
dealt in the World Series of Poker
this year and whose beard is
more brown than blue.

— Bill Willingham

Introduction by James McManus

Bill Willingham and Paul Guinan's PROPOSITION
PLAYER is an intriguing extension of both the art
and the literature of poker, America's — and
increasingly the world's — favorite card game. Pen
and ink, cards and money have naturally gone
together for as long as we've played games, drawn
pictures, and written down stories. When the
Chinese invented paper around 200 B.C., in fact,
the first uses they found for it were as writing and
drawing materials, money, and playing cards.
All four applications spread along trade routes,
especially to places where divination and gambling with straws, beads, and pebbles (called
"lots," as in "lottery") were already common. Since
card games could be made more complex than
the casting of lots, they tended to appeal to more
literate cultures. Once priests, scribes, and warriors
took up cards, they were further disseminated,
along with the means to produce them, via con-
quest. The earliest cards in the Islamic world were
oblong, with decks subdivided into as many as ten
suits. Christian crusaders and Venetian merchants
brought cards back to Europe, where Spaniards
and Italians began playing with forty-card decks,
and Germans made do for a while with thirty-six.
By the early fourteenth century, Persians had
developed a deck of fifty-two cards arranged in
four suits, each with ten numerical ranks and three
hand-painted court cards. The suits were Coins,
Cups, Swords, and Polo Sticks, emblematic of the

officers providing a sultan's court with money, food and drink, military protection, and sporting entertainment. Renaissance Venetians kept separate apartments, called *casini*, in which to play *faro* and consort with *cortigiani onesti*, those well educated "honest" courtesans fêted as symbols of Venice's splendor and liberal values. Outsized Venetian *casini*, including a pixilated $2 billion facsimile of the city itself, now dominate the landscape of the planet's preferred adult playground: Las Vegas.

The cards dealt in modern casinos have always represented the strata into which societies arrange themselves. A report from 1377, for example, has many Swiss decks with the sun at the top of the hierarchy, followed in descending order by the king, queen, knight, lady, valet, and maid. In another popular deck, the order was snarling lions, haughty kings and their ravishing ladies, soldiers in breastplates and helmets, then bare-breasted dancing girls. On Florentine decks of this era, most of the women were naked.

By 1470, French card makers in Rouen had settled on the four suits with which we're familiar today. The church was represented by hearts, the state by spades, merchants by diamonds, farmers by clubs (which resembled more and more the clover they harvested). Earlier cards had been expensively hand-painted for the actual king and his court, but widespread demand among common folk soon led to mass production of uniform decks using woodcuts and stencils, anticipating the offset printing that brought the comic books' bright colors to readers in the 20th century.

The modern poker deck continues to provide clear expression of erotic, theological, and military politics. Like towering alpha spires, sex-neutral aces dominate the tabletop cosmos. Kings, just below them, outrank their consorts, who in turn outrank the young male soldiers who protect them, who outrank the dancing girls, valets, maids, sevens, sixes, etc. In addition to gender-based status markers, we can follow a seniority-based progression up the social ladder — the idea that white-bearded kings used to be clean-jawed soldiers, or that queens had spent time promenading with uncovered bosoms. Even the more abstract numbered cards can signify social arrangements. Some historians argue that the ace, or one, for example, made its counternumerical switch from lowest to highest rank during the American and French revolutions, when it suddenly became possible for the merest commoner to become emperor, prime minister, or president. These days the ace represents

whatever intangible force (such as God, Allah, aleph, I, the Arabic number one, or what physicists call a singularity) can overcome the most august human being. Harvard sociobiologist Edward O. Wilson has shown that in complex societies, culture and religion have always combined to determine status. "Power belonged to kings by divine right, but high priests often ruled over kings by virtue of the higher ranks of the gods." Magic and totemism occur almost universally in human societies, for deep biological reasons. Rituals such as cardplaying, says Wilson, "celebrate the creation myths, propitiate the gods, and resanctify the tribal moral codes." When we play cards and abide by the rules, surrendering without comment or resistance a massive pot to the tiny old woman holding jacks to our tens, we "resanctify" these ancient hierarchies. We also can make them ironic.

The earliest versions of poker seem to have derived from the Persian game *As Nas*, or a French version, known as *poque*. French soldiers brought *poque* to New Orleans around 1820, when it was played with a twenty-card deck. After a shuffle, five-card hands were dealt facedown to four players, who proceeded to bet on the relative strength of their cards. Without straights or flushes — let alone straight flushes — four aces, or four kings with an ace, were the only unbeatable hands. But even if you held no pair at all, the look in your eye combined with the size of your wager could force players holding much stronger hands to relinquish the pot, a tactic that seemed very much in the spirit of our fledgling market democracy.

As *poque* spread north on Mississippi riverboats, more and more folks wanted in on the newfangled chancing. The southern pronunciation was "pokuh," which, as the game migrated north and east, became "poker." The rules changed as well. The fifty-two-card deck was incorporated around 1837 to accommodate up to ten players and make for more lucrative pots. Flushes and straights were introduced, as was the option to draw three new cards. Fortunes in land, fur, gold, cotton, and tobacco changed hands on the turn of one card, or a bluff — who knew which?

In addition to gorgeously hand-painted court cards, the gambling tradition has given us visual masterpieces of the caliber of Cézanne's *Cardplayers*, Cubist variations on that theme by Picasso and Braque, Alexander Calder's *As de pique (Ace of Spades)*, and more recent gestural drawings by the American painter Donald Sultan. Even *Dogs Playing Poker* has taken its place in the pantheon of comic Americana.

In the literary realm, we've read of human lives altered irrevocably at the gaming tables in Homer, in Dante, in Shakespeare. Alexander Pushkin's "The Queen of Spades" continues this tradition, as do several famous chapters of Tolstoy's *War and Peace*, not to mention Dostoevsky's *The Gambler*. Poker is at the heart of such twentieth-century American novels as Richard Jessup's *The Cincinnati Kid*, Jesse May's *Shut Up and Deal*, Bruce Olds's *Bucking the Tiger*, as well as *American Buffalo*, David Mamet's wickedly hilarious play about small-time burglars and cardsharps. The classic nonfiction accounts of the game include Herbert O. Yardley's *The Education of a Poker Player*, A. Alvarez's *The Biggest Game in Town*, former world poker champion Bobby Baldwin's *Tales Out of Tulsa*, Anthony Holden's *Big Deal*, and, more recently, Katy Lederer's *Poker Face*.

Out of all these traditions comes Joey Martin, a low-stakes proposition player at Thunder Road, a fictional Vegas casino. Props are paid a small salary to fill out the tables until more well-heeled customers arrive, at which point the prop must find other ways of passing the time. As Willingham's tale gets under way, we find Joey spending his time plotting ways to increase his all-important bankroll and dreaming of the day that he can quit Thunder Road and start playing in some real, high-stakes games — a plan that isn't helped by an unexpected (and costly) series of wagers that leaves him in possession of thirty-two souls from the casino's bar. Besides being cheap, Joey's also something of a cad, as he demonstrates by kicking his girlfriend and co-worker Lacy out of bed once they'd finished their "business" that night.

Rude though he may be, Joey soon has bigger things to worry about — things that arrive in the form of a nine-foot-tall bully and a shapely green-eyed temptress, both determined to lay claim to the souls that Joey has recently acquired. As the pressure from these supernatural agents builds, Joey will need every scrap of poker-learned skill that he's got just to survive this new and deadly game in which he's landed.

Drawn with verve and precision, PROPOSITION PLAYER may remind older readers of Bobby Baldwin's rise from Oklahoma road gambler in the 1970s to the presidency of the Bellagio, the poshest resort in Las Vegas and the unrivaled capital of poker. It's also a worthy successor to even the most astonishing of Baldwin's own *Tales Out of Tulsa*. Whatever their age, whatever their level of innocence, readers of this story are likely to find their unruliest guilt and desire tweaked to the point of steep vertigo.

James McManus is the author of seven books of fiction and poetry, as well as of Positively Fifth Street: Murderers, Cheetahs, and Binion's World Series of Poker. *His work has appeared in* Harper's, The New York Times, The Boston Globe, Paris Review, The Best American Poetry, The Best American Sports Writing, *and* The Good Parts: The Best Erotic Writing in Modern Fiction. *He teaches at the School of the Art Institute of Chicago.*

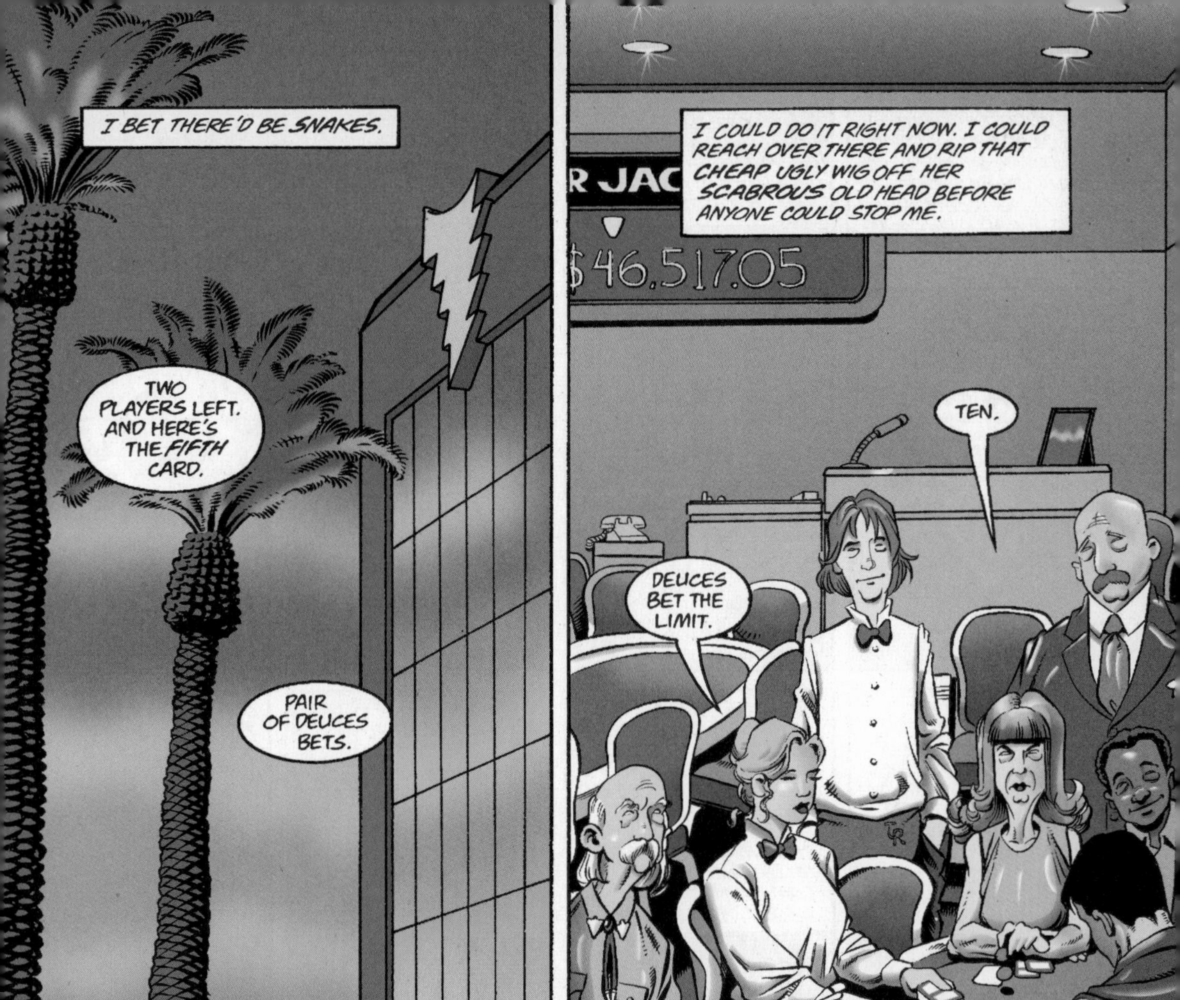
I BET THERE'D BE SNAKES.
TWO PLAYERS LEFT. AND HERE'S THE FIFTH CARD.
PAIR OF DEUCES BETS.
THUNDER ROAD CASINO
I COULD DO IT RIGHT NOW. I COULD REACH OVER THERE AND RIP THAT CHEAP UGLY WIG OFF HER SCABROUS OLD HEAD BEFORE ANYONE COULD STOP ME.
R JAC
$46,517.05
TEN.
DEUCES BET THE LIMIT.
CALL.
LAST UP CARD.
STILL ON THE DEUCES.

A NEW PLAYER
Or The Truth About CAT and DOG Owners!

created ,written and inked by: BILL WILLINGHAM
pencilled by: BILL WILLINGHAM (Pgs 1-8 / 18 & 22) and PAUL GUINAN (Pgs 9-17 / 19-21)
lettered by: JOHN COSTANZA
colors by: JAMES SINCLAIR
color separations by: JAMISON
cover art by: JOHN BOLTON
assistant editor: JENNIFER LEE
edited by: SHELLY ROEBERG

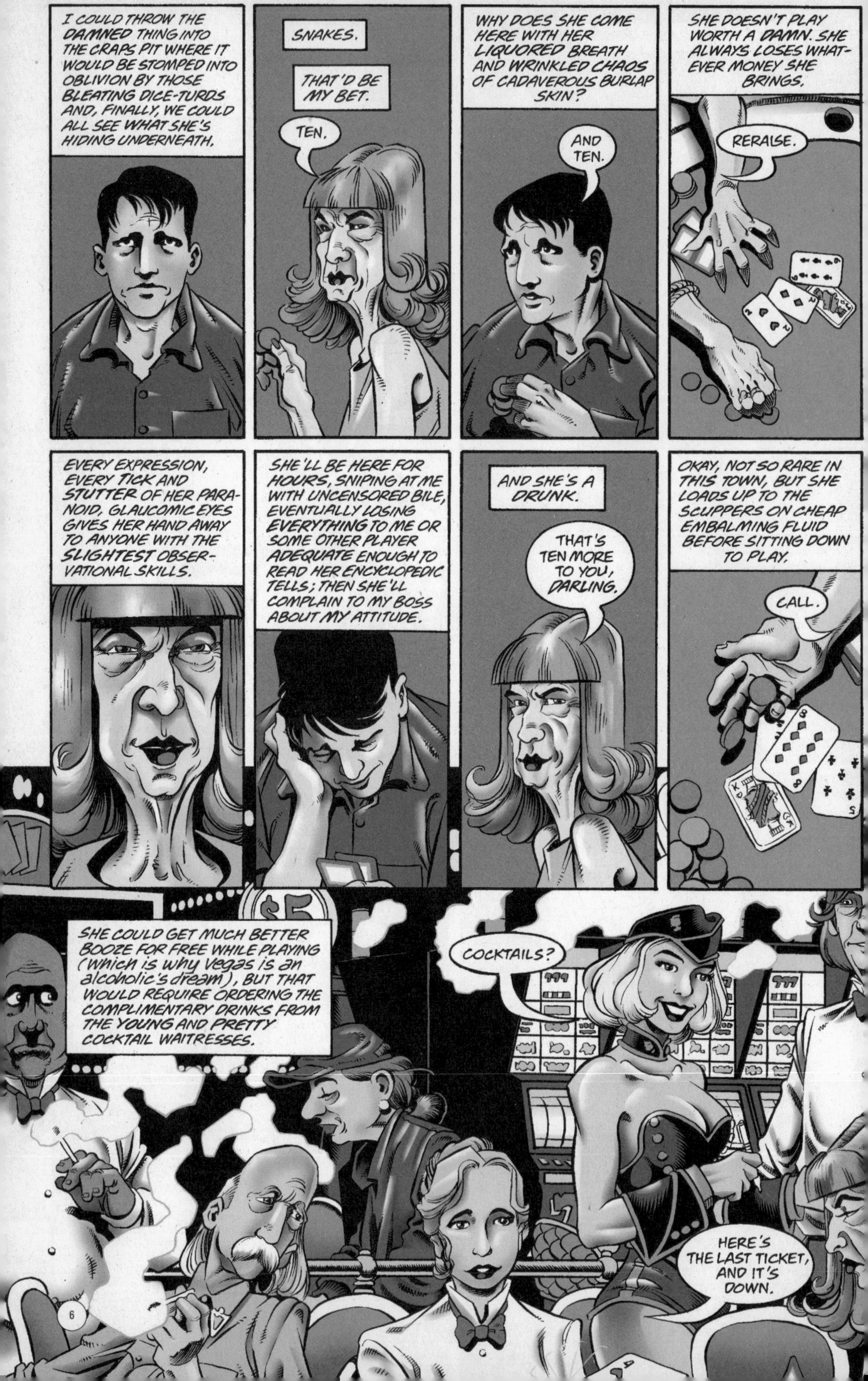

I COULD THROW THE DAMNED THING INTO THE CRAPS PIT WHERE IT WOULD BE STOMPED INTO OBLIVION BY THOSE BLEATING DICE-TURDS AND, FINALLY, WE COULD ALL SEE WHAT SHE'S HIDING UNDERNEATH.
SNAKES.
THAT'D BE MY BET.
TEN.
WHY DOES SHE COME HERE WITH HER LIQUORED BREATH AND WRINKLED CHAOS OF CADAVEROUS BURLAP SKIN?
AND TEN.
SHE DOESN'T PLAY WORTH A DAMN. SHE ALWAYS LOSES WHAT-EVER MONEY SHE BRINGS.
RERAISE.
EVERY EXPRESSION, EVERY TICK AND STUTTER OF HER PARA-NOID, GLAUCOMIC EYES GIVES HER HAND AWAY TO ANYONE WITH THE SLIGHTEST OBSER-VATIONAL SKILLS.
SHE'LL BE HERE FOR HOURS, SNIPING AT ME WITH UNCENSORED BILE, EVENTUALLY LOSING EVERYTHING TO ME OR SOME OTHER PLAYER ADEQUATE ENOUGH TO READ HER ENCYCLOPEDIC TELLS; THEN SHE'LL COMPLAIN TO MY BOSS ABOUT MY ATTITUDE.
AND SHE'S A DRUNK.
THAT'S TEN MORE TO YOU, DARLING.
OKAY, NOT SO RARE IN THIS TOWN, BUT SHE LOADS UP TO THE SCUPPERS ON CHEAP EMBALMING FLUID BEFORE SITTING DOWN TO PLAY.
CALL.
SHE COULD GET MUCH BETTER BOOZE FOR FREE WHILE PLAYING (which is why Vegas is an alcoholic's dream), BUT THAT WOULD REQUIRE ORDERING THE COMPLIMENTARY DRINKS FROM THE YOUNG AND PRETTY COCKTAIL WAITRESSES.
COCKTAILS?
HERE'S THE LAST TICKET, AND IT'S DOWN.

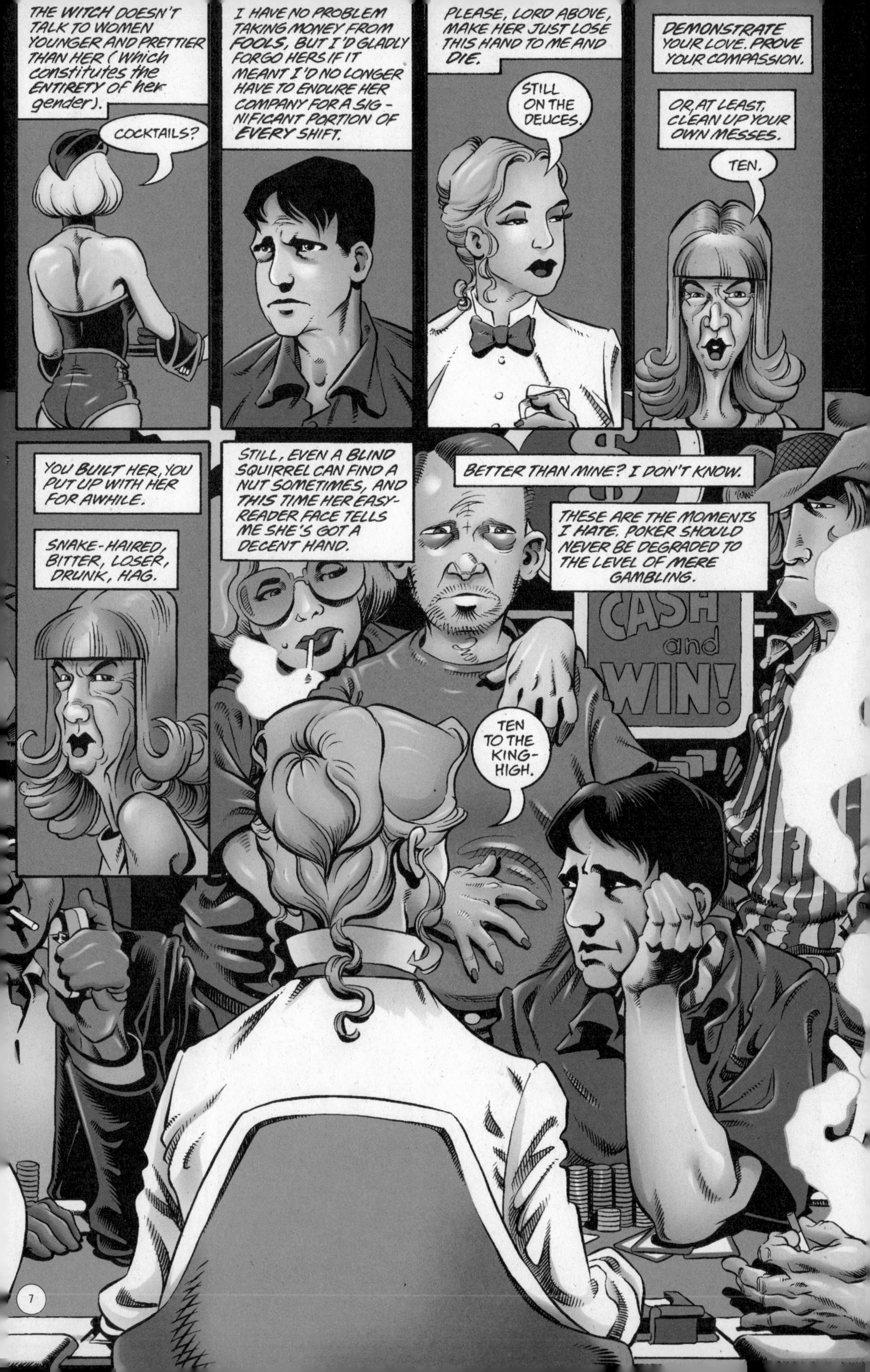
THE WITCH DOESN'T TALK TO WOMEN YOUNGER AND PRETTIER THAN HER (which constitutes the ENTIRETY of her gender).
COCKTAILS?
I HAVE NO PROBLEM TAKING MONEY FROM FOOLS, BUT I'D GLADLY FORGO HERS IF IT MEANT I'D NO LONGER HAVE TO ENDURE HER COMPANY FOR A SIGNIFICANT PORTION OF EVERY SHIFT.
PLEASE, LORD ABOVE, MAKE HER JUST LOSE THIS HAND TO ME AND DIE.
STILL ON THE DEUCES.
DEMONSTRATE YOUR LOVE. PROVE YOUR COMPASSION.
OR, AT LEAST, CLEAN UP YOUR OWN MESSES.
TEN.
YOU BUILT HER, YOU PUT UP WITH HER FOR AWHILE.
SNAKE-HAIRED, BITTER, LOSER, DRUNK, HAG.
STILL, EVEN A BLIND SQUIRREL CAN FIND A NUT SOMETIMES, AND THIS TIME HER EASY-READER FACE TELLS ME SHE'S GOT A DECENT HAND.
BETTER THAN MINE? I DON'T KNOW.
THESE ARE THE MOMENTS I HATE. POKER SHOULD NEVER BE DEGRADED TO THE LEVEL OF MERE GAMBLING.
CASH and WIN!
TEN TO THE KING-HIGH.

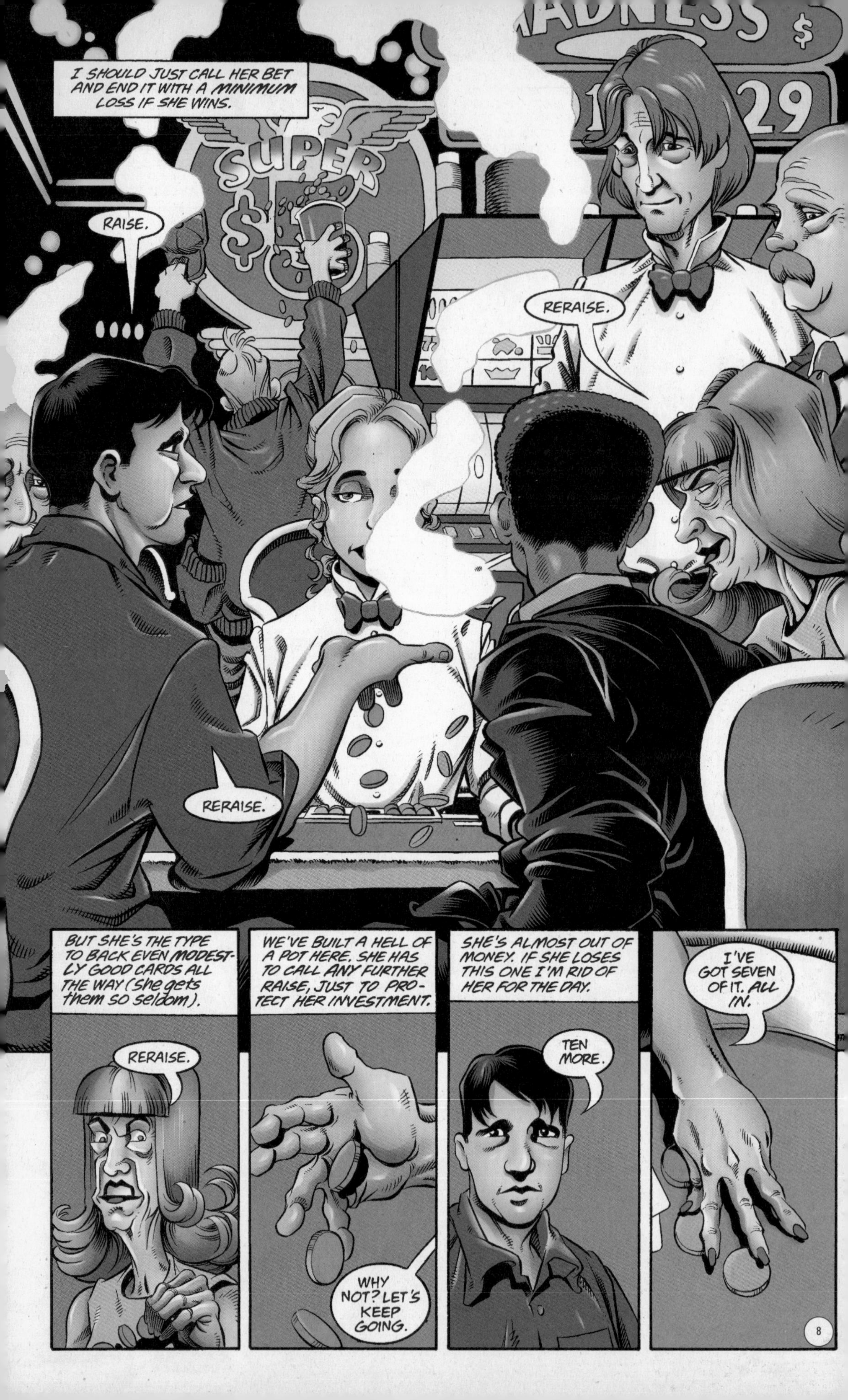

I SHOULD JUST CALL HER BET AND END IT WITH A MINIMUM LOSS IF SHE WINS.
RAISE.
RERAISE.
RERAISE.
BUT SHE'S THE TYPE TO BACK EVEN MODESTLY GOOD CARDS ALL THE WAY (she gets them so seldom).
RERAISE.
WE'VE BUILT A HELL OF A POT HERE. SHE HAS TO CALL ANY FURTHER RAISE, JUST TO PROTECT HER INVESTMENT.
WHY NOT? LET'S KEEP GOING.
SHE'S ALMOST OUT OF MONEY. IF SHE LOSES THIS ONE I'M RID OF HER FOR THE DAY.
TEN MORE.
I'VE GOT SEVEN OF IT. ALL IN.

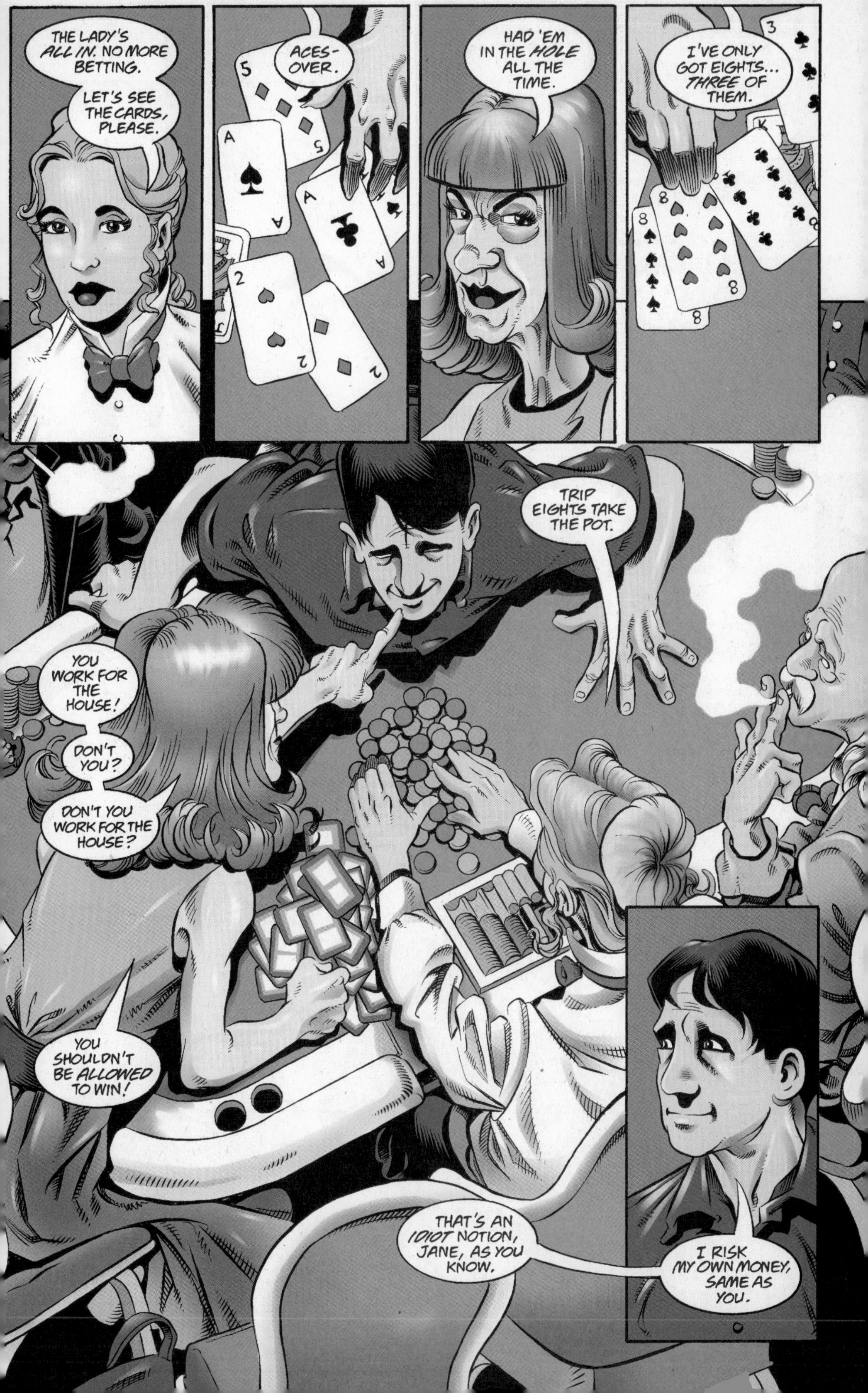
THE LADY'S ALL IN. NO MORE BETTING.
LET'S SEE THE CARDS, PLEASE.
ACES-OVER.
HAD 'EM IN THE HOLE ALL THE TIME.
I'VE ONLY GOT EIGHTS... THREE OF THEM.
TRIP EIGHTS TAKE THE POT.
YOU WORK FOR THE HOUSE!
DON'T YOU?
DON'T YOU WORK FOR THE HOUSE?
YOU SHOULDN'T BE ALLOWED TO WIN!
THAT'S AN IDIOT NOTION, JANE, AS YOU KNOW.
I RISK MY OWN MONEY, SAME AS YOU.

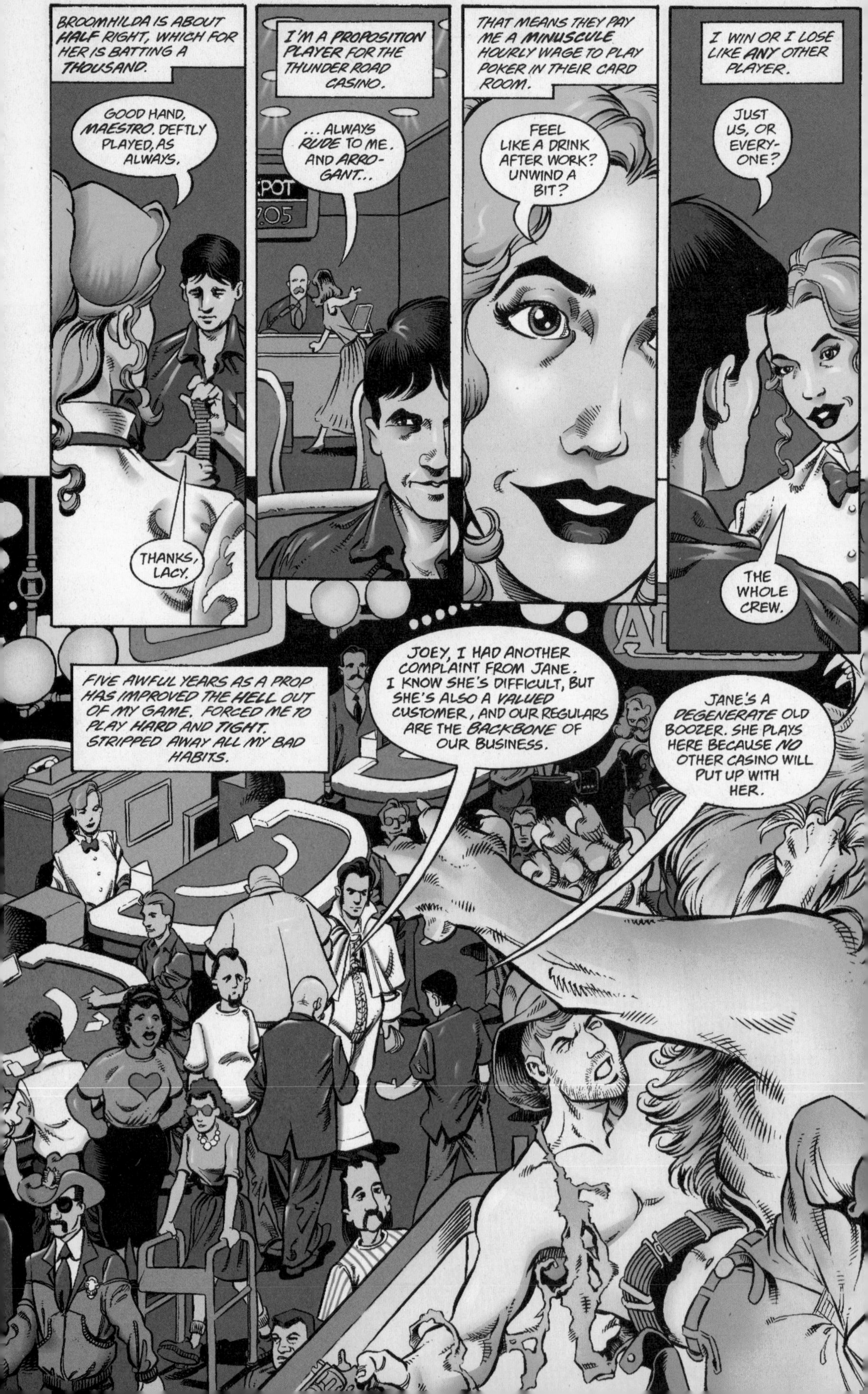
BROOMHILDA IS ABOUT HALF RIGHT, WHICH FOR HER IS BATTING A THOUSAND.
GOOD HAND, MAESTRO. DEFTLY PLAYED, AS ALWAYS.
THANKS, LACY.
I'M A PROPOSITION PLAYER FOR THE THUNDER ROAD CASINO.
...ALWAYS RUDE TO ME. AND ARRO-GANT...
THAT MEANS THEY PAY ME A MINUSCULE HOURLY WAGE TO PLAY POKER IN THEIR CARD ROOM.
FEEL LIKE A DRINK AFTER WORK? UNWIND A BIT?
I WIN OR I LOSE LIKE ANY OTHER PLAYER.
JUST US, OR EVERY-ONE?
THE WHOLE CREW.
FIVE AWFUL YEARS AS A PROP HAS IMPROVED THE HELL OUT OF MY GAME. FORCED ME TO PLAY HARD AND TIGHT. STRIPPED AWAY ALL MY BAD HABITS.
JOEY, I HAD ANOTHER COMPLAINT FROM JANE. I KNOW SHE'S DIFFICULT, BUT SHE'S ALSO A VALUED CUSTOMER, AND OUR REGULARS ARE THE BACKBONE OF OUR BUSINESS.
JANE'S A DEGENERATE OLD BOOZER. SHE PLAYS HERE BECAUSE NO OTHER CASINO WILL PUT UP WITH HER.

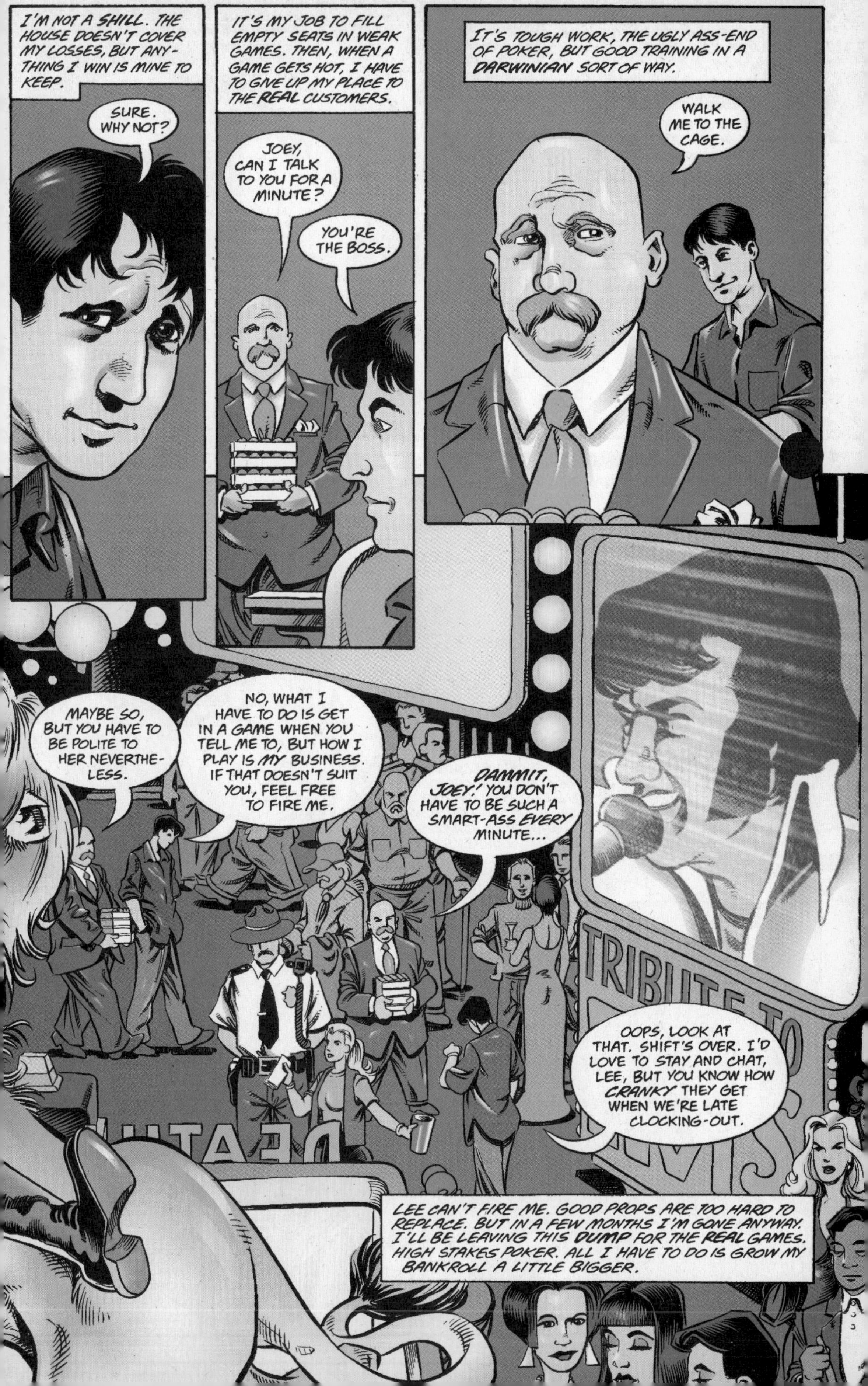

I'M NOT A SHILL. THE HOUSE DOESN'T COVER MY LOSSES, BUT ANYTHING I WIN IS MINE TO KEEP.
SURE. WHY NOT?
IT'S MY JOB TO FILL EMPTY SEATS IN WEAK GAMES. THEN, WHEN A GAME GETS HOT, I HAVE TO GIVE UP MY PLACE TO THE REAL CUSTOMERS.
JOEY, CAN I TALK TO YOU FOR A MINUTE?
YOU'RE THE BOSS.
IT'S TOUGH WORK, THE UGLY ASS-END OF POKER, BUT GOOD TRAINING IN A DARWINIAN SORT OF WAY.
WALK ME TO THE CAGE.
MAYBE SO, BUT YOU HAVE TO BE POLITE TO HER NEVERTHELESS.
NO, WHAT I HAVE TO DO IS GET IN A GAME WHEN YOU TELL ME TO, BUT HOW I PLAY IS MY BUSINESS. IF THAT DOESN'T SUIT YOU, FEEL FREE TO FIRE ME.
DAMMIT, JOEY! YOU DON'T HAVE TO BE SUCH A SMART-ASS EVERY MINUTE...
TRIBUTE TO
OOPS, LOOK AT THAT. SHIFT'S OVER. I'D LOVE TO STAY AND CHAT, LEE, BUT YOU KNOW HOW CRANKY THEY GET WHEN WE'RE LATE CLOCKING-OUT.
LEE CAN'T FIRE ME. GOOD PROPS ARE TOO HARD TO REPLACE. BUT IN A FEW MONTHS I'M GONE ANYWAY. I'LL BE LEAVING THIS DUMP FOR THE REAL GAMES. HIGH STAKES POKER. ALL I HAVE TO DO IS GROW MY BANKROLL A LITTLE BIGGER.

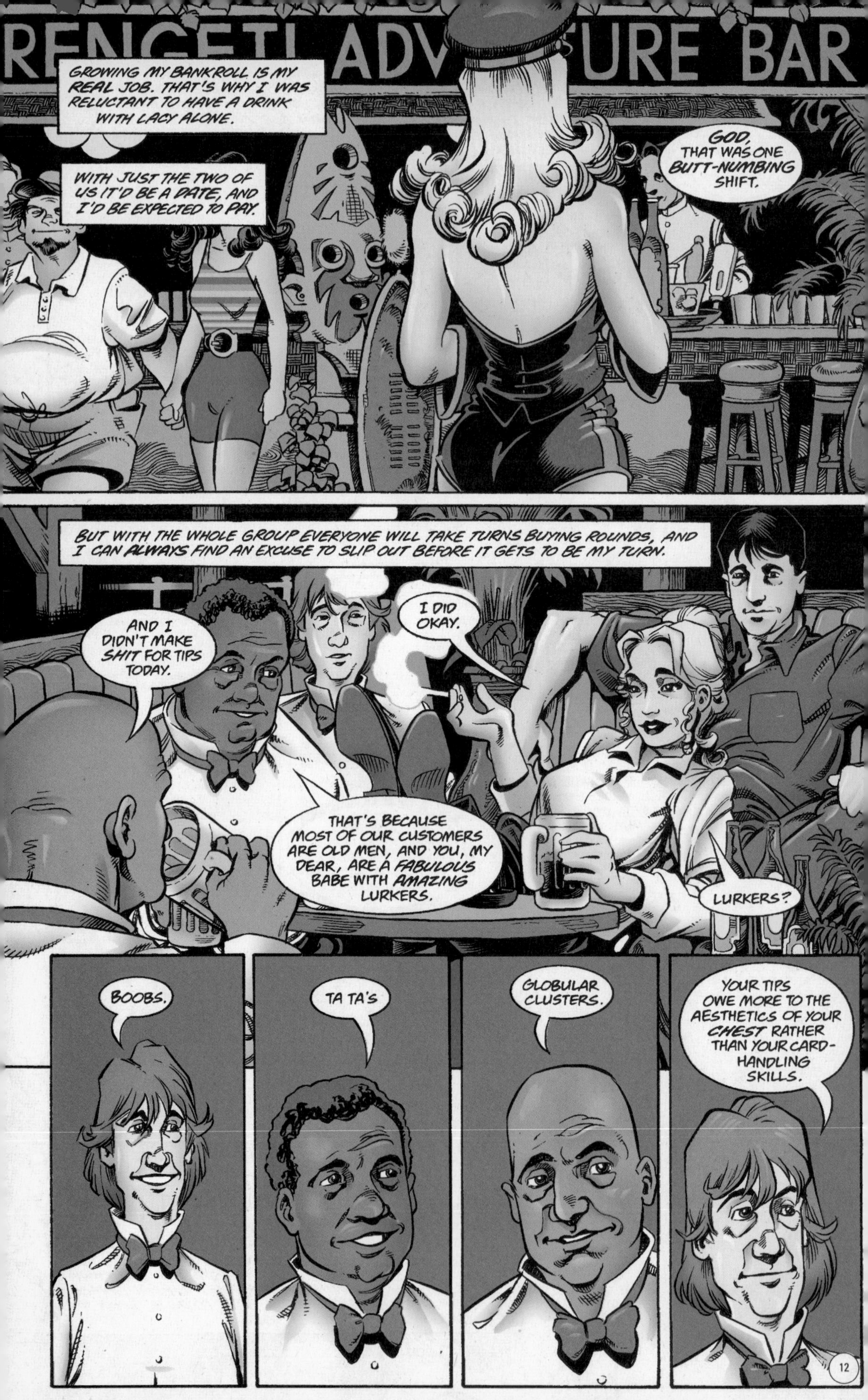

RENGETI ADV FURE BAR
GROWING MY BANKROLL IS MY REAL JOB. THAT'S WHY I WAS RELUCTANT TO HAVE A DRINK WITH LACY ALONE.
WITH JUST THE TWO OF US IT'D BE A DATE, AND I'D BE EXPECTED TO PAY.
GOD, THAT WAS ONE BUTT-NUMBING SHIFT.
BUT WITH THE WHOLE GROUP EVERYONE WILL TAKE TURNS BUYING ROUNDS, AND I CAN ALWAYS FIND AN EXCUSE TO SLIP OUT BEFORE IT GETS TO BE MY TURN.
AND I DIDN'T MAKE SHIT FOR TIPS TODAY.
I DID OKAY.
THAT'S BECAUSE MOST OF OUR CUSTOMERS ARE OLD MEN, AND YOU, MY DEAR, ARE A FABULOUS BABE WITH AMAZING LURKERS.
LURKERS?
BOOBS.
TA TA'S
GLOBULAR CLUSTERS.
YOUR TIPS OWE MORE TO THE AESTHETICS OF YOUR CHEST RATHER THAN YOUR CARD-HANDLING SKILLS.

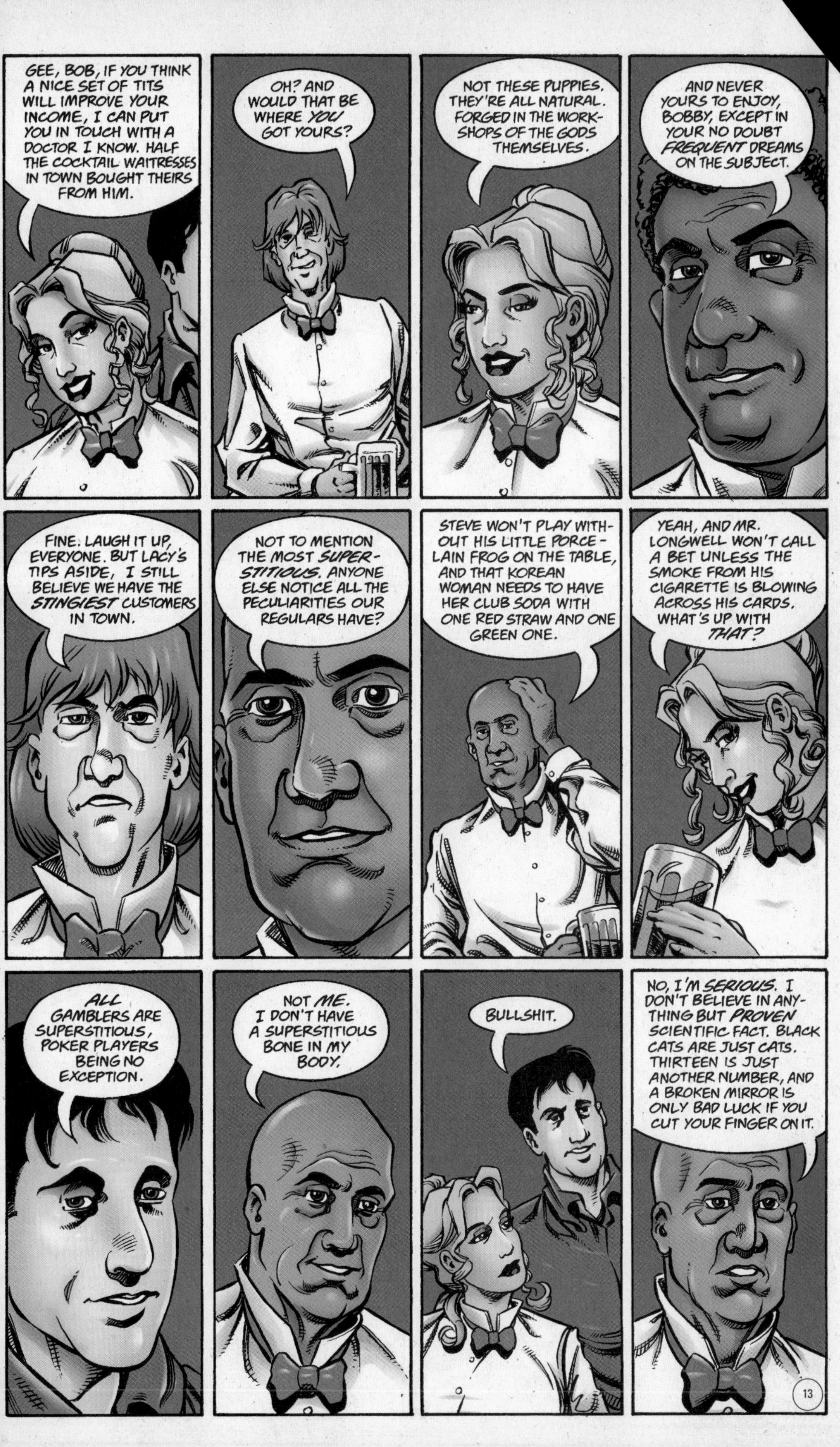
GEE, BOB, IF YOU THINK A NICE SET OF TITS WILL IMPROVE YOUR INCOME, I CAN PUT YOU IN TOUCH WITH A DOCTOR I KNOW. HALF THE COCKTAIL WAITRESSES IN TOWN BOUGHT THEIRS FROM HIM.
OH? AND WOULD THAT BE WHERE YOU GOT YOURS?
NOT THESE PUPPIES. THEY'RE ALL NATURAL. FORGED IN THE WORK-SHOPS OF THE GODS THEMSELVES.
AND NEVER YOURS TO ENJOY, BOBBY, EXCEPT IN YOUR NO DOUBT FREQUENT DREAMS ON THE SUBJECT.
FINE. LAUGH IT UP, EVERYONE. BUT LACY'S TIPS ASIDE, I STILL BELIEVE WE HAVE THE STINGIEST CUSTOMERS IN TOWN.
NOT TO MENTION THE MOST SUPER-STITIOUS. ANYONE ELSE NOTICE ALL THE PECULIARITIES OUR REGULARS HAVE?
STEVE WON'T PLAY WITH-OUT HIS LITTLE PORCE-LAIN FROG ON THE TABLE, AND THAT KOREAN WOMAN NEEDS TO HAVE HER CLUB SODA WITH ONE RED STRAW AND ONE GREEN ONE.
YEAH, AND MR. LONGWELL WON'T CALL A BET UNLESS THE SMOKE FROM HIS CIGARETTE IS BLOWING ACROSS HIS CARDS. WHAT'S UP WITH THAT?
ALL GAMBLERS ARE SUPERSTITIOUS, POKER PLAYERS BEING NO EXCEPTION.
NOT ME. I DON'T HAVE A SUPERSTITIOUS BONE IN MY BODY.
BULLSHIT.
NO, I'M SERIOUS. I DON'T BELIEVE IN ANY-THING BUT PROVEN SCIENTIFIC FACT. BLACK CATS ARE JUST CATS. THIRTEEN IS JUST ANOTHER NUMBER, AND A BROKEN MIRROR IS ONLY BAD LUCK IF YOU CUT YOUR FINGER ON IT.

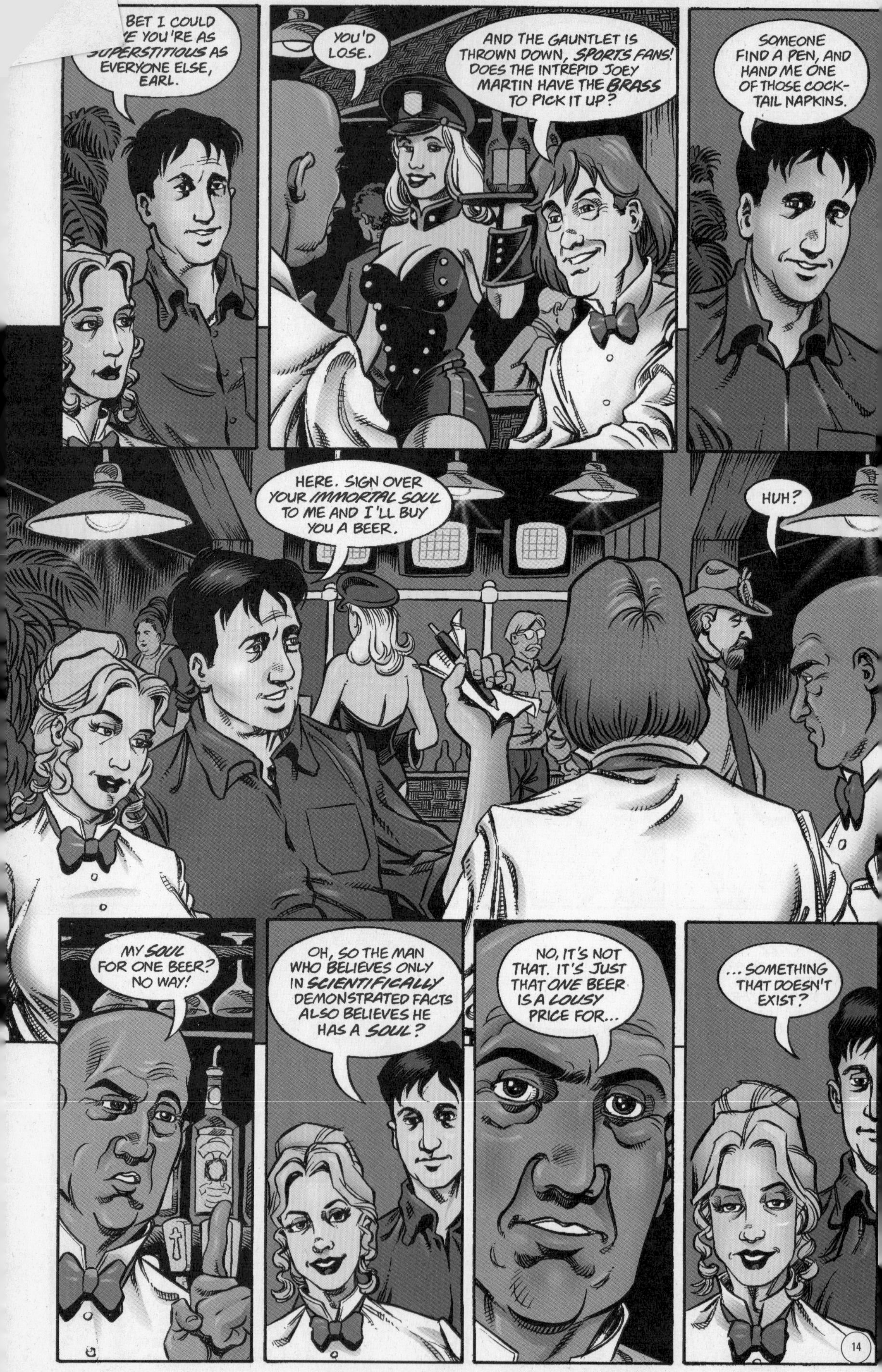
BET I COULD
E YOU'RE AS SUPERSTITIOUS AS EVERYONE ELSE, EARL.
YOU'D LOSE.
AND THE GAUNTLET IS THROWN DOWN, SPORTS FANS! DOES THE INTREPID JOEY MARTIN HAVE THE BRASS TO PICK IT UP?
SOMEONE FIND A PEN, AND HAND ME ONE OF THOSE COCKTAIL NAPKINS.
HERE. SIGN OVER YOUR IMMORTAL SOUL TO ME AND I'LL BUY YOU A BEER.
HUH?
MY SOUL FOR ONE BEER? NO WAY!
OH, SO THE MAN WHO BELIEVES ONLY IN SCIENTIFICALLY DEMONSTRATED FACTS ALSO BELIEVES HE HAS A SOUL?
NO, IT'S NOT THAT. IT'S JUST THAT ONE BEER IS A LOUSY PRICE FOR...
...SOMETHING THAT DOESN'T EXIST?

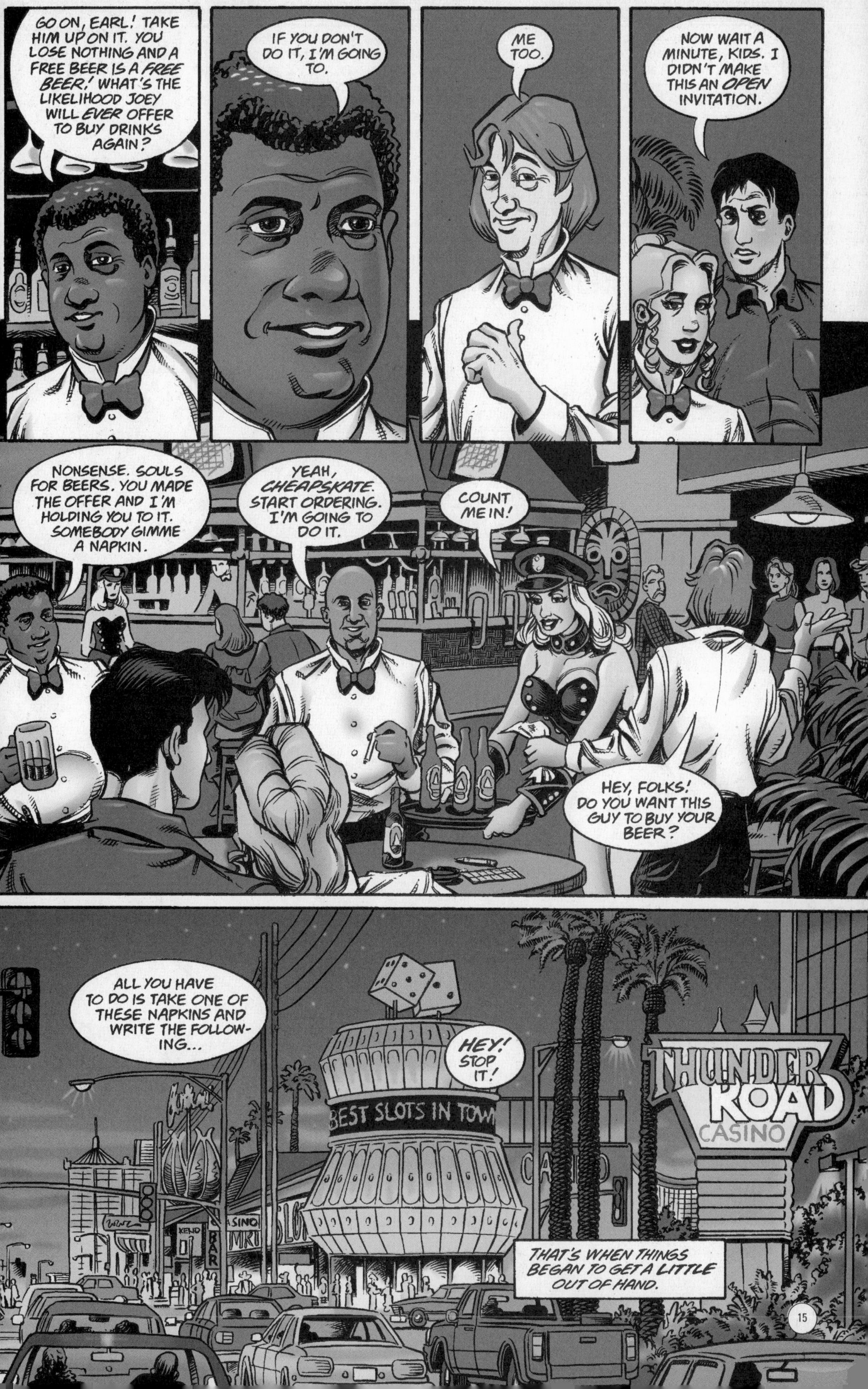
GO ON, EARL! TAKE HIM UP ON IT. YOU LOSE NOTHING AND A FREE BEER IS A FREE BEER! WHAT'S THE LIKELIHOOD JOEY WILL EVER OFFER TO BUY DRINKS AGAIN?
IF YOU DON'T DO IT, I'M GOING TO.
ME TOO.
NOW WAIT A MINUTE, KIDS. I DIDN'T MAKE THIS AN OPEN INVITATION.
NONSENSE. SOULS FOR BEERS. YOU MADE THE OFFER AND I'M HOLDING YOU TO IT. SOMEBODY GIMME A NAPKIN.
YEAH, CHEAPSKATE. START ORDERING. I'M GOING TO DO IT.
COUNT ME IN!
HEY, FOLKS! DO YOU WANT THIS GUY TO BUY YOUR BEER?
ALL YOU HAVE TO DO IS TAKE ONE OF THESE NAPKINS AND WRITE THE FOLLOW-ING...
HEY! STOP IT!
BEST SLOTS IN TOWN
THUNDER ROAD CASINO
THAT'S WHEN THINGS BEGAN TO GET A LITTLE OUT OF HAND.

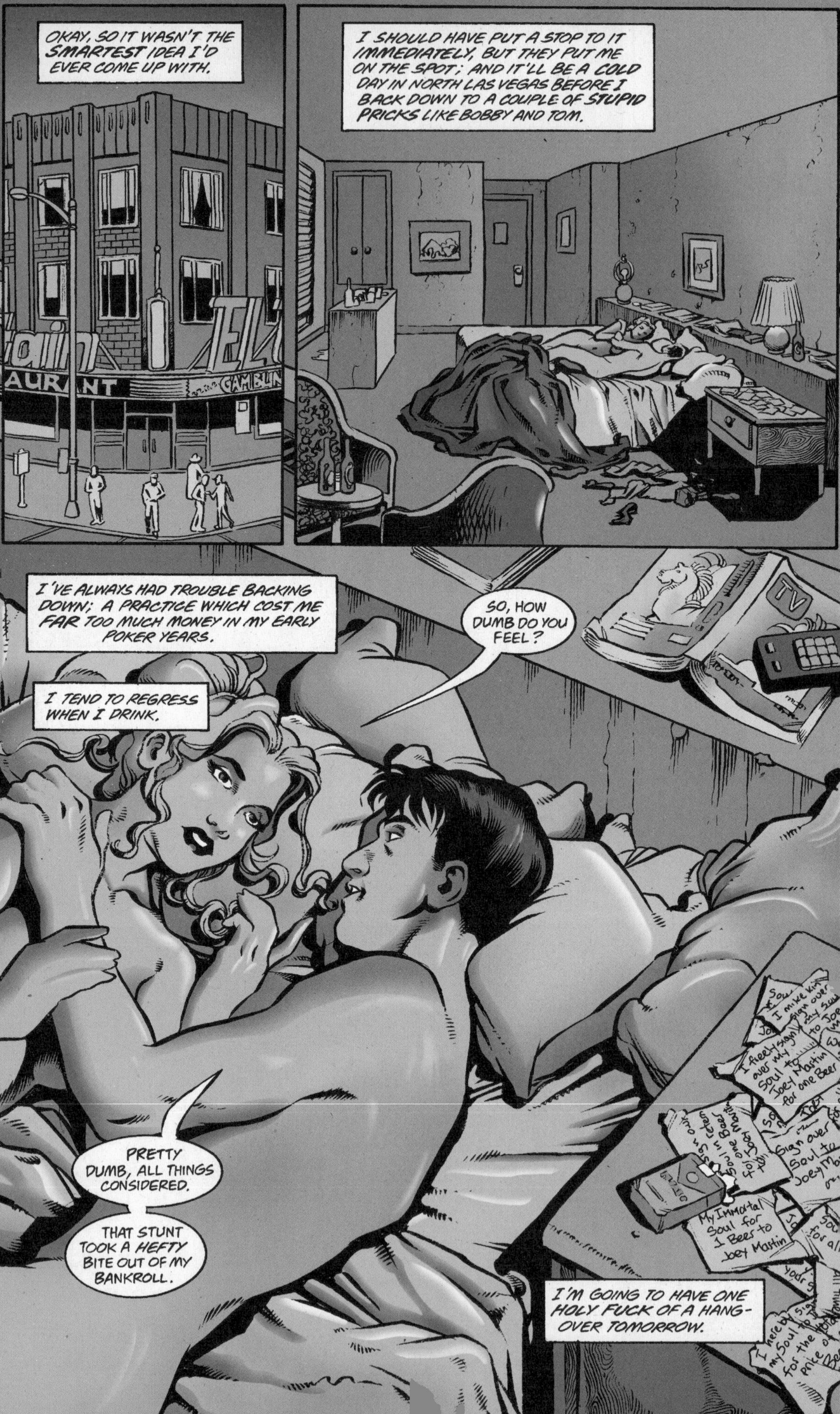
OKAY, SO IT WASN'T THE SMARTEST IDEA I'D EVER COME UP WITH.
I SHOULD HAVE PUT A STOP TO IT IMMEDIATELY, BUT THEY PUT ME ON THE SPOT; AND IT'LL BE A COLD DAY IN NORTH LAS VEGAS BEFORE I BACK DOWN TO A COUPLE OF STUPID PRICKS LIKE BOBBY AND TOM.
I'VE ALWAYS HAD TROUBLE BACKING DOWN; A PRACTICE WHICH COST ME FAR TOO MUCH MONEY IN MY EARLY POKER YEARS.
I TEND TO REGRESS WHEN I DRINK.
SO, HOW DUMB DO YOU FEEL?
PRETTY DUMB, ALL THINGS CONSIDERED.
THAT STUNT TOOK A HEFTY BITE OUT OF MY BANKROLL.
I'M GOING TO HAVE ONE HOLY FUCK OF A HANG-OVER TOMORROW.
TV
My Immortal Soul for 1 Beer to Joey Martin

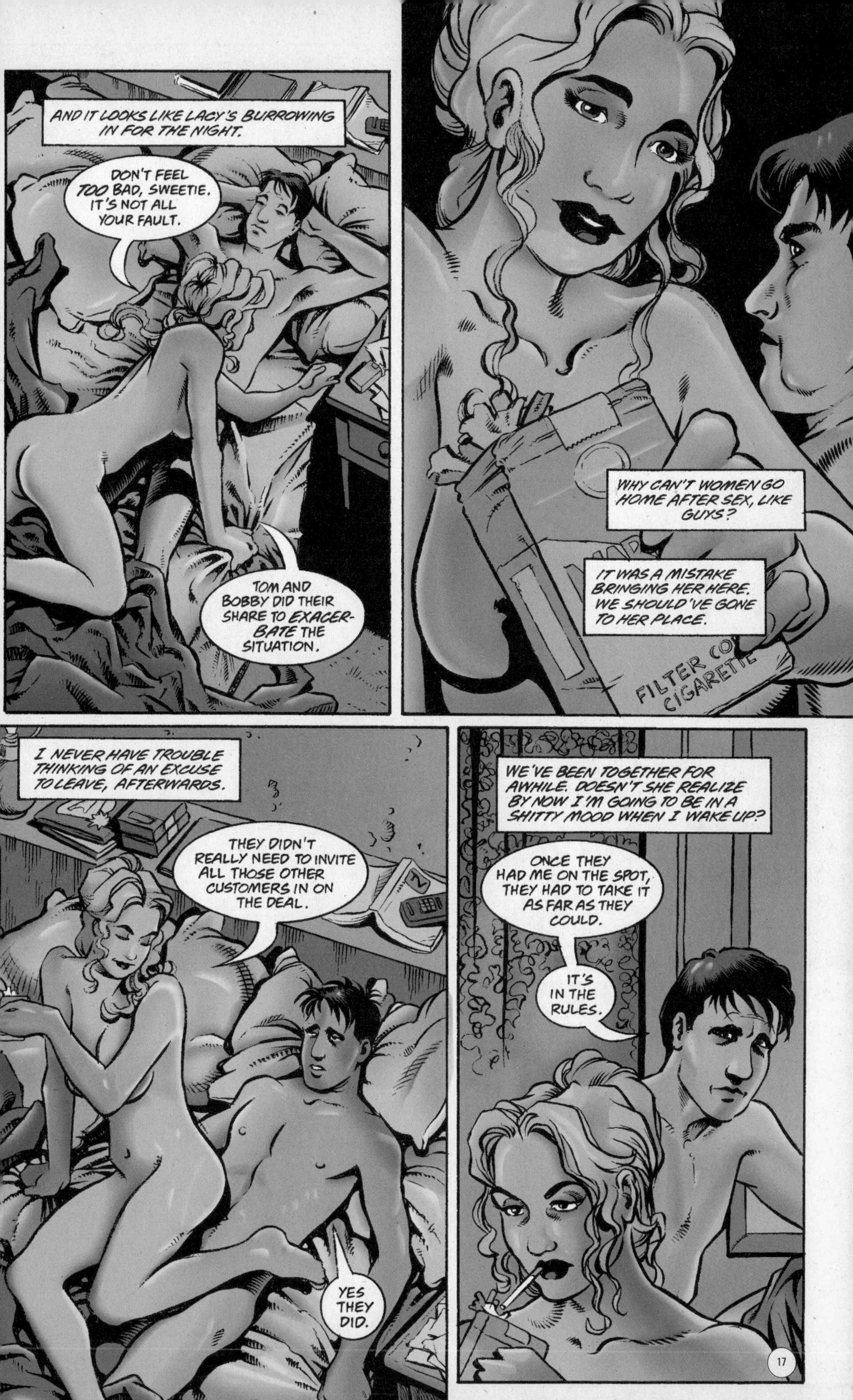
AND IT LOOKS LIKE LACY'S BURROWING IN FOR THE NIGHT.
DON'T FEEL TOO BAD, SWEETIE. IT'S NOT ALL YOUR FAULT.
TOM AND BOBBY DID THEIR SHARE TO EXACER-BATE THE SITUATION.
WHY CAN'T WOMEN GO HOME AFTER SEX, LIKE GUYS?
IT WAS A MISTAKE BRINGING HER HERE. WE SHOULD'VE GONE TO HER PLACE.
FILTER CO CIGARETTE
I NEVER HAVE TROUBLE THINKING OF AN EXCUSE TO LEAVE, AFTERWARDS.
THEY DIDN'T REALLY NEED TO INVITE ALL THOSE OTHER CUSTOMERS IN ON THE DEAL.
YES THEY DID.
WE'VE BEEN TOGETHER FOR AWHILE. DOESN'T SHE REALIZE BY NOW I'M GOING TO BE IN A SHITTY MOOD WHEN I WAKE UP?
ONCE THEY HAD ME ON THE SPOT, THEY HAD TO TAKE IT AS FAR AS THEY COULD.
IT'S IN THE RULES.

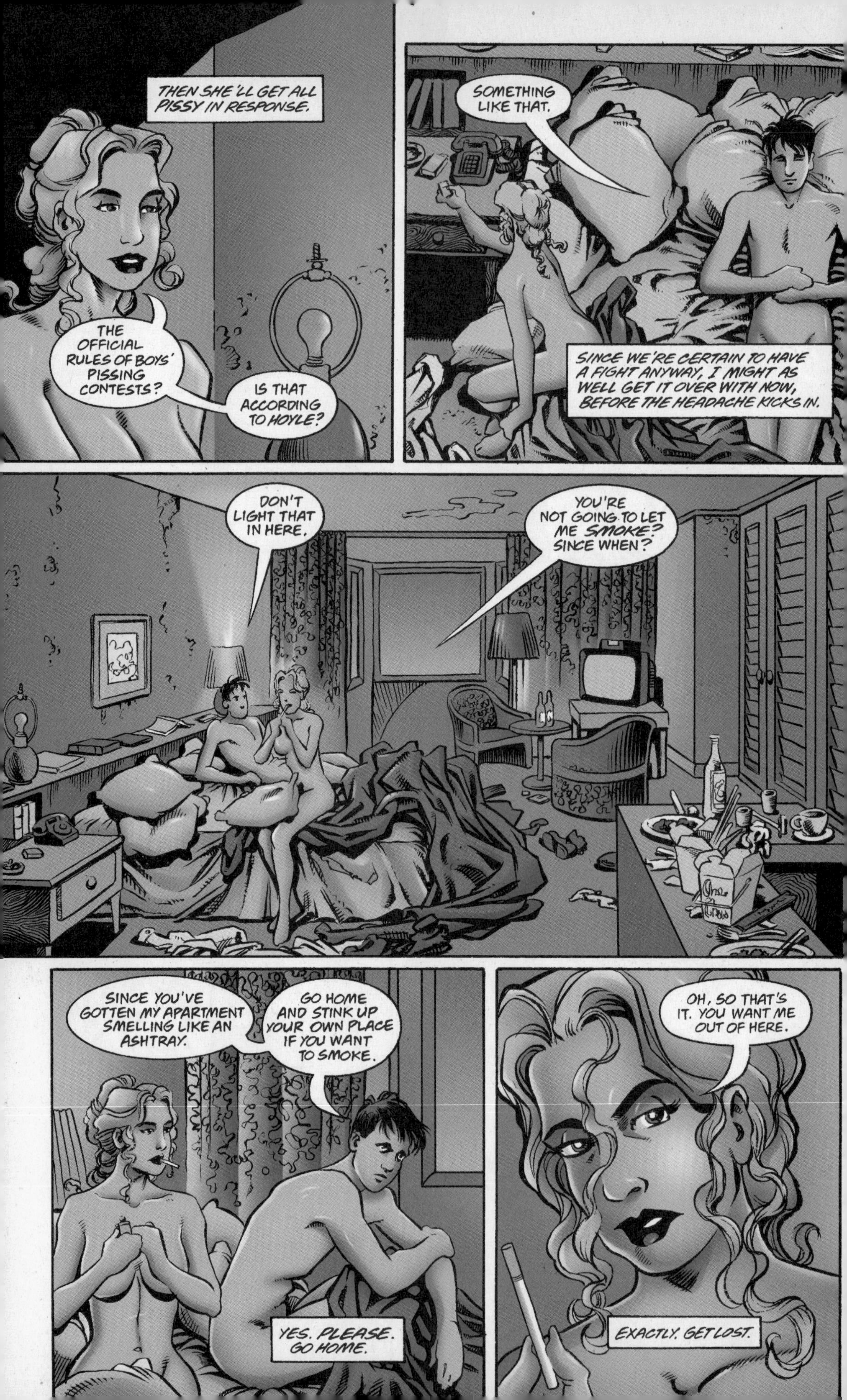
THEN SHE'LL GET ALL PISSY IN RESPONSE.
THE OFFICIAL RULES OF BOYS' PISSING CONTESTS?
IS THAT ACCORDING TO HOYLE?
SOMETHING LIKE THAT.
SINCE WE'RE CERTAIN TO HAVE A FIGHT ANYWAY, I MIGHT AS WELL GET IT OVER WITH NOW, BEFORE THE HEADACHE KICKS IN.
DON'T LIGHT THAT IN HERE.
YOU'RE NOT GOING TO LET ME SMOKE? SINCE WHEN?
SINCE YOU'VE GOTTEN MY APARTMENT SMELLING LIKE AN ASHTRAY.
GO HOME AND STINK UP YOUR OWN PLACE IF YOU WANT TO SMOKE.
YES. PLEASE. GO HOME.
OH, SO THAT'S IT. YOU WANT ME OUT OF HERE.
EXACTLY. GET LOST.

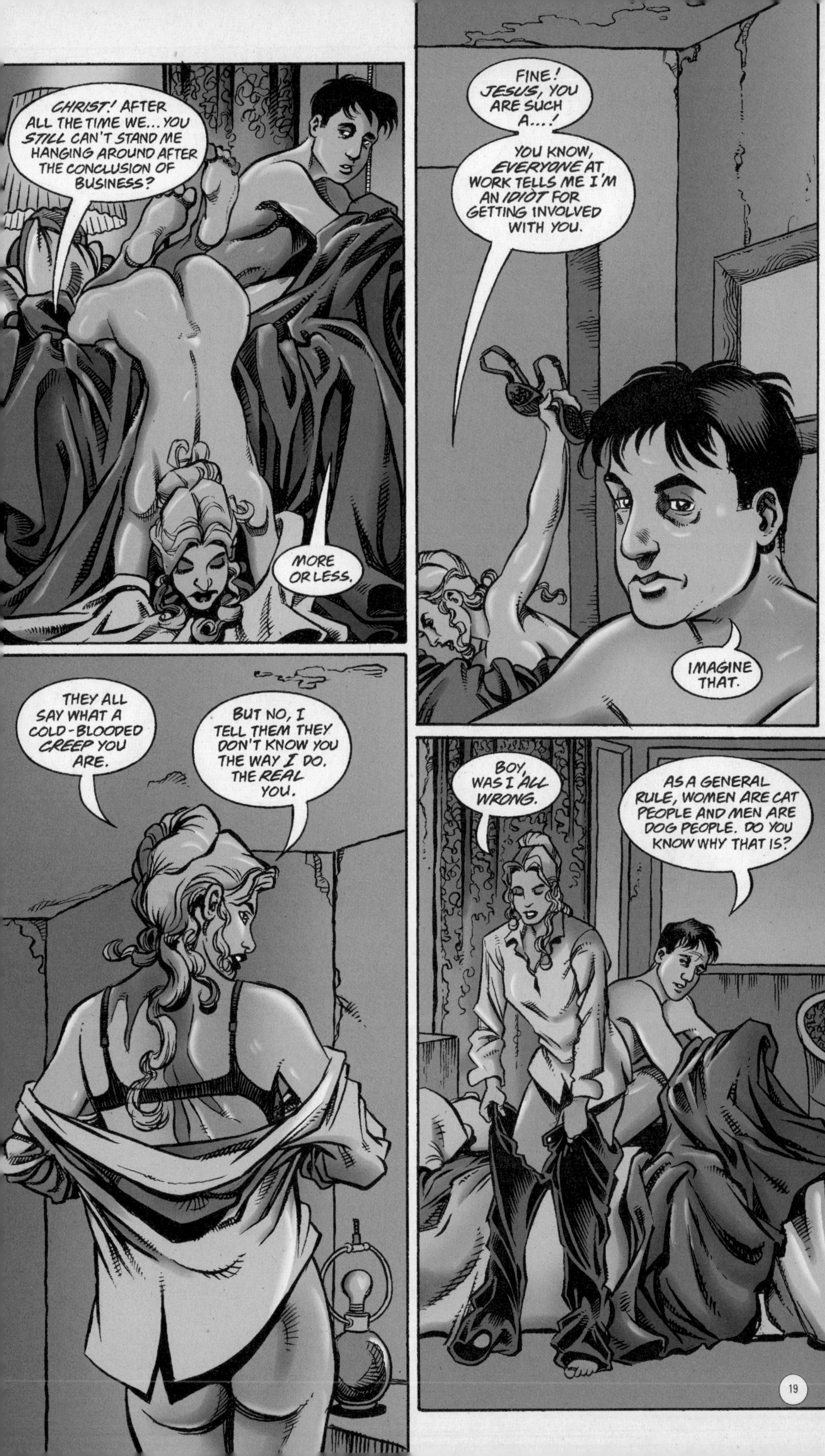
CHRIST! AFTER ALL THE TIME WE... YOU STILL CAN'T STAND ME HANGING AROUND AFTER THE CONCLUSION OF BUSINESS?
MORE OR LESS.
FINE! JESUS, YOU ARE SUCH A...!
YOU KNOW, EVERYONE AT WORK TELLS ME I'M AN IDIOT FOR GETTING INVOLVED WITH YOU.
IMAGINE THAT.
THEY ALL SAY WHAT A COLD-BLOODED CREEP YOU ARE.
BUT NO, I TELL THEM THEY DON'T KNOW YOU THE WAY I DO. THE REAL YOU.
BOY, WAS I ALL WRONG.
AS A GENERAL RULE, WOMEN ARE CAT PEOPLE AND MEN ARE DOG PEOPLE. DO YOU KNOW WHY THAT IS?

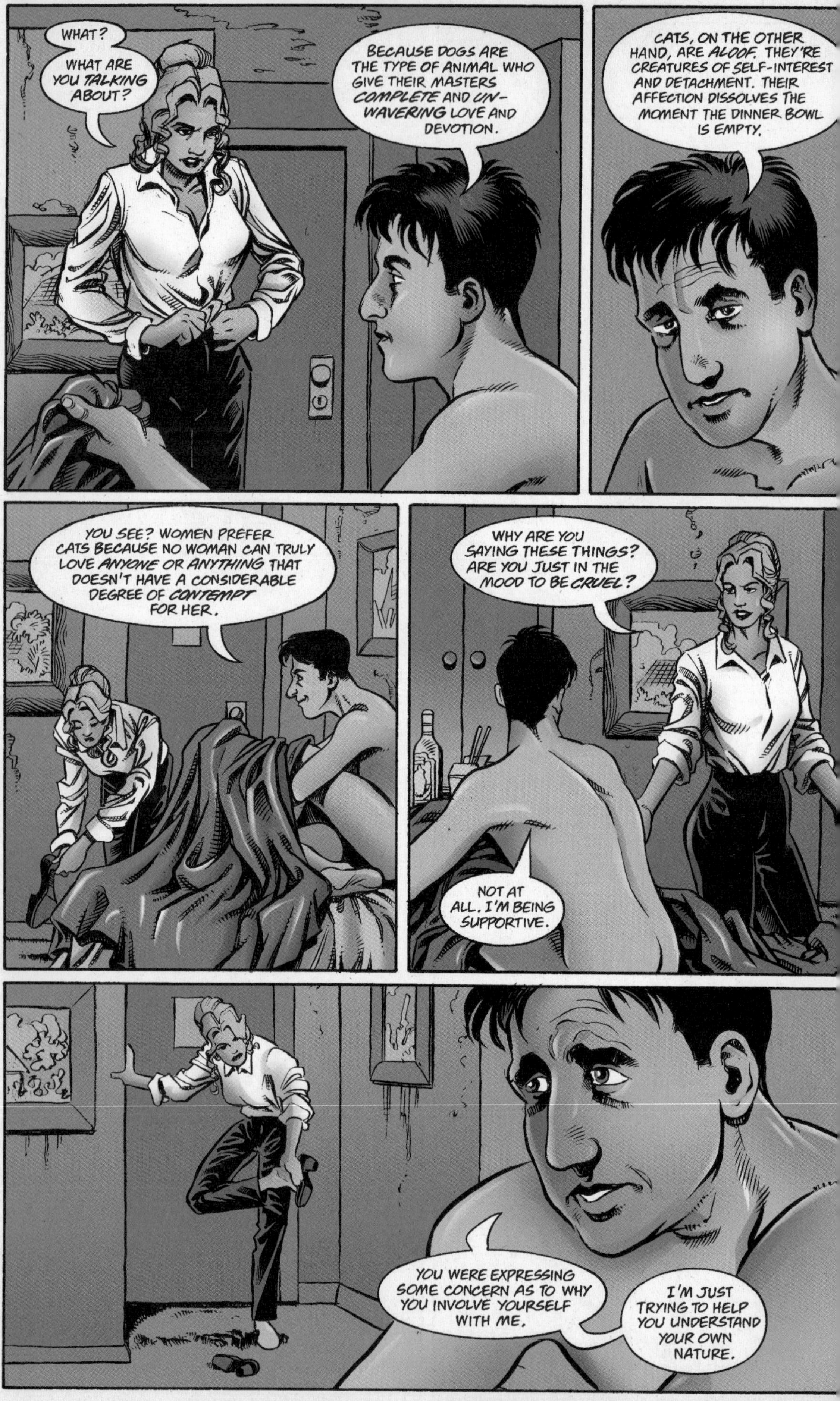
WHAT?
WHAT ARE YOU TALKING ABOUT?
BECAUSE DOGS ARE THE TYPE OF ANIMAL WHO GIVE THEIR MASTERS COMPLETE AND UN-WAVERING LOVE AND DEVOTION.
CATS, ON THE OTHER HAND, ARE ALOOF. THEY'RE CREATURES OF SELF-INTEREST AND DETACHMENT. THEIR AFFECTION DISSOLVES THE MOMENT THE DINNER BOWL IS EMPTY.
YOU SEE? WOMEN PREFER CATS BECAUSE NO WOMAN CAN TRULY LOVE ANYONE OR ANYTHING THAT DOESN'T HAVE A CONSIDERABLE DEGREE OF CONTEMPT FOR HER.
WHY ARE YOU SAYING THESE THINGS? ARE YOU JUST IN THE MOOD TO BE CRUEL?
NOT AT ALL. I'M BEING SUPPORTIVE.
YOU WERE EXPRESSING SOME CONCERN AS TO WHY YOU INVOLVE YOURSELF WITH ME.
I'M JUST TRYING TO HELP YOU UNDERSTAND YOUR OWN NATURE.

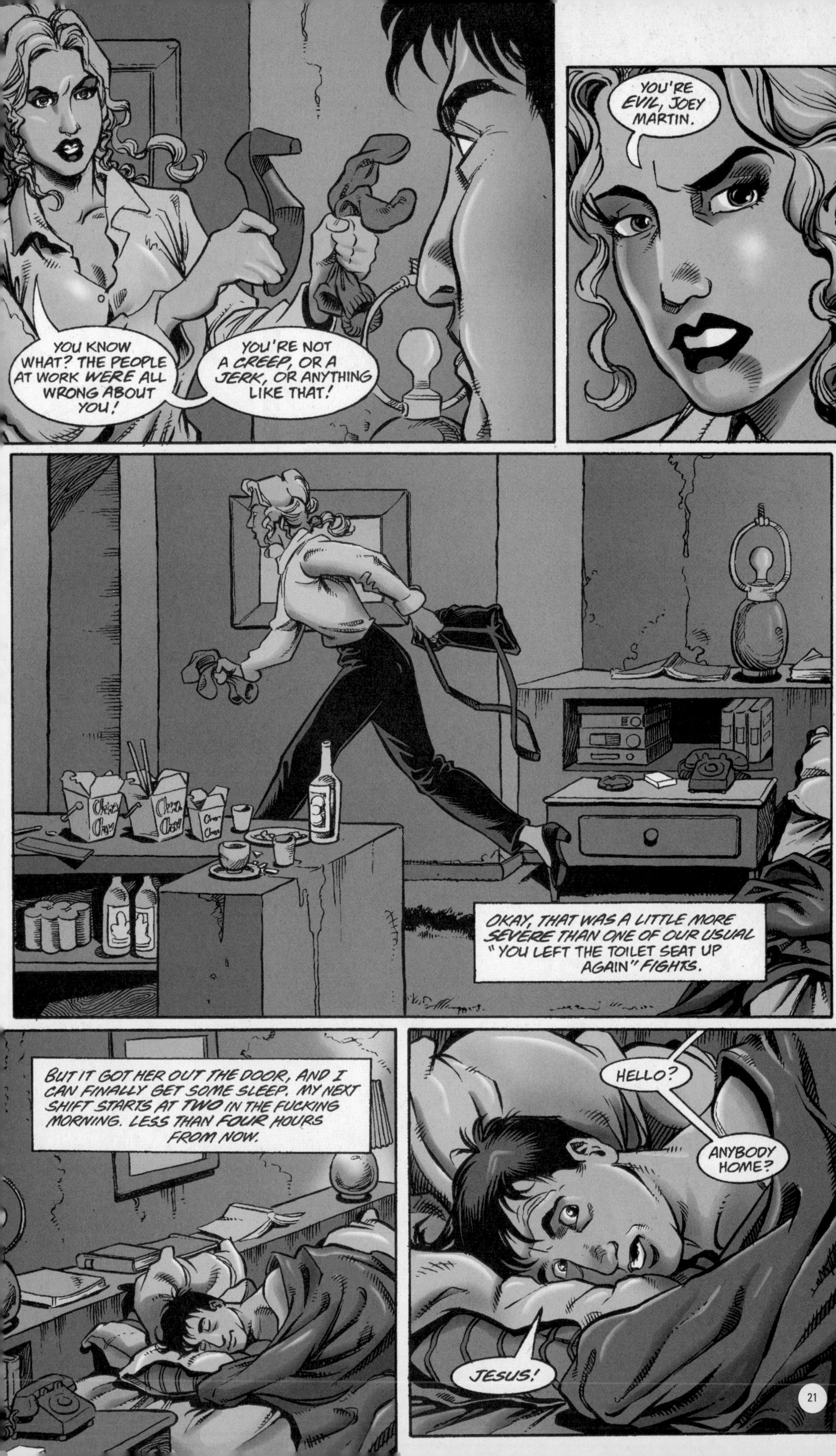
YOU KNOW WHAT? THE PEOPLE AT WORK WERE ALL WRONG ABOUT YOU!
YOU'RE NOT A CREEP, OR A JERK, OR ANYTHING LIKE THAT!
YOU'RE EVIL, JOEY MARTIN.
OKAY, THAT WAS A LITTLE MORE SEVERE THAN ONE OF OUR USUAL "YOU LEFT THE TOILET SEAT UP AGAIN" FIGHTS.
BUT IT GOT HER OUT THE DOOR, AND I CAN FINALLY GET SOME SLEEP. MY NEXT SHIFT STARTS AT TWO IN THE FUCKING MORNING. LESS THAN FOUR HOURS FROM NOW.
HELLO?
ANYBODY HOME?
JESUS!

THAT CRAZY SLUT LEFT MY DOOR OPEN, AND NOW SOME PIMP-HEROIN-ADDICT-STREET-SCUM HAS COME SNIFFING AROUND!

HUH?

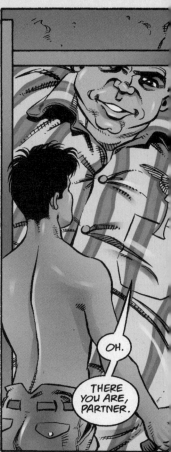

OH.

THERE YOU ARE, PARTNER.

HI. YOU MUST BE JOEY, RIGHT?

JOEY MARTIN?

HELL, YOU LOOK LIKE HIM, AND YOU'RE WEARING HIS PANTS, SO I'LL BET YOU'RE HIM.

YOU...? WHAT...?

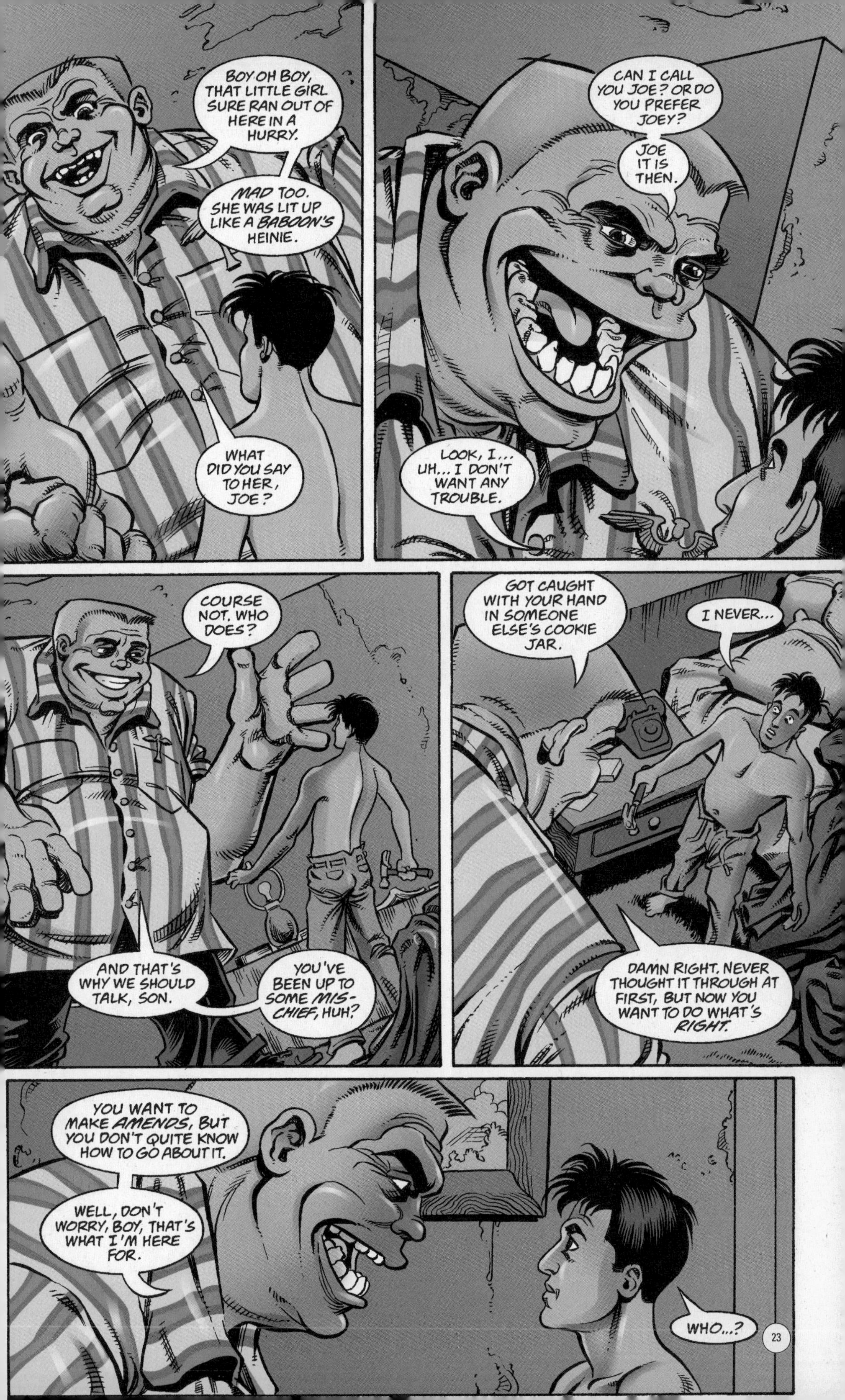
BOY OH BOY, THAT LITTLE GIRL SURE RAN OUT OF HERE IN A HURRY.
MAD TOO. SHE WAS LIT UP LIKE A BABOON'S HEINIE.
WHAT DID YOU SAY TO HER, JOE?
CAN I CALL YOU JOE? OR DO YOU PREFER JOEY?
JOE IT IS THEN.
LOOK, I... UH... I DON'T WANT ANY TROUBLE.
COURSE NOT. WHO DOES?
AND THAT'S WHY WE SHOULD TALK, SON.
YOU'VE BEEN UP TO SOME MIS-CHIEF, HUH?
GOT CAUGHT WITH YOUR HAND IN SOMEONE ELSE'S COOKIE JAR.
I NEVER...
DAMN RIGHT. NEVER THOUGHT IT THROUGH AT FIRST, BUT NOW YOU WANT TO DO WHAT'S RIGHT.
YOU WANT TO MAKE AMENDS, BUT YOU DON'T QUITE KNOW HOW TO GO ABOUT IT.
WELL, DON'T WORRY, BOY, THAT'S WHAT I'M HERE FOR.
WHO...?

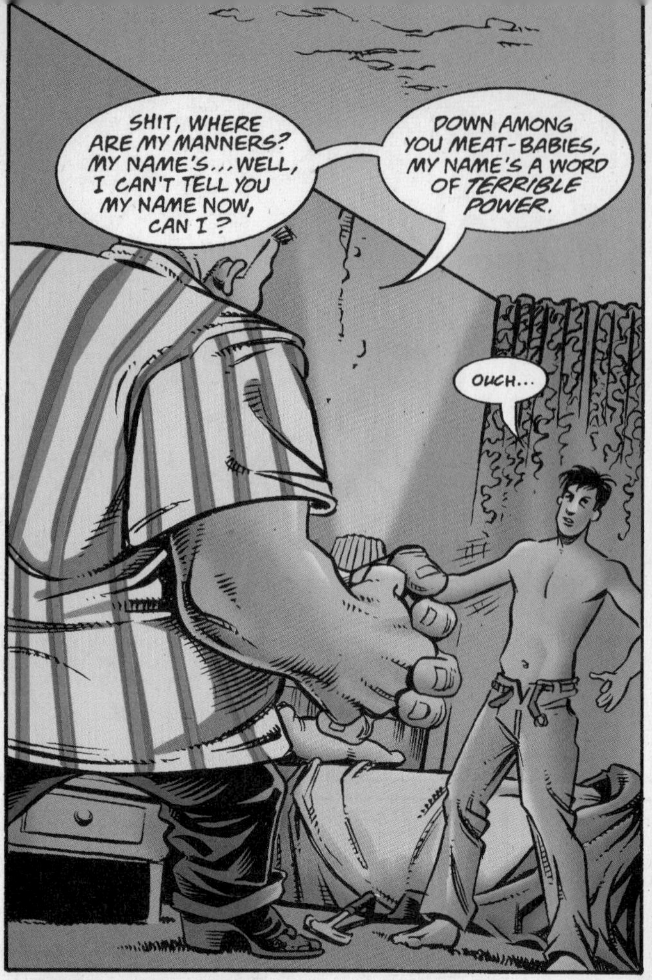
SHIT, WHERE ARE MY MANNERS? MY NAME'S... WELL, I CAN'T TELL YOU MY NAME NOW, CAN I?
DOWN AMONG YOU MEAT-BABIES, MY NAME'S A WORD OF TERRIBLE POWER.
OUCH...

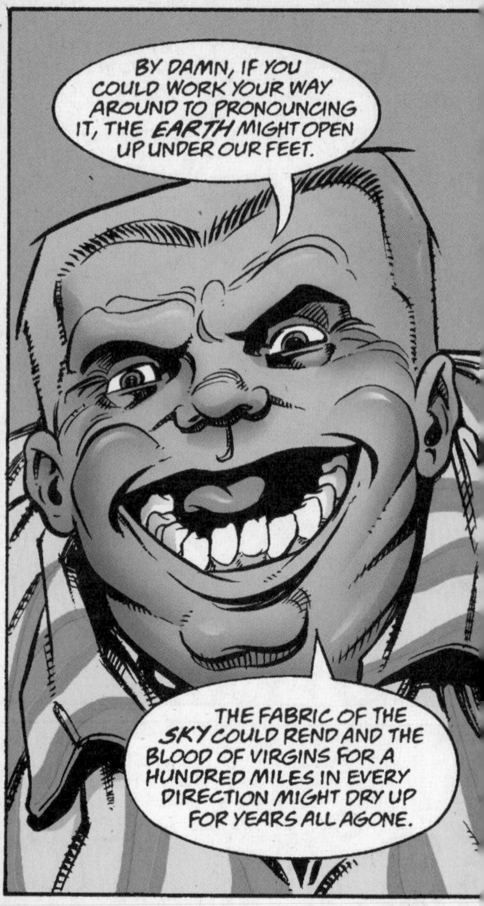
BY DAMN, IF YOU COULD WORK YOUR WAY AROUND TO PRONOUNCING IT, THE EARTH MIGHT OPEN UP UNDER OUR FEET.
THE FABRIC OF THE SKY COULD REND AND THE BLOOD OF VIRGINS FOR A HUNDRED MILES IN EVERY DIRECTION MIGHT DRY UP FOR YEARS ALL AGONE.

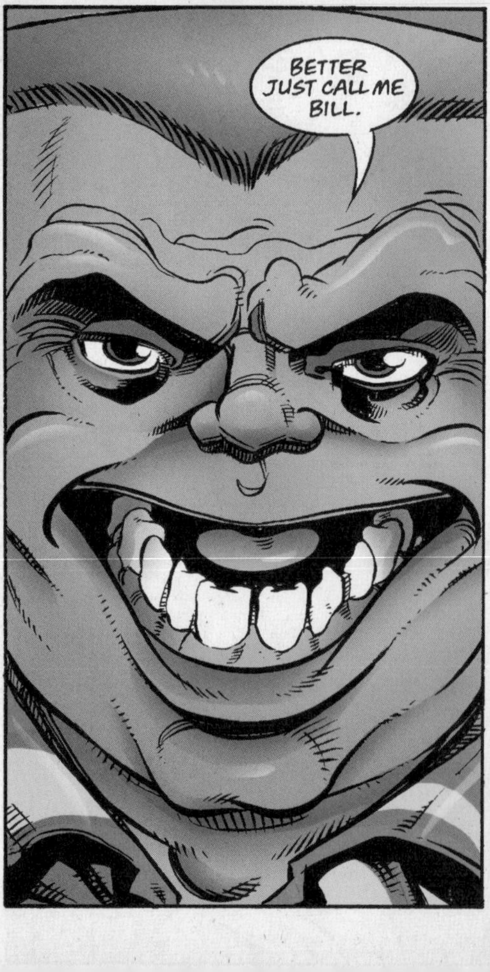
BETTER JUST CALL ME BILL.

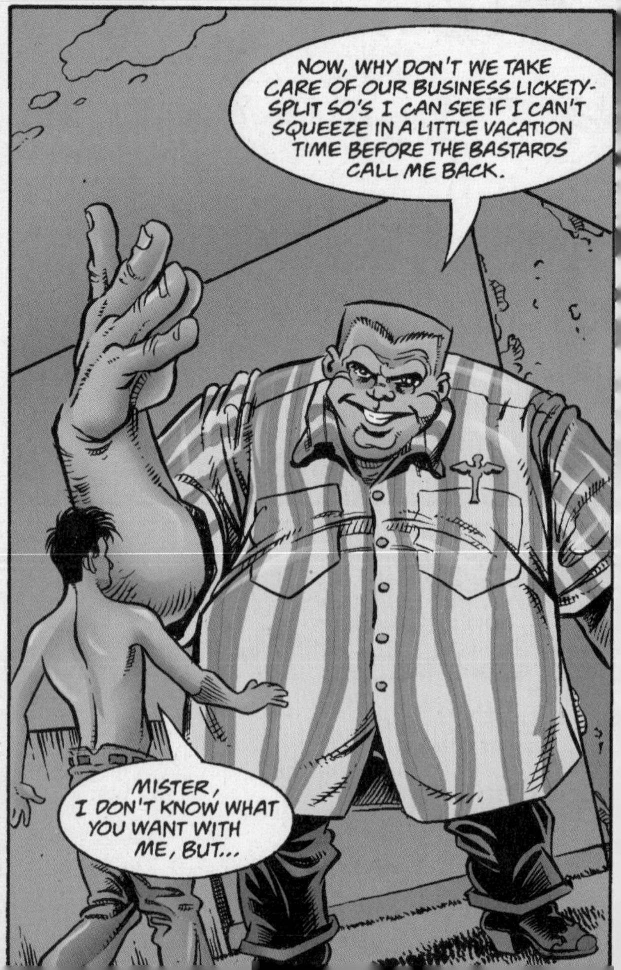
NOW, WHY DON'T WE TAKE CARE OF OUR BUSINESS LICKETY-SPLIT SO'S I CAN SEE IF I CAN'T SQUEEZE IN A LITTLE VACATION TIME BEFORE THE BASTARDS CALL ME BACK.
MISTER, I DON'T KNOW WHAT YOU WANT WITH ME, BUT...

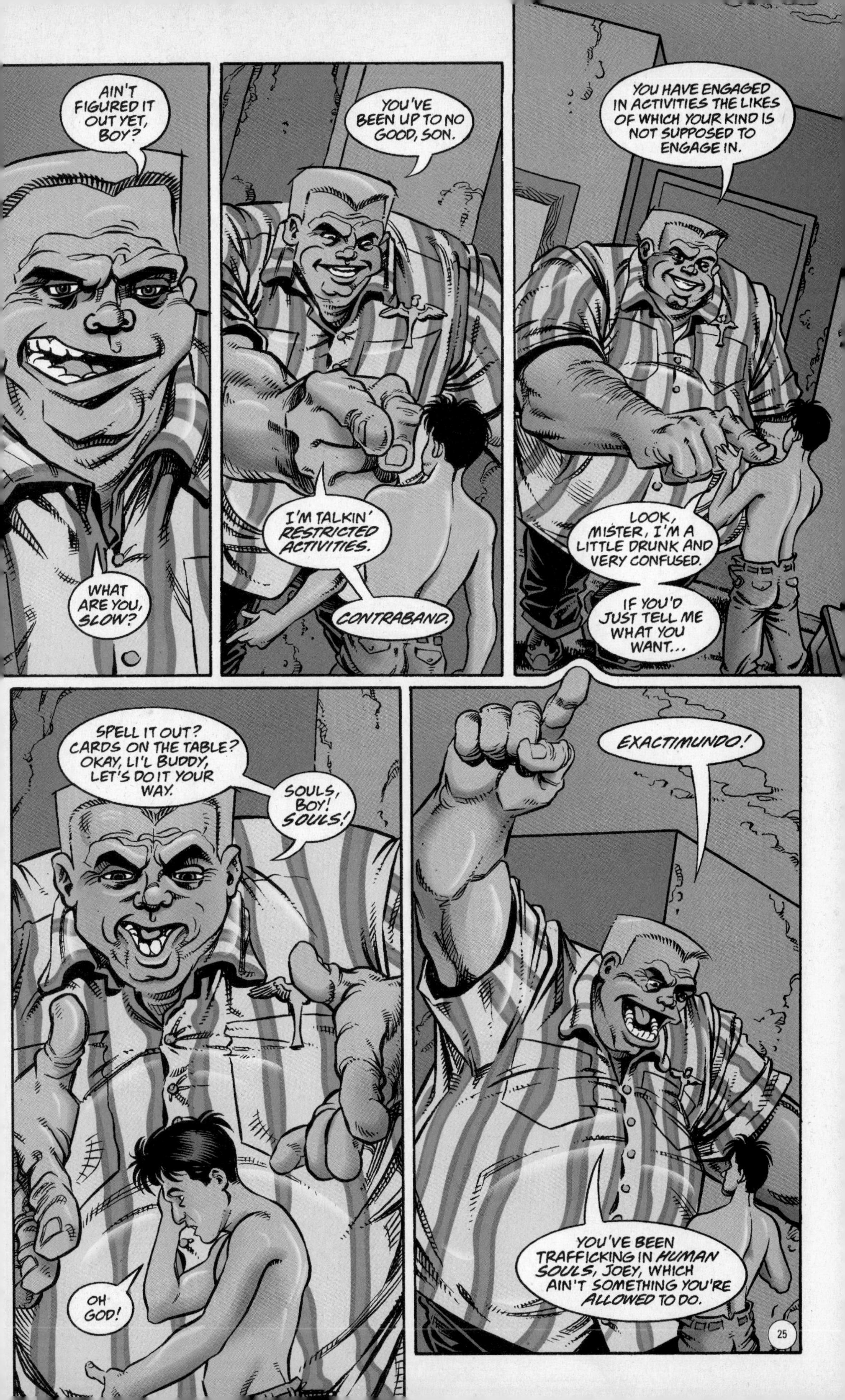
AIN'T FIGURED IT OUT YET, BOY?
WHAT ARE YOU, SLOW?
YOU'VE BEEN UP TO NO GOOD, SON.
I'M TALKIN' RESTRICTED ACTIVITIES.
CONTRABAND.
YOU HAVE ENGAGED IN ACTIVITIES THE LIKES OF WHICH YOUR KIND IS NOT SUPPOSED TO ENGAGE IN.
LOOK, MISTER, I'M A LITTLE DRUNK AND VERY CONFUSED.
IF YOU'D JUST TELL ME WHAT YOU WANT...
SPELL IT OUT? CARDS ON THE TABLE? OKAY, LI'L BUDDY, LET'S DO IT YOUR WAY.
SOULS, BOY! SOULS!
OH GOD!
EXACTIMUNDO!
YOU'VE BEEN TRAFFICKING IN HUMAN SOULS, JOEY, WHICH AIN'T SOMETHING YOU'RE ALLOWED TO DO.

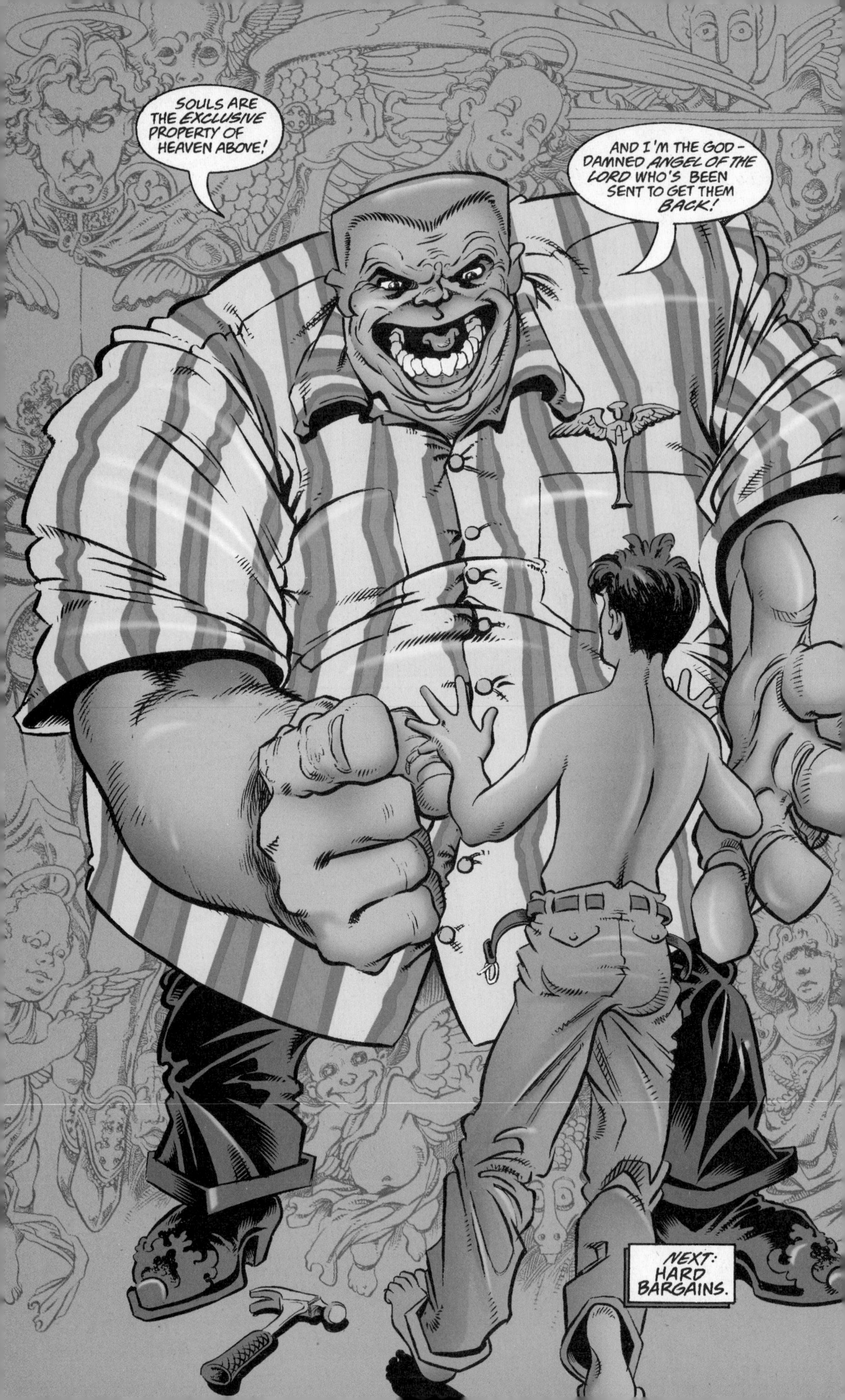
SOULS ARE THE EXCLUSIVE PROPERTY OF HEAVEN ABOVE!
AND I'M THE GOD-DAMNED ANGEL OF THE LORD WHO'S BEEN SENT TO GET THEM BACK!
NEXT: HARD BARGAINS.

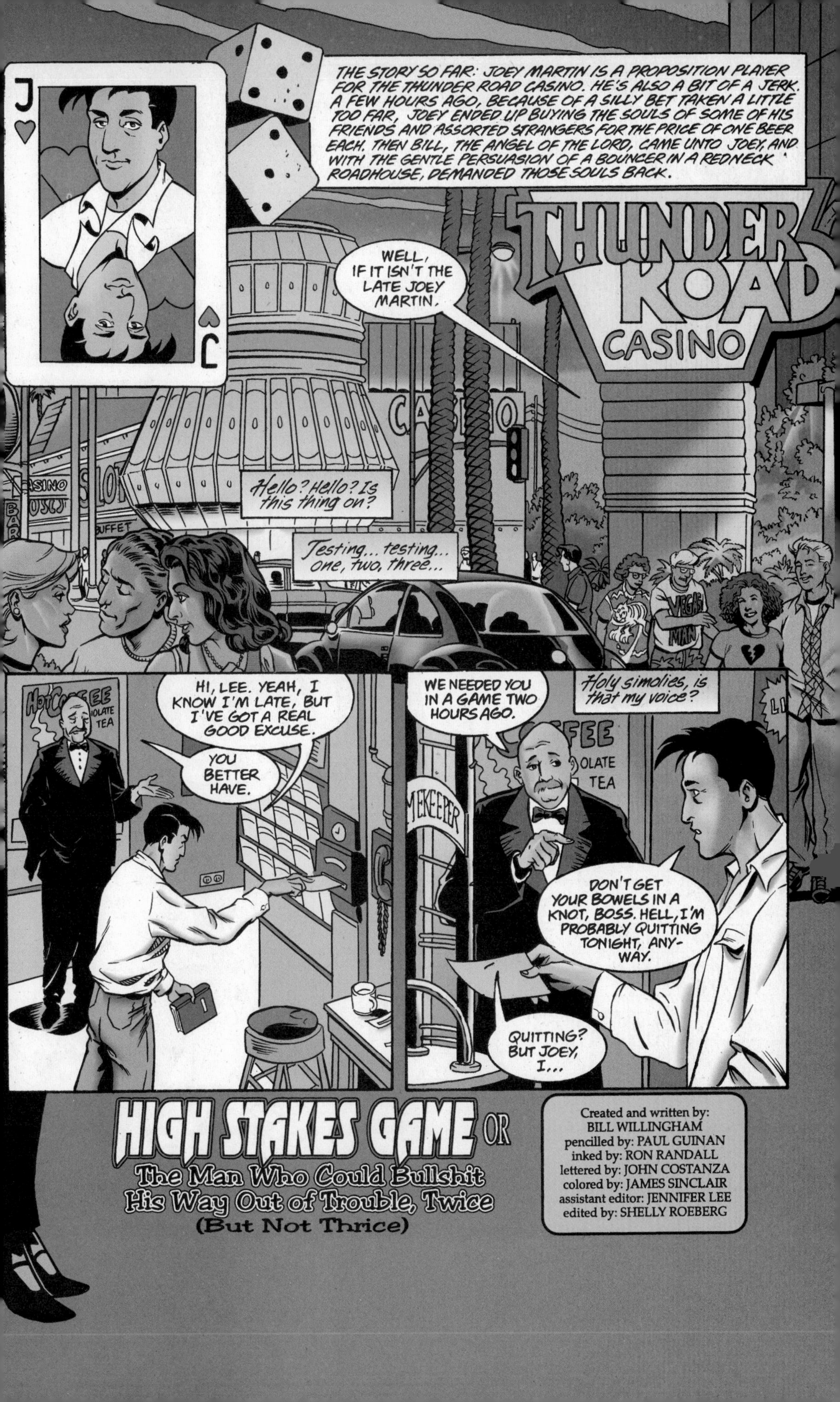
THE STORY SO FAR: JOEY MARTIN IS A PROPOSITION PLAYER FOR THE THUNDER ROAD CASINO. HE'S ALSO A BIT OF A JERK. A FEW HOURS AGO, BECAUSE OF A SILLY BET TAKEN A LITTLE TOO FAR, JOEY ENDED UP BUYING THE SOULS OF SOME OF HIS FRIENDS AND ASSORTED STRANGERS FOR THE PRICE OF ONE BEER EACH. THEN BILL, THE ANGEL OF THE LORD, CAME UNTO JOEY, AND WITH THE GENTLE PERSUASION OF A BOUNCER IN A REDNECK ROADHOUSE, DEMANDED THOSE SOULS BACK.
THUNDER ROAD CASINO
WELL, IF IT ISN'T THE LATE JOEY MARTIN.
Hello? Hello? Is this thing on?
Testing... testing... one, two, three...
HI, LEE. YEAH, I KNOW I'M LATE, BUT I'VE GOT A REAL GOOD EXCUSE.
YOU BETTER HAVE.
WE NEEDED YOU IN A GAME TWO HOURS AGO.
Holy simolies, is that my voice?
DON'T GET YOUR BOWELS IN A KNOT, BOSS. HELL, I'M PROBABLY QUITTING TONIGHT, ANY-WAY.
QUITTING? BUT JOEY, I...

HIGH STAKES GAME OR
The Man Who Could Bullshit His Way Out of Trouble, Twice (But Not Thrice)

Created and written by: BILL WILLINGHAM
pencilled by: PAUL GUINAN
inked by: RON RANDALL
lettered by: JOHN COSTANZA
colored by: JAMES SINCLAIR
assistant editor: JENNIFER LEE
edited by: SHELLY ROEBERG

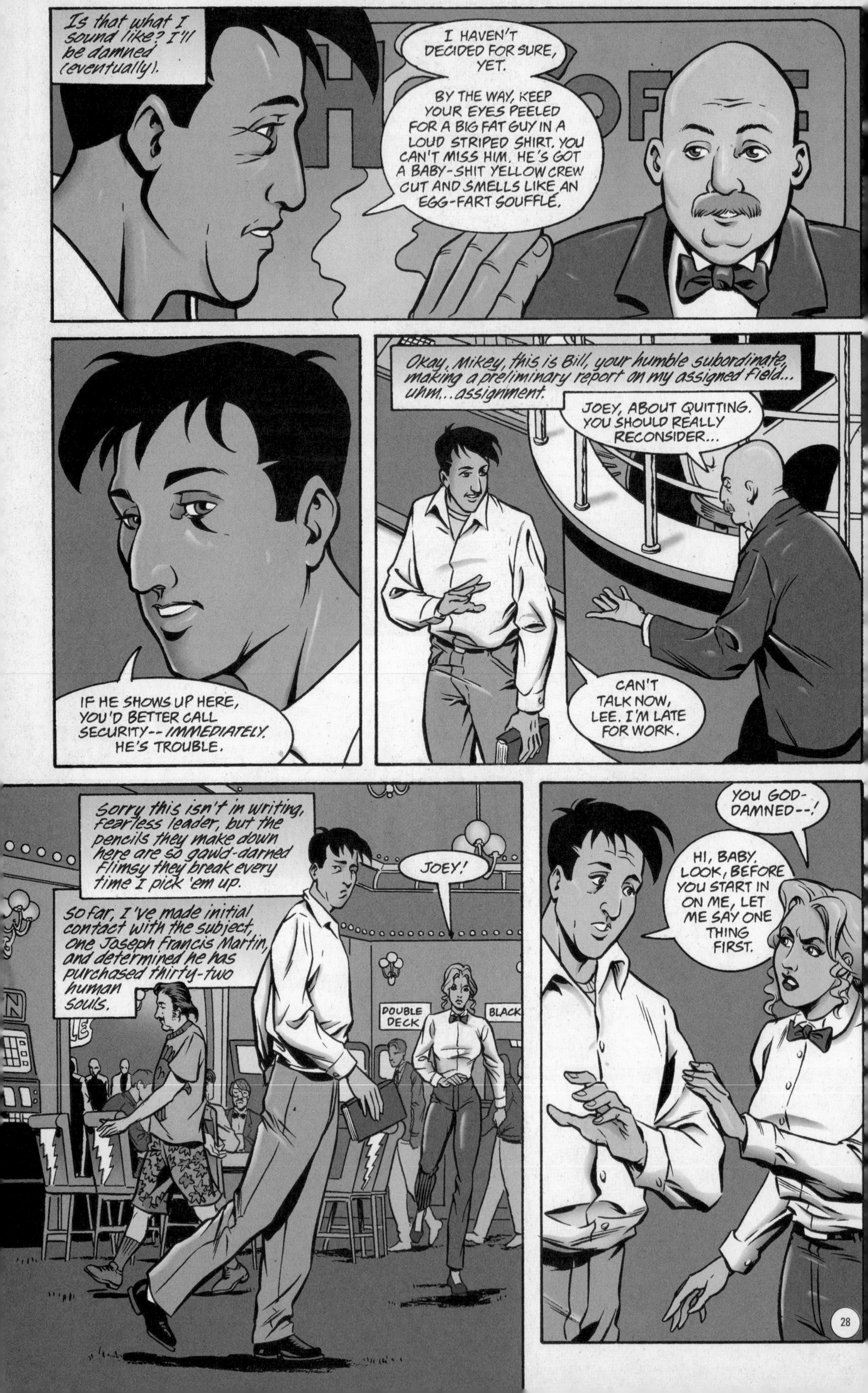

Is that what I sound like? I'll be damned (eventually).
I HAVEN'T DECIDED FOR SURE, YET.
BY THE WAY, KEEP YOUR EYES PEELED FOR A BIG FAT GUY IN A LOUD STRIPED SHIRT. YOU CAN'T MISS HIM. HE'S GOT A BABY-SHIT YELLOW CREW CUT AND SMELLS LIKE AN EGG-FART SOUFFLÉ.
IF HE SHOWS UP HERE, YOU'D BETTER CALL SECURITY-- IMMEDIATELY. HE'S TROUBLE.
Okay, Mikey, this is Bill, your humble subordinate, making a preliminary report on my assigned field... uhm... assignment.
JOEY, ABOUT QUITTING. YOU SHOULD REALLY RECONSIDER...
CAN'T TALK NOW, LEE. I'M LATE FOR WORK.
Sorry this isn't in writing, fearless leader, but the pencils they make down here are so gawd-darned flimsy they break every time I pick 'em up.
So far, I've made initial contact with the subject, one Joseph Francis Martin, and determined he has purchased thirty-two human souls.
JOEY!
DOUBLE DECK
BLACK
YOU GOD-DAMNED--!
HI, BABY. LOOK, BEFORE YOU START IN ON ME, LET ME SAY ONE THING FIRST.

I've also visually ascertained the existence of the purchase contracts in Mr. Martin's apartment.

I'VE GOT NO EXCUSE, AND I WON'T BLAME YOU IF YOU NEVER TALK TO ME AGAIN; BUT I WAS DRINKING AND...

DRINKING'S NO EXCUSE.

RIGHT.

YOU'RE RIGHT, BUT... OH, HERE, BEFORE I FORGET, I GOT YOU THIS.

I TREATED YOU LIKE SHIT EARLIER AND I'M SORRY.

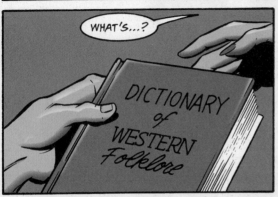

WHAT'S...?

A DICTIONARY OF WESTERN FOLKLORE?

DICTIONARY of WESTERN Folklore

However, as we suspected, I was unable to physically touch said documents, thus confirming their authenticity and celestial recognition of their new ownership.

IT'S FULL OF UNICORNS AND MYTHOLOGY AND ALL THAT KIND OF SHIT YOU LIKE.

OH, JOEY, IT'S PERFECT. IT'S...

WAIT A MINUTE.

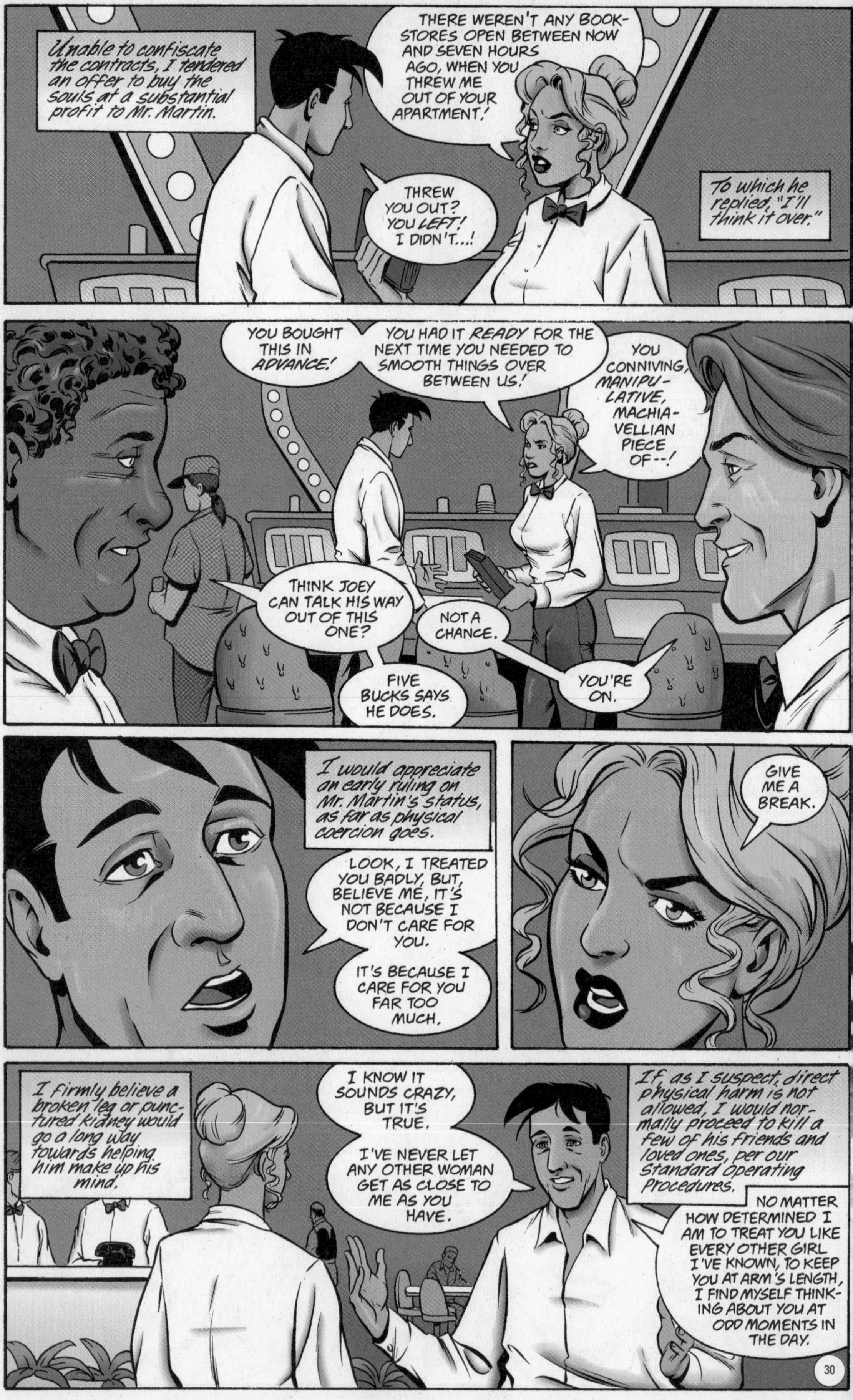

Unable to confiscate the contracts, I tendered an offer to buy the souls at a substantial profit to Mr. Martin.
THERE WEREN'T ANY BOOK-STORES OPEN BETWEEN NOW AND SEVEN HOURS AGO, WHEN YOU THREW ME OUT OF YOUR APARTMENT!
THREW YOU OUT? YOU LEFT! I DIDN'T...!
To which he replied, "I'll think it over."
YOU BOUGHT THIS IN ADVANCE!
YOU HAD IT READY FOR THE NEXT TIME YOU NEEDED TO SMOOTH THINGS OVER BETWEEN US!
YOU CONNIVING, MANIPU-LATIVE, MACHIA-VELLIAN PIECE OF--!
THINK JOEY CAN TALK HIS WAY OUT OF THIS ONE?
NOT A CHANCE.
FIVE BUCKS SAYS HE DOES.
YOU'RE ON.
I would appreciate an early ruling on Mr. Martin's status, as far as physical coercion goes.
LOOK, I TREATED YOU BADLY, BUT, BELIEVE ME, IT'S NOT BECAUSE I DON'T CARE FOR YOU.
IT'S BECAUSE I CARE FOR YOU FAR TOO MUCH.
GIVE ME A BREAK.
I firmly believe a broken leg or punc-tured kidney would go a long way towards helping him make up his mind.
I KNOW IT SOUNDS CRAZY, BUT IT'S TRUE.
I'VE NEVER LET ANY OTHER WOMAN GET AS CLOSE TO ME AS YOU HAVE.
If, as I suspect, direct physical harm is not allowed, I would nor-mally proceed to kill a few of his friends and loved ones, per our Standard Operating Procedures.
NO MATTER HOW DETERMINED I AM TO TREAT YOU LIKE EVERY OTHER GIRL I'VE KNOWN, TO KEEP YOU AT ARM'S LENGTH, I FIND MYSELF THINK-ING ABOUT YOU AT ODD MOMENTS IN THE DAY.

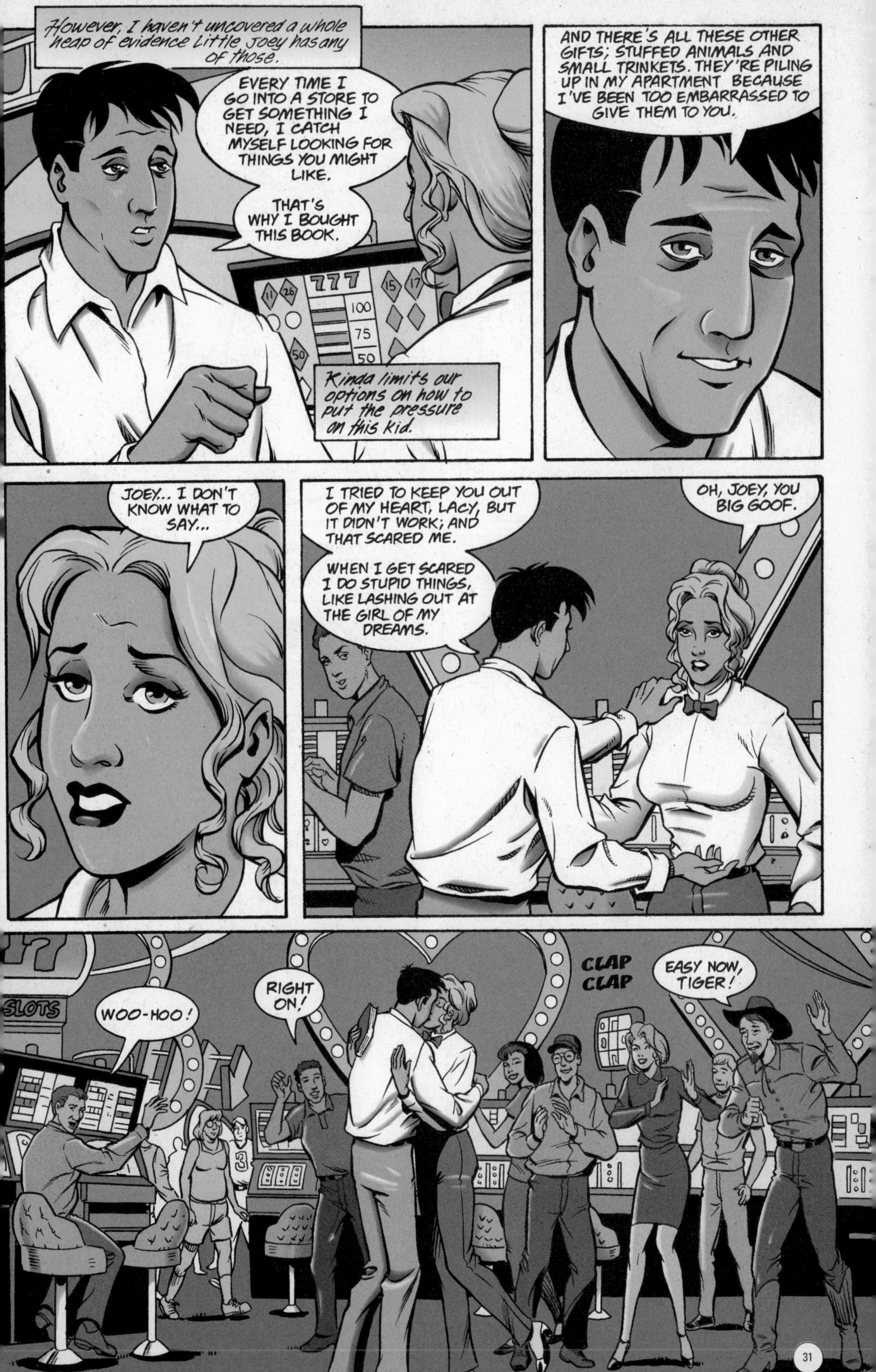
However, I haven't uncovered a whole heap of evidence Little Joey has any of those.
EVERY TIME I GO INTO A STORE TO GET SOMETHING I NEED, I CATCH MYSELF LOOKING FOR THINGS YOU MIGHT LIKE.
THAT'S WHY I BOUGHT THIS BOOK.
777
100
75
50
Kinda limits our options on how to put the pressure on this kid.
AND THERE'S ALL THESE OTHER GIFTS; STUFFED ANIMALS AND SMALL TRINKETS. THEY'RE PILING UP IN MY APARTMENT BECAUSE I'VE BEEN TOO EMBARRASSED TO GIVE THEM TO YOU.
JOEY... I DON'T KNOW WHAT TO SAY...
I TRIED TO KEEP YOU OUT OF MY HEART, LACY, BUT IT DIDN'T WORK; AND THAT SCARED ME.
WHEN I GET SCARED I DO STUPID THINGS, LIKE LASHING OUT AT THE GIRL OF MY DREAMS.
OH, JOEY, YOU BIG GOOF.
SLOTS
WOO-HOO!
RIGHT ON!
CLAP CLAP
EASY NOW, TIGER!

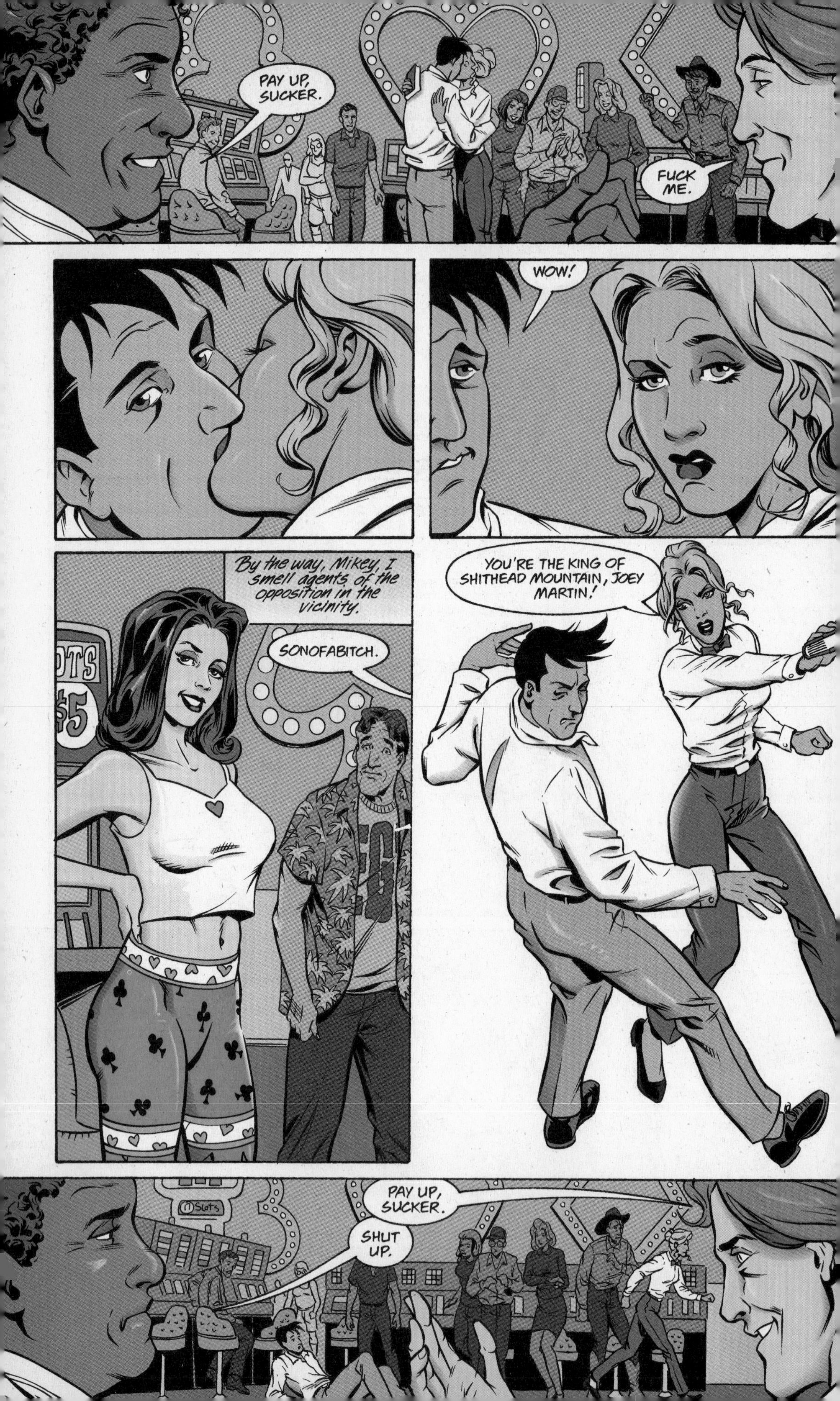
PAY UP, SUCKER.
FUCK ME.
WOW!
By the way, Mikey, I smell agents of the opposition in the vicinity.
SONOFABITCH.
YOU'RE THE KING OF SHITHEAD MOUNTAIN, JOEY MARTIN!
PAY UP, SUCKER.
SHUT UP.

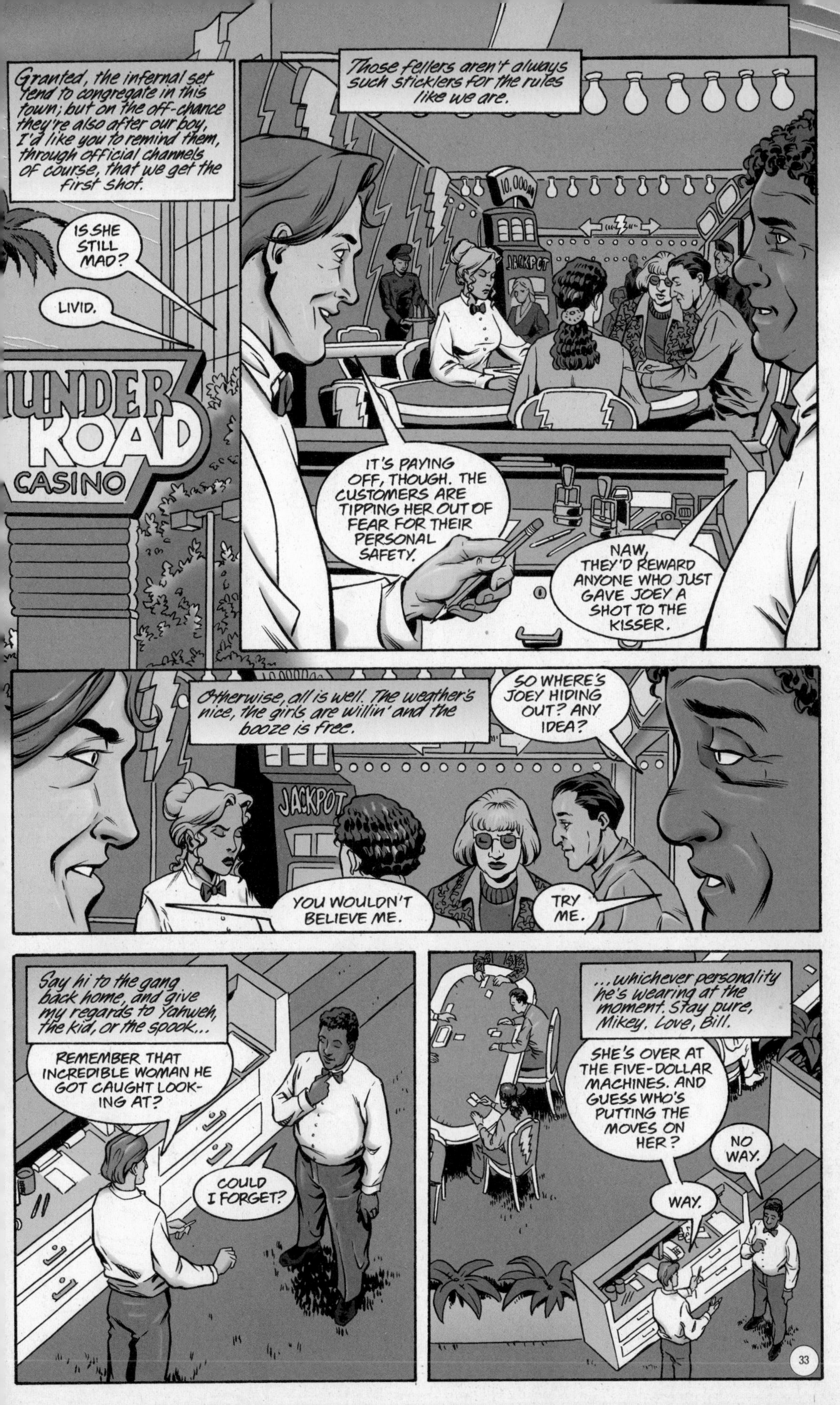
Granted, the infernal set tend to congregate in this town; but on the off-chance they're also after our boy, I'd like you to remind them, through official channels of course, that we get the first shot.
IS SHE STILL MAD?
LIVID.
UNDER ROAD CASINO
Those fellers aren't always such sticklers for the rules like we are.
10,000
JACKPOT
IT'S PAYING OFF, THOUGH. THE CUSTOMERS ARE TIPPING HER OUT OF FEAR FOR THEIR PERSONAL SAFETY.
NAW, THEY'D REWARD ANYONE WHO JUST GAVE JOEY A SHOT TO THE KISSER.
Otherwise, all is well. The weather's nice, the girls are willin' and the booze is free.
SO WHERE'S JOEY HIDING OUT? ANY IDEA?
JACKPOT
YOU WOULDN'T BELIEVE ME.
TRY ME.
Say hi to the gang back home, and give my regards to Yahweh, the kid, or the spook...
REMEMBER THAT INCREDIBLE WOMAN HE GOT CAUGHT LOOKING AT?
COULD I FORGET?
...whichever personality he's wearing at the moment. Stay pure, Mikey. Love, Bill.
SHE'S OVER AT THE FIVE-DOLLAR MACHINES. AND GUESS WHO'S PUTTING THE MOVES ON HER?
NO WAY.
WAY.

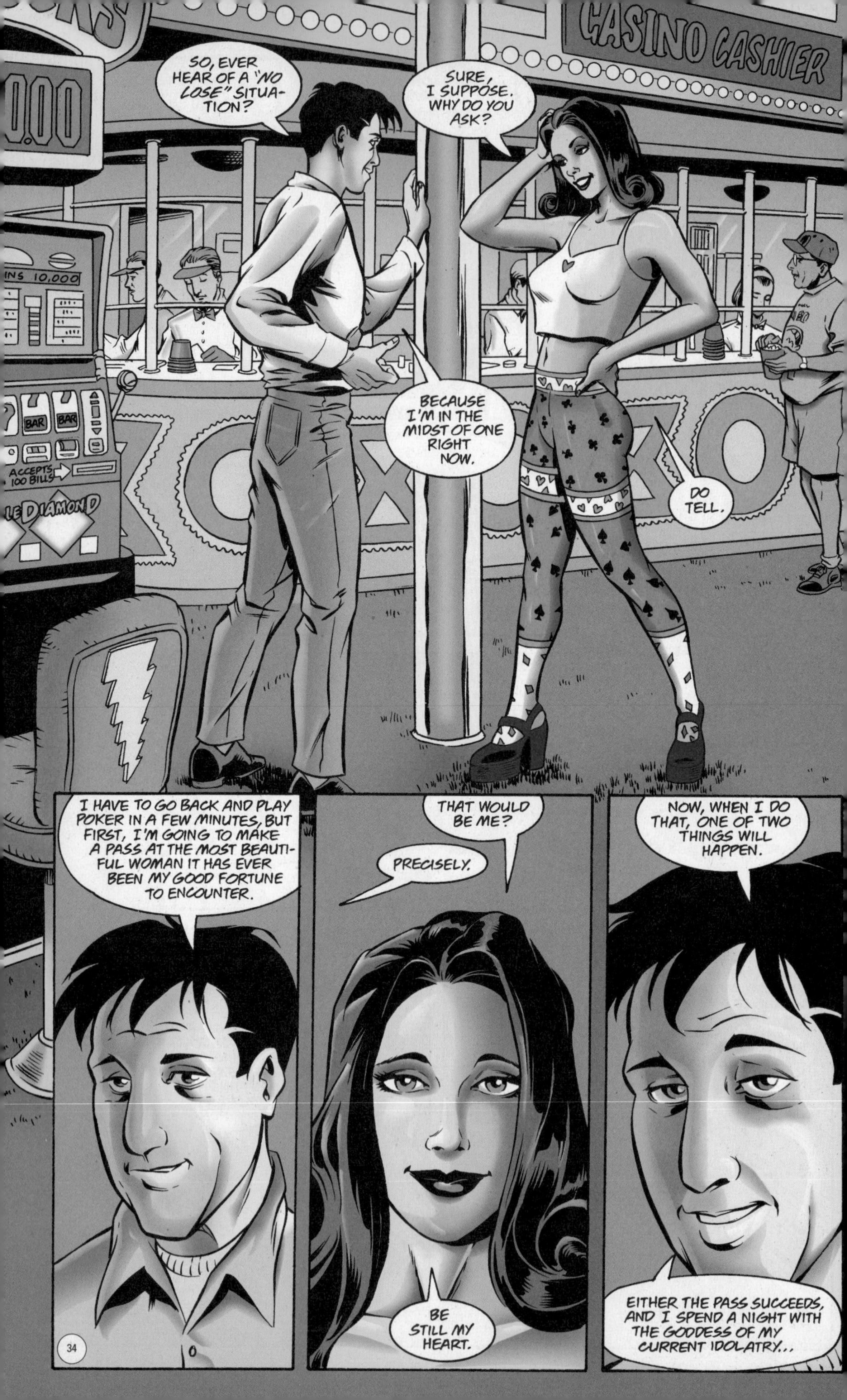
CASINO CASHIER
SO, EVER HEAR OF A "NO LOSE" SITUATION?
SURE, I SUPPOSE. WHY DO YOU ASK?
ACCEPTS 100 BILLS
BECAUSE I'M IN THE MIDST OF ONE RIGHT NOW.
DO TELL.
I HAVE TO GO BACK AND PLAY POKER IN A FEW MINUTES, BUT FIRST, I'M GOING TO MAKE A PASS AT THE MOST BEAUTIFUL WOMAN IT HAS EVER BEEN MY GOOD FORTUNE TO ENCOUNTER.
THAT WOULD BE ME?
PRECISELY.
BE STILL MY HEART.
NOW, WHEN I DO THAT, ONE OF TWO THINGS WILL HAPPEN.
EITHER THE PASS SUCCEEDS, AND I SPEND A NIGHT WITH THE GODDESS OF MY CURRENT IDOLATRY...

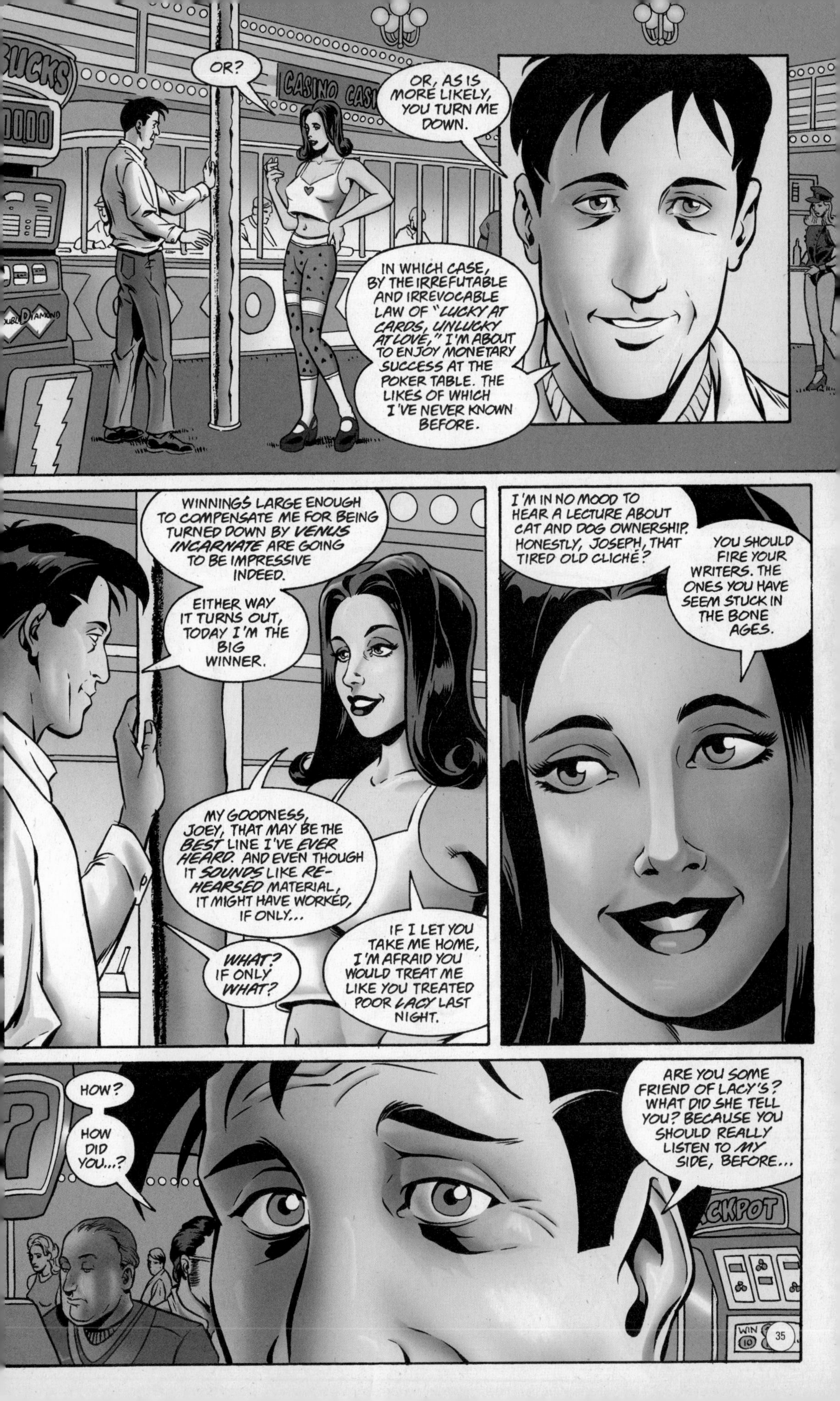
OR?
OR, AS IS MORE LIKELY, YOU TURN ME DOWN.
IN WHICH CASE, BY THE IRREFUTABLE AND IRREVOCABLE LAW OF "LUCKY AT CARDS, UNLUCKY AT LOVE," I'M ABOUT TO ENJOY MONETARY SUCCESS AT THE POKER TABLE. THE LIKES OF WHICH I'VE NEVER KNOWN BEFORE.
WINNINGS LARGE ENOUGH TO COMPENSATE ME FOR BEING TURNED DOWN BY VENUS INCARNATE ARE GOING TO BE IMPRESSIVE INDEED.
EITHER WAY IT TURNS OUT, TODAY I'M THE BIG WINNER.
MY GOODNESS, JOEY, THAT MAY BE THE BEST LINE I'VE EVER HEARD. AND EVEN THOUGH IT SOUNDS LIKE RE-HEARSED MATERIAL, IT MIGHT HAVE WORKED, IF ONLY...
WHAT? IF ONLY WHAT?
IF I LET YOU TAKE ME HOME, I'M AFRAID YOU WOULD TREAT ME LIKE YOU TREATED POOR LACY LAST NIGHT.
I'M IN NO MOOD TO HEAR A LECTURE ABOUT CAT AND DOG OWNERSHIP. HONESTLY, JOSEPH, THAT TIRED OLD CLICHÉ?
YOU SHOULD FIRE YOUR WRITERS. THE ONES YOU HAVE SEEM STUCK IN THE BONE AGES.
HOW?
HOW DID YOU...?
ARE YOU SOME FRIEND OF LACY'S? WHAT DID SHE TELL YOU? BECAUSE YOU SHOULD REALLY LISTEN TO MY SIDE, BEFORE...

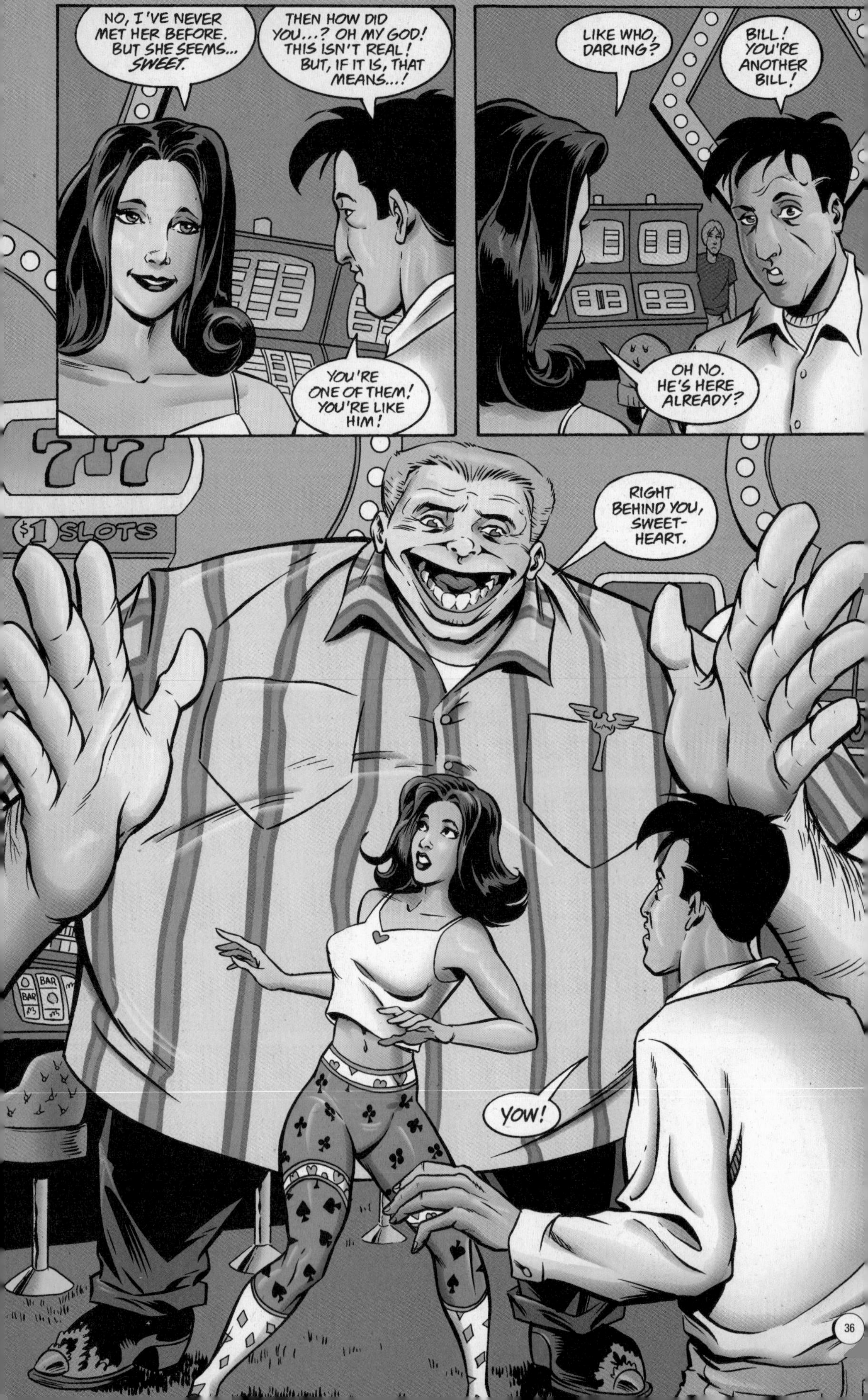
NO, I'VE NEVER MET HER BEFORE. BUT SHE SEEMS... SWEET.
THEN HOW DID YOU...? OH MY GOD! THIS ISN'T REAL! BUT, IF IT IS, THAT MEANS...!
YOU'RE ONE OF THEM! YOU'RE LIKE HIM!
LIKE WHO, DARLING?
BILL! YOU'RE ANOTHER BILL!
OH NO. HE'S HERE ALREADY?
777
$1 SLOTS
RIGHT BEHIND YOU, SWEET-HEART.
BAR
BAR
YOW!

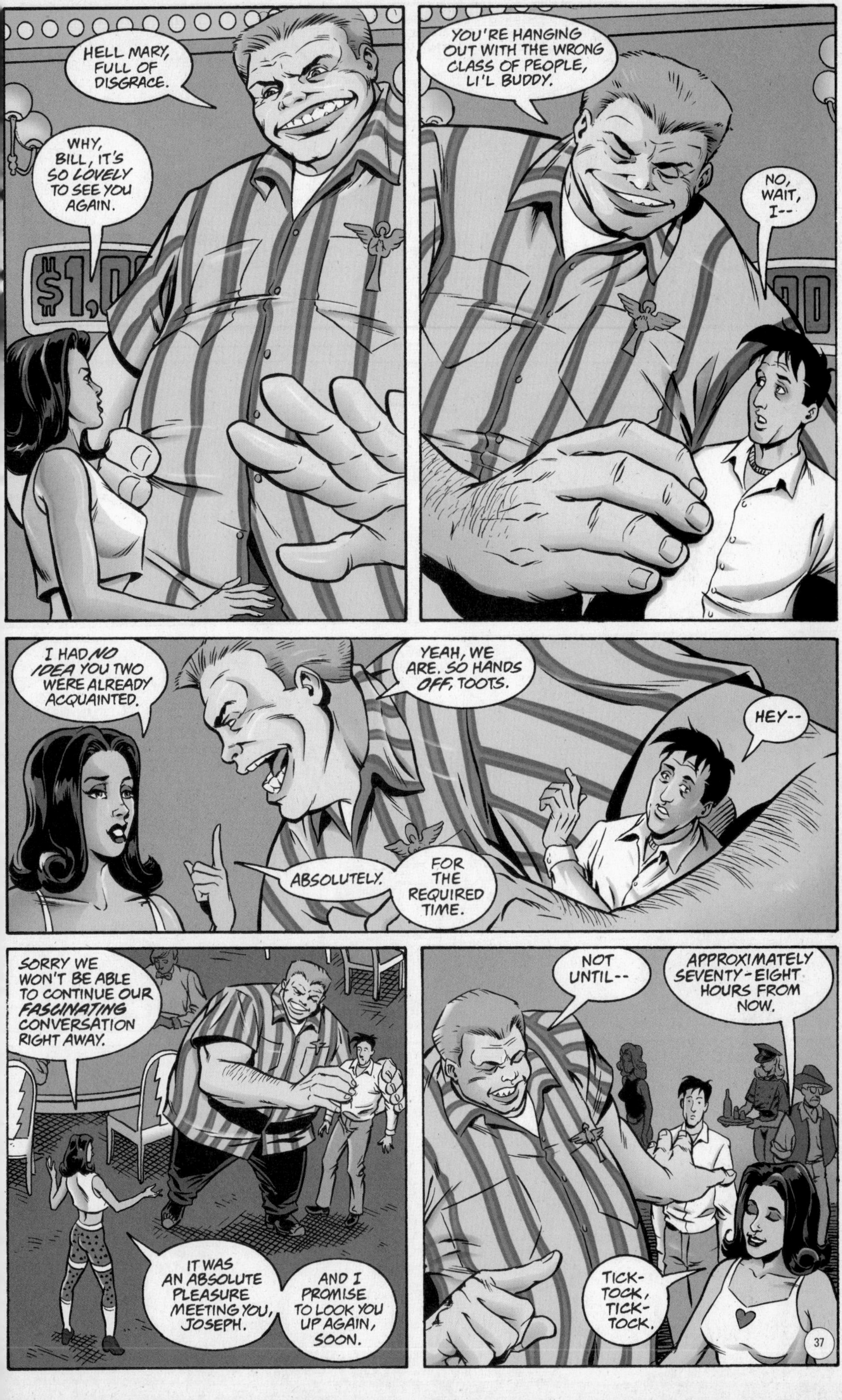
HELL MARY, FULL OF DISGRACE.
WHY, BILL, IT'S SO LOVELY TO SEE YOU AGAIN.
$1,0
YOU'RE HANGING OUT WITH THE WRONG CLASS OF PEOPLE, LI'L BUDDY.
NO, WAIT, I--
I HAD NO IDEA YOU TWO WERE ALREADY ACQUAINTED.
YEAH, WE ARE. SO HANDS OFF, TOOTS.
HEY--
ABSOLUTELY.
FOR THE REQUIRED TIME.
SORRY WE WON'T BE ABLE TO CONTINUE OUR FASCINATING CONVERSATION RIGHT AWAY.
IT WAS AN ABSOLUTE PLEASURE MEETING YOU, JOSEPH.
AND I PROMISE TO LOOK YOU UP AGAIN, SOON.
NOT UNTIL--
APPROXIMATELY SEVENTY-EIGHT HOURS FROM NOW.
TICK-TOCK, TICK-TOCK.

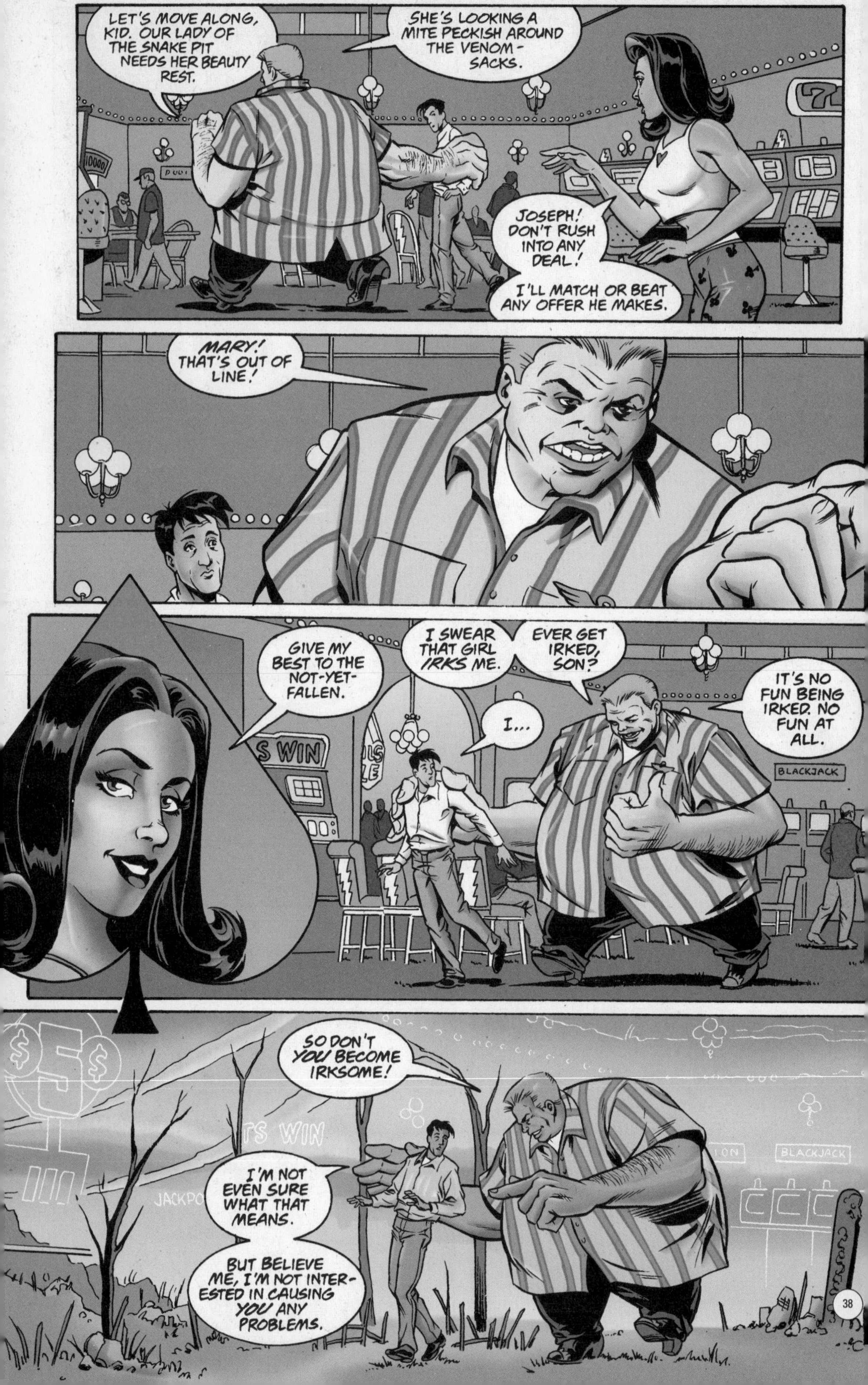
LET'S MOVE ALONG, KID. OUR LADY OF THE SNAKE PIT NEEDS HER BEAUTY REST.
SHE'S LOOKING A MITE PECKISH AROUND THE VENOM-SACKS.
JOSEPH! DON'T RUSH INTO ANY DEAL!
I'LL MATCH OR BEAT ANY OFFER HE MAKES.
MARY! THAT'S OUT OF LINE!
GIVE MY BEST TO THE NOT-YET-FALLEN.
I SWEAR THAT GIRL IRKS ME.
EVER GET IRKED, SON?
I...
IT'S NO FUN BEING IRKED. NO FUN AT ALL.
BLACKJACK
S WIN
SO DON'T YOU BECOME IRKSOME!
I'M NOT EVEN SURE WHAT THAT MEANS.
BUT BELIEVE ME, I'M NOT INTERESTED IN CAUSING YOU ANY PROBLEMS.
BLACKJACK

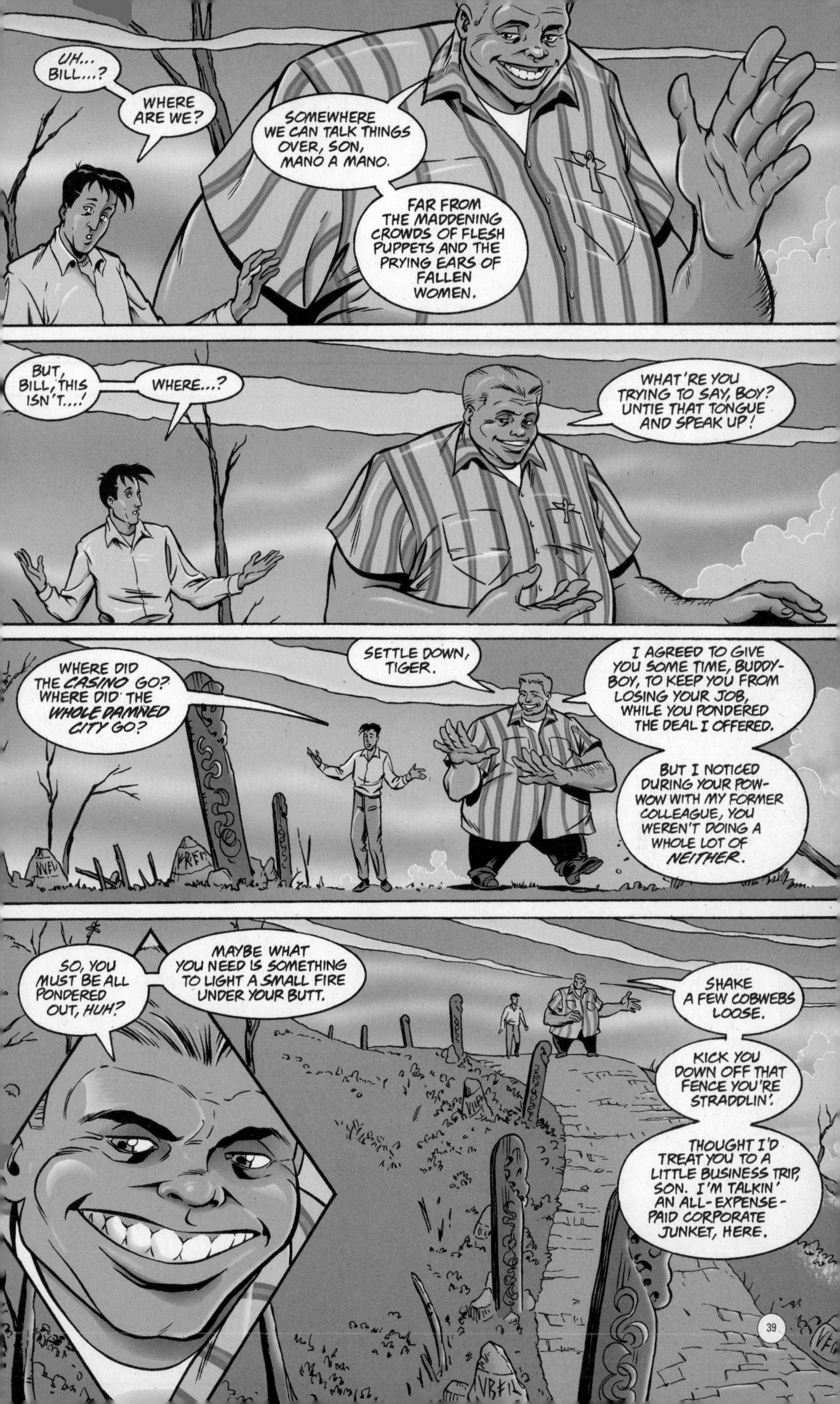
UH... BILL...?
WHERE ARE WE?
SOMEWHERE WE CAN TALK THINGS OVER, SON, MANO A MANO.
FAR FROM THE MADDENING CROWDS OF FLESH PUPPETS AND THE PRYING EARS OF FALLEN WOMEN.
BUT, BILL, THIS ISN'T...!
WHERE...?
WHAT'RE YOU TRYING TO SAY, BOY? UNTIE THAT TONGUE AND SPEAK UP!
WHERE DID THE CASINO GO? WHERE DID THE WHOLE DAMNED CITY GO?
SETTLE DOWN, TIGER.
I AGREED TO GIVE YOU SOME TIME, BUDDY-BOY, TO KEEP YOU FROM LOSING YOUR JOB, WHILE YOU PONDERED THE DEAL I OFFERED.
BUT I NOTICED DURING YOUR POW-WOW WITH MY FORMER COLLEAGUE, YOU WEREN'T DOING A WHOLE LOT OF NEITHER.
SO, YOU MUST BE ALL PONDERED OUT, HUH?
MAYBE WHAT YOU NEED IS SOMETHING TO LIGHT A SMALL FIRE UNDER YOUR BUTT.
SHAKE A FEW COBWEBS LOOSE.
KICK YOU DOWN OFF THAT FENCE YOU'RE STRADDLIN'.
THOUGHT I'D TREAT YOU TO A LITTLE BUSINESS TRIP, SON. I'M TALKIN' AN ALL-EXPENSE-PAID CORPORATE JUNKET, HERE.

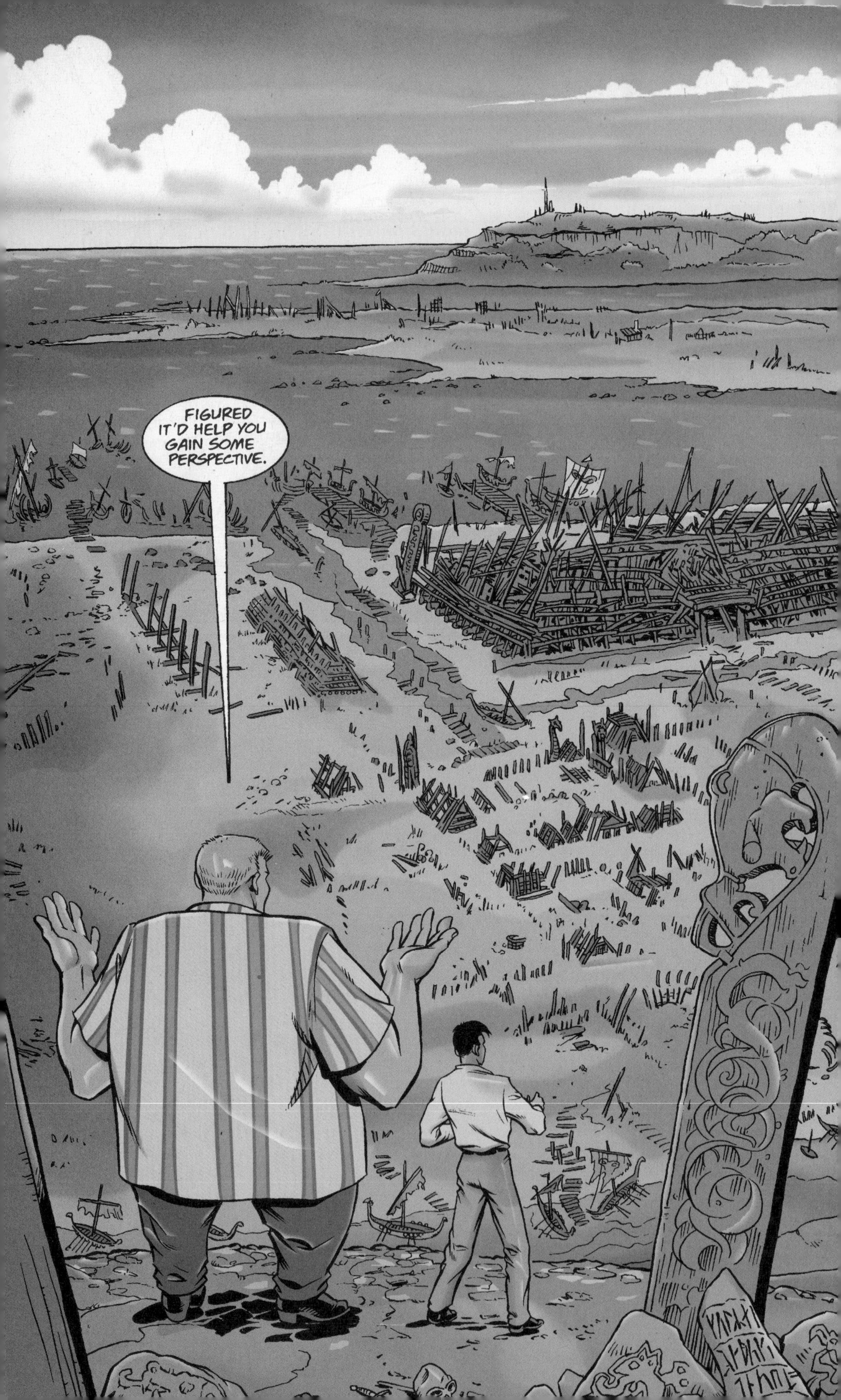
FIGURED IT'D HELP YOU GAIN SOME PERSPECTIVE.

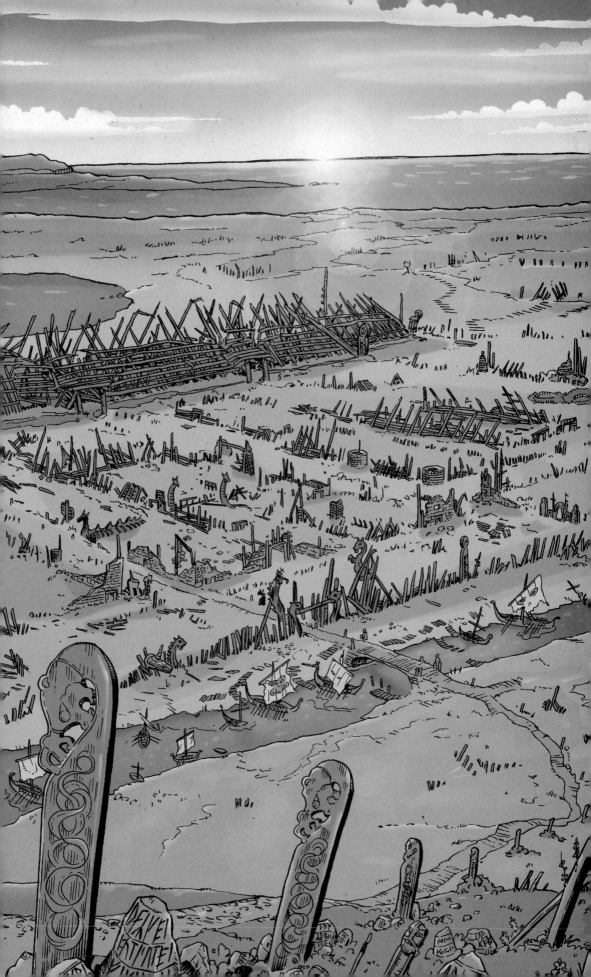

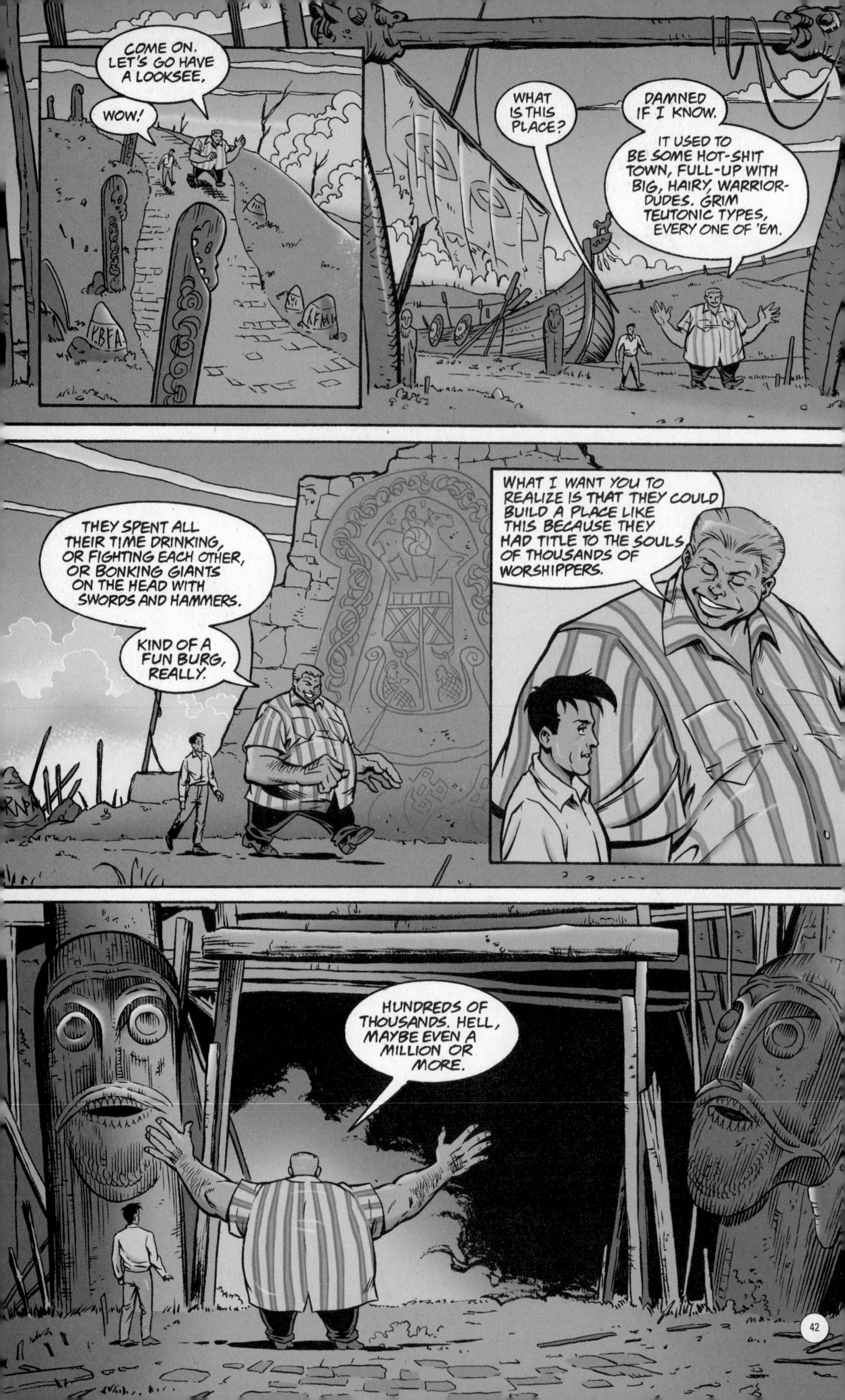

COME ON. LET'S GO HAVE A LOOKSEE.
WOW!
WHAT IS THIS PLACE?
DAMNED IF I KNOW.
IT USED TO BE SOME HOT-SHIT TOWN, FULL-UP WITH BIG, HAIRY, WARRIOR-DUDES. GRIM TEUTONIC TYPES, EVERY ONE OF 'EM.
THEY SPENT ALL THEIR TIME DRINKING, OR FIGHTING EACH OTHER, OR BONKING GIANTS ON THE HEAD WITH SWORDS AND HAMMERS.
KIND OF A FUN BURG, REALLY.
WHAT I WANT YOU TO REALIZE IS THAT THEY COULD BUILD A PLACE LIKE THIS BECAUSE THEY HAD TITLE TO THE SOULS OF THOUSANDS OF WORSHIPPERS.
HUNDREDS OF THOUSANDS. HELL, MAYBE EVEN A MILLION OR MORE.

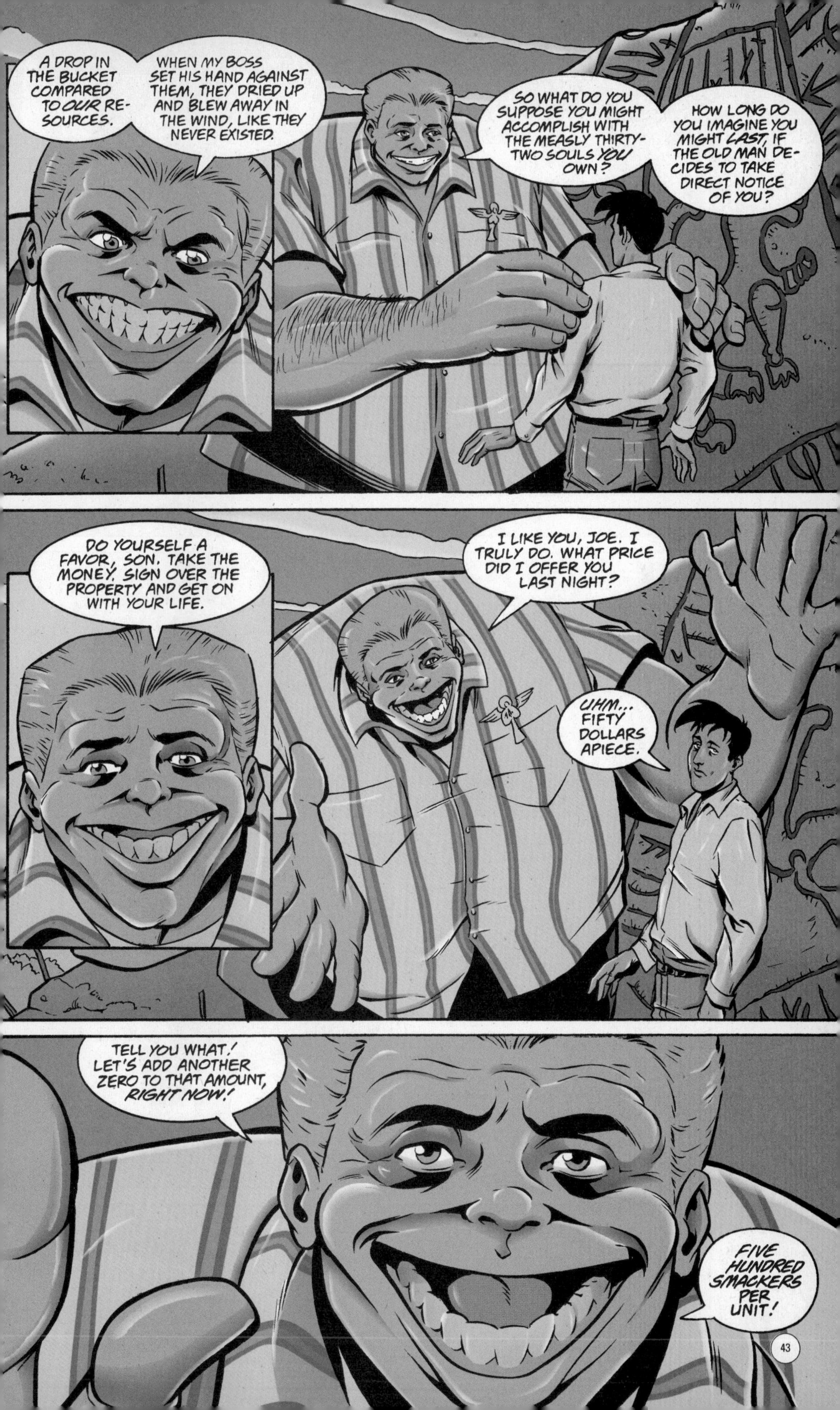
A DROP IN THE BUCKET COMPARED TO OUR RE-SOURCES.
WHEN MY BOSS SET HIS HAND AGAINST THEM, THEY DRIED UP AND BLEW AWAY IN THE WIND, LIKE THEY NEVER EXISTED.
SO WHAT DO YOU SUPPOSE YOU MIGHT ACCOMPLISH WITH THE MEASLY THIRTY-TWO SOULS YOU OWN?
HOW LONG DO YOU IMAGINE YOU MIGHT LAST, IF THE OLD MAN DE-CIDES TO TAKE DIRECT NOTICE OF YOU?
DO YOURSELF A FAVOR, SON. TAKE THE MONEY. SIGN OVER THE PROPERTY AND GET ON WITH YOUR LIFE.
I LIKE YOU, JOE. I TRULY DO. WHAT PRICE DID I OFFER YOU LAST NIGHT?
UHM... FIFTY DOLLARS APIECE.
TELL YOU WHAT! LET'S ADD ANOTHER ZERO TO THAT AMOUNT, RIGHT NOW!
FIVE HUNDRED SMACKERS PER UNIT!

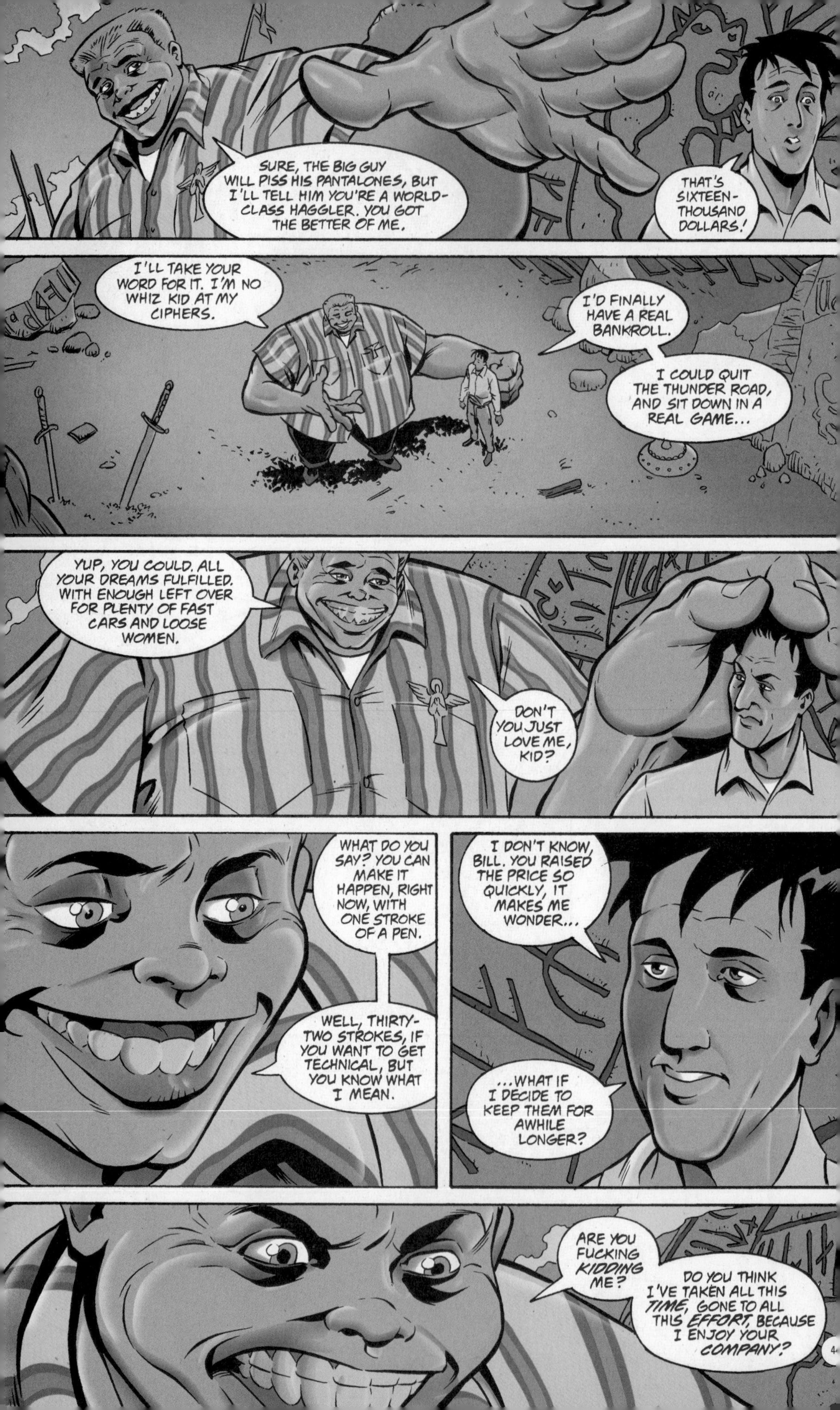

SURE, THE BIG GUY WILL PISS HIS PANTALONES, BUT I'LL TELL HIM YOU'RE A WORLD-CLASS HAGGLER. YOU GOT THE BETTER OF ME.
THAT'S SIXTEEN-THOUSAND DOLLARS!
I'LL TAKE YOUR WORD FOR IT. I'M NO WHIZ KID AT MY CIPHERS.
I'D FINALLY HAVE A REAL BANKROLL.
I COULD QUIT THE THUNDER ROAD, AND SIT DOWN IN A REAL GAME...
YUP, YOU COULD. ALL YOUR DREAMS FULFILLED. WITH ENOUGH LEFT OVER FOR PLENTY OF FAST CARS AND LOOSE WOMEN.
DON'T YOU JUST LOVE ME, KID?
WHAT DO YOU SAY? YOU CAN MAKE IT HAPPEN, RIGHT NOW, WITH ONE STROKE OF A PEN.
WELL, THIRTY-TWO STROKES, IF YOU WANT TO GET TECHNICAL, BUT YOU KNOW WHAT I MEAN.
I DON'T KNOW, BILL. YOU RAISED THE PRICE SO QUICKLY, IT MAKES ME WONDER...
...WHAT IF I DECIDE TO KEEP THEM FOR AWHILE LONGER?
ARE YOU FUCKING *KIDDING* ME?
DO YOU THINK I'VE TAKEN ALL THIS *TIME*, GONE TO ALL THIS *EFFORT*, BECAUSE I ENJOY YOUR *COMPANY*?

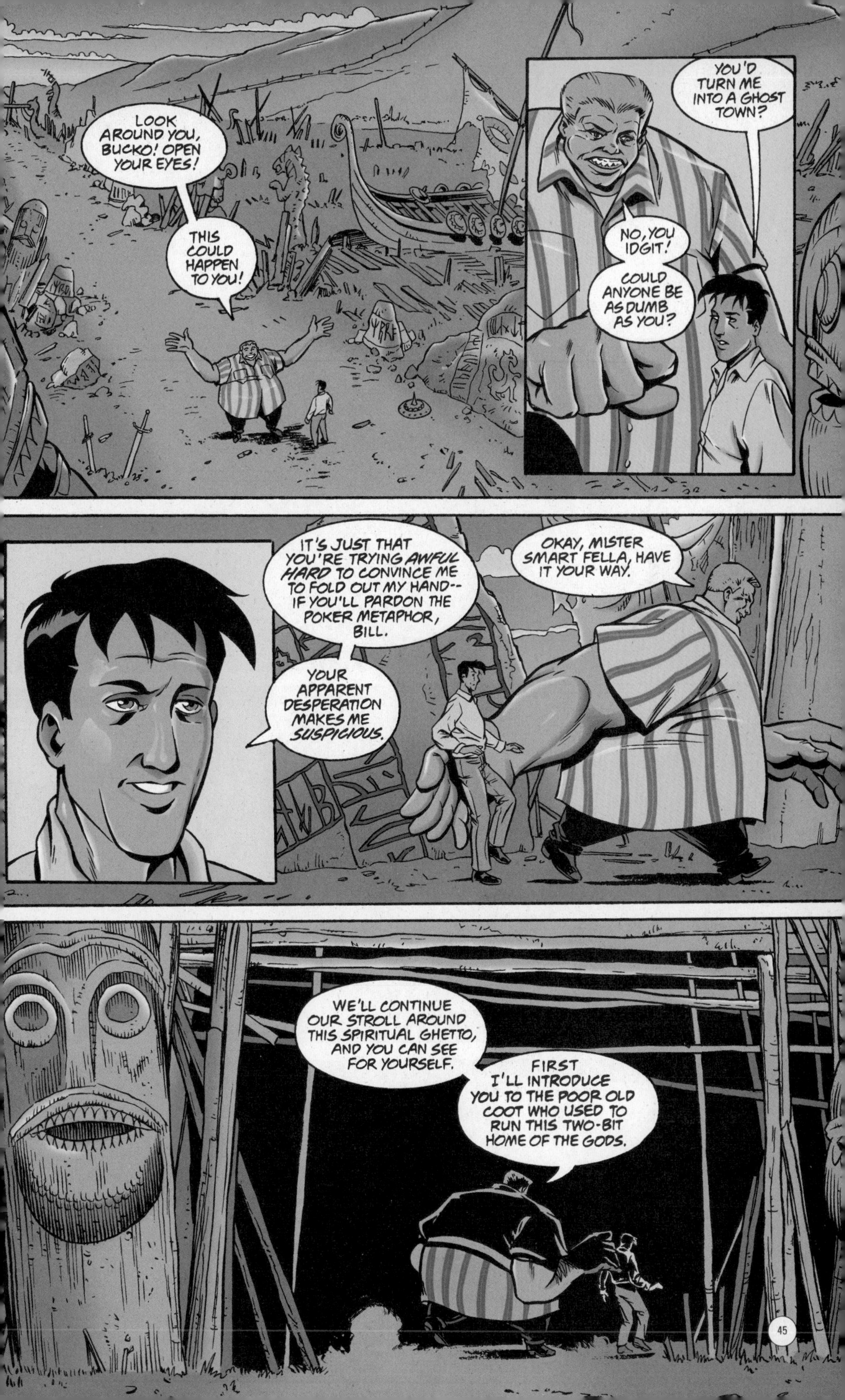
LOOK AROUND YOU, BUCKO! OPEN YOUR EYES!
THIS COULD HAPPEN TO YOU!
YOU'D TURN ME INTO A GHOST TOWN?
NO, YOU IDGIT!
COULD ANYONE BE AS DUMB AS YOU?
IT'S JUST THAT YOU'RE TRYING AWFUL HARD TO CONVINCE ME TO FOLD OUT MY HAND-- IF YOU'LL PARDON THE POKER METAPHOR, BILL.
YOUR APPARENT DESPERATION MAKES ME SUSPICIOUS.
OKAY, MISTER SMART FELLA, HAVE IT YOUR WAY.
WE'LL CONTINUE OUR STROLL AROUND THIS SPIRITUAL GHETTO, AND YOU CAN SEE FOR YOURSELF.
FIRST I'LL INTRODUCE YOU TO THE POOR OLD COOT WHO USED TO RUN THIS TWO-BIT HOME OF THE GODS.

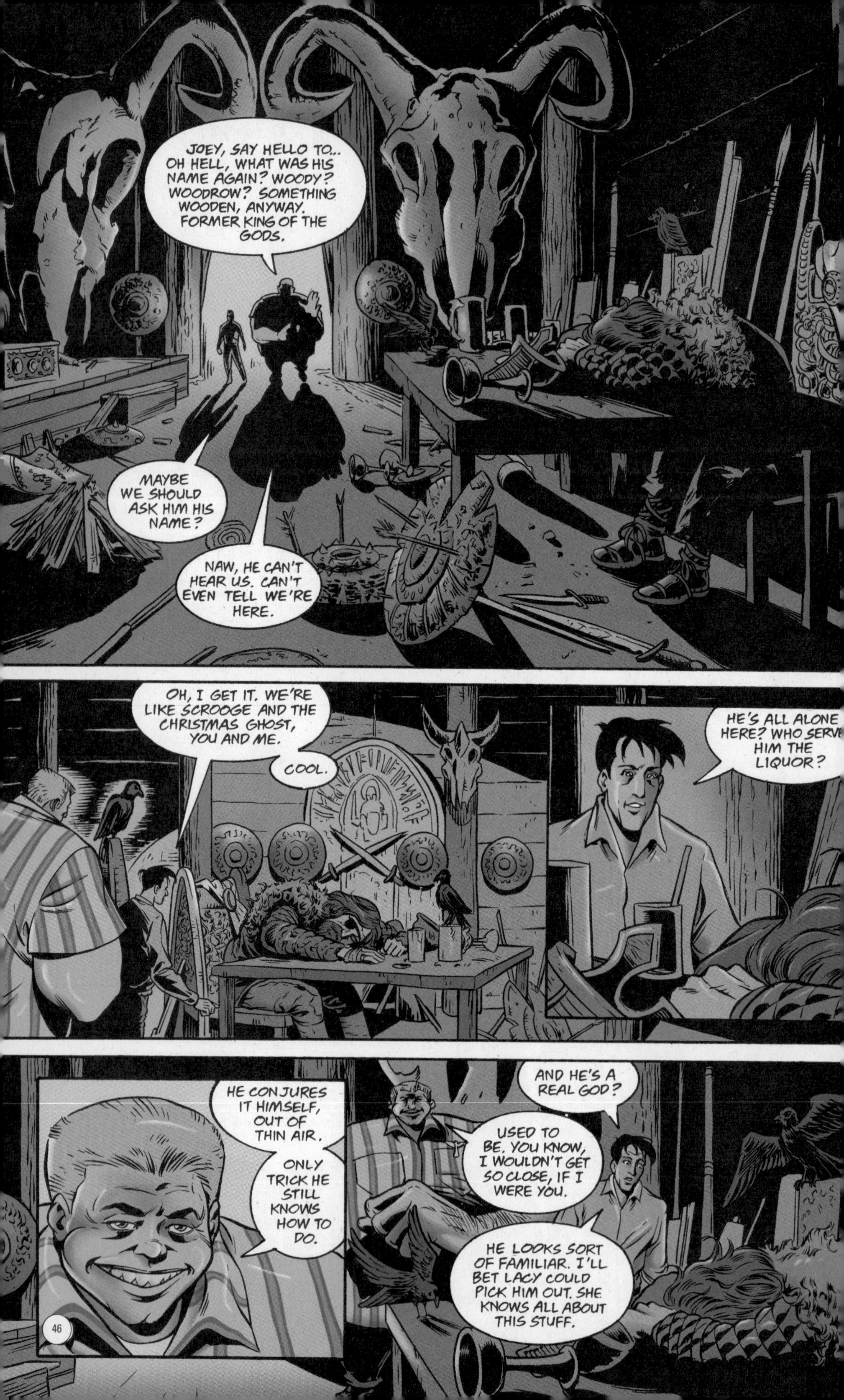
JOEY, SAY HELLO TO... OH HELL, WHAT WAS HIS NAME AGAIN? WOODY? WOODROW? SOMETHING WOODEN, ANYWAY. FORMER KING OF THE GODS.
MAYBE WE SHOULD ASK HIM HIS NAME?
NAW, HE CAN'T HEAR US. CAN'T EVEN TELL WE'RE HERE.
OH, I GET IT. WE'RE LIKE SCROOGE AND THE CHRISTMAS GHOST, YOU AND ME.
COOL.
HE'S ALL ALONE HERE? WHO SERVE HIM THE LIQUOR?
HE CONJURES IT HIMSELF, OUT OF THIN AIR.
ONLY TRICK HE STILL KNOWS HOW TO DO.
AND HE'S A REAL GOD?
USED TO BE. YOU KNOW, I WOULDN'T GET SO CLOSE, IF I WERE YOU.
HE LOOKS SORT OF FAMILIAR. I'LL BET LACY COULD PICK HIM OUT. SHE KNOWS ALL ABOUT THIS STUFF.

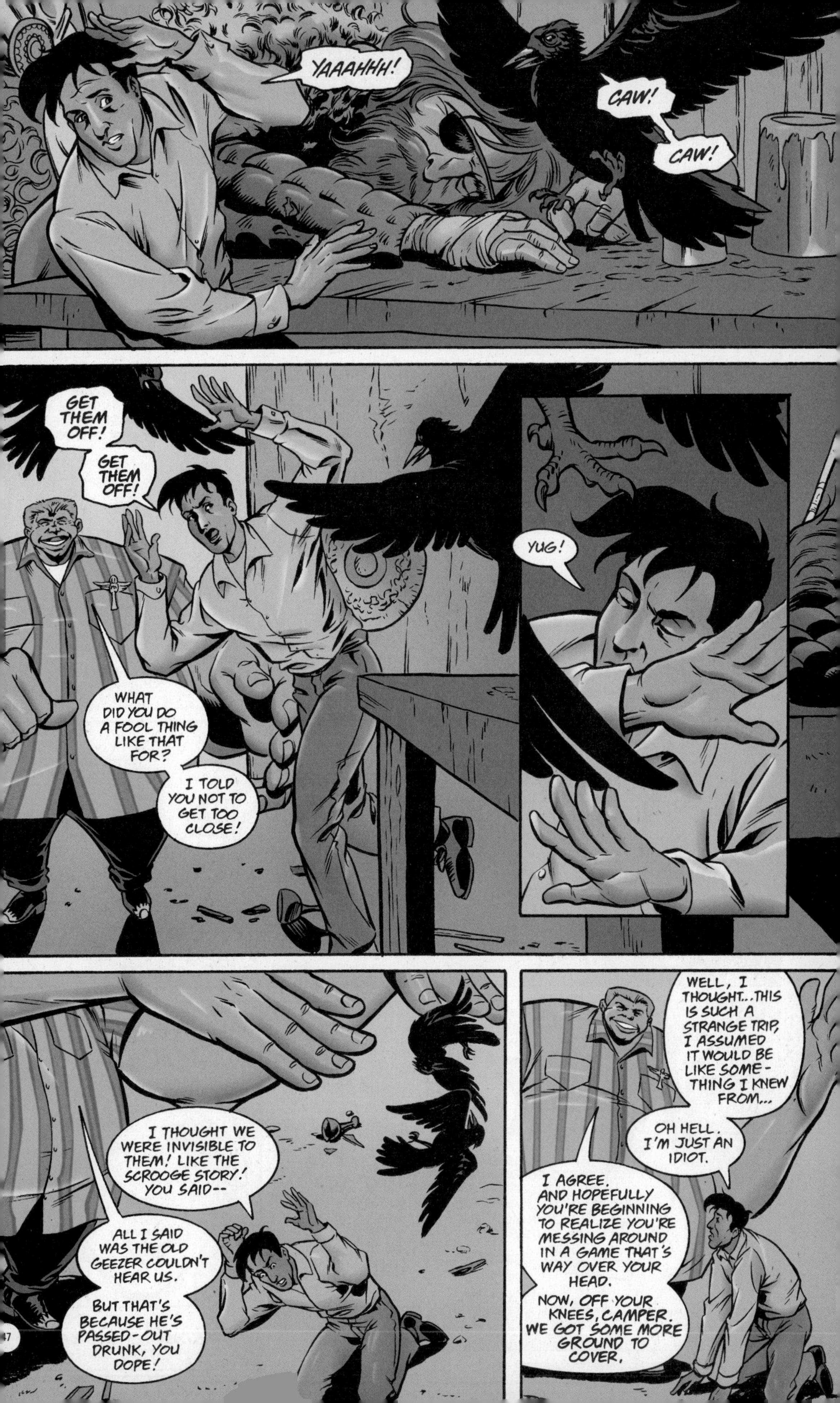

YAAAHHH!
CAW!
CAW!
GET THEM OFF!
GET THEM OFF!
YUG!
WHAT DID YOU DO A FOOL THING LIKE THAT FOR?
I TOLD YOU NOT TO GET TOO CLOSE!
I THOUGHT WE WERE INVISIBLE TO THEM! LIKE THE SCROOGE STORY! YOU SAID--
ALL I SAID WAS THE OLD GEEZER COULDN'T HEAR US.
BUT THAT'S BECAUSE HE'S PASSED-OUT DRUNK, YOU DOPE!
WELL, I THOUGHT...THIS IS SUCH A STRANGE TRIP, I ASSUMED IT WOULD BE LIKE SOME-THING I KNEW FROM...
OH HELL. I'M JUST AN IDIOT.
I AGREE. AND HOPEFULLY YOU'RE BEGINNING TO REALIZE YOU'RE MESSING AROUND IN A GAME THAT'S WAY OVER YOUR HEAD.
NOW, OFF YOUR KNEES, CAMPER. WE GOT SOME MORE GROUND TO COVER.

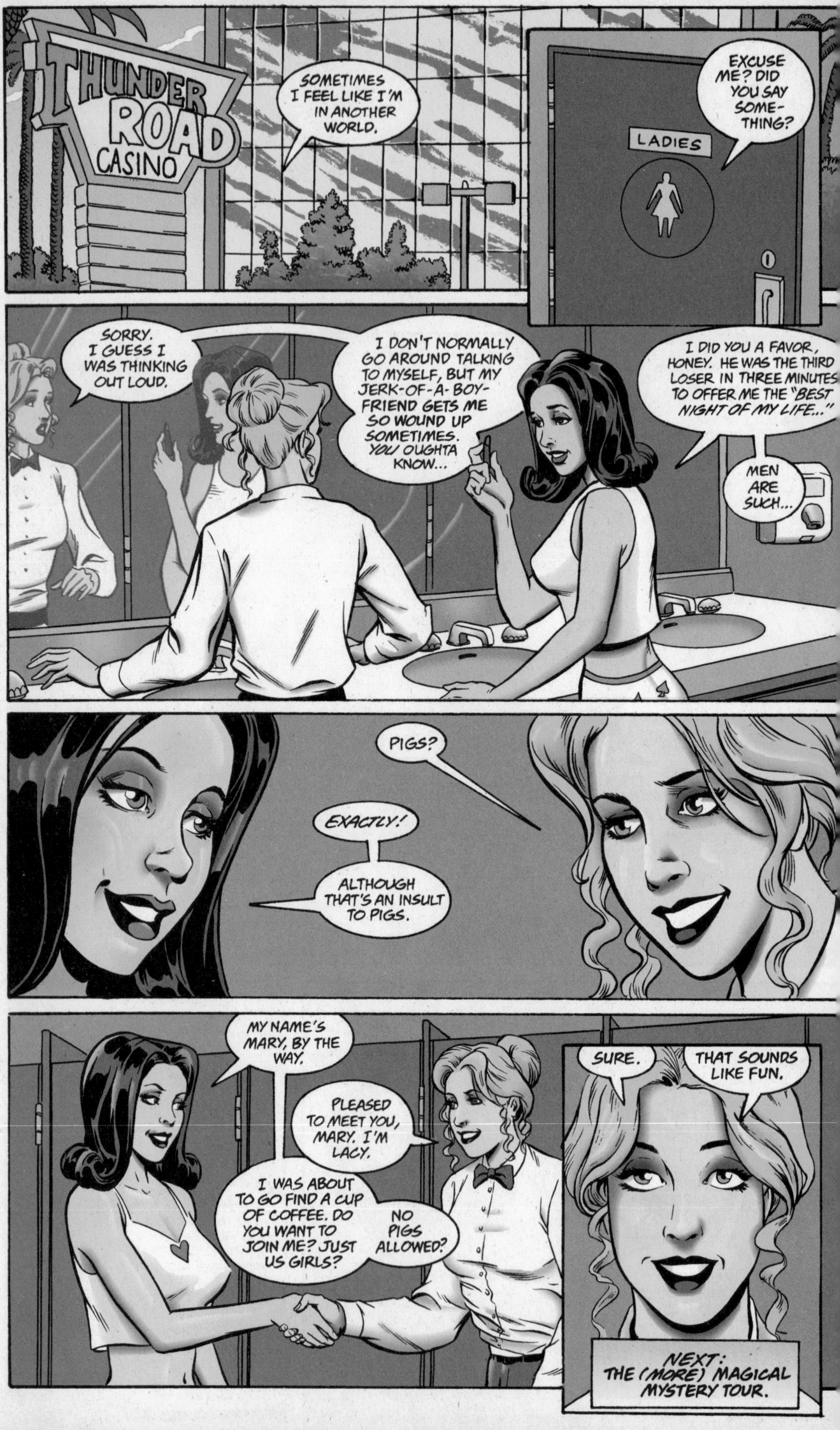
THUNDER ROAD CASINO
SOMETIMES I FEEL LIKE I'M IN ANOTHER WORLD.
LADIES
EXCUSE ME? DID YOU SAY SOME-THING?
SORRY. I GUESS I WAS THINKING OUT LOUD.
I DON'T NORMALLY GO AROUND TALKING TO MYSELF, BUT MY JERK-OF-A-BOY-FRIEND GETS ME SO WOUND UP SOMETIMES. YOU OUGHTA KNOW...
I DID YOU A FAVOR, HONEY. HE WAS THE THIRD LOSER IN THREE MINUTES TO OFFER ME THE "BEST NIGHT OF MY LIFE..."
MEN ARE SUCH...
PIGS?
EXACTLY!
ALTHOUGH THAT'S AN INSULT TO PIGS.
MY NAME'S MARY, BY THE WAY.
PLEASED TO MEET YOU, MARY. I'M LACY.
I WAS ABOUT TO GO FIND A CUP OF COFFEE. DO YOU WANT TO JOIN ME? JUST US GIRLS?
NO PIGS ALLOWED?
SURE.
THAT SOUNDS LIKE FUN.
NEXT: THE (MORE) MAGICAL MYSTERY TOUR.

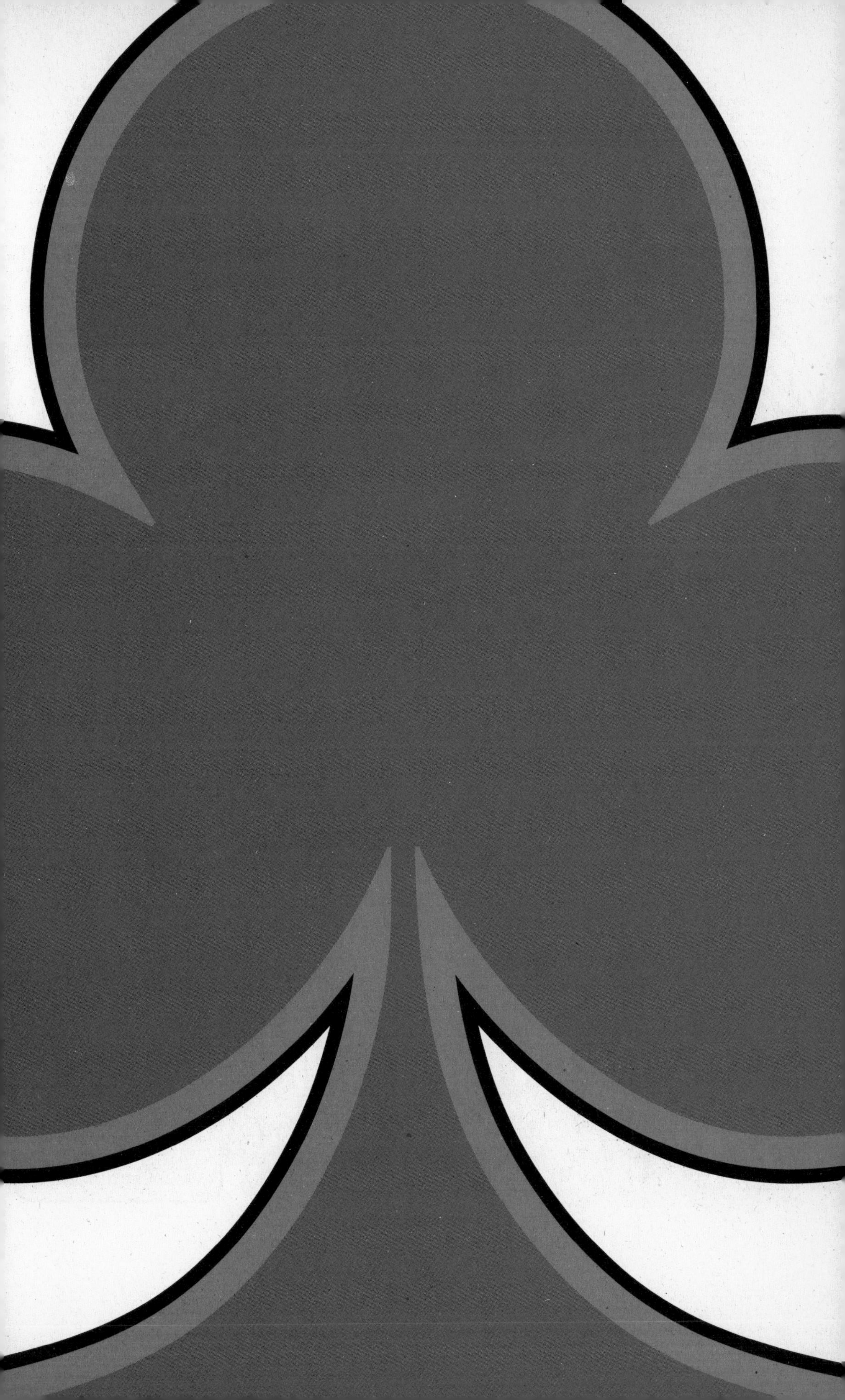

THE STORY SO FAR: IN THE COMPANY OF BILL, THE ANGEL OF THE LORD, JOEY BEGAN A TOUR OF STRANGE OTHER LANDS, FAR FROM ANY PART OF OUR OWN WORLD. BILL'S JOB IS TO FORCE JOEY TO SIGN OVER HIS THIRTY-TWO SOULS BY SHOWING HIM WHAT HAPPENS TO THOSE WHO GO AGAINST THE WISHES OF HIS HEAVENLY BOSSES. MEANWHILE, HELL MARY, AN AGENT OF THE INFERNAL REALM, AND BILL'S DIRECT COUNTERPART IN THIS ASSIGNMENT, HAS ENTERED THE SCENE. THE CELESTIAL RULES OF ENGAGEMENT REQUIRE THAT SHE LET BILL HAVE AN UNHINDERED FIRST SHO AT THEIR QUARRY. BUT THE HOURS ARE PASSING EVER CLOSER TO THE TIME WHEN SHE, TOO, CAN HAVE HER CHANCE TO WIN, STEAL OR BUY JOEY'S SMALL TREASURE OF CONTRABAND SOULS. AND WHILE HELL MARY WAITS HER TURN, SHE GETS "CHUMMY" WITH JOEY'S (EX?) GIRLFRIEND.

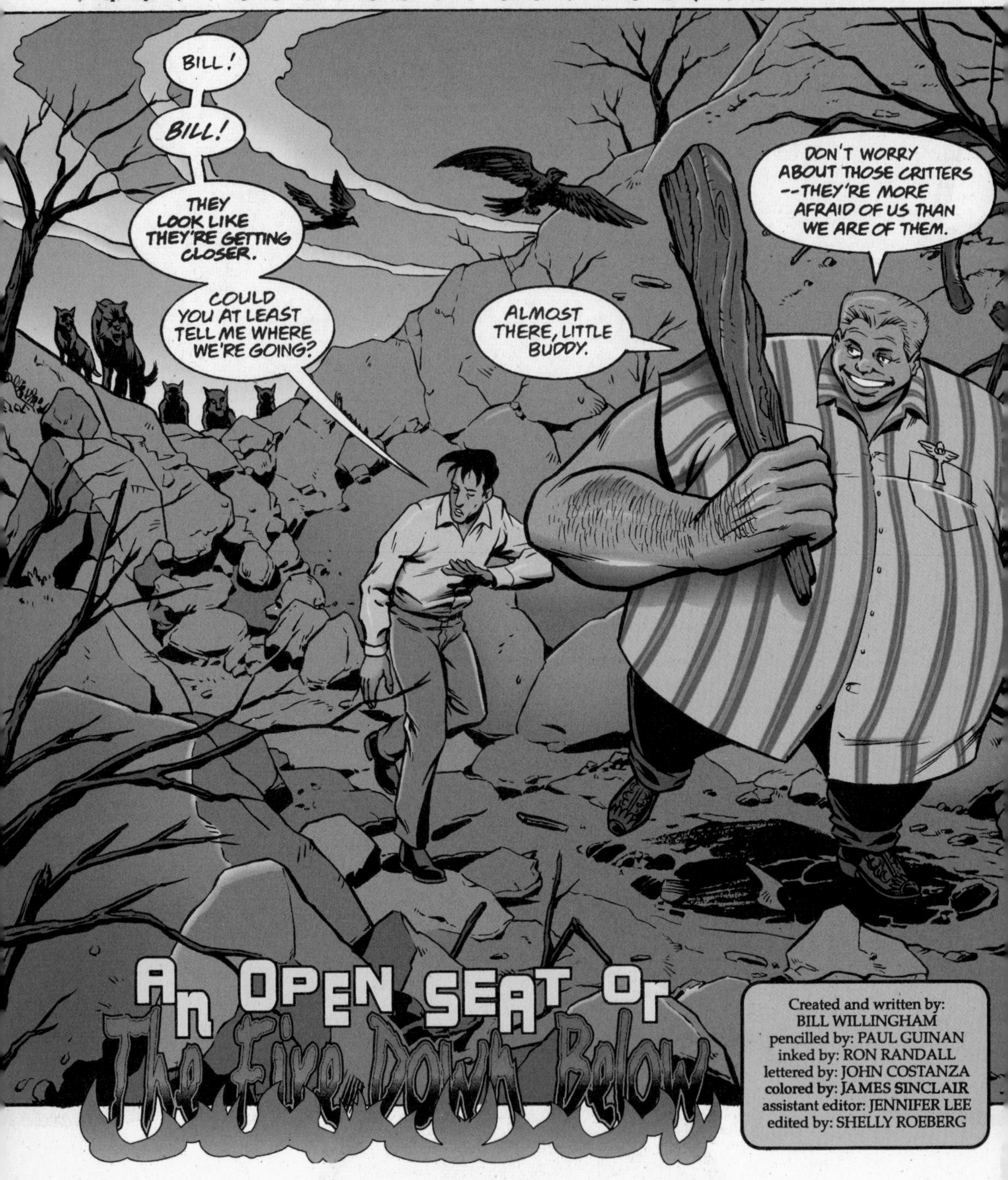

BILL!
BILL!
THEY LOOK LIKE THEY'RE GETTING CLOSER.
COULD YOU AT LEAST TELL ME WHERE WE'RE GOING?
ALMOST THERE, LITTLE BUDDY.
DON'T WORRY ABOUT THOSE CRITTERS --THEY'RE MORE AFRAID OF US THAN WE ARE OF THEM.
An OPEN SEAT or
The Fire Down Below
Created and written by: BILL WILLINGHAM
pencilled by: PAUL GUINAN
inked by: RON RANDALL
lettered by: JOHN COSTANZA
colored by: JAMES SINCLAIR
assistant editor: JENNIFER LEE
edited by: SHELLY ROEBERG

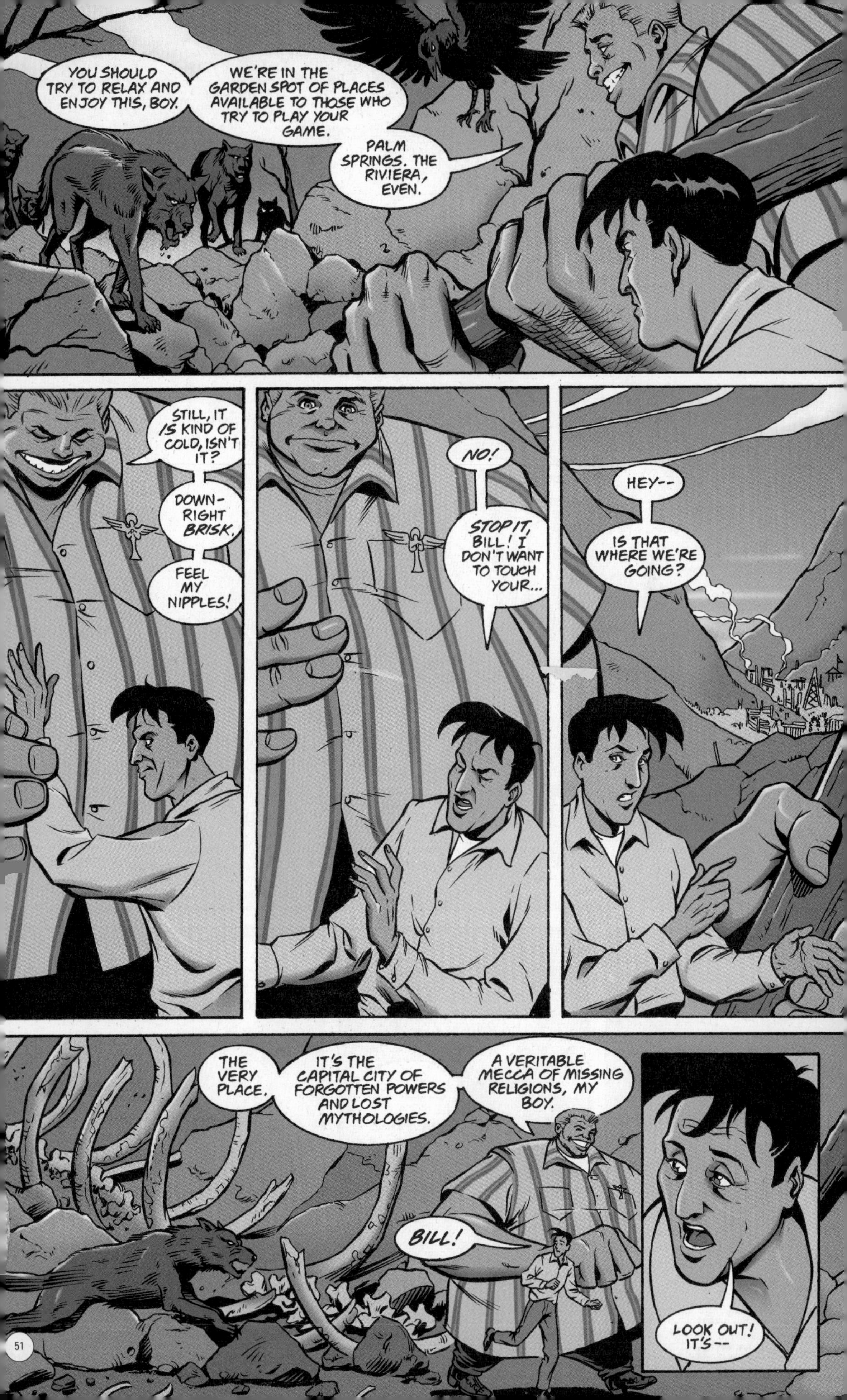
YOU SHOULD TRY TO RELAX AND ENJOY THIS, BOY.
WE'RE IN THE GARDEN SPOT OF PLACES AVAILABLE TO THOSE WHO TRY TO PLAY YOUR GAME.
PALM SPRINGS. THE RIVIERA, EVEN.
STILL, IT IS KIND OF COLD, ISN'T IT?
DOWN-RIGHT BRISK.
FEEL MY NIPPLES!
NO!
STOP IT, BILL! I DON'T WANT TO TOUCH YOUR...
HEY--
IS THAT WHERE WE'RE GOING?
THE VERY PLACE.
IT'S THE CAPITAL CITY OF FORGOTTEN POWERS AND LOST MYTHOLOGIES.
A VERITABLE MECCA OF MISSING RELIGIONS, MY BOY.
BILL!
LOOK OUT! IT'S --

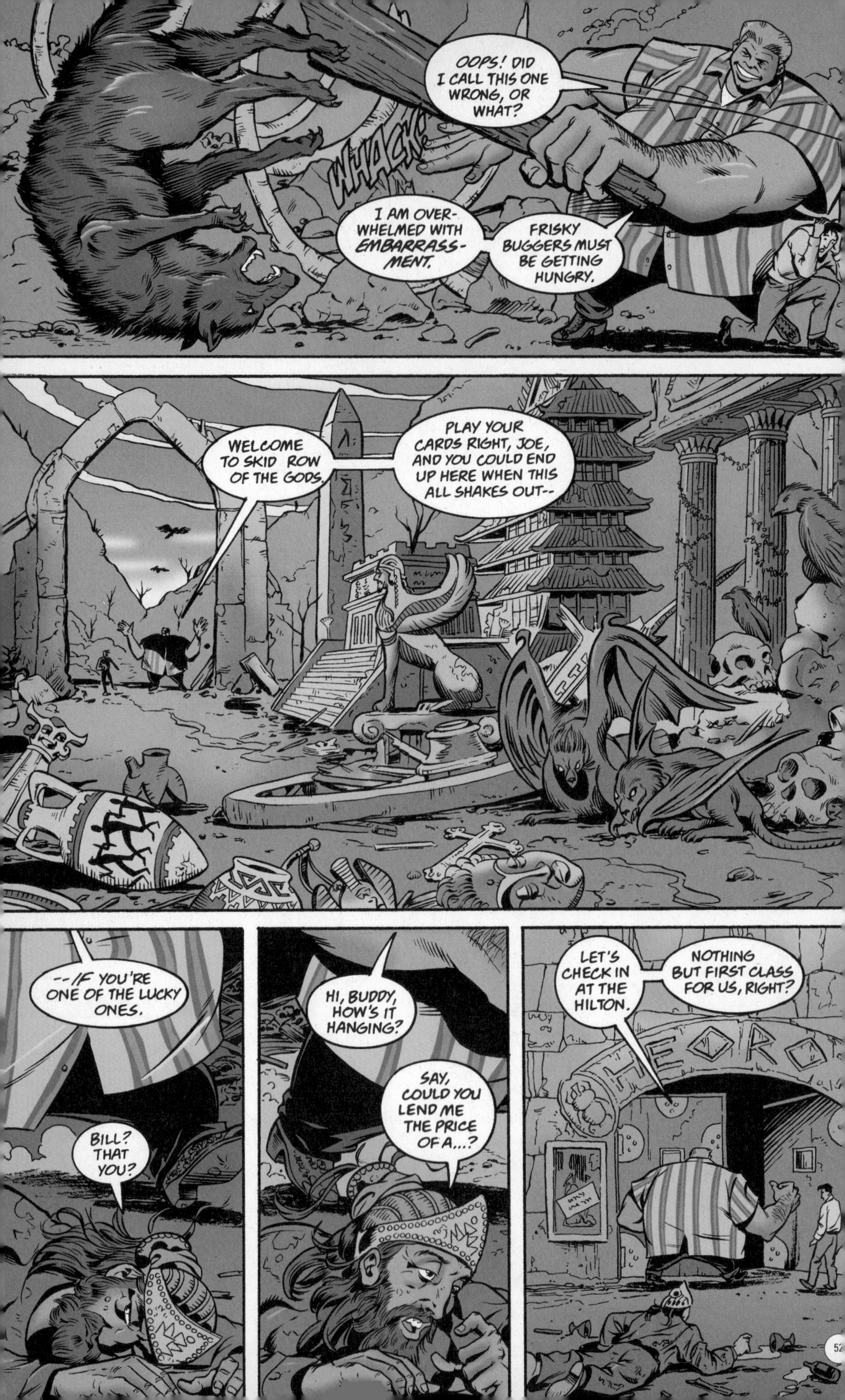
OOPS! DID I CALL THIS ONE WRONG, OR WHAT?
WHACK!
I AM OVER-WHELMED WITH EMBARRASS-MENT.
FRISKY BUGGERS MUST BE GETTING HUNGRY.
WELCOME TO SKID ROW OF THE GODS.
PLAY YOUR CARDS RIGHT, JOE, AND YOU COULD END UP HERE WHEN THIS ALL SHAKES OUT--
--IF YOU'RE ONE OF THE LUCKY ONES.
BILL? THAT YOU?
HI, BUDDY, HOW'S IT HANGING?
SAY, COULD YOU LEND ME THE PRICE OF A...?
LET'S CHECK IN AT THE HILTON.
NOTHING BUT FIRST CLASS FOR US, RIGHT?
HEORO

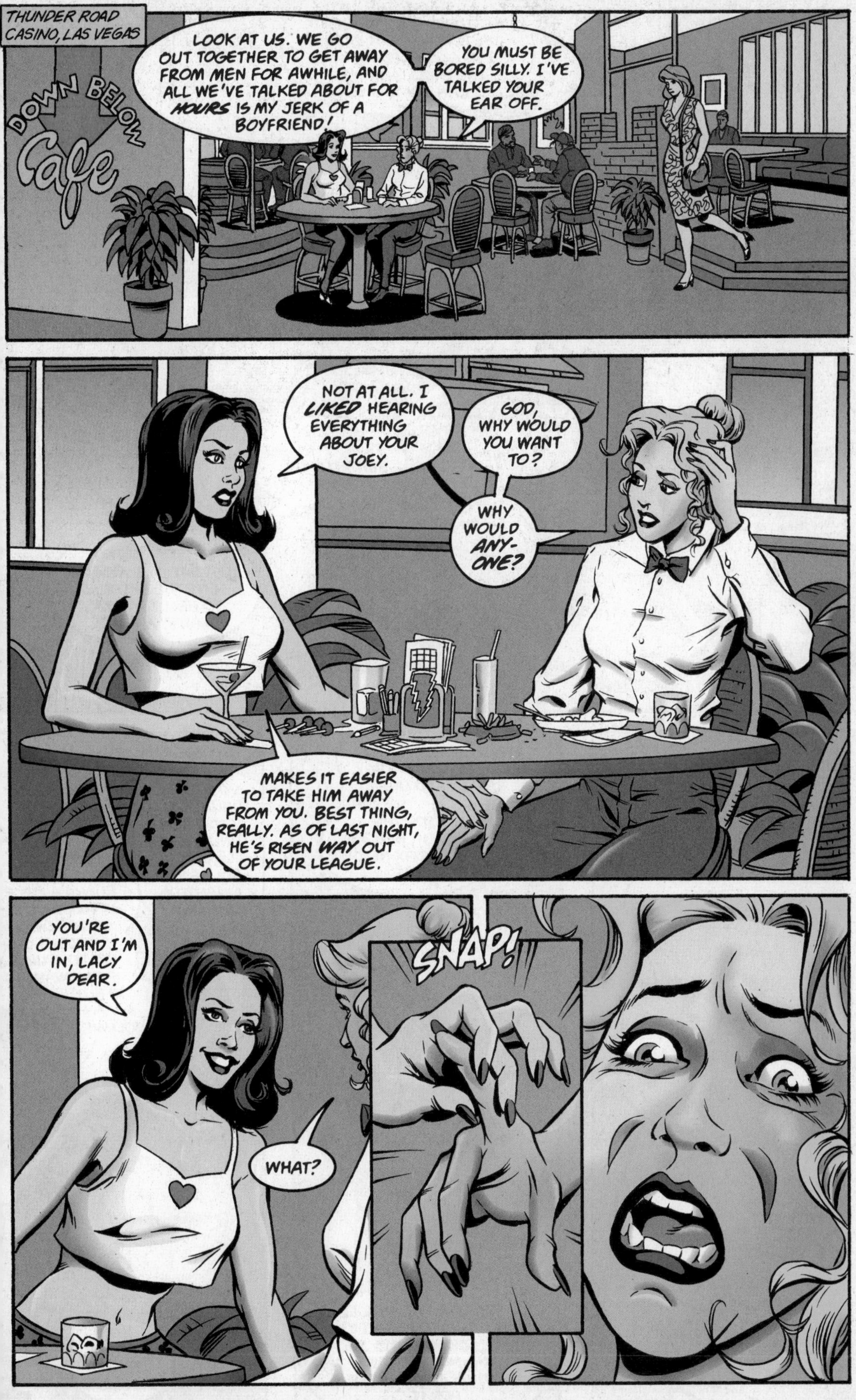
THUNDER ROAD CASINO, LAS VEGAS
DOWN BELOW Cafe
LOOK AT US. WE GO OUT TOGETHER TO GET AWAY FROM MEN FOR AWHILE, AND ALL WE'VE TALKED ABOUT FOR HOURS IS MY JERK OF A BOYFRIEND!
YOU MUST BE BORED SILLY. I'VE TALKED YOUR EAR OFF.
NOT AT ALL. I LIKED HEARING EVERYTHING ABOUT YOUR JOEY.
GOD, WHY WOULD YOU WANT TO?
WHY WOULD ANY-ONE?
MAKES IT EASIER TO TAKE HIM AWAY FROM YOU. BEST THING, REALLY. AS OF LAST NIGHT, HE'S RISEN WAY OUT OF YOUR LEAGUE.
YOU'RE OUT AND I'M IN, LACY DEAR.
WHAT?
SNAP!

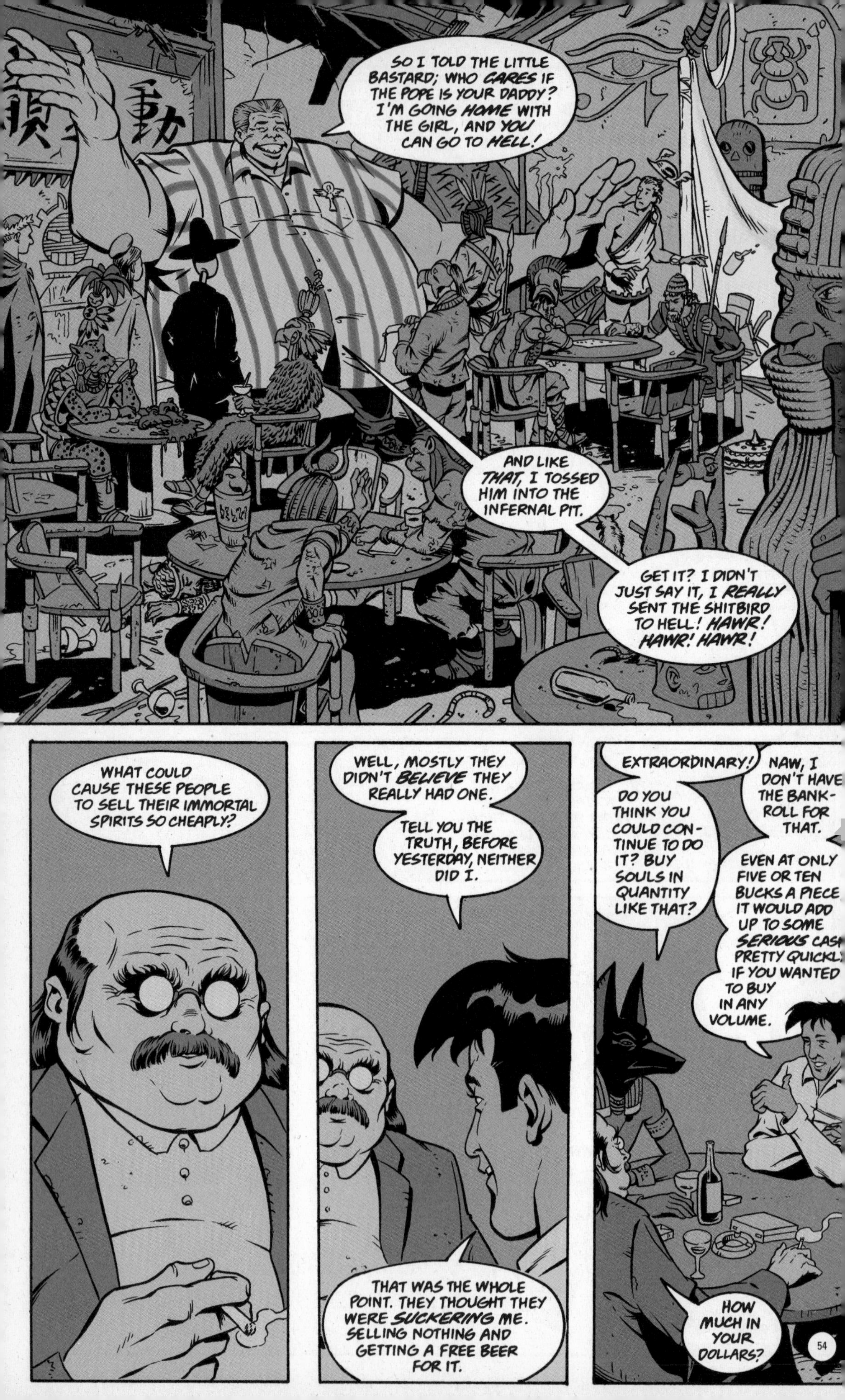
SO I TOLD THE LITTLE BASTARD; WHO CARES IF THE POPE IS YOUR DADDY? I'M GOING HOME WITH THE GIRL, AND YOU CAN GO TO HELL!
AND LIKE THAT, I TOSSED HIM INTO THE INFERNAL PIT.
GET IT? I DIDN'T JUST SAY IT, I REALLY SENT THE SHITBIRD TO HELL! HAWR! HAWR! HAWR!
WHAT COULD CAUSE THESE PEOPLE TO SELL THEIR IMMORTAL SPIRITS SO CHEAPLY?
WELL, MOSTLY THEY DIDN'T BELIEVE THEY REALLY HAD ONE.
TELL YOU THE TRUTH, BEFORE YESTERDAY, NEITHER DID I.
THAT WAS THE WHOLE POINT. THEY THOUGHT THEY WERE SUCKERING ME. SELLING NOTHING AND GETTING A FREE BEER FOR IT.
EXTRAORDINARY!
DO YOU THINK YOU COULD CON-TINUE TO DO IT? BUY SOULS IN QUANTITY LIKE THAT?
NAW, I DON'T HAVE THE BANK-ROLL FOR THAT.
EVEN AT ONLY FIVE OR TEN BUCKS A PIECE IT WOULD ADD UP TO SOME SERIOUS CAS PRETTY QUICKL IF YOU WANTED TO BUY IN ANY VOLUME.
HOW MUCH IN YOUR DOLLARS?

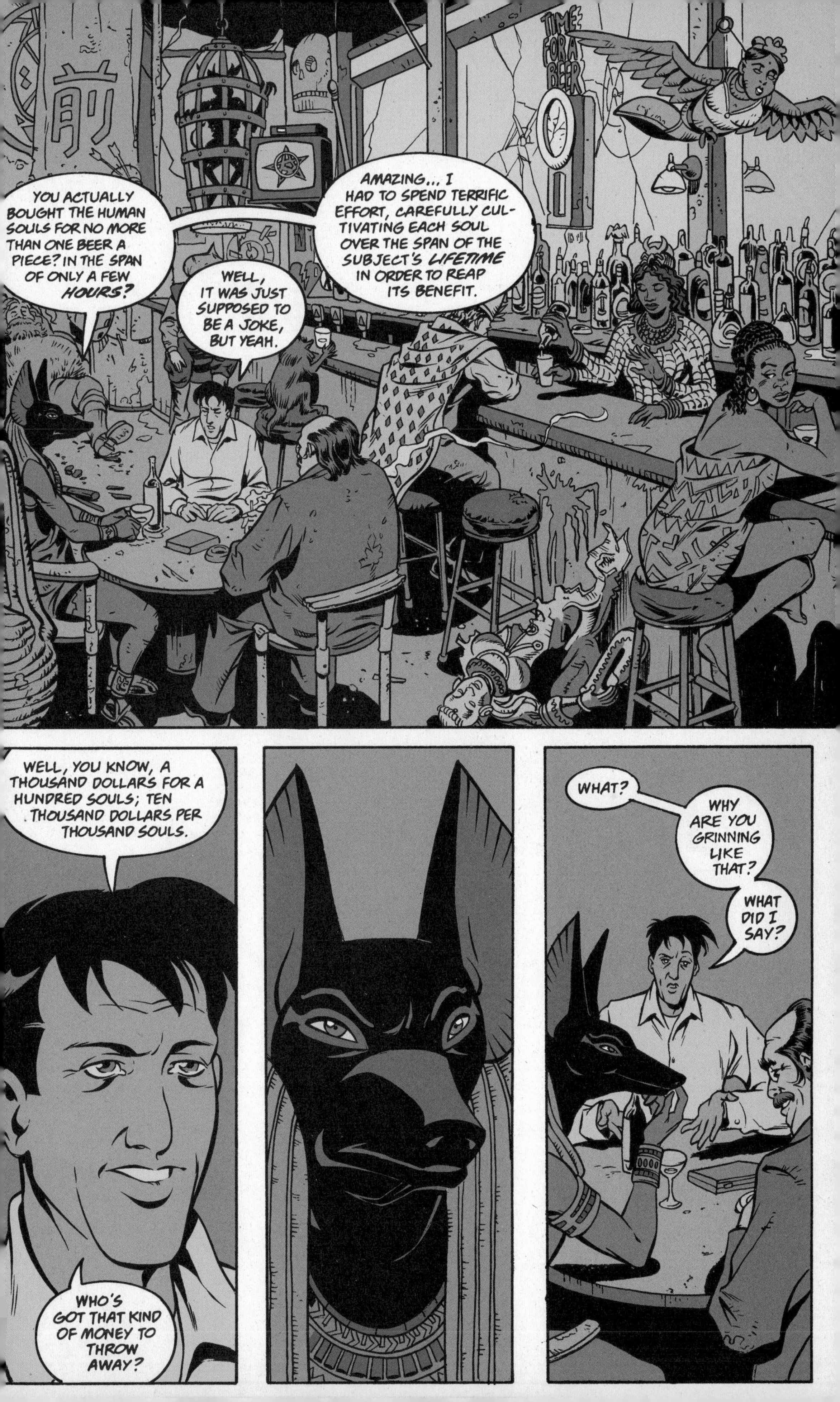

TIME FOR A BEER
YOU ACTUALLY BOUGHT THE HUMAN SOULS FOR NO MORE THAN ONE BEER A PIECE? IN THE SPAN OF ONLY A FEW *HOURS?*
AMAZING... I HAD TO SPEND TERRIFIC EFFORT, CAREFULLY CULTIVATING EACH SOUL OVER THE SPAN OF THE SUBJECT'S *LIFETIME* IN ORDER TO REAP ITS BENEFIT.
WELL, IT WAS JUST SUPPOSED TO BE A JOKE, BUT YEAH.
WELL, YOU KNOW, A THOUSAND DOLLARS FOR A HUNDRED SOULS; TEN THOUSAND DOLLARS PER THOUSAND SOULS.
WHO'S GOT THAT KIND OF MONEY TO THROW AWAY?
WHAT?
WHY ARE YOU GRINNING LIKE THAT?
WHAT DID I SAY?

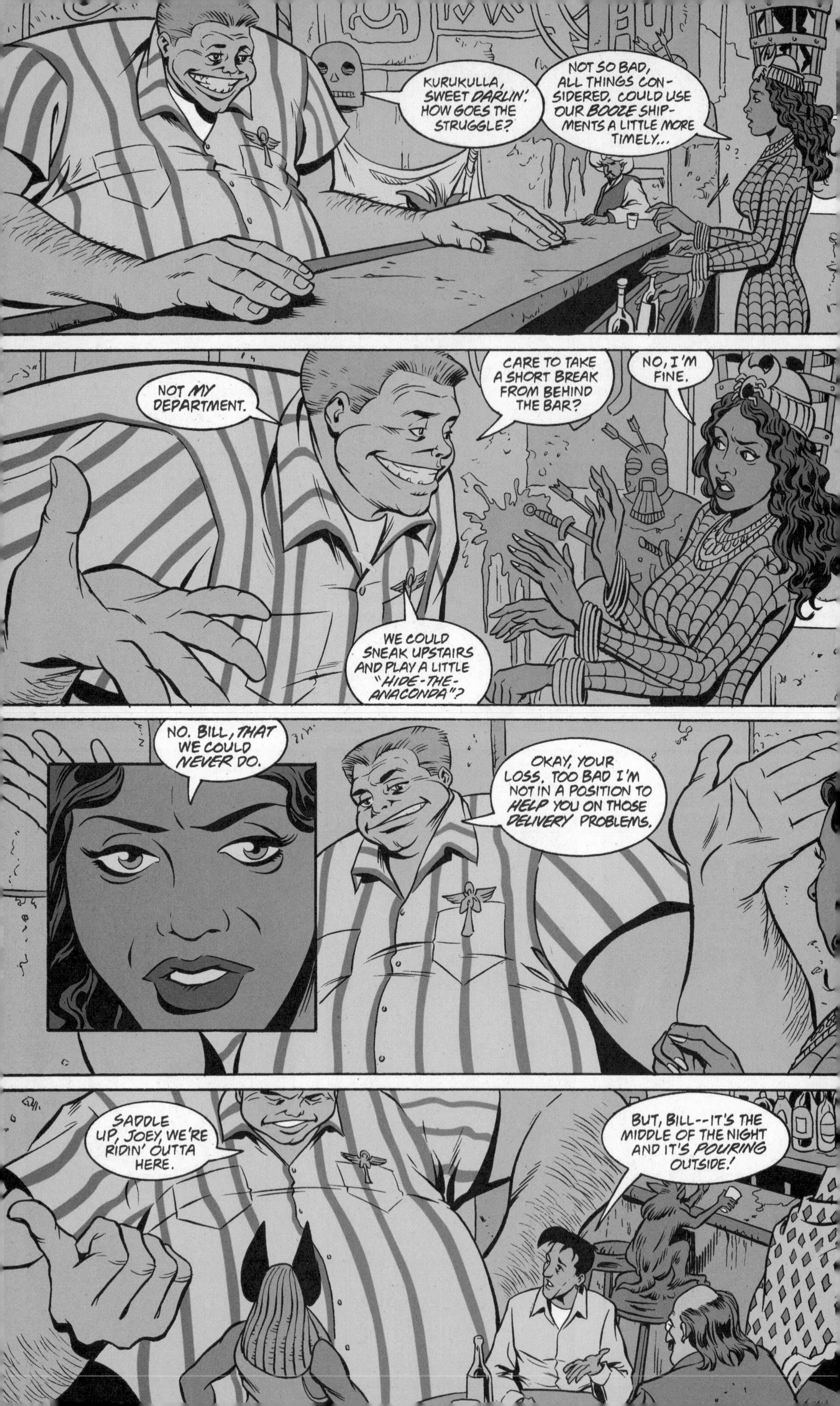
KURUKULLA, SWEET DARLIN'. HOW GOES THE STRUGGLE?
NOT SO BAD, ALL THINGS CONSIDERED. COULD USE OUR BOOZE SHIPMENTS A LITTLE MORE TIMELY...
NOT MY DEPARTMENT.
CARE TO TAKE A SHORT BREAK FROM BEHIND THE BAR?
NO, I'M FINE.
WE COULD SNEAK UPSTAIRS AND PLAY A LITTLE "HIDE-THE-ANACONDA"?
NO. BILL, THAT WE COULD NEVER DO.
OKAY, YOUR LOSS. TOO BAD I'M NOT IN A POSITION TO HELP YOU ON THOSE DELIVERY PROBLEMS.
SADDLE UP, JOEY, WE'RE RIDIN' OUTTA HERE.
BUT, BILL--IT'S THE MIDDLE OF THE NIGHT AND IT'S POURING OUTSIDE!

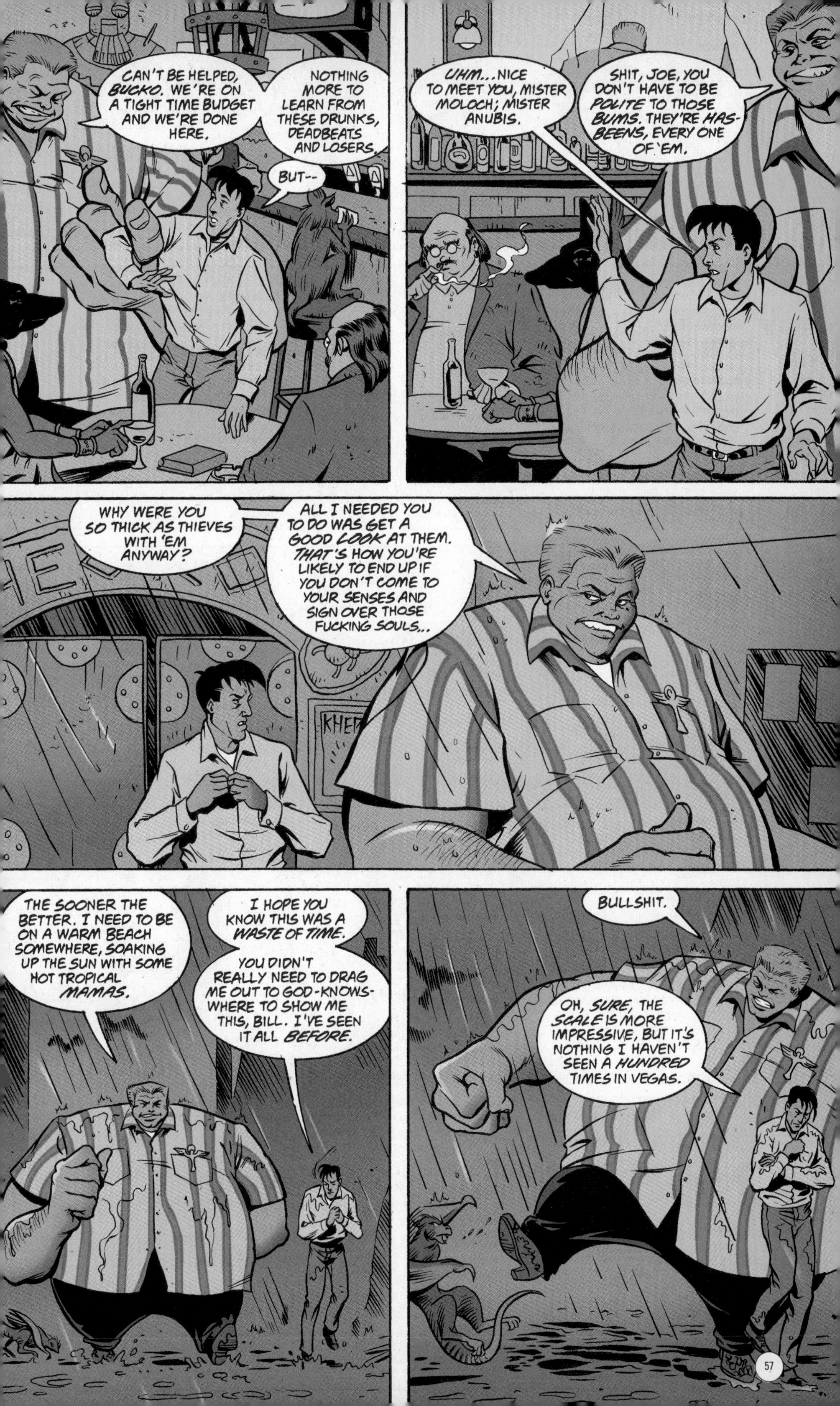

CAN'T BE HELPED, BUCKO. WE'RE ON A TIGHT TIME BUDGET AND WE'RE DONE HERE.
NOTHING MORE TO LEARN FROM THESE DRUNKS, DEADBEATS AND LOSERS.
BUT--
UHM... NICE TO MEET YOU, MISTER MOLOCH; MISTER ANUBIS.
SHIT, JOE, YOU DON'T HAVE TO BE POLITE TO THOSE BUMS. THEY'RE HAS-BEENS, EVERY ONE OF 'EM.
WHY WERE YOU SO THICK AS THIEVES WITH 'EM ANYWAY?
ALL I NEEDED YOU TO DO WAS GET A GOOD LOOK AT THEM. THAT'S HOW YOU'RE LIKELY TO END UP IF YOU DON'T COME TO YOUR SENSES AND SIGN OVER THOSE FUCKING SOULS...
THE SOONER THE BETTER. I NEED TO BE ON A WARM BEACH SOMEWHERE, SOAKING UP THE SUN WITH SOME HOT TROPICAL MAMAS.
I HOPE YOU KNOW THIS WAS A WASTE OF TIME.
YOU DIDN'T REALLY NEED TO DRAG ME OUT TO GOD-KNOWS-WHERE TO SHOW ME THIS, BILL. I'VE SEEN IT ALL BEFORE.
BULLSHIT.
OH, SURE, THE SCALE IS MORE IMPRESSIVE, BUT IT'S NOTHING I HAVEN'T SEEN A HUNDRED TIMES IN VEGAS.

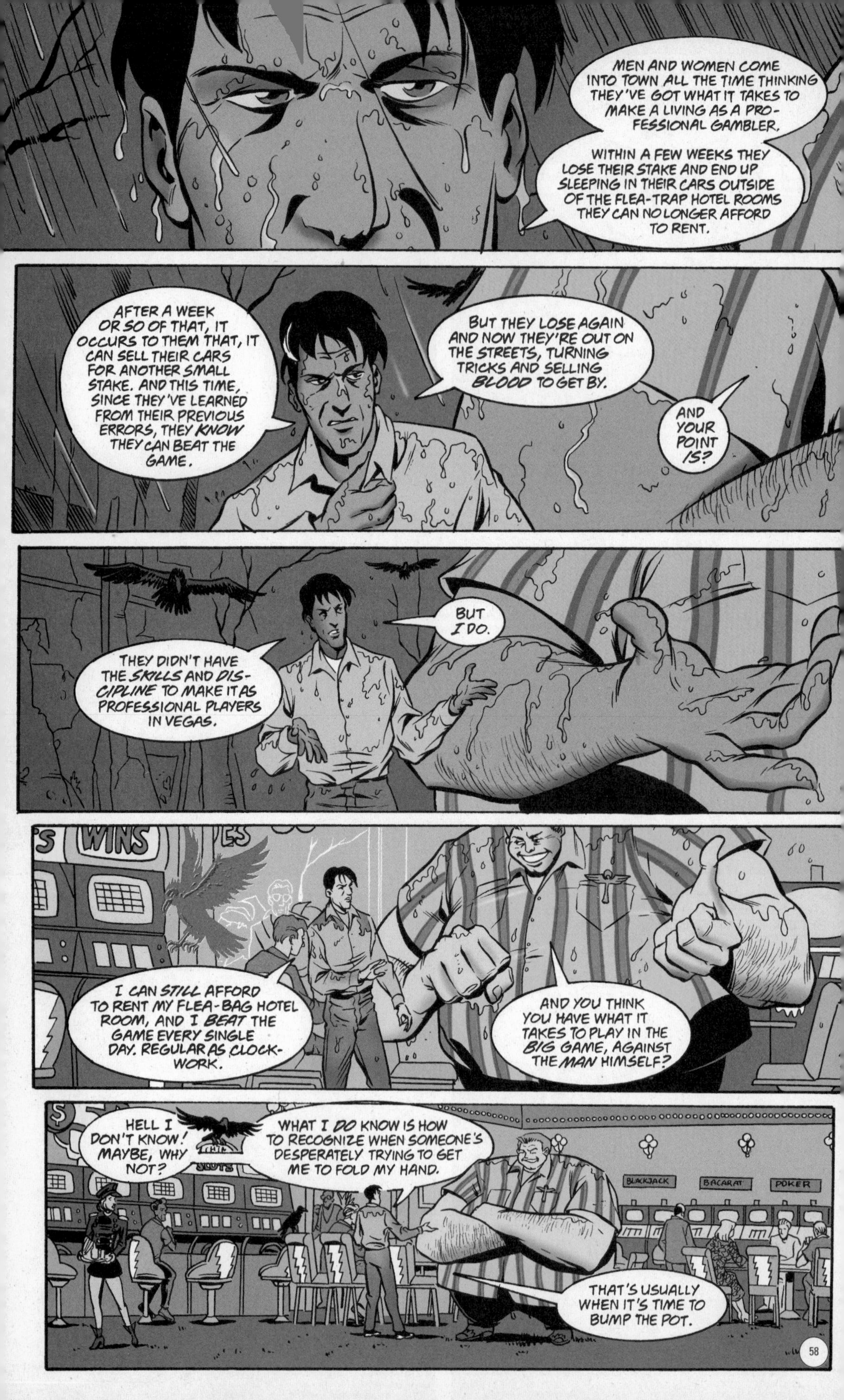
MEN AND WOMEN COME INTO TOWN ALL THE TIME THINKING THEY'VE GOT WHAT IT TAKES TO MAKE A LIVING AS A PRO-FESSIONAL GAMBLER.
WITHIN A FEW WEEKS THEY LOSE THEIR STAKE AND END UP SLEEPING IN THEIR CARS OUTSIDE OF THE FLEA-TRAP HOTEL ROOMS THEY CAN NO LONGER AFFORD TO RENT.
AFTER A WEEK OR SO OF THAT, IT OCCURS TO THEM THAT, IT CAN SELL THEIR CARS FOR ANOTHER SMALL STAKE. AND THIS TIME, SINCE THEY'VE LEARNED FROM THEIR PREVIOUS ERRORS, THEY KNOW THEY CAN BEAT THE GAME.
BUT THEY LOSE AGAIN AND NOW THEY'RE OUT ON THE STREETS, TURNING TRICKS AND SELLING BLOOD TO GET BY.
AND YOUR POINT IS?
THEY DIDN'T HAVE THE SKILLS AND DIS-CIPLINE TO MAKE IT AS PROFESSIONAL PLAYERS IN VEGAS.
BUT I DO.
WINS
I CAN STILL AFFORD TO RENT MY FLEA-BAG HOTEL ROOM, AND I BEAT THE GAME EVERY SINGLE DAY. REGULAR AS CLOCK-WORK.
AND YOU THINK YOU HAVE WHAT IT TAKES TO PLAY IN THE BIG GAME, AGAINST THE MAN HIMSELF?
HELL I DON'T KNOW! MAYBE, WHY NOT?
WHAT I DO KNOW IS HOW TO RECOGNIZE WHEN SOMEONE'S DESPERATELY TRYING TO GET ME TO FOLD MY HAND.
SLOTS
BLACKJACK
BACARAT
POKER
THAT'S USUALLY WHEN IT'S TIME TO BUMP THE POT.

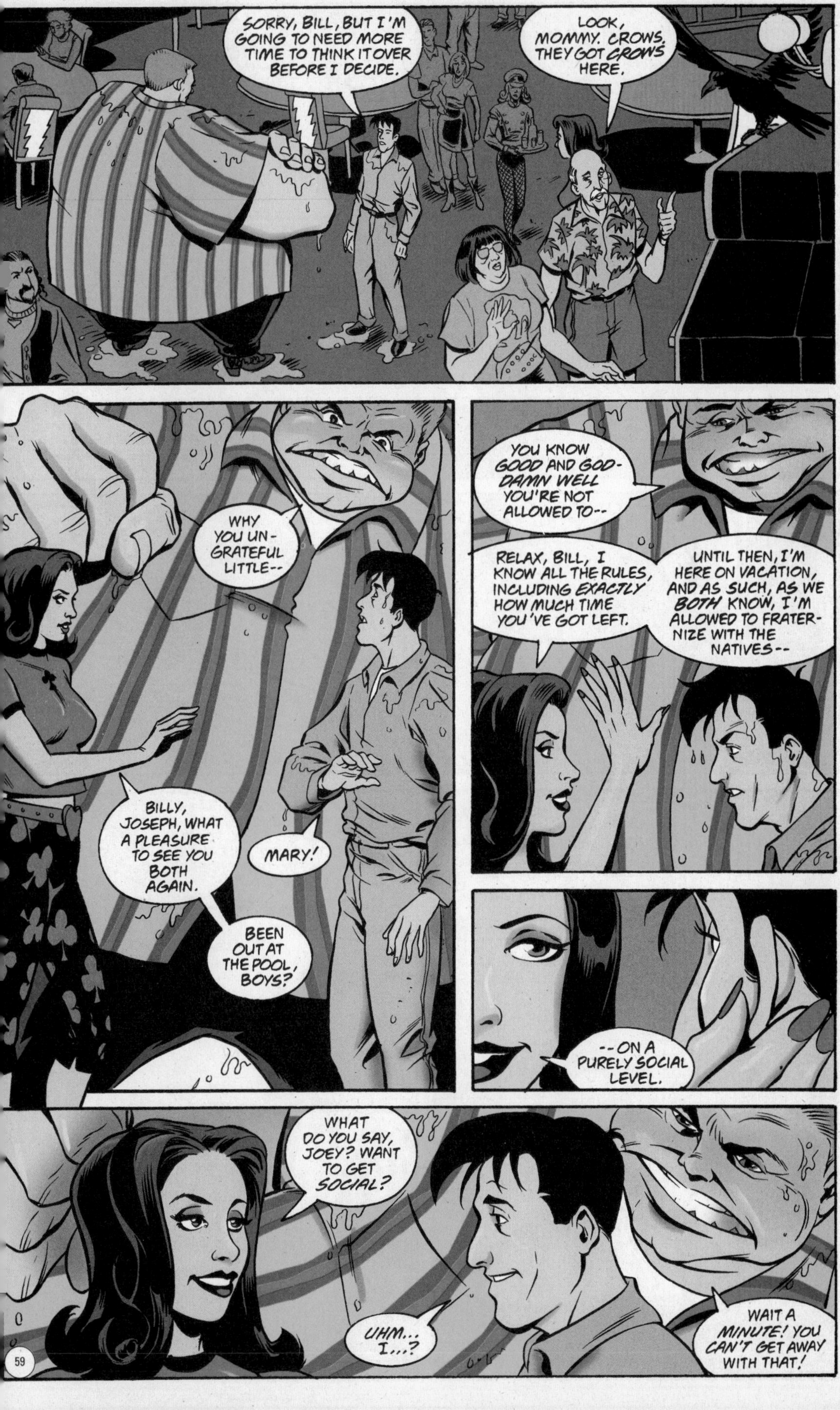
SORRY, BILL, BUT I'M GOING TO NEED MORE TIME TO THINK IT OVER BEFORE I DECIDE.
LOOK, MOMMY. CROWS. THEY GOT CROWS HERE.
WHY YOU UN-GRATEFUL LITTLE--
BILLY, JOSEPH, WHAT A PLEASURE TO SEE YOU BOTH AGAIN.
MARY!
BEEN OUT AT THE POOL, BOYS?
YOU KNOW GOOD AND GOD-DAMN WELL YOU'RE NOT ALLOWED TO--
RELAX, BILL, I KNOW ALL THE RULES, INCLUDING EXACTLY HOW MUCH TIME YOU'VE GOT LEFT.
UNTIL THEN, I'M HERE ON VACATION, AND AS SUCH, AS WE BOTH KNOW, I'M ALLOWED TO FRATER-NIZE WITH THE NATIVES--
--ON A PURELY SOCIAL LEVEL.
WHAT DO YOU SAY, JOEY? WANT TO GET SOCIAL?
UHM... I...?
WAIT A MINUTE! YOU CAN'T GET AWAY WITH THAT!

SURE I CAN, AS LONG AS I DON'T TALK BUSINESS.

HOW ABOUT IT, HANDSOME? YOU'RE NOT IN THE MOOD TO TALK BUSINESS, ARE YOU?

WHY NO, OF COURSE NOT.

I'M PUTTING A STOP TO THIS RIGHT NOW!

I DON'T THINK SO, TIGER. I JUST SAW YOUR BOSS PULL UP OUTSIDE IN HIS LONG, BLACK CAR.

I WOULD IMAGINE HE'D LIKE TO SEE YOU -- RIGHT AWAY.

WHAT DO YOU THINK, BILL?

THINK HE WOULDN'T MIND IF YOU KEPT HIM WAITING?

OKAY, I'M GOING TO HAVE TO STEP OUT FOR A MINUTE, SO I WANT YOU TO GO BACK TO YOUR APARTMENT, ALONE, CLEAN UP, DRY OFF, AND DO THE PONDERING YOU WERE GOING TO DO.

GOT THAT, MR. BIG POKER HOTSHOT?

WELL...

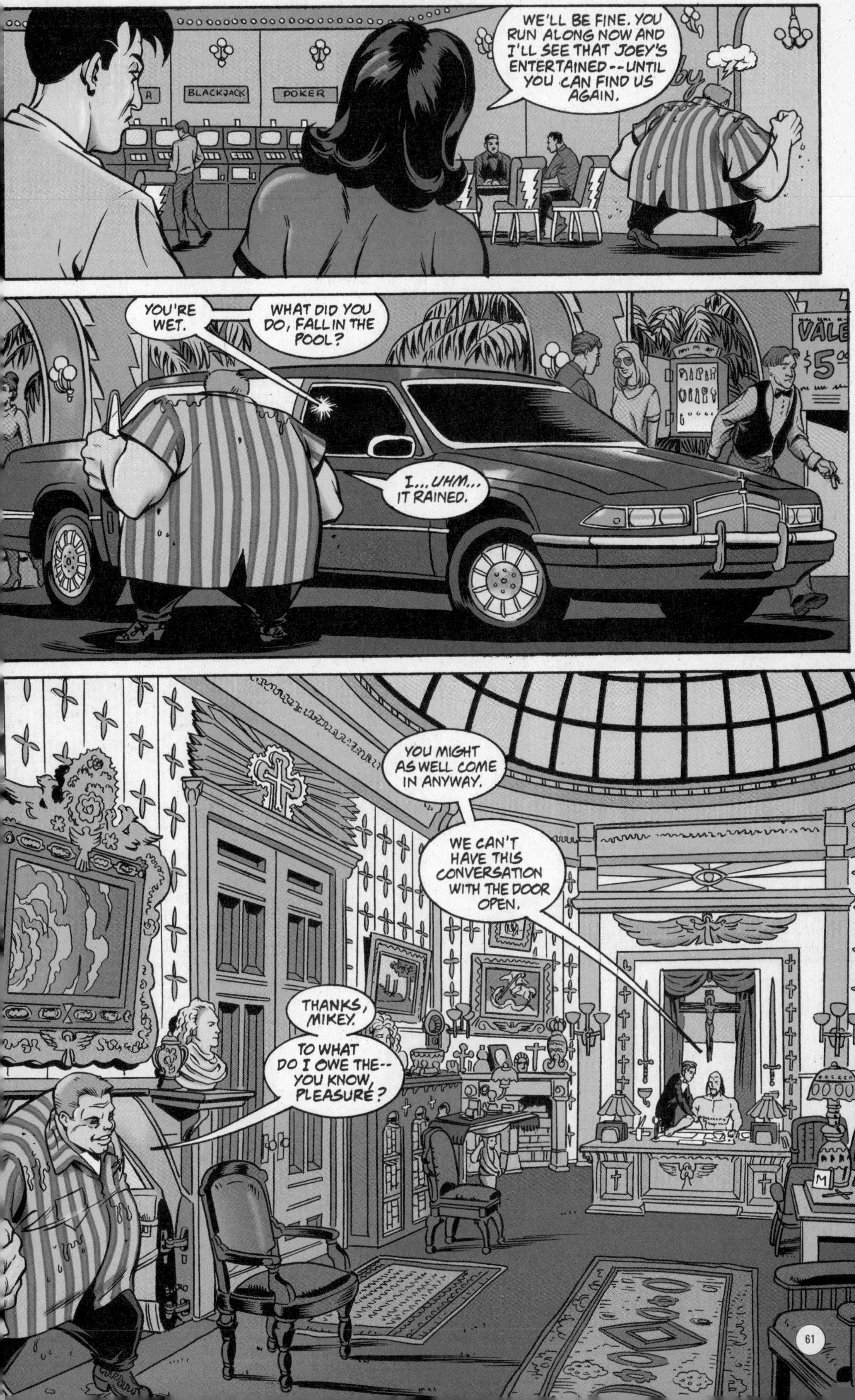
BLACKJACK
POKER
WE'LL BE FINE. YOU RUN ALONG NOW AND I'LL SEE THAT JOEY'S ENTERTAINED--UNTIL YOU CAN FIND US AGAIN.
YOU'RE WET.
WHAT DID YOU DO, FALL IN THE POOL?
I... UHM... IT RAINED.
VALE
$5
YOU MIGHT AS WELL COME IN ANYWAY.
WE CAN'T HAVE THIS CONVERSATION WITH THE DOOR OPEN.
THANKS, MIKEY.
TO WHAT DO I OWE THE-- YOU KNOW, PLEASURÉ?
M

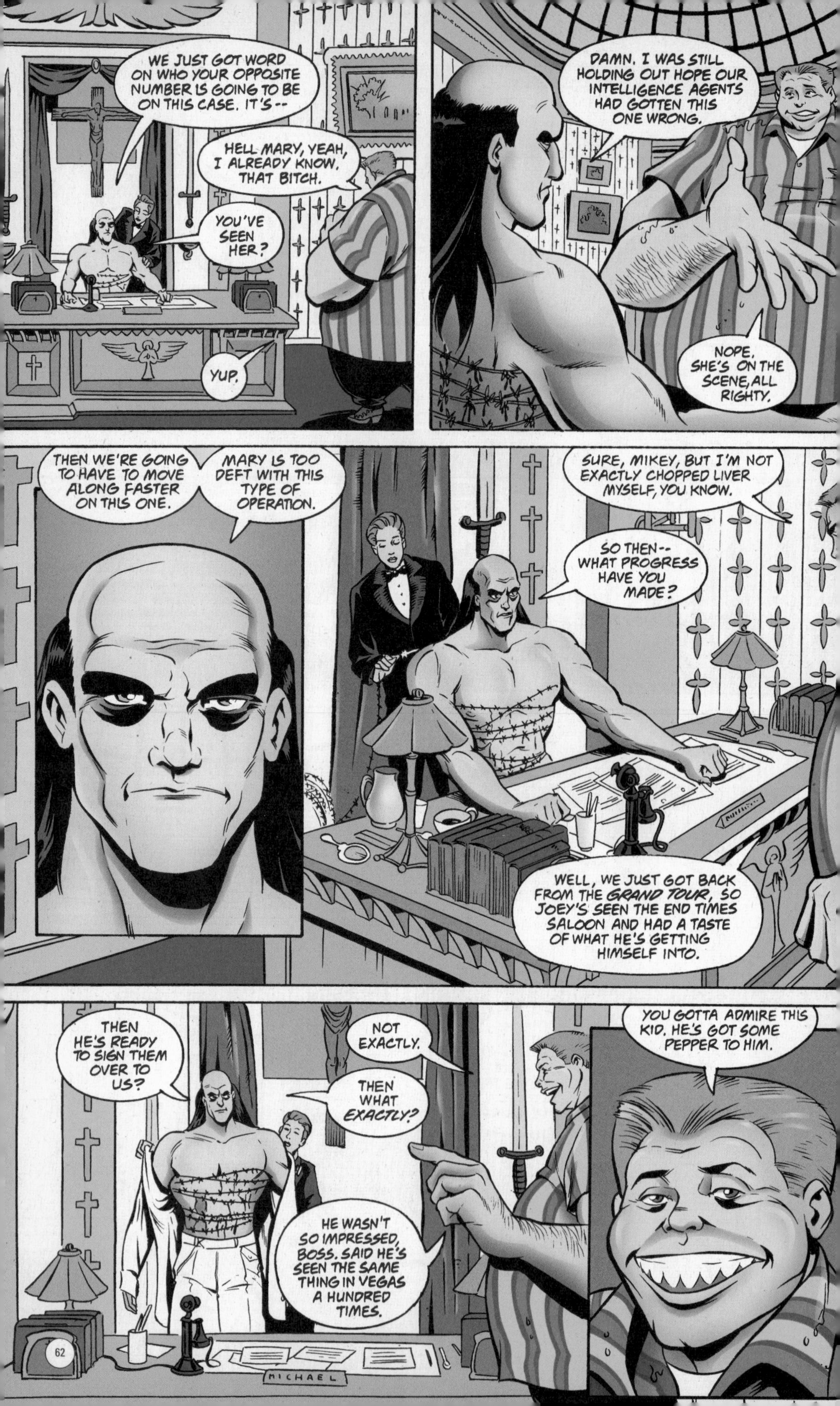
WE JUST GOT WORD ON WHO YOUR OPPOSITE NUMBER IS GOING TO BE ON THIS CASE. IT'S--
HELL MARY, YEAH, I ALREADY KNOW. THAT BITCH.
YOU'VE SEEN HER?
YUP.
DAMN. I WAS STILL HOLDING OUT HOPE OUR INTELLIGENCE AGENTS HAD GOTTEN THIS ONE WRONG.
NOPE. SHE'S ON THE SCENE, ALL RIGHTY.
THEN WE'RE GOING TO HAVE TO MOVE ALONG FASTER ON THIS ONE.
MARY IS TOO DEFT WITH THIS TYPE OF OPERATION.
SURE, MIKEY, BUT I'M NOT EXACTLY CHOPPED LIVER MYSELF, YOU KNOW.
SO THEN-- WHAT PROGRESS HAVE YOU MADE?
WELL, WE JUST GOT BACK FROM THE GRAND TOUR, SO JOEY'S SEEN THE END TIMES SALOON AND HAD A TASTE OF WHAT HE'S GETTING HIMSELF INTO.
THEN HE'S READY TO SIGN THEM OVER TO US?
NOT EXACTLY.
THEN WHAT EXACTLY?
HE WASN'T SO IMPRESSED, BOSS. SAID HE'S SEEN THE SAME THING IN VEGAS A HUNDRED TIMES.
YOU GOTTA ADMIRE THIS KID. HE'S GOT SOME PEPPER TO HIM.
MICHAEL

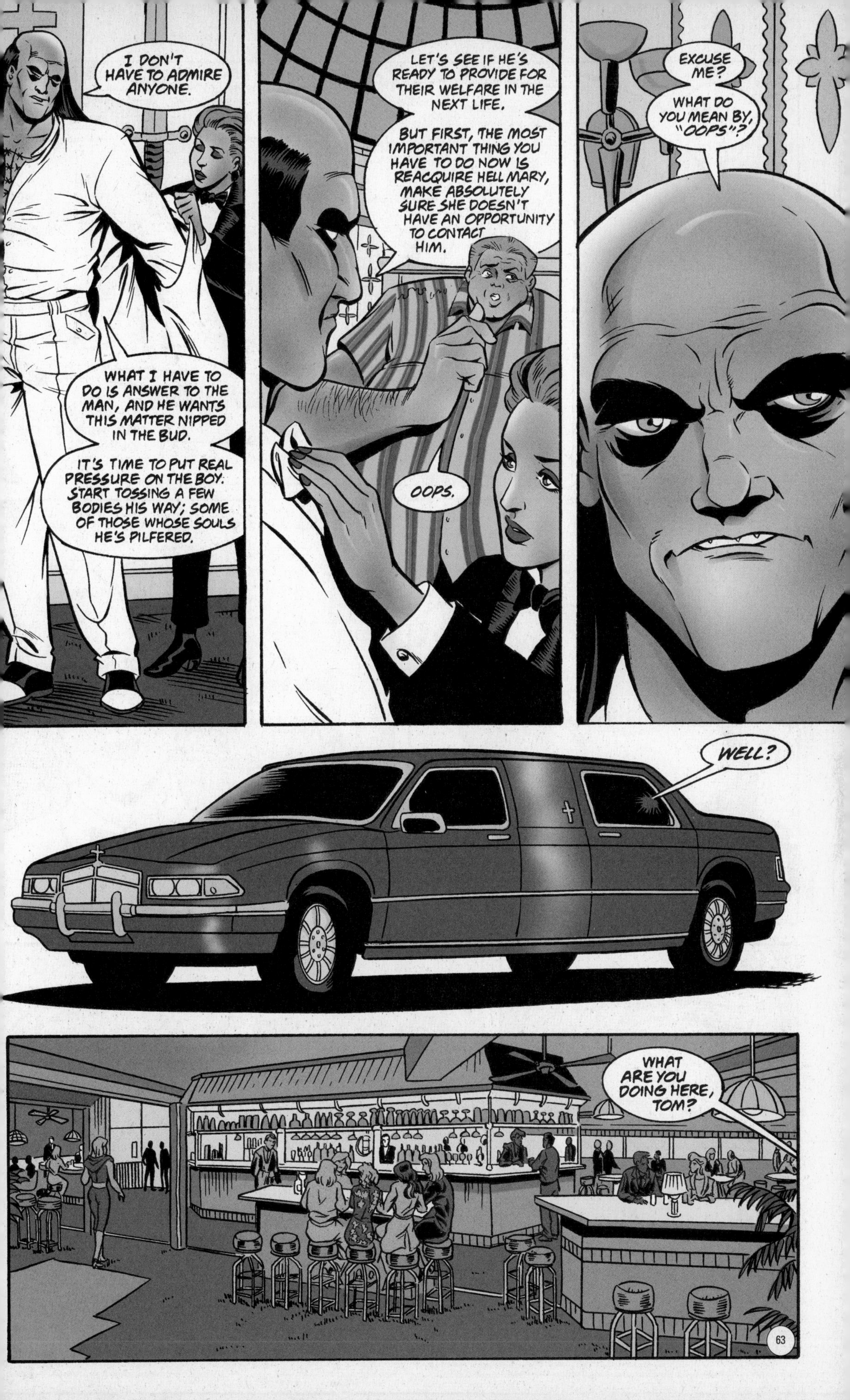
I DON'T HAVE TO ADMIRE ANYONE.
WHAT I HAVE TO DO IS ANSWER TO THE MAN, AND HE WANTS THIS MATTER NIPPED IN THE BUD.
IT'S TIME TO PUT REAL PRESSURE ON THE BOY. START TOSSING A FEW BODIES HIS WAY; SOME OF THOSE WHOSE SOULS HE'S PILFERED.
LET'S SEE IF HE'S READY TO PROVIDE FOR THEIR WELFARE IN THE NEXT LIFE.
BUT FIRST, THE MOST IMPORTANT THING YOU HAVE TO DO NOW IS REACQUIRE HELL MARY, MAKE ABSOLUTELY SURE SHE DOESN'T HAVE AN OPPORTUNITY TO CONTACT HIM.
OOPS.
EXCUSE ME?
WHAT DO YOU MEAN BY, "OOPS"?
WELL?
WHAT ARE YOU DOING HERE, TOM?

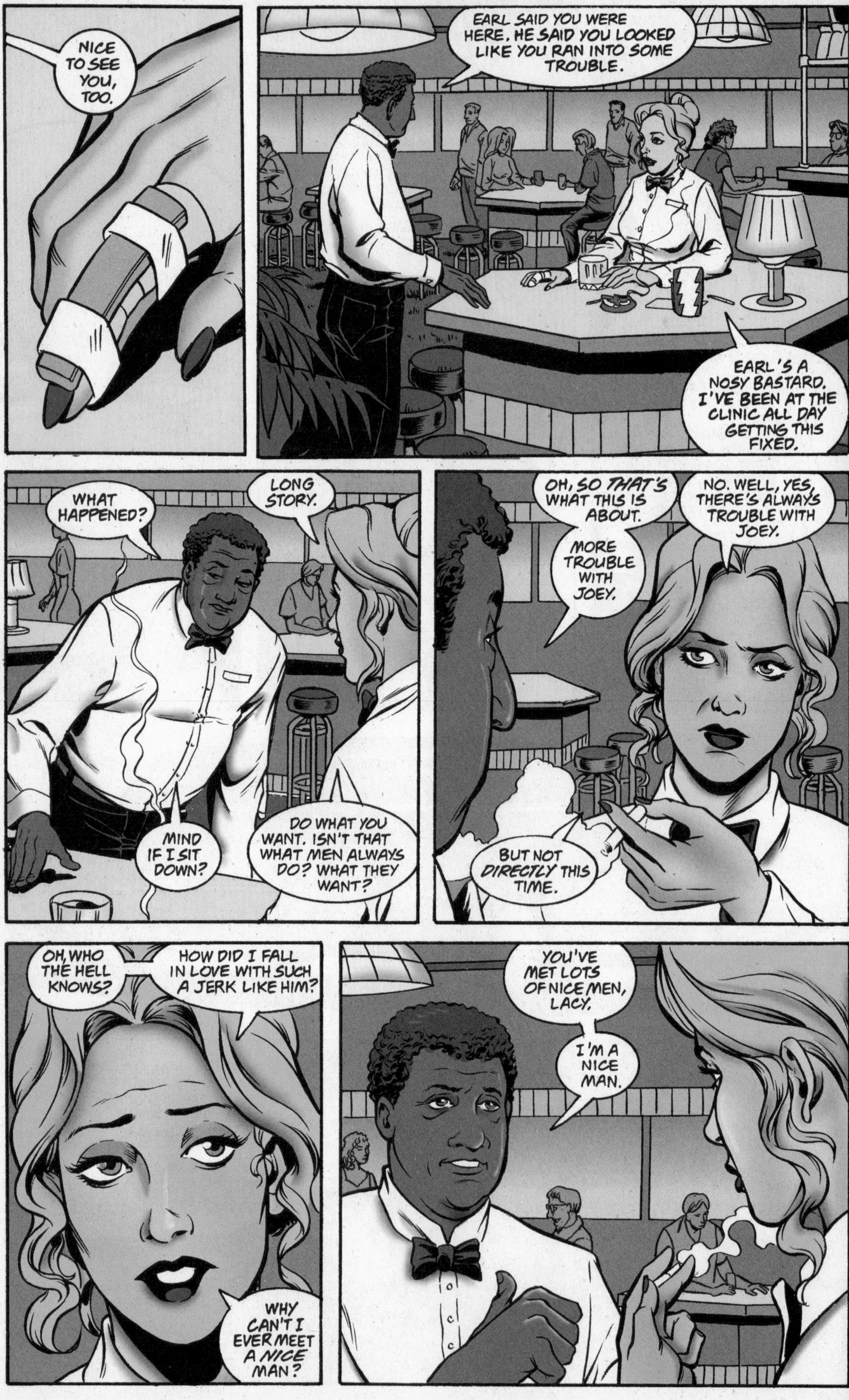
NICE TO SEE YOU, TOO.
EARL SAID YOU WERE HERE. HE SAID YOU LOOKED LIKE YOU RAN INTO SOME TROUBLE.
EARL'S A NOSY BASTARD. I'VE BEEN AT THE CLINIC ALL DAY GETTING THIS FIXED.
WHAT HAPPENED?
LONG STORY.
MIND IF I SIT DOWN?
DO WHAT YOU WANT. ISN'T THAT WHAT MEN ALWAYS DO? WHAT THEY WANT?
OH, SO *THAT'S* WHAT THIS IS ABOUT.
MORE TROUBLE WITH JOEY.
NO. WELL, YES, THERE'S ALWAYS TROUBLE WITH JOEY.
BUT NOT *DIRECTLY* THIS TIME.
OH, WHO THE HELL KNOWS?
HOW DID I FALL IN LOVE WITH SUCH A JERK LIKE HIM?
WHY CAN'T I EVER MEET A *NICE* MAN?
YOU'VE MET LOTS OF NICE MEN, LACY.
I'M A NICE MAN.

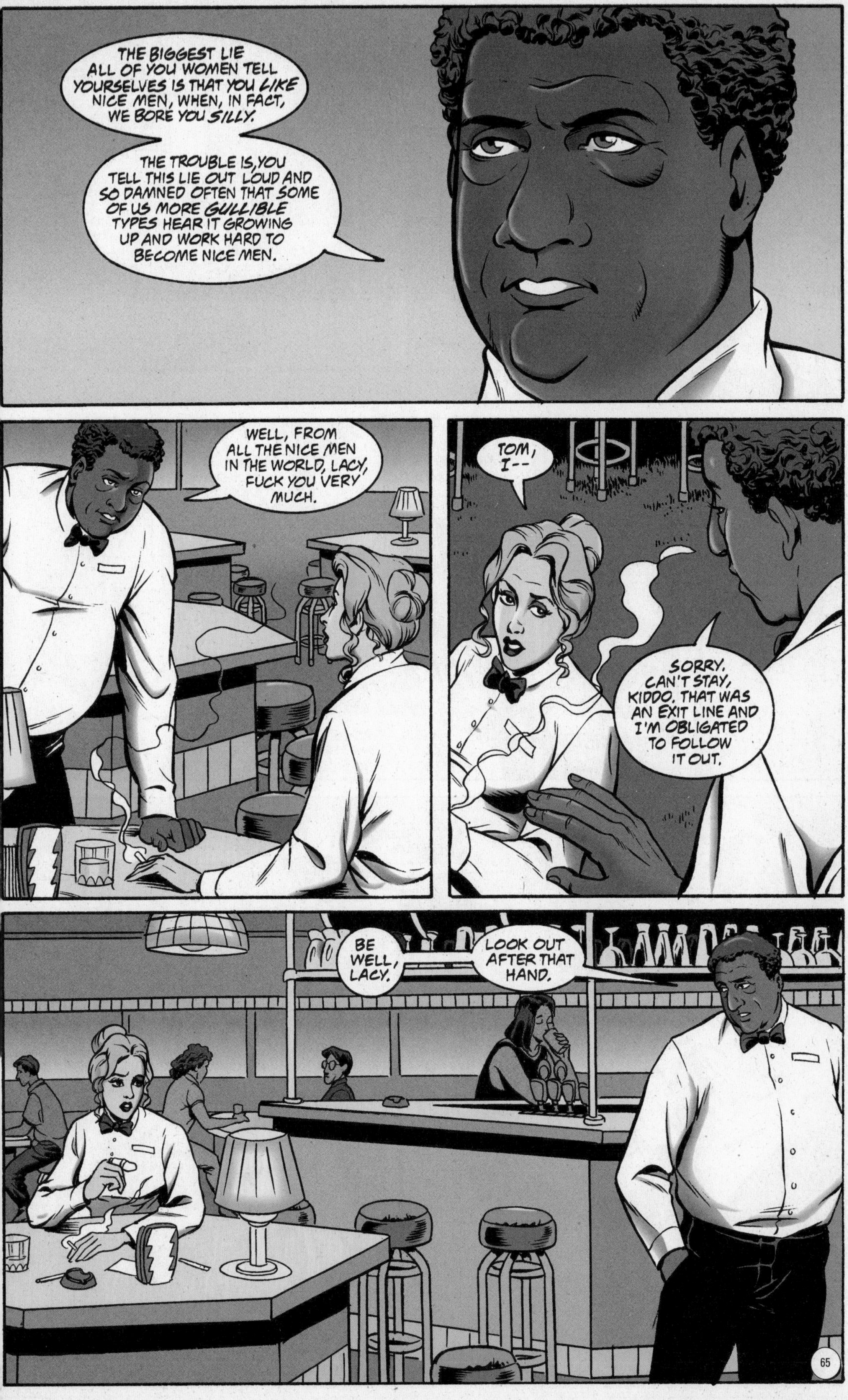
THE BIGGEST LIE ALL OF YOU WOMEN TELL YOURSELVES IS THAT YOU LIKE NICE MEN, WHEN, IN FACT, WE BORE YOU SILLY.
THE TROUBLE IS, YOU TELL THIS LIE OUT LOUD AND SO DAMNED OFTEN THAT SOME OF US MORE GULLIBLE TYPES HEAR IT GROWING UP AND WORK HARD TO BECOME NICE MEN.
WELL, FROM ALL THE NICE MEN IN THE WORLD, LACY, FUCK YOU VERY MUCH.
TOM, I--
SORRY. CAN'T STAY, KIDDO. THAT WAS AN EXIT LINE AND I'M OBLIGATED TO FOLLOW IT OUT.
BE WELL, LACY.
LOOK OUT AFTER THAT HAND.

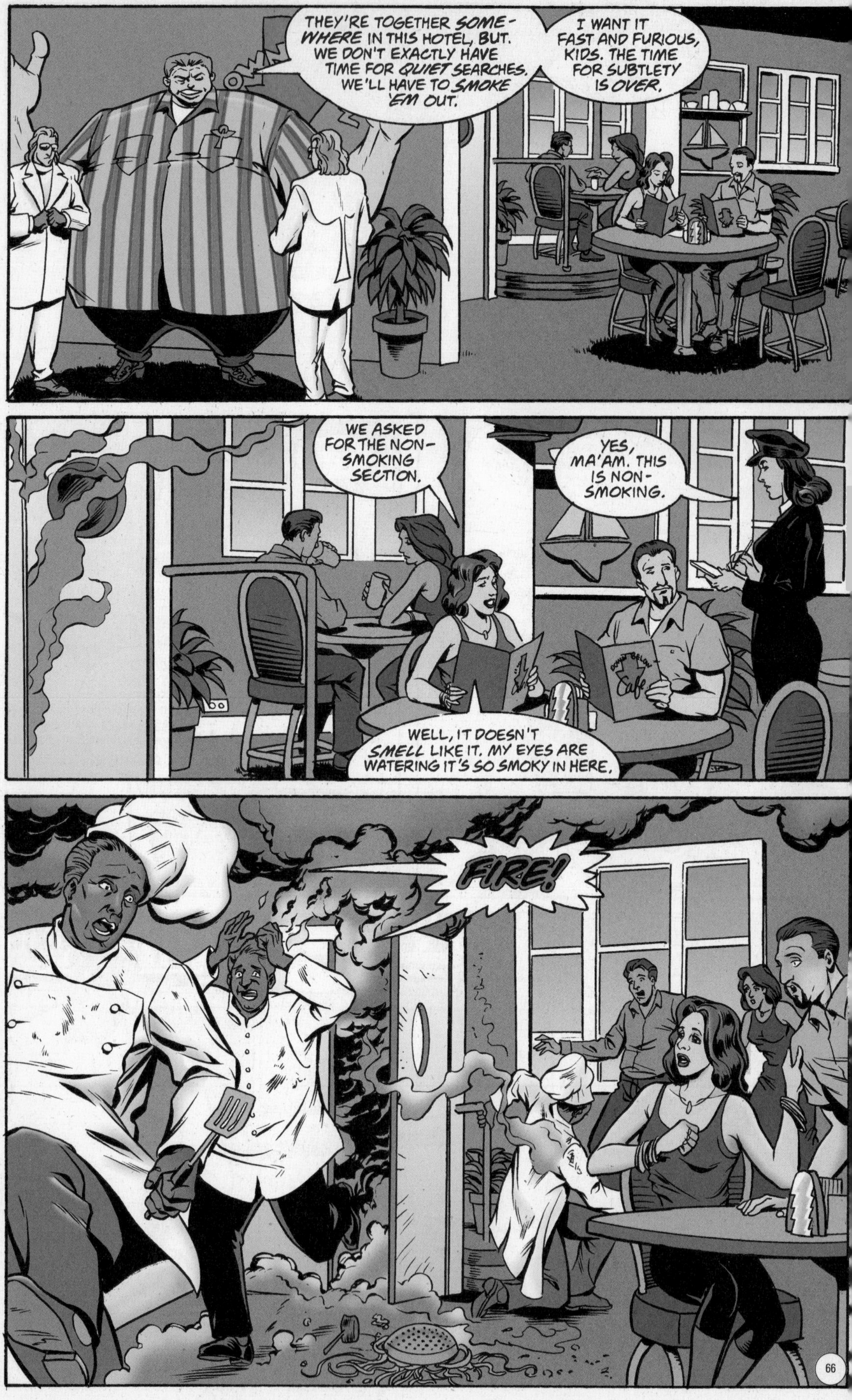
THEY'RE TOGETHER SOME-WHERE IN THIS HOTEL, BUT. WE DON'T EXACTLY HAVE TIME FOR QUIET SEARCHES. WE'LL HAVE TO SMOKE 'EM OUT.
I WANT IT FAST AND FURIOUS, KIDS. THE TIME FOR SUBTLETY IS OVER.
WE ASKED FOR THE NON-SMOKING SECTION.
YES, MA'AM. THIS IS NON-SMOKING.
WELL, IT DOESN'T SMELL LIKE IT. MY EYES ARE WATERING IT'S SO SMOKY IN HERE.
FIRE!

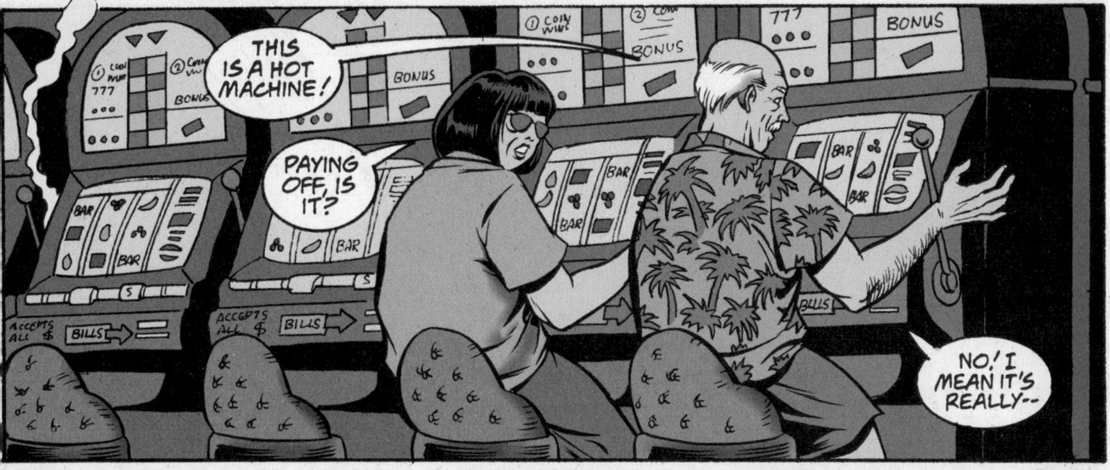
THIS IS A HOT MACHINE!
PAYING OFF, IS IT?
NO! I MEAN IT'S REALLY--

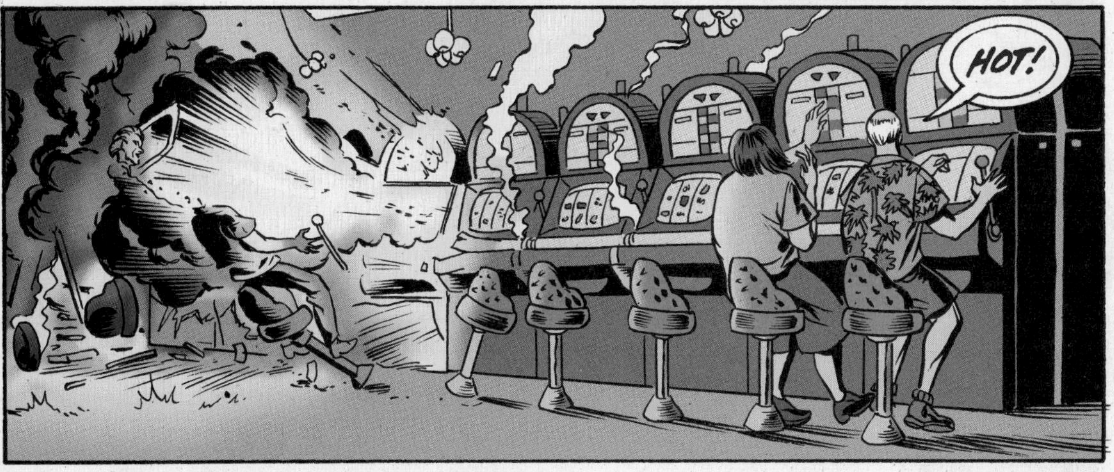
HOT!

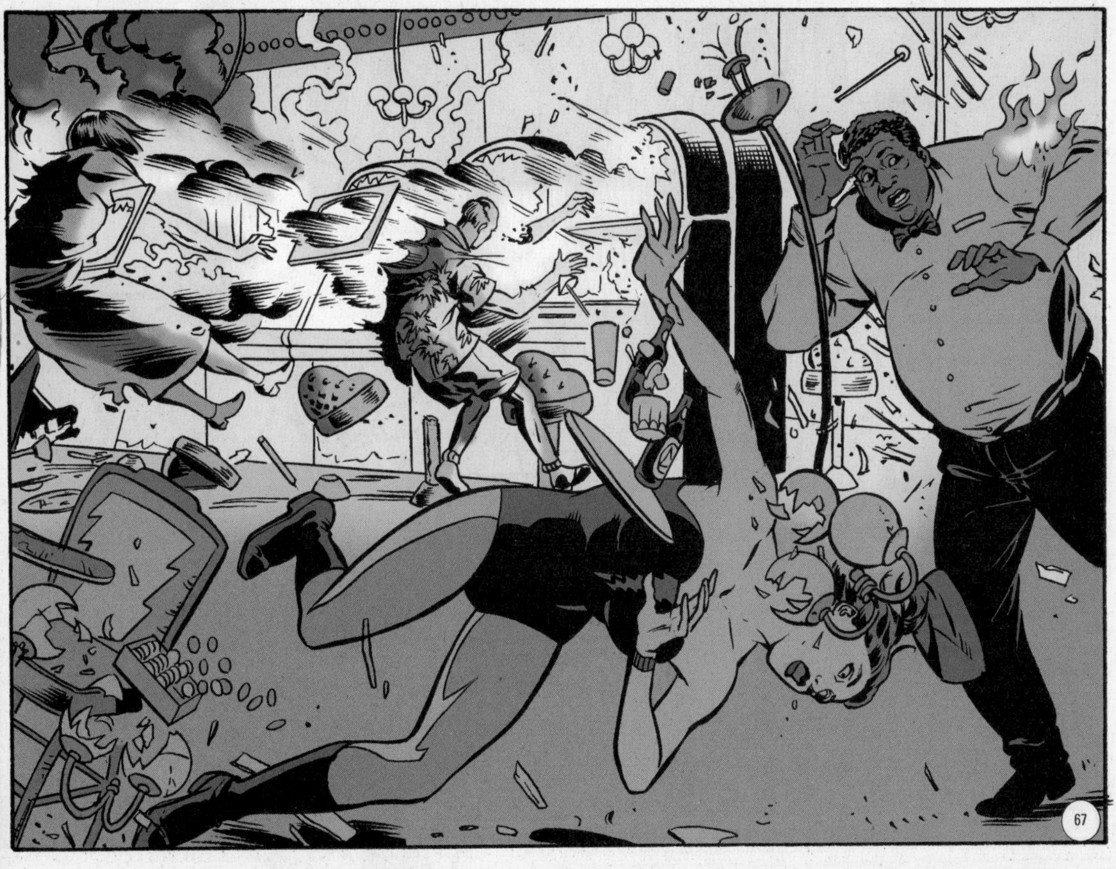

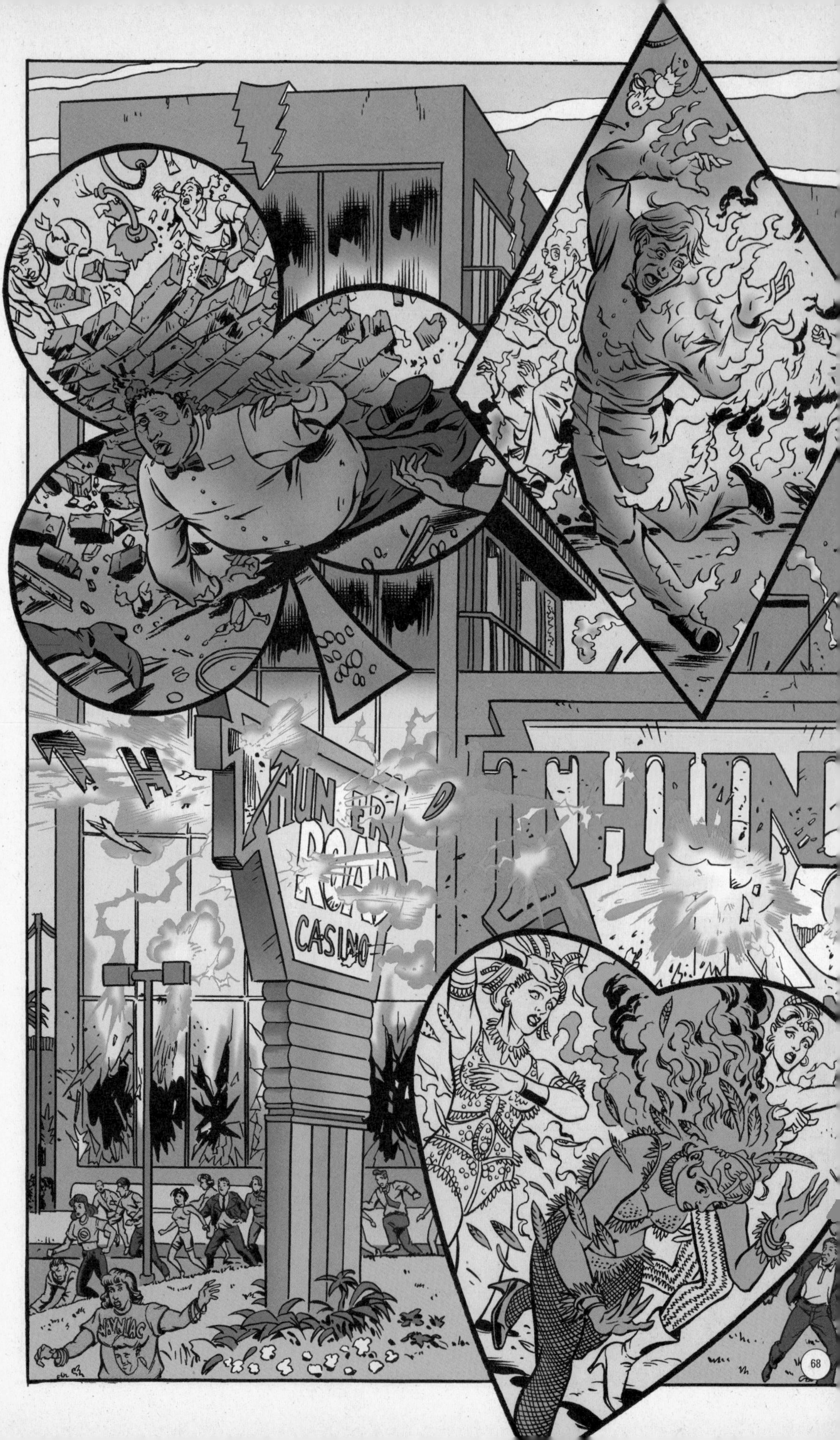
CASINO

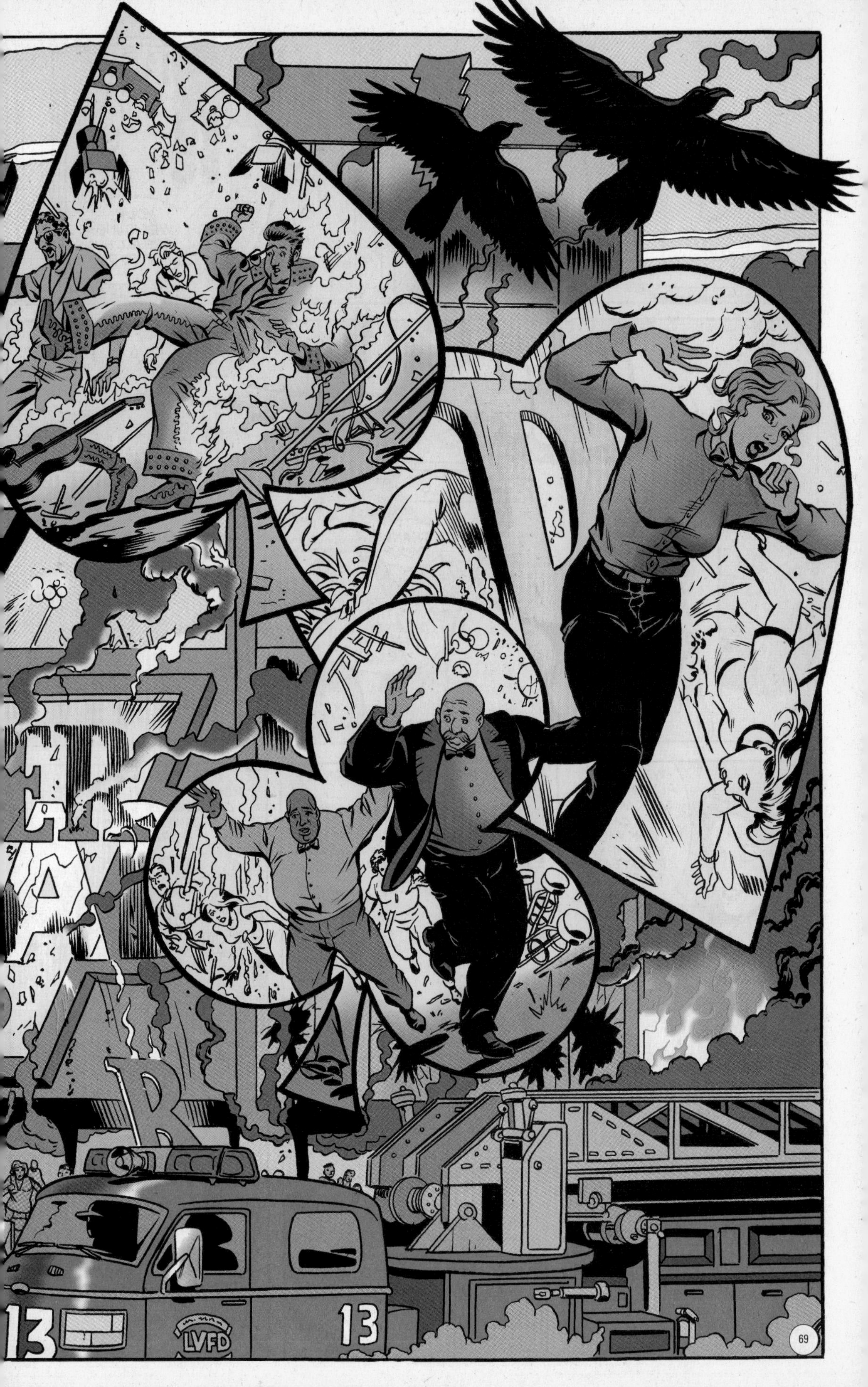
13
LVFD
13

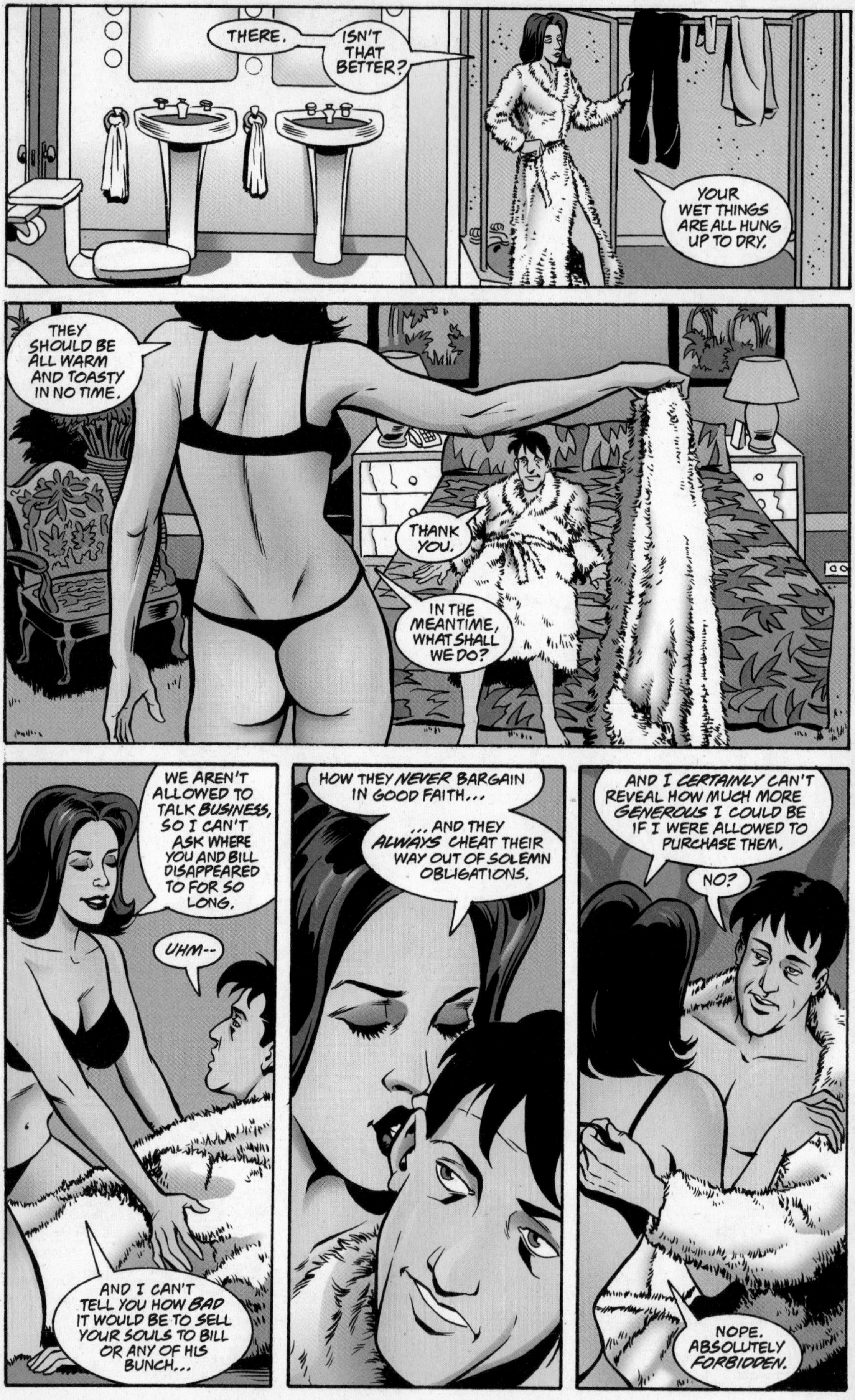
THERE.
ISN'T THAT BETTER?
YOUR WET THINGS ARE ALL HUNG UP TO DRY.
THEY SHOULD BE ALL WARM AND TOASTY IN NO TIME.
THANK YOU.
IN THE MEANTIME, WHAT SHALL WE DO?
WE AREN'T ALLOWED TO TALK BUSINESS, SO I CAN'T ASK WHERE YOU AND BILL DISAPPEARED TO FOR SO LONG.
UHM--
AND I CAN'T TELL YOU HOW BAD IT WOULD BE TO SELL YOUR SOULS TO BILL OR ANY OF HIS BUNCH...
HOW THEY NEVER BARGAIN IN GOOD FAITH...
...AND THEY ALWAYS CHEAT THEIR WAY OUT OF SOLEMN OBLIGATIONS.
AND I CERTAINLY CAN'T REVEAL HOW MUCH MORE GENEROUS I COULD BE IF I WERE ALLOWED TO PURCHASE THEM.
NO?
NOPE. ABSOLUTELY FORBIDDEN.

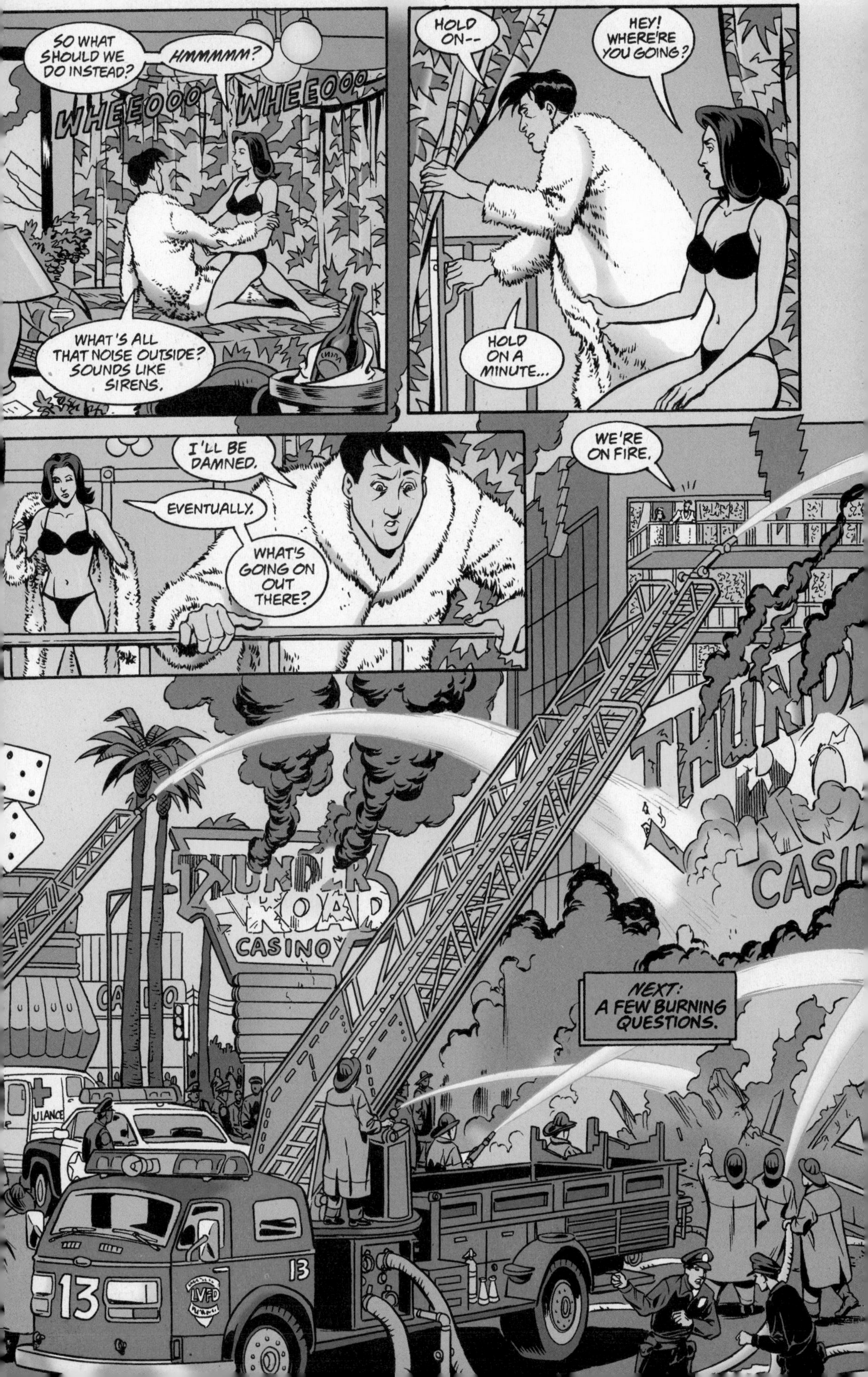
SO WHAT SHOULD WE DO INSTEAD?
HMMMMM?
WHEEOOO WHEEOOO
WHAT'S ALL THAT NOISE OUTSIDE? SOUNDS LIKE SIRENS.
HOLD ON--
HEY! WHERE'RE YOU GOING?
HOLD ON A MINUTE...
I'LL BE DAMNED.
EVENTUALLY.
WHAT'S GOING ON OUT THERE?
WE'RE ON FIRE.
THUNDER ROAD CASINO
CASINO
13
LVFD
NEXT: A FEW BURNING QUESTIONS.

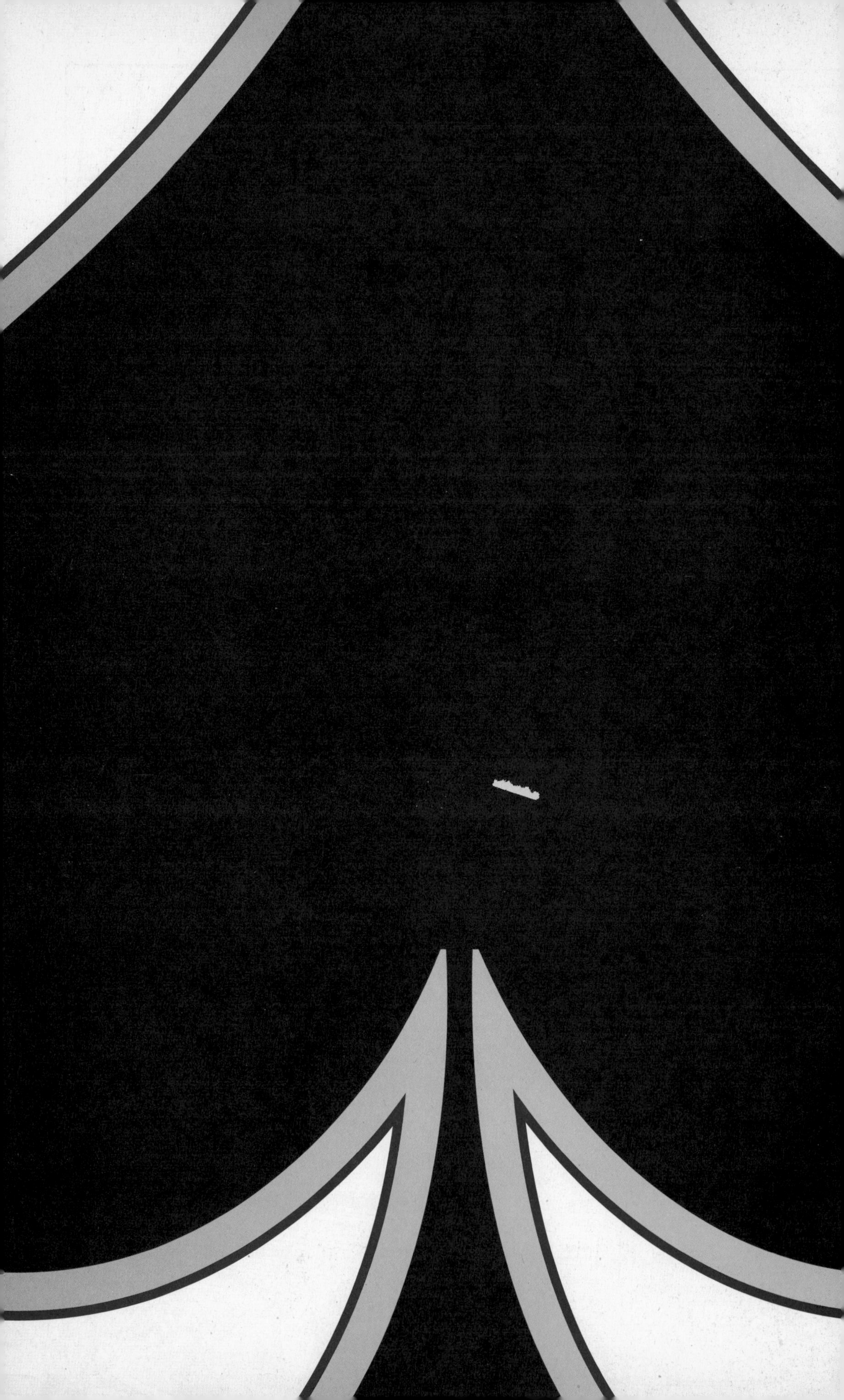

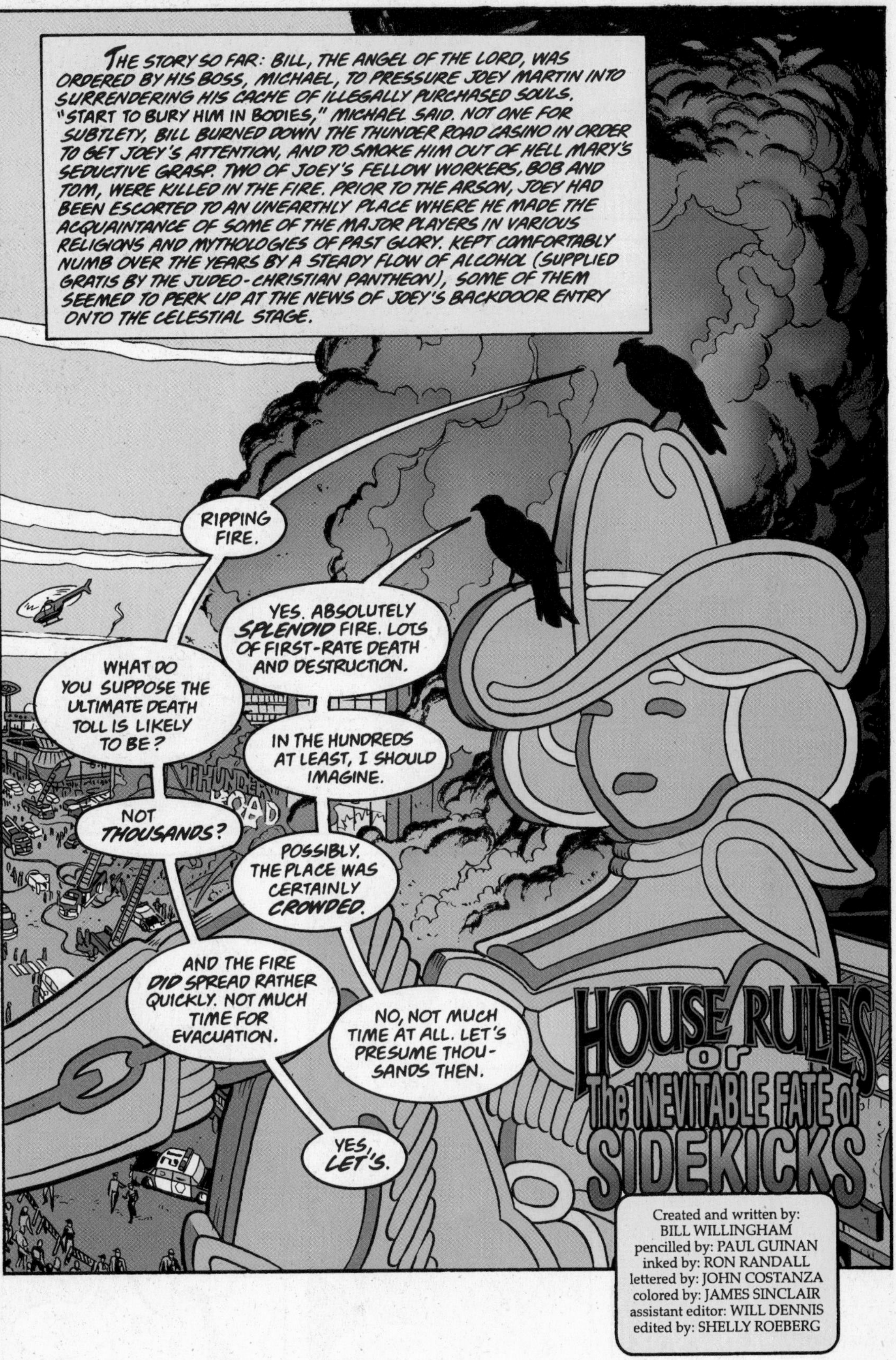

THE STORY SO FAR: BILL, THE ANGEL OF THE LORD, WAS ORDERED BY HIS BOSS, MICHAEL, TO PRESSURE JOEY MARTIN INTO SURRENDERING HIS CACHE OF ILLEGALLY PURCHASED SOULS. "START TO BURY HIM IN BODIES," MICHAEL SAID. NOT ONE FOR SUBTLETY, BILL BURNED DOWN THE THUNDER ROAD CASINO IN ORDER TO GET JOEY'S ATTENTION, AND TO SMOKE HIM OUT OF HELL MARY'S SEDUCTIVE GRASP. TWO OF JOEY'S FELLOW WORKERS, BOB AND TOM, WERE KILLED IN THE FIRE. PRIOR TO THE ARSON, JOEY HAD BEEN ESCORTED TO AN UNEARTHLY PLACE WHERE HE MADE THE ACQUAINTANCE OF SOME OF THE MAJOR PLAYERS IN VARIOUS RELIGIONS AND MYTHOLOGIES OF PAST GLORY. KEPT COMFORTABLY NUMB OVER THE YEARS BY A STEADY FLOW OF ALCOHOL (SUPPLIED GRATIS BY THE JUDEO-CHRISTIAN PANTHEON), SOME OF THEM SEEMED TO PERK UP AT THE NEWS OF JOEY'S BACKDOOR ENTRY ONTO THE CELESTIAL STAGE.
RIPPING FIRE.
YES. ABSOLUTELY *SPLENDID* FIRE. LOTS OF FIRST-RATE DEATH AND DESTRUCTION.
WHAT DO YOU SUPPOSE THE ULTIMATE DEATH TOLL IS LIKELY TO BE?
IN THE HUNDREDS AT LEAST, I SHOULD IMAGINE.
NOT *THOUSANDS?*
POSSIBLY. THE PLACE WAS CERTAINLY *CROWDED.*
AND THE FIRE *DID* SPREAD RATHER QUICKLY. NOT MUCH TIME FOR EVACUATION.
NO, NOT MUCH TIME AT ALL. LET'S PRESUME THOUSANDS THEN.
YES, *LET'S.*
HOUSE RULES or The INEVITABLE FATE of SIDEKICKS

HOUSE RULES or The INEVITABLE FATE of SIDEKICKS

Created and written by: BILL WILLINGHAM
pencilled by: PAUL GUINAN
inked by: RON RANDALL
lettered by: JOHN COSTANZA
colored by: JAMES SINCLAIR
assistant editor: WILL DENNIS
edited by: SHELLY ROEBERG

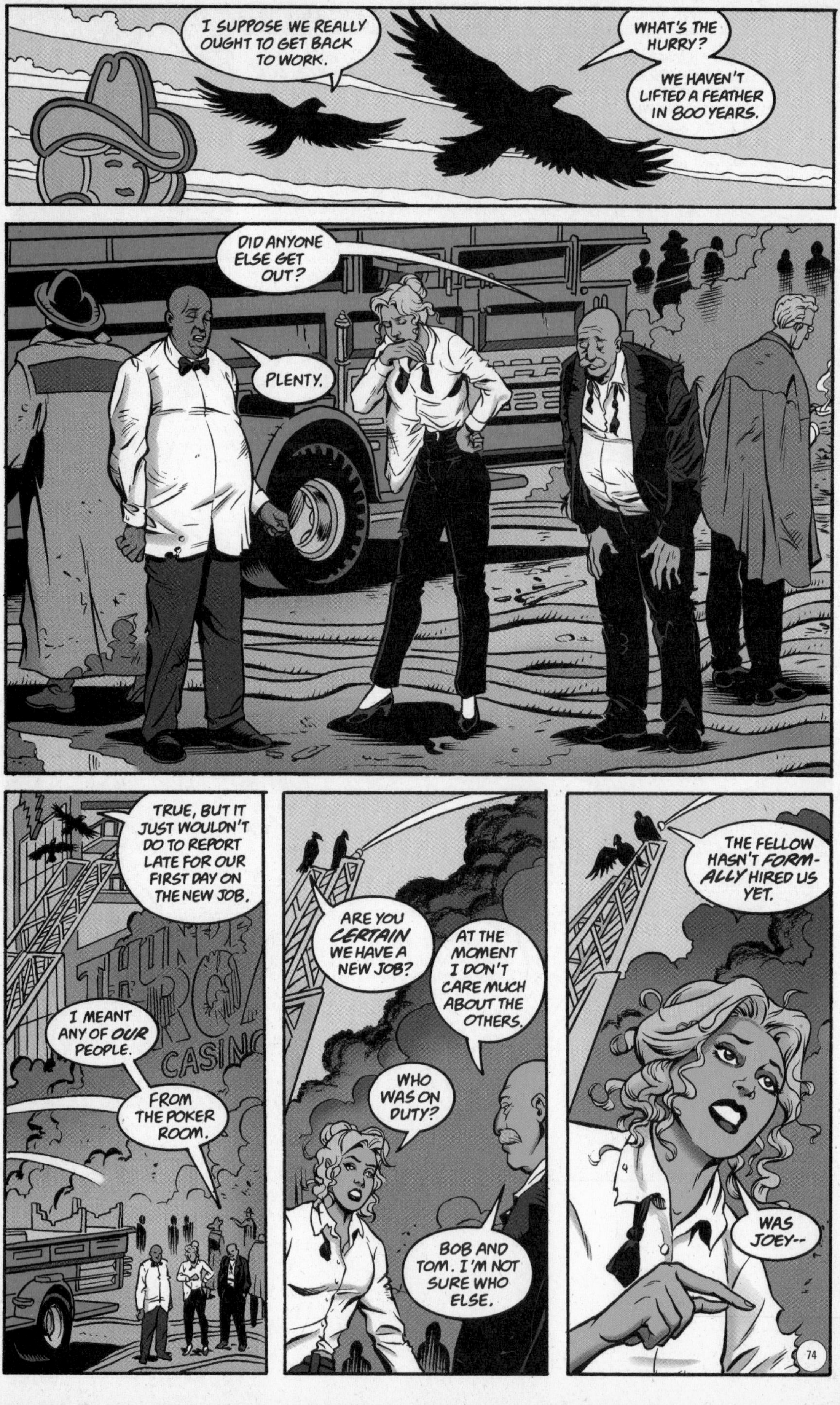
I SUPPOSE WE REALLY OUGHT TO GET BACK TO WORK.
WHAT'S THE HURRY?
WE HAVEN'T LIFTED A FEATHER IN 800 YEARS.
DID ANYONE ELSE GET OUT?
PLENTY.
TRUE, BUT IT JUST WOULDN'T DO TO REPORT LATE FOR OUR FIRST DAY ON THE NEW JOB.
CASINO
I MEANT ANY OF OUR PEOPLE.
FROM THE POKER ROOM.
ARE YOU CERTAIN WE HAVE A NEW JOB?
AT THE MOMENT I DON'T CARE MUCH ABOUT THE OTHERS.
WHO WAS ON DUTY?
BOB AND TOM. I'M NOT SURE WHO ELSE.
THE FELLOW HASN'T FORMALLY HIRED US YET.
WAS JOEY--
74

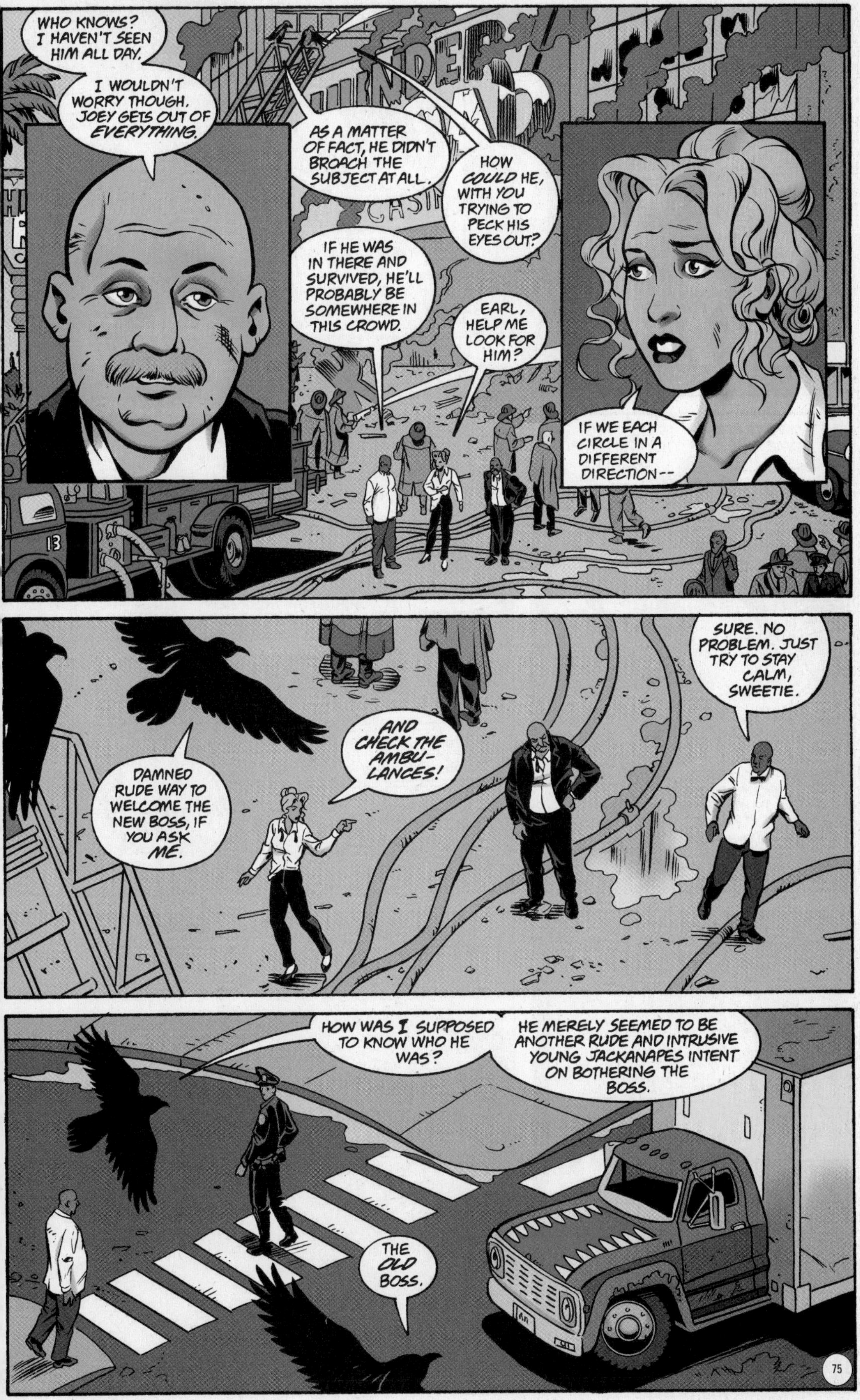
WHO KNOWS? I HAVEN'T SEEN HIM ALL DAY.
I WOULDN'T WORRY THOUGH. JOEY GETS OUT OF EVERYTHING.
AS A MATTER OF FACT, HE DIDN'T BROACH THE SUBJECT AT ALL.
HOW COULD HE, WITH YOU TRYING TO PECK HIS EYES OUT?
IF HE WAS IN THERE AND SURVIVED, HE'LL PROBABLY BE SOMEWHERE IN THIS CROWD.
EARL, HELP ME LOOK FOR HIM?
IF WE EACH CIRCLE IN A DIFFERENT DIRECTION--
13
SURE. NO PROBLEM. JUST TRY TO STAY CALM, SWEETIE.
AND CHECK THE AMBU-LANCES!
DAMNED RUDE WAY TO WELCOME THE NEW BOSS, IF YOU ASK ME.
HOW WAS I SUPPOSED TO KNOW WHO HE WAS?
HE MERELY SEEMED TO BE ANOTHER RUDE AND INTRUSIVE YOUNG JACKANAPES INTENT ON BOTHERING THE BOSS.
THE OLD BOSS.

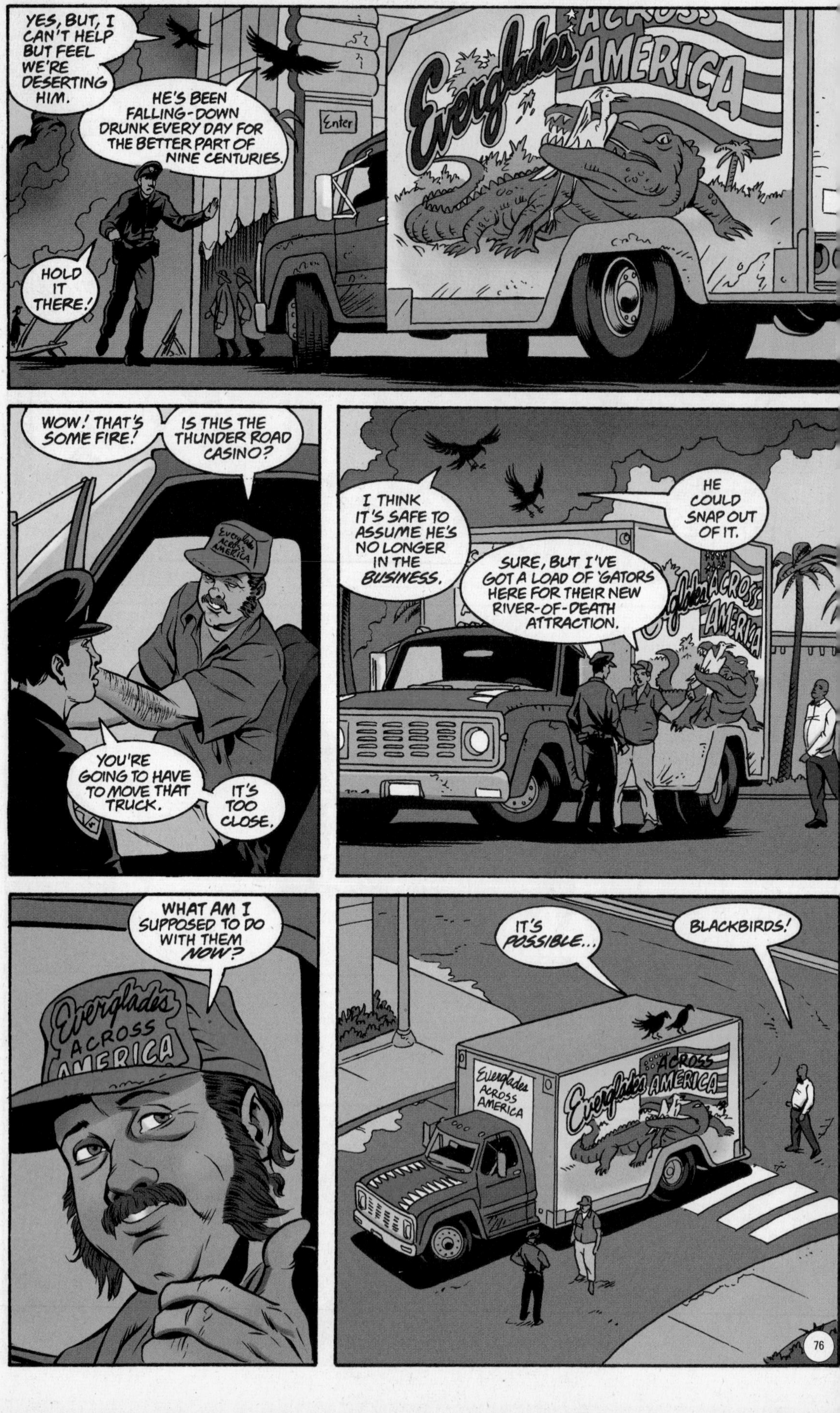
Everglades ACROSS AMERICA
Enter
YES, BUT, I CAN'T HELP BUT FEEL WE'RE DESERTING HIM.
HE'S BEEN FALLING-DOWN DRUNK EVERY DAY FOR THE BETTER PART OF NINE CENTURIES.
HOLD IT THERE!
WOW! THAT'S SOME FIRE!
IS THIS THE THUNDER ROAD CASINO?
YOU'RE GOING TO HAVE TO MOVE THAT TRUCK.
IT'S TOO CLOSE.
I THINK IT'S SAFE TO ASSUME HE'S NO LONGER IN THE BUSINESS.
HE COULD SNAP OUT OF IT.
SURE, BUT I'VE GOT A LOAD OF 'GATORS HERE FOR THEIR NEW RIVER-OF-DEATH ATTRACTION.
WHAT AM I SUPPOSED TO DO WITH THEM NOW?
Everglades ACROSS AMERICA
IT'S POSSIBLE...
BLACKBIRDS!
Everglades ACROSS AMERICA

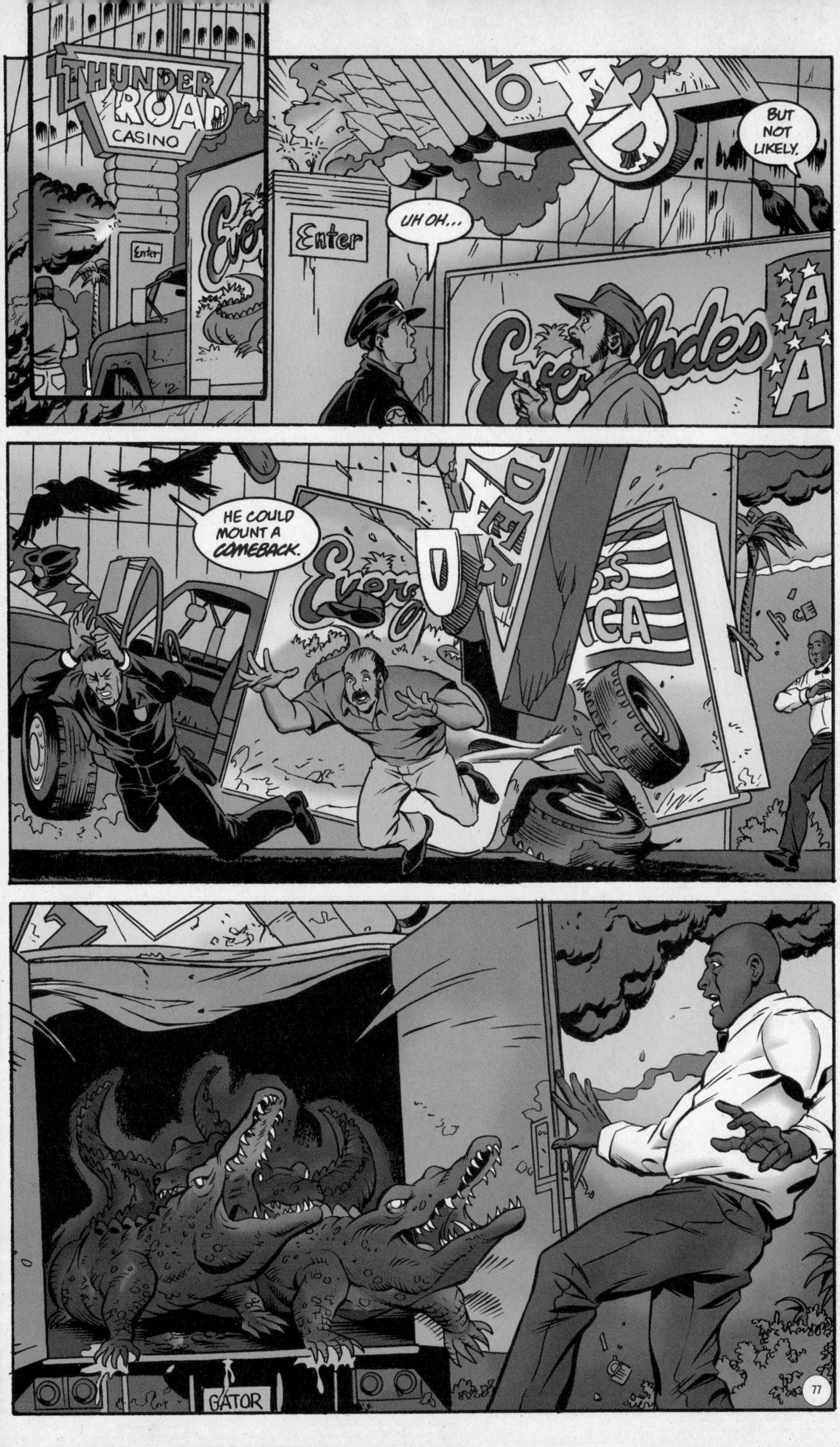
THUNDER ROAD
CASINO
Enter
Enter
UH OH...
BUT NOT LIKELY.
Everglades
HE COULD MOUNT A COMEBACK.
GATOR

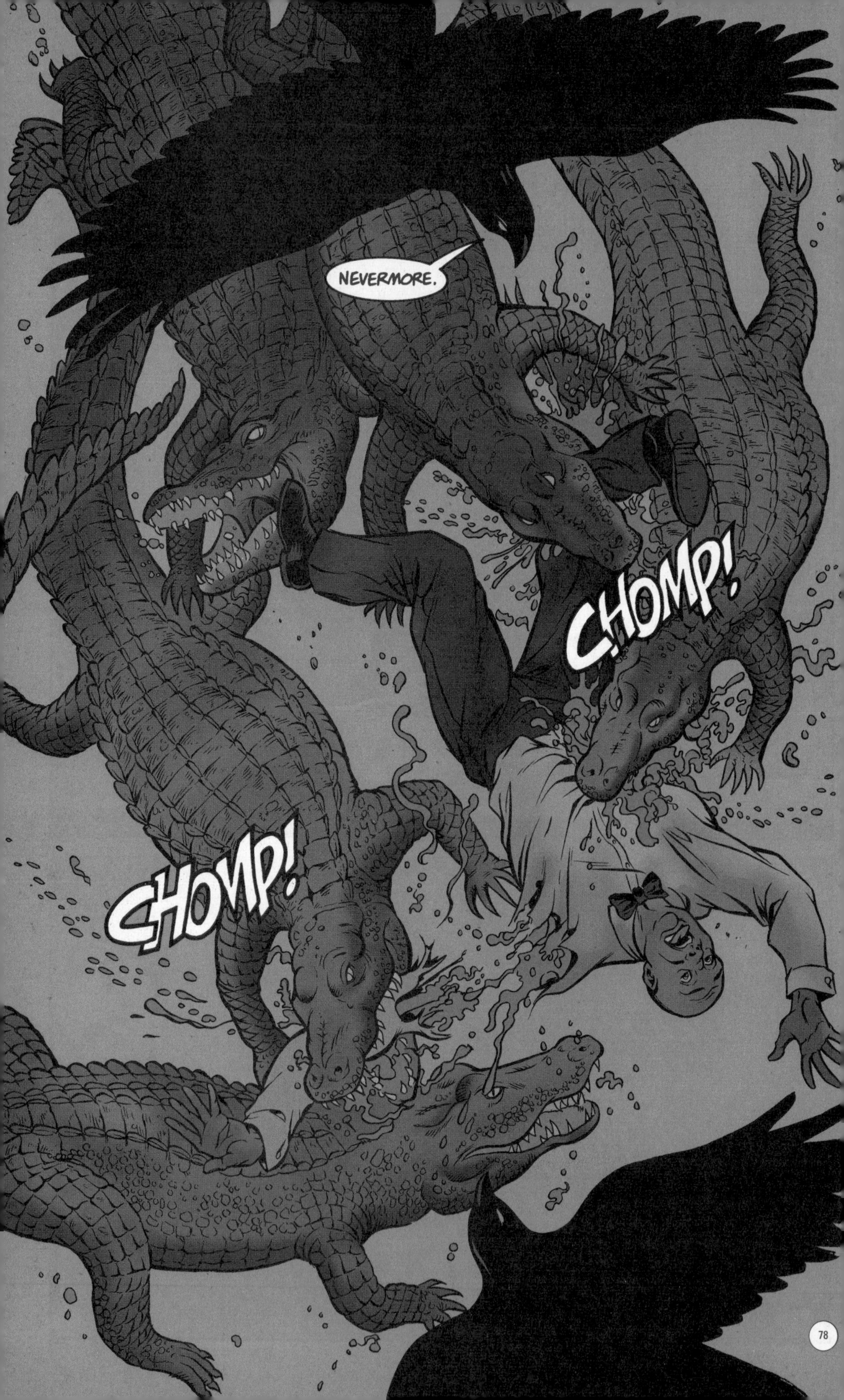
NEVERMORE.
CHOMP!
CHOMP!

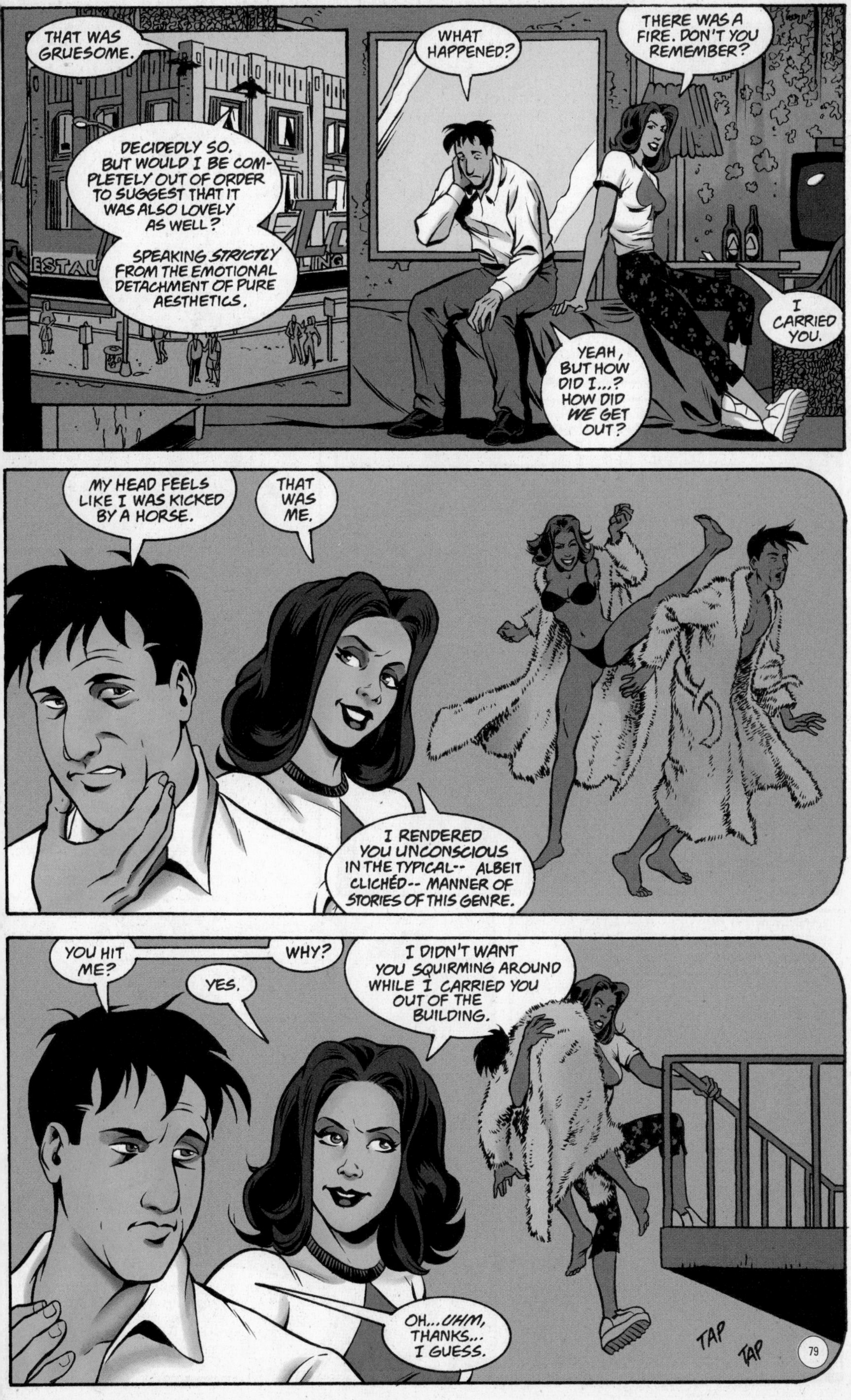
THAT WAS GRUESOME.
DECIDEDLY SO. BUT WOULD I BE COMPLETELY OUT OF ORDER TO SUGGEST THAT IT WAS ALSO LOVELY AS WELL?
SPEAKING STRICTLY FROM THE EMOTIONAL DETACHMENT OF PURE AESTHETICS.
WHAT HAPPENED?
THERE WAS A FIRE. DON'T YOU REMEMBER?
YEAH, BUT HOW DID I...? HOW DID WE GET OUT?
I CARRIED YOU.
MY HEAD FEELS LIKE I WAS KICKED BY A HORSE.
THAT WAS ME.
I RENDERED YOU UNCONSCIOUS IN THE TYPICAL-- ALBEIT CLICHÉD-- MANNER OF STORIES OF THIS GENRE.
YOU HIT ME?
WHY?
YES.
I DIDN'T WANT YOU SQUIRMING AROUND WHILE I CARRIED YOU OUT OF THE BUILDING.
OH...UHM, THANKS... I GUESS.
TAP
TAP

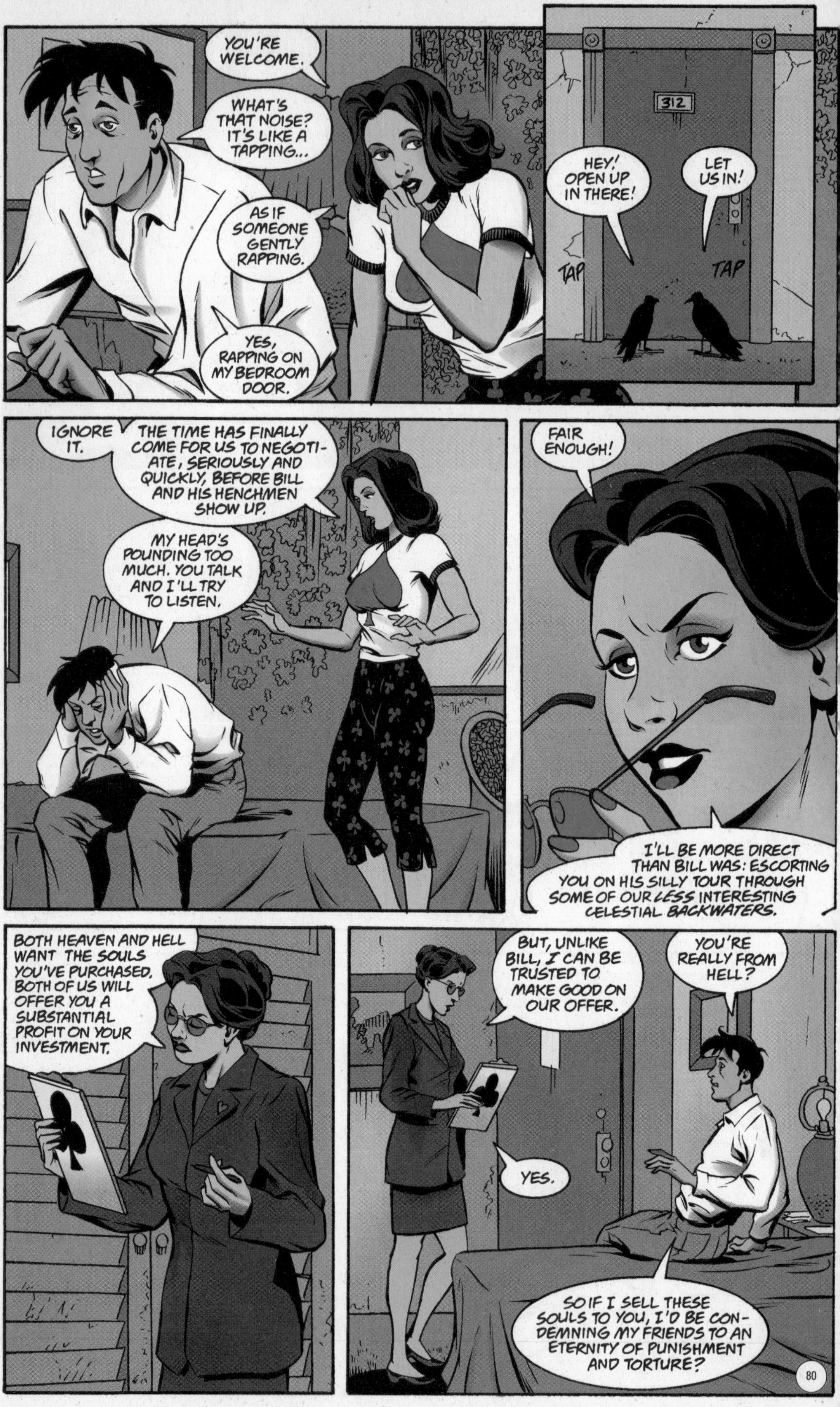
YOU'RE WELCOME.
WHAT'S THAT NOISE? IT'S LIKE A TAPPING...
AS IF SOMEONE GENTLY RAPPING.
YES, RAPPING ON MY BEDROOM DOOR.
312
HEY! OPEN UP IN THERE!
LET US IN!
TAP
TAP
IGNORE IT.
THE TIME HAS FINALLY COME FOR US TO NEGOTI-ATE, SERIOUSLY AND QUICKLY, BEFORE BILL AND HIS HENCHMEN SHOW UP.
MY HEAD'S POUNDING TOO MUCH. YOU TALK AND I'LL TRY TO LISTEN.
FAIR ENOUGH!
I'LL BE MORE DIRECT THAN BILL WAS: ESCORTING YOU ON HIS SILLY TOUR THROUGH SOME OF OUR *LESS* INTERESTING CELESTIAL *BACKWATERS*.
BOTH HEAVEN AND HELL WANT THE SOULS YOU'VE PURCHASED, BOTH OF US WILL OFFER YOU A SUBSTANTIAL PROFIT ON YOUR INVESTMENT.
BUT, UNLIKE BILL, *I* CAN BE TRUSTED TO MAKE GOOD ON OUR OFFER.
YOU'RE REALLY FROM HELL?
YES.
SO IF I SELL THESE SOULS TO YOU, I'D BE CON-DEMNING *MY FRIENDS* TO AN ETERNITY OF PUNISHMENT AND TORTURE?

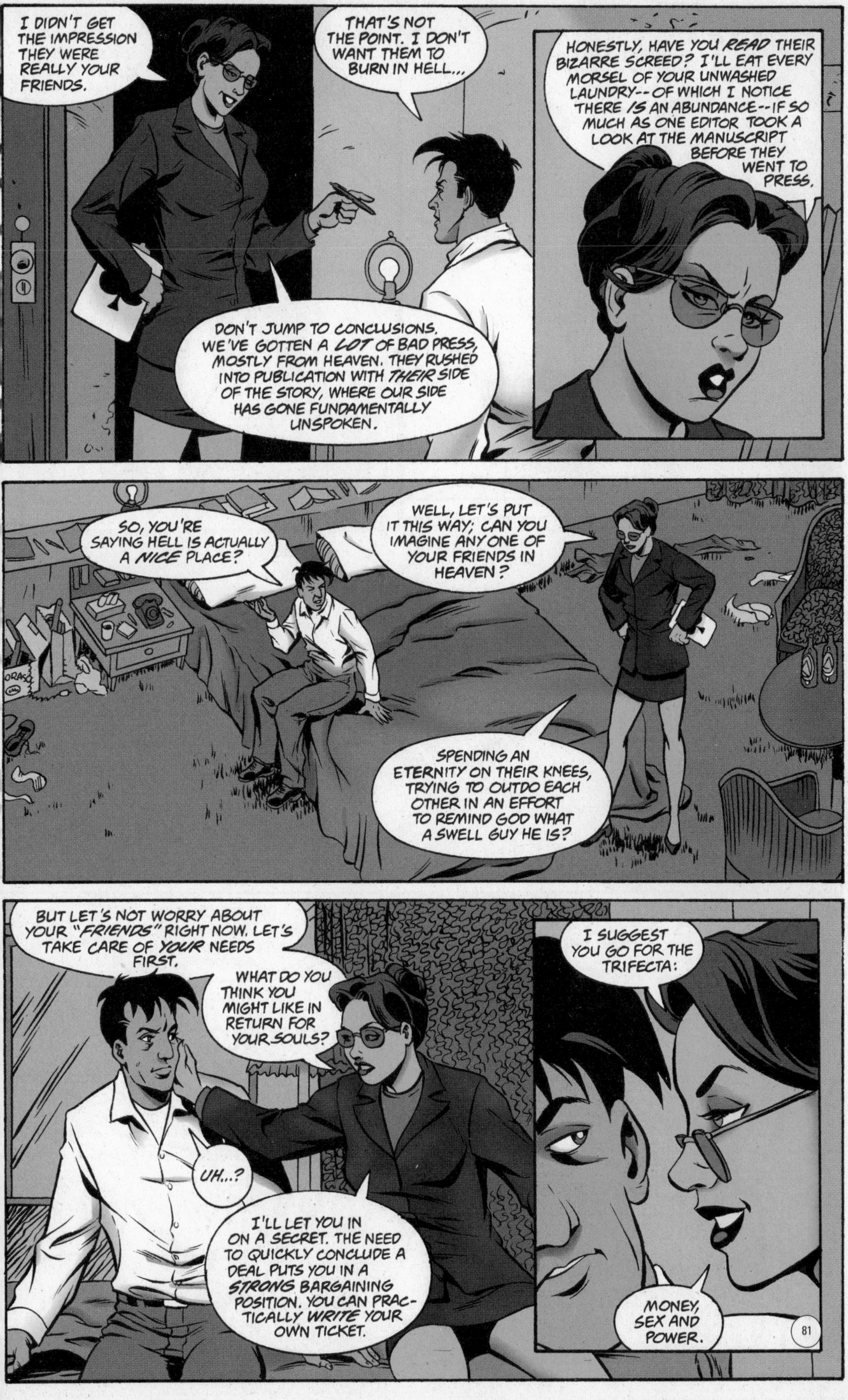
I DIDN'T GET THE IMPRESSION THEY WERE REALLY YOUR FRIENDS.
THAT'S NOT THE POINT. I DON'T WANT THEM TO BURN IN HELL...
DON'T JUMP TO CONCLUSIONS. WE'VE GOTTEN A LOT OF BAD PRESS, MOSTLY FROM HEAVEN. THEY RUSHED INTO PUBLICATION WITH THEIR SIDE OF THE STORY, WHERE OUR SIDE HAS GONE FUNDAMENTALLY UNSPOKEN.
HONESTLY, HAVE YOU READ THEIR BIZARRE SCREED? I'LL EAT EVERY MORSEL OF YOUR UNWASHED LAUNDRY--OF WHICH I NOTICE THERE IS AN ABUNDANCE--IF SO MUCH AS ONE EDITOR TOOK A LOOK AT THE MANUSCRIPT BEFORE THEY WENT TO PRESS.
SO, YOU'RE SAYING HELL IS ACTUALLY A NICE PLACE?
WELL, LET'S PUT IT THIS WAY; CAN YOU IMAGINE ANY ONE OF YOUR FRIENDS IN HEAVEN?
SPENDING AN ETERNITY ON THEIR KNEES, TRYING TO OUTDO EACH OTHER IN AN EFFORT TO REMIND GOD WHAT A SWELL GUY HE IS?
BUT LET'S NOT WORRY ABOUT YOUR "FRIENDS" RIGHT NOW. LET'S TAKE CARE OF YOUR NEEDS FIRST.
WHAT DO YOU THINK YOU MIGHT LIKE IN RETURN FOR YOUR SOULS?
UH...?
I'LL LET YOU IN ON A SECRET. THE NEED TO QUICKLY CONCLUDE A DEAL PUTS YOU IN A STRONG BARGAINING POSITION. YOU CAN PRACTICALLY WRITE YOUR OWN TICKET.
I SUGGEST YOU GO FOR THE TRIFECTA:
MONEY, SEX AND POWER.

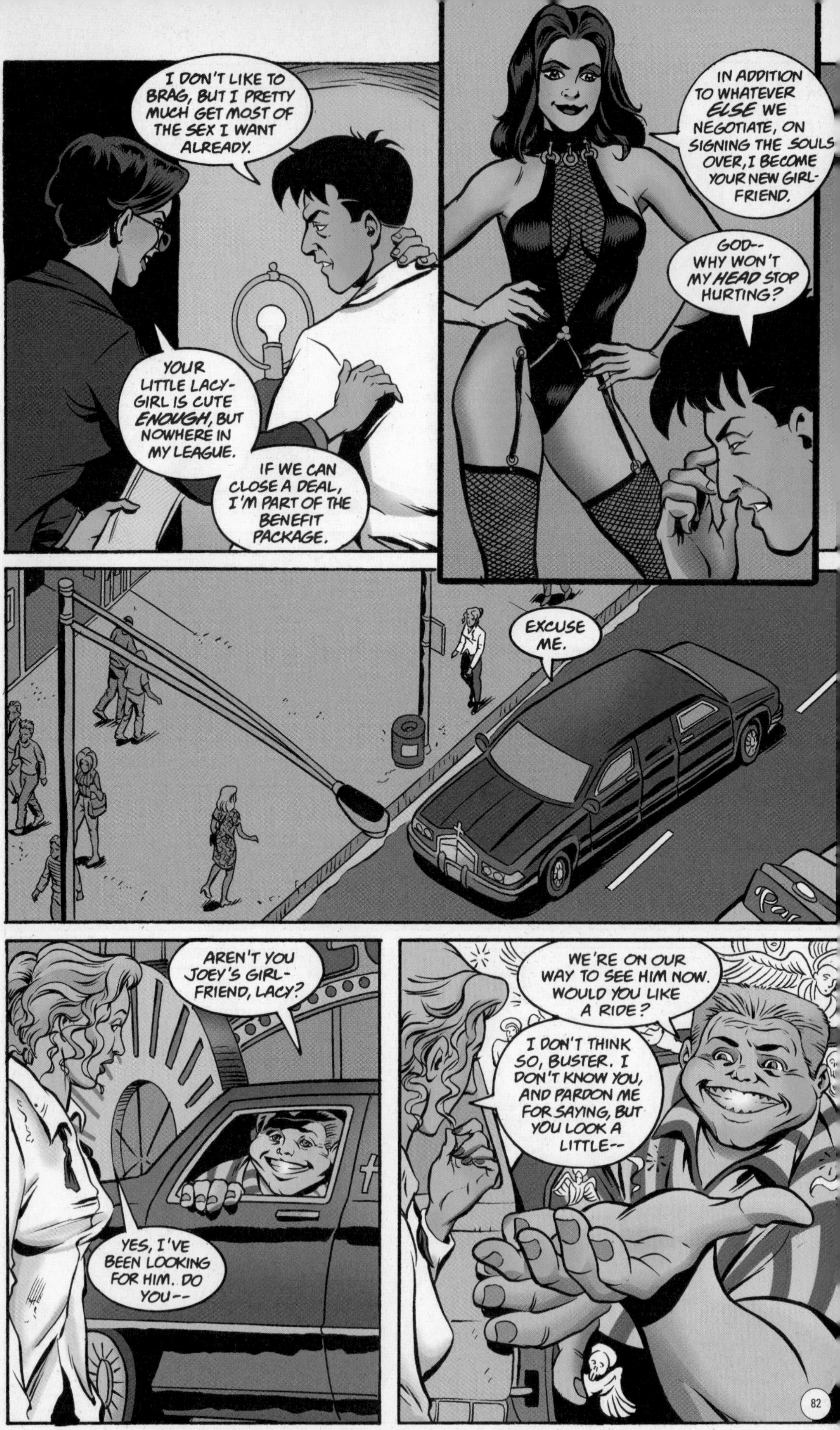
I DON'T LIKE TO BRAG, BUT I PRETTY MUCH GET MOST OF THE SEX I WANT ALREADY.
YOUR LITTLE LACY-GIRL IS CUTE ENOUGH, BUT NOWHERE IN MY LEAGUE.
IF WE CAN CLOSE A DEAL, I'M PART OF THE BENEFIT PACKAGE.
IN ADDITION TO WHATEVER ELSE WE NEGOTIATE, ON SIGNING THE SOULS OVER, I BECOME YOUR NEW GIRL-FRIEND.
GOD-- WHY WON'T MY HEAD STOP HURTING?
EXCUSE ME.
AREN'T YOU JOEY'S GIRL-FRIEND, LACY?
YES, I'VE BEEN LOOKING FOR HIM. DO YOU--
WE'RE ON OUR WAY TO SEE HIM NOW. WOULD YOU LIKE A RIDE?
I DON'T THINK SO, BUSTER. I DON'T KNOW YOU, AND PARDON ME FOR SAYING, BUT YOU LOOK A LITTLE--

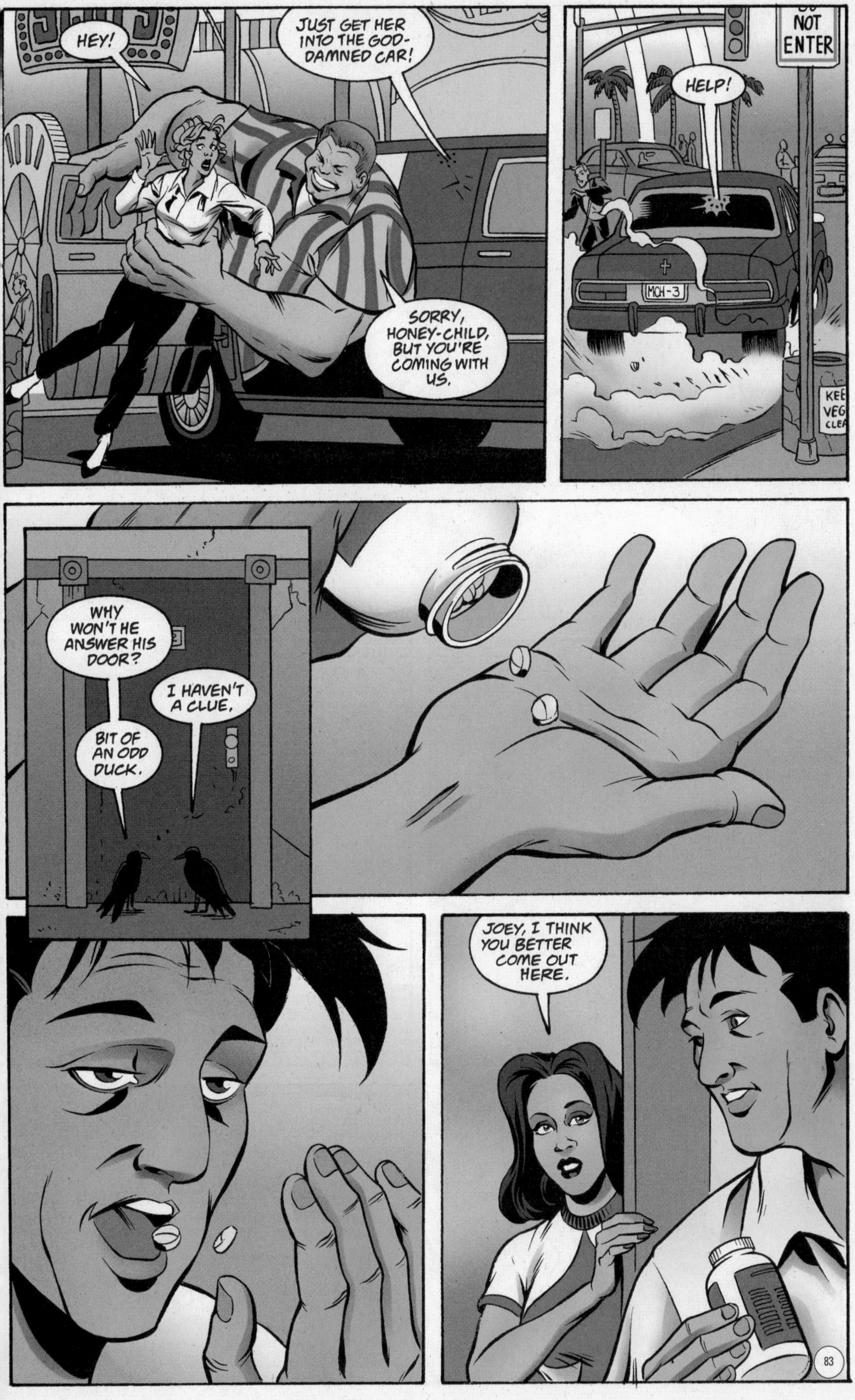
HEY!
JUST GET HER INTO THE GOD-DAMNED CAR!
SORRY, HONEY-CHILD, BUT YOU'RE COMING WITH US.
NOT ENTER
HELP!
MCH-3
WHY WON'T HE ANSWER HIS DOOR?
I HAVEN'T A CLUE.
BIT OF AN ODD DUCK.
JOEY, I THINK YOU BETTER COME OUT HERE.

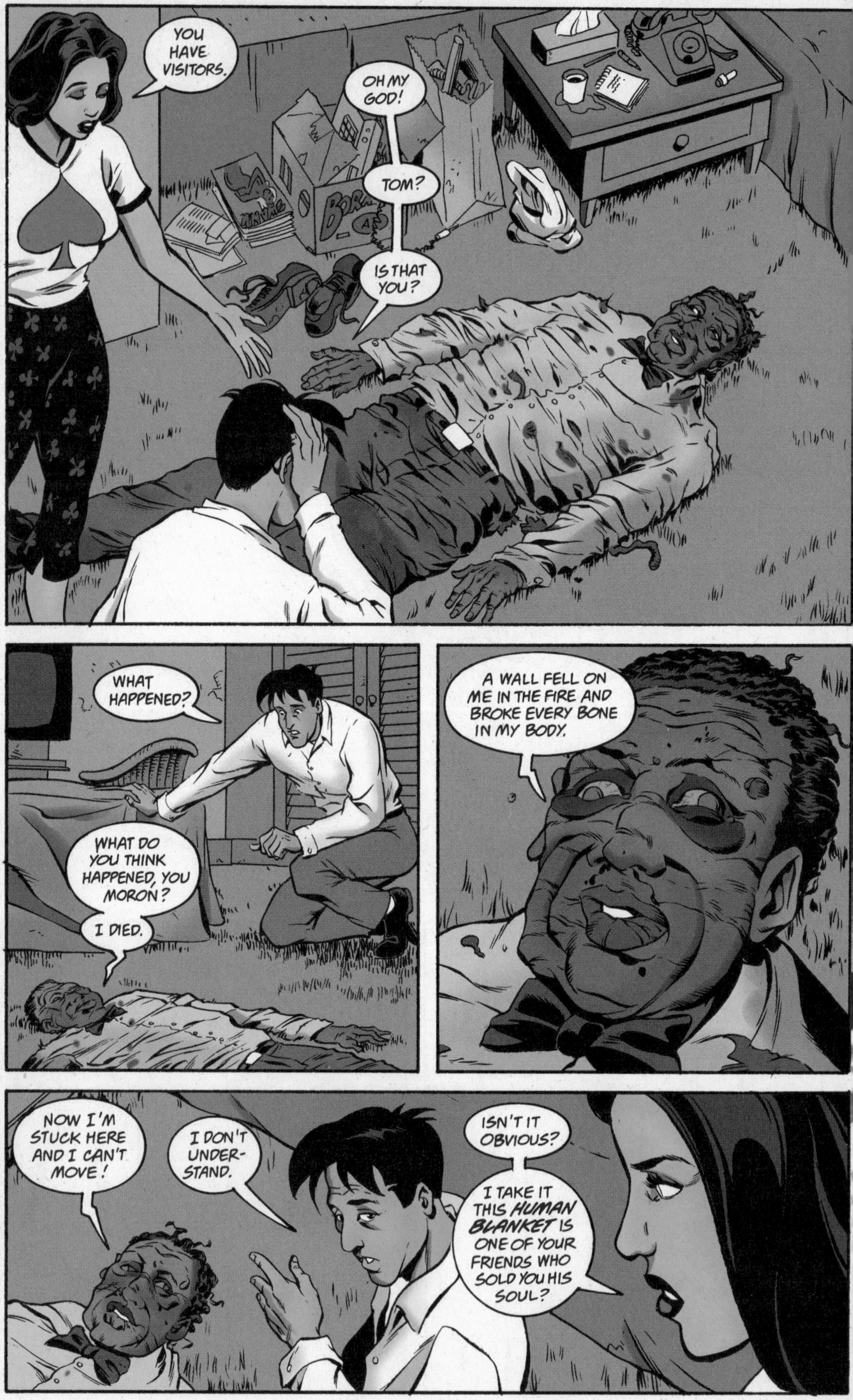
YOU HAVE VISITORS.
OH MY GOD!
TOM?
IS THAT YOU?
WHAT HAPPENED?
WHAT DO YOU THINK HAPPENED, YOU MORON?
I DIED.
A WALL FELL ON ME IN THE FIRE AND BROKE EVERY BONE IN MY BODY.
NOW I'M STUCK HERE AND I CAN'T MOVE!
I DON'T UNDER-STAND.
ISN'T IT OBVIOUS?
I TAKE IT THIS HUMAN BLANKET IS ONE OF YOUR FRIENDS WHO SOLD YOU HIS SOUL?

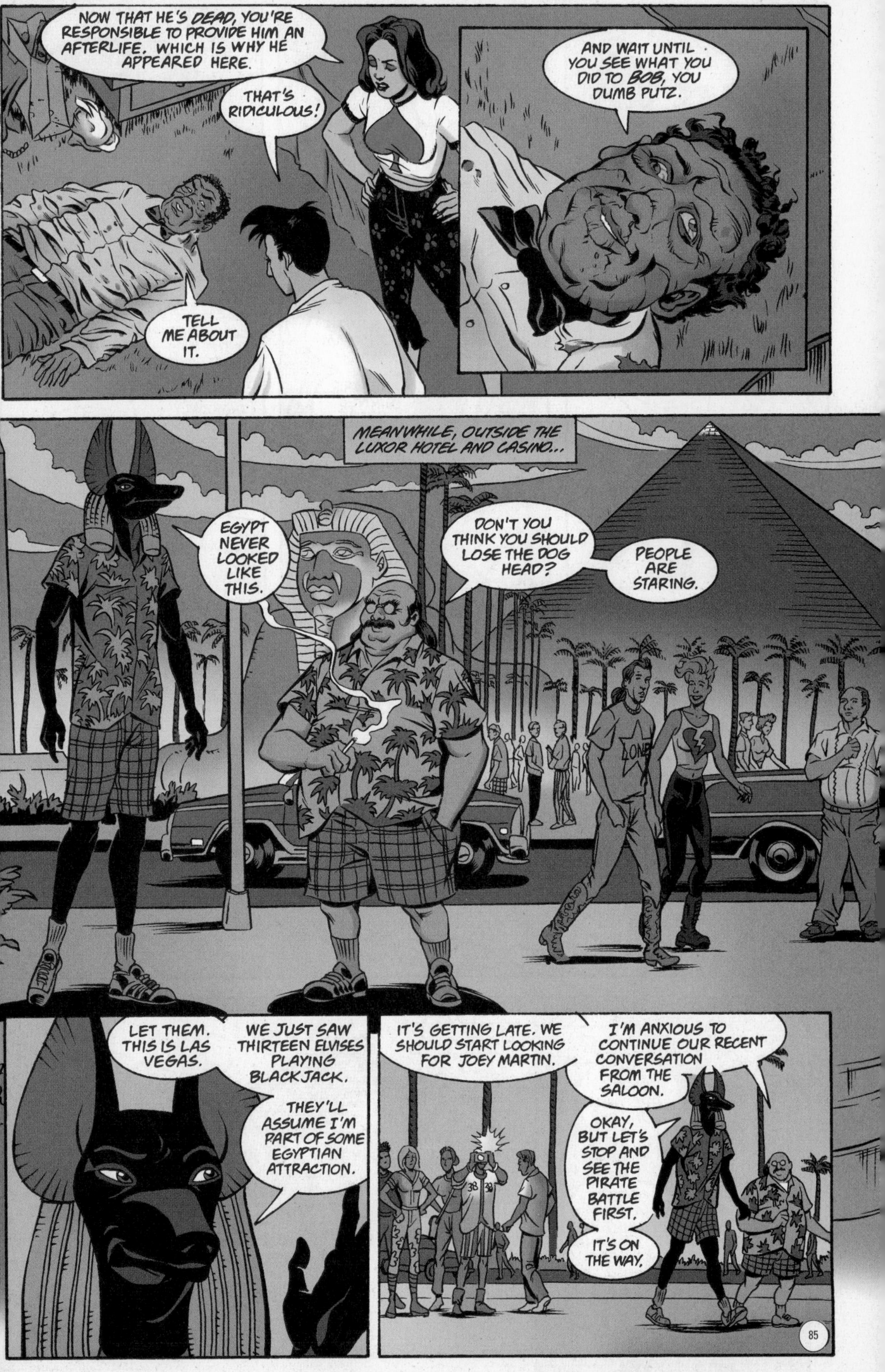
NOW THAT HE'S DEAD, YOU'RE RESPONSIBLE TO PROVIDE HIM AN AFTERLIFE. WHICH IS WHY HE APPEARED HERE.
THAT'S RIDICULOUS!
TELL ME ABOUT IT.
AND WAIT UNTIL YOU SEE WHAT YOU DID TO BOB, YOU DUMB PUTZ.
MEANWHILE, OUTSIDE THE LUXOR HOTEL AND CASINO...
EGYPT NEVER LOOKED LIKE THIS.
DON'T YOU THINK YOU SHOULD LOSE THE DOG HEAD?
PEOPLE ARE STARING.
LET THEM. THIS IS LAS VEGAS.
WE JUST SAW THIRTEEN ELVISES PLAYING BLACKJACK.
THEY'LL ASSUME I'M PART OF SOME EGYPTIAN ATTRACTION.
IT'S GETTING LATE. WE SHOULD START LOOKING FOR JOEY MARTIN.
I'M ANXIOUS TO CONTINUE OUR RECENT CONVERSATION FROM THE SALOON.
OKAY, BUT LET'S STOP AND SEE THE PIRATE BATTLE FIRST.
IT'S ON THE WAY.

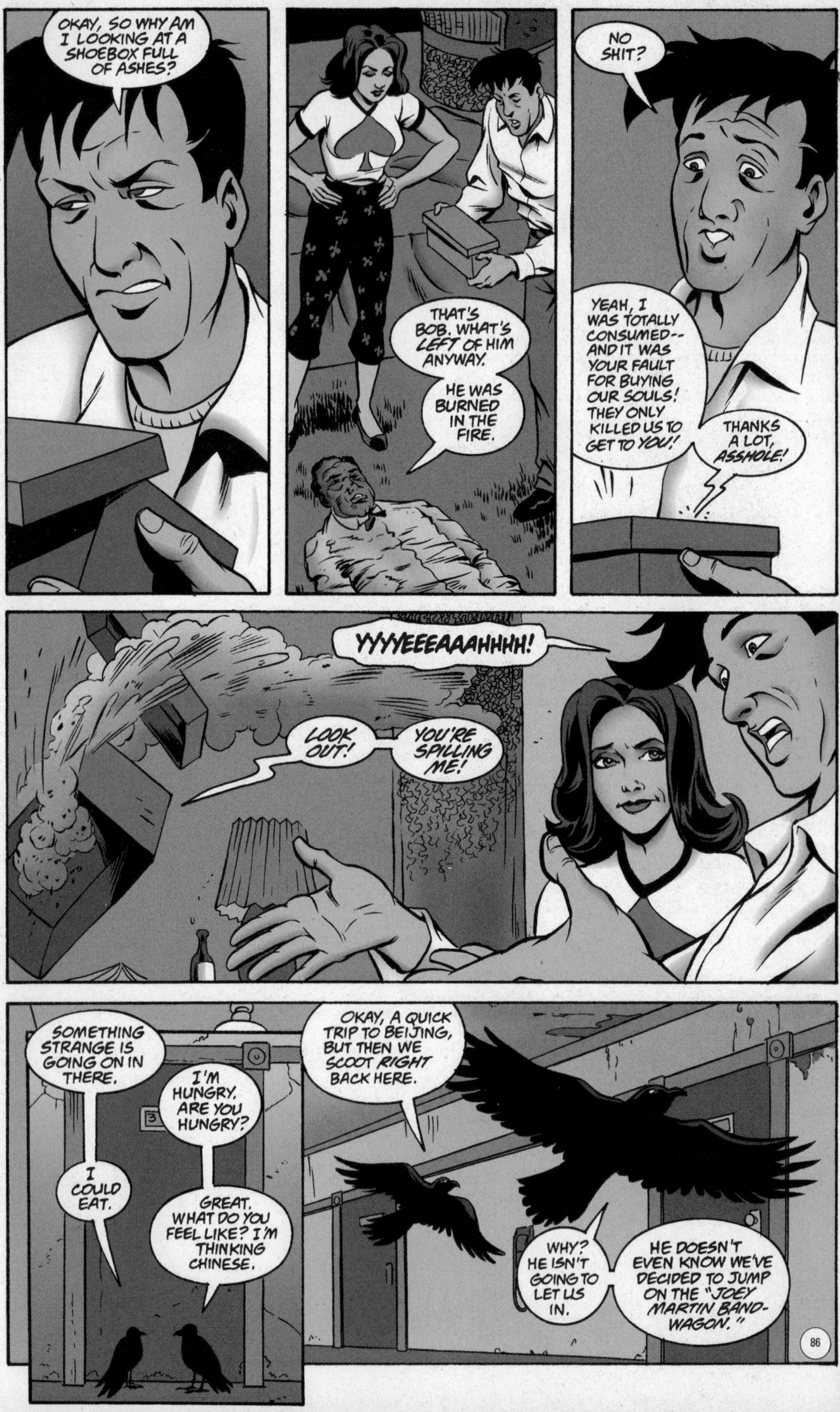
OKAY, SO WHY AM I LOOKING AT A SHOEBOX FULL OF ASHES?
THAT'S BOB. WHAT'S LEFT OF HIM ANYWAY.
HE WAS BURNED IN THE FIRE.
NO SHIT?
YEAH, I WAS TOTALLY CONSUMED-- AND IT WAS YOUR FAULT FOR BUYING OUR SOULS! THEY ONLY KILLED US TO GET TO YOU!
THANKS A LOT, ASSHOLE!
YYYYEEEAAAHHHH!
LOOK OUT!
YOU'RE SPILLING ME!
SOMETHING STRANGE IS GOING ON IN THERE.
I COULD EAT.
I'M HUNGRY. ARE YOU HUNGRY?
GREAT. WHAT DO YOU FEEL LIKE? I'M THINKING CHINESE.
OKAY, A QUICK TRIP TO BEIJING, BUT THEN WE SCOOT RIGHT BACK HERE.
WHY? HE ISN'T GOING TO LET US IN.
HE DOESN'T EVEN KNOW WE'VE DECIDED TO JUMP ON THE "JOEY MARTIN BAND-WAGON."

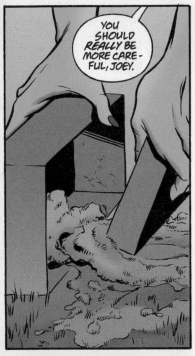

YOU SHOULD *REALLY* BE MORE CARE-FUL, JOEY.

YOU ALMOST *SCATTERED* POOR BOB.

I THINK SOME OF ME SPILLED UNDER THE BED.

CHRIST, YOU WON'T BELIEVE SOME OF THE THINGS HE HAS GROWING UNDER THERE!

LIKE IT OR NOT, THEIR *WELFARE* IS NOW IN YOUR HANDS.

YOU HAVE TO LEARN TO BE *RESPONSIBLE.*

WHY? HOW?

YOU'RE *BABBLING,* DEAR.

I DON'T SUPPOSE ANYONE'S WILLING TO PICK ME UP OFF THE FLOOR?

HOW COME THEY'RE LIKE THIS, MARY?

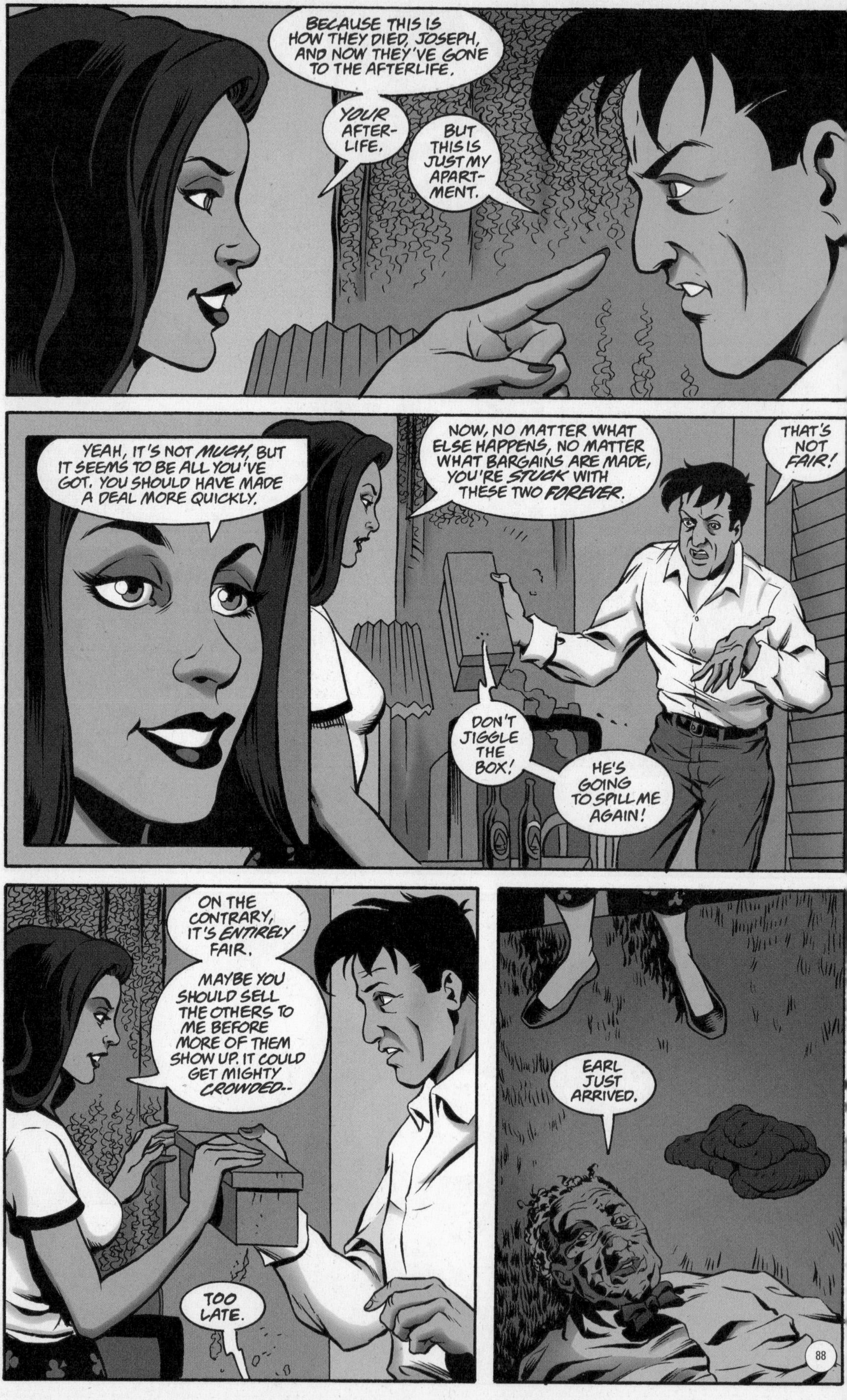
BECAUSE THIS IS HOW THEY DIED, JOSEPH, AND NOW THEY'VE GONE TO THE AFTERLIFE.
YOUR AFTER-LIFE.
BUT THIS IS JUST MY APART-MENT.
YEAH, IT'S NOT MUCH, BUT IT SEEMS TO BE ALL YOU'VE GOT. YOU SHOULD HAVE MADE A DEAL MORE QUICKLY.
NOW, NO MATTER WHAT ELSE HAPPENS, NO MATTER WHAT BARGAINS ARE MADE, YOU'RE STUCK WITH THESE TWO FOREVER.
THAT'S NOT FAIR!
DON'T JIGGLE THE BOX!
HE'S GOING TO SPILL ME AGAIN!
ON THE CONTRARY, IT'S ENTIRELY FAIR.
MAYBE YOU SHOULD SELL THE OTHERS TO ME BEFORE MORE OF THEM SHOW UP. IT COULD GET MIGHTY CROWDED--
TOO LATE.
EARL JUST ARRIVED.

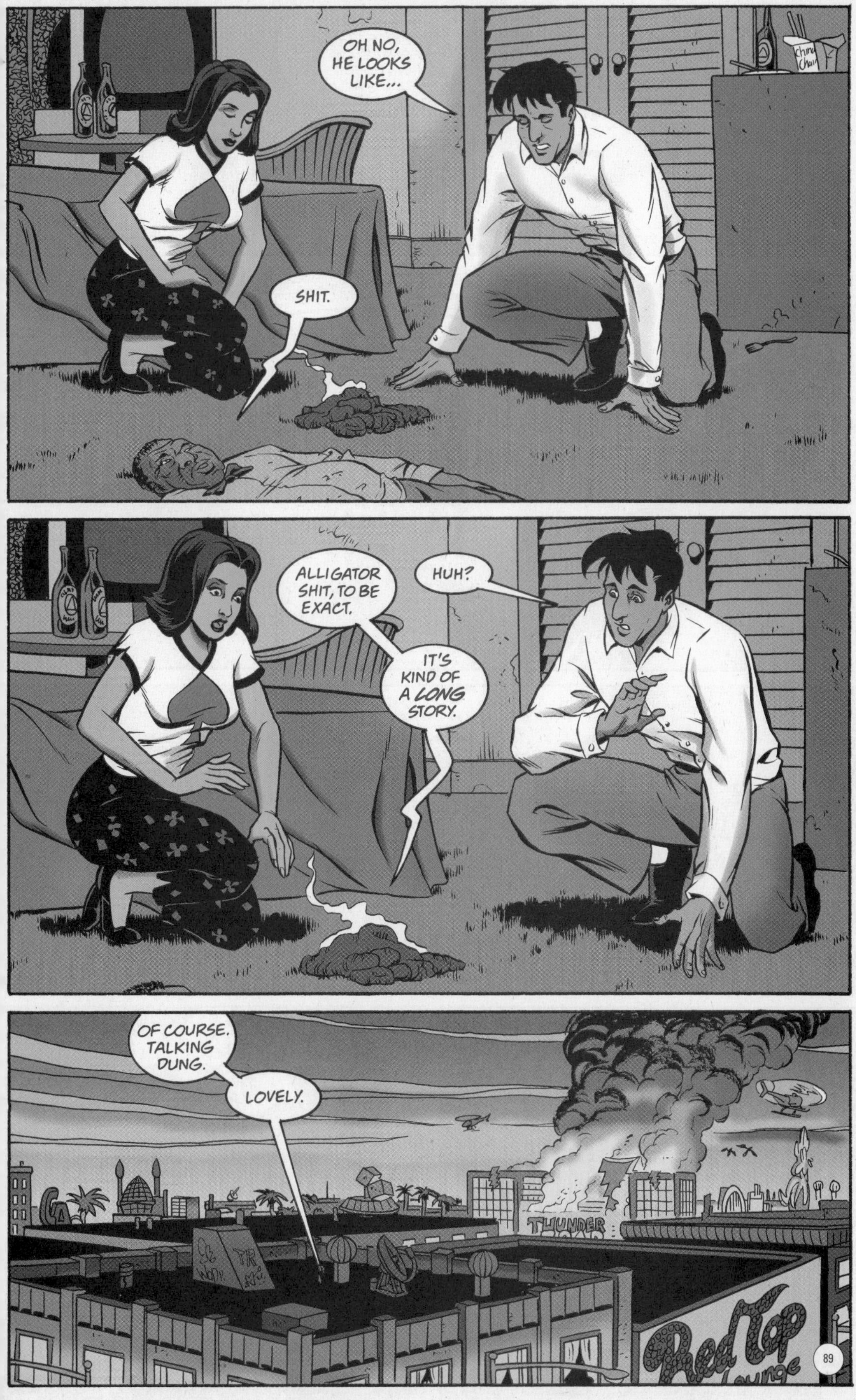

OH NO, HE LOOKS LIKE...
SHIT.
ALLIGATOR SHIT, TO BE EXACT.
HUH?
IT'S KIND OF A *LONG* STORY.
OF COURSE. TALKING DUNG.
LOVELY.
THUNDER
Red Top

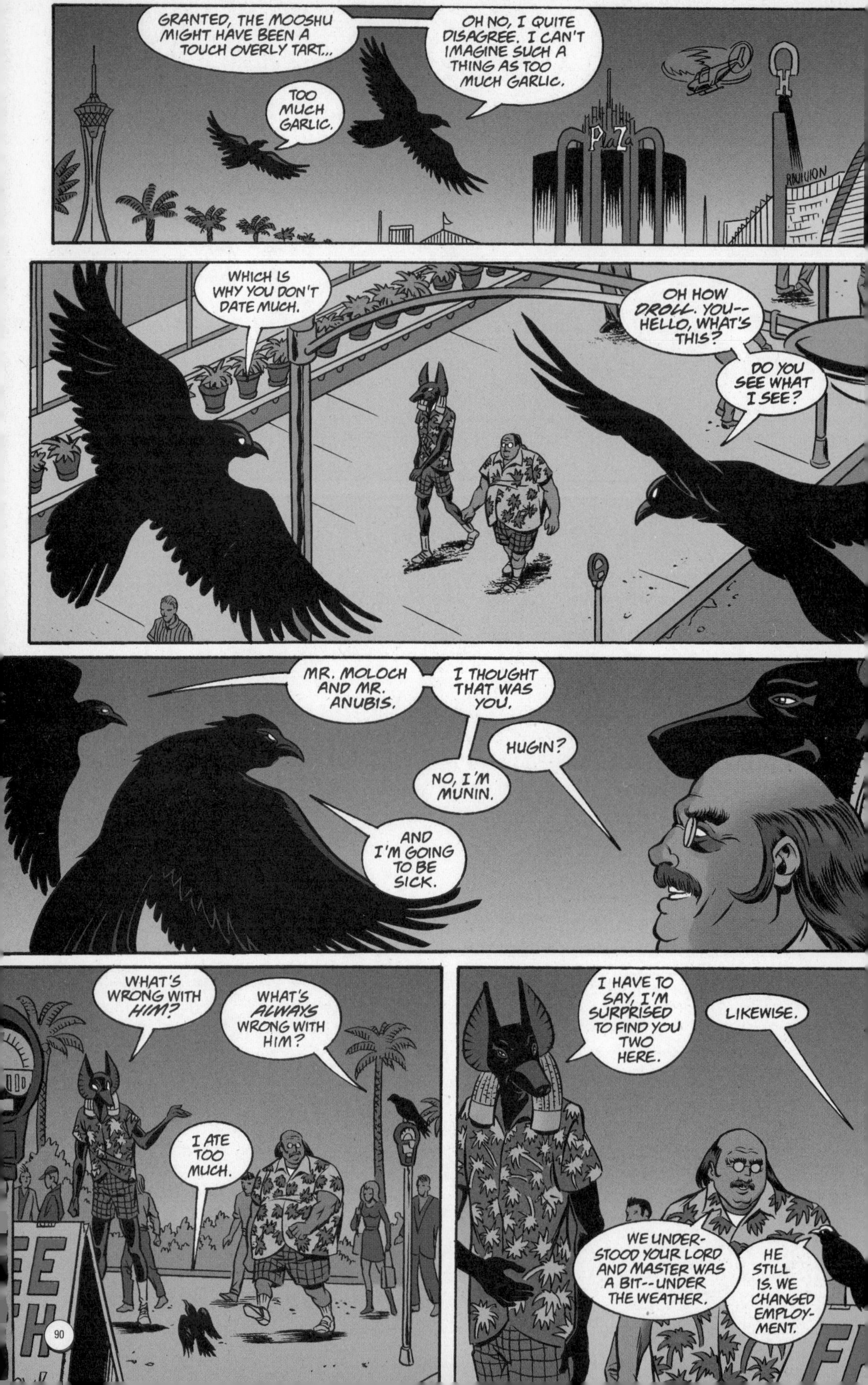

GRANTED, THE MOOSHU MIGHT HAVE BEEN A TOUCH OVERLY TART...
TOO MUCH GARLIC.
OH NO, I QUITE DISAGREE. I CAN'T IMAGINE SUCH A THING AS TOO MUCH GARLIC.
PLAZA
WHICH IS WHY YOU DON'T DATE MUCH.
OH HOW *DROLL*. YOU-- HELLO, WHAT'S THIS?
DO YOU SEE WHAT I SEE?
MR. MOLOCH AND MR. ANUBIS.
I THOUGHT THAT WAS YOU.
HUGIN?
NO, I'M MUNIN.
AND I'M GOING TO BE SICK.
WHAT'S WRONG WITH *HIM?*
WHAT'S *ALWAYS* WRONG WITH HIM?
I ATE TOO MUCH.
I HAVE TO SAY, I'M SURPRISED TO FIND YOU TWO HERE.
LIKEWISE.
WE UNDERSTOOD YOUR LORD AND MASTER WAS A BIT--UNDER THE WEATHER.
HE STILL IS. WE CHANGED EMPLOYMENT.

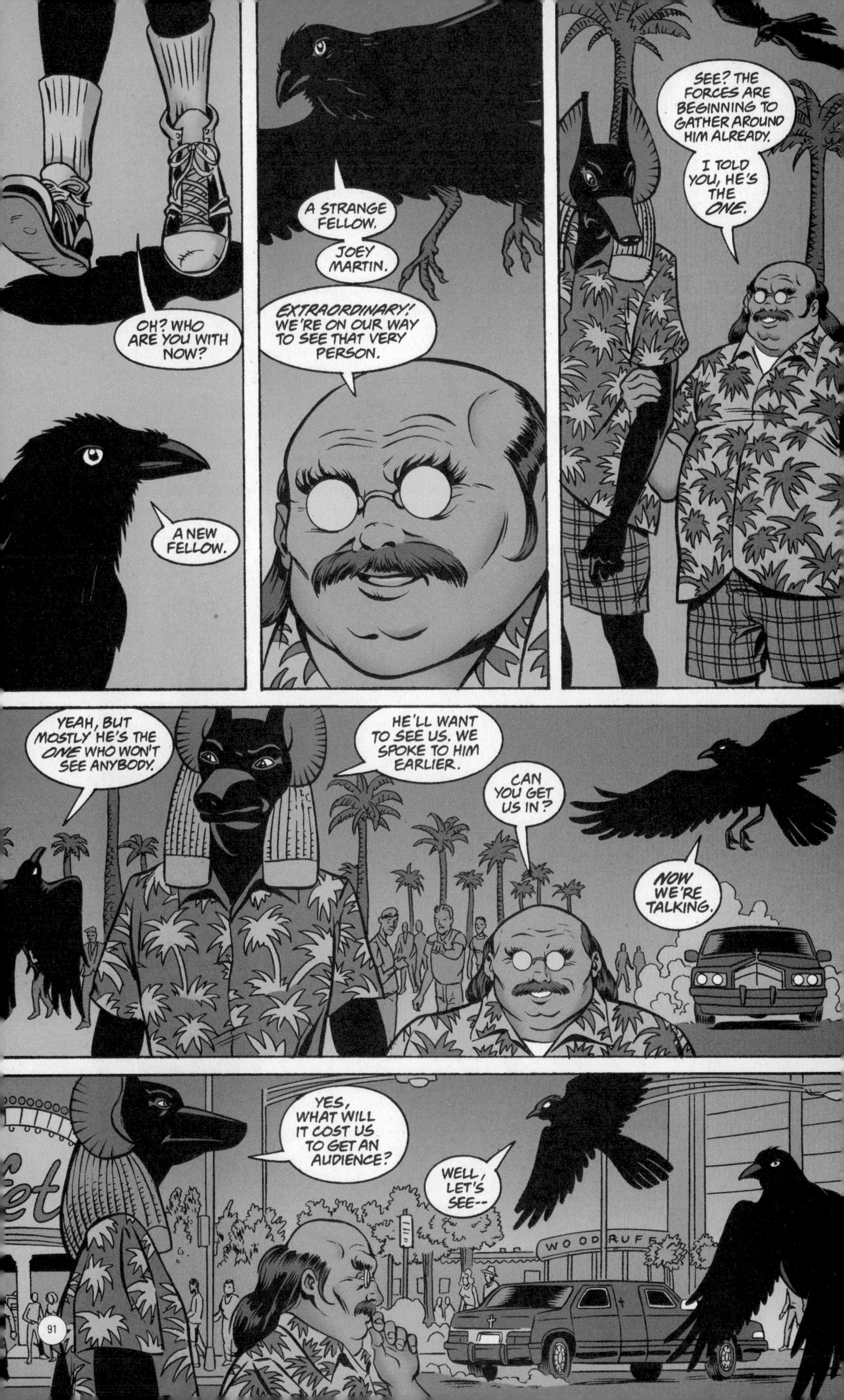
OH? WHO ARE YOU WITH NOW?
A NEW FELLOW.
A STRANGE FELLOW.
JOEY MARTIN.
EXTRAORDINARY! WE'RE ON OUR WAY TO SEE THAT VERY PERSON.
SEE? THE FORCES ARE BEGINNING TO GATHER AROUND HIM ALREADY.
I TOLD YOU, HE'S THE ONE.
YEAH, BUT MOSTLY HE'S THE ONE WHO WON'T SEE ANYBODY.
HE'LL WANT TO SEE US. WE SPOKE TO HIM EARLIER.
CAN YOU GET US IN?
NOW WE'RE TALKING.
YES, WHAT WILL IT COST US TO GET AN AUDIENCE?
WELL, LET'S SEE--
WOODRUFF

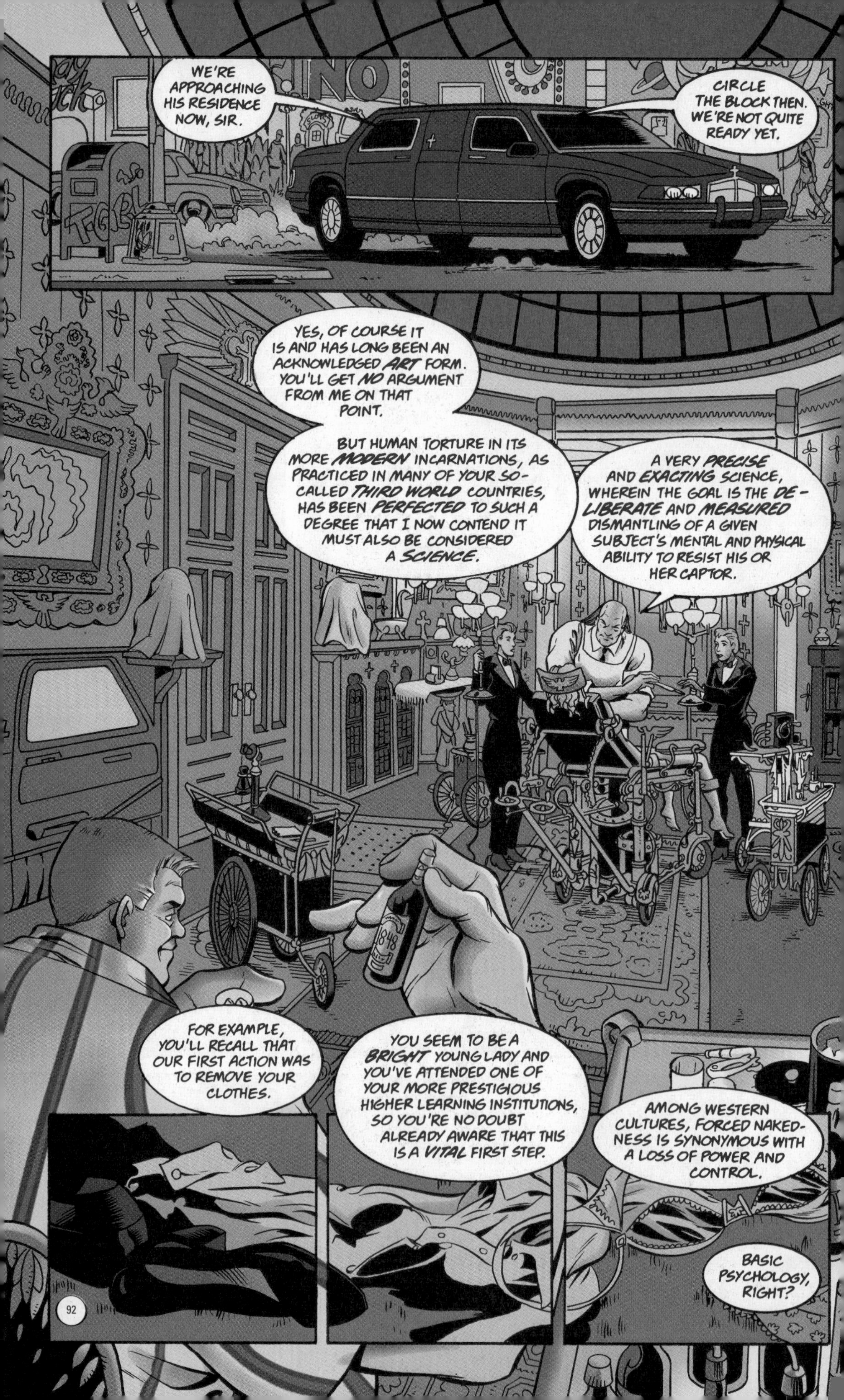
WE'RE APPROACHING HIS RESIDENCE NOW, SIR.
CIRCLE THE BLOCK THEN. WE'RE NOT QUITE READY YET.
YES, OF COURSE IT IS AND HAS LONG BEEN AN ACKNOWLEDGED ART FORM. YOU'LL GET NO ARGUMENT FROM ME ON THAT POINT.
BUT HUMAN TORTURE IN ITS MORE MODERN INCARNATIONS, AS PRACTICED IN MANY OF YOUR SO-CALLED THIRD WORLD COUNTRIES, HAS BEEN PERFECTED TO SUCH A DEGREE THAT I NOW CONTEND IT MUST ALSO BE CONSIDERED A SCIENCE.
A VERY PRECISE AND EXACTING SCIENCE, WHEREIN THE GOAL IS THE DE-LIBERATE AND MEASURED DISMANTLING OF A GIVEN SUBJECT'S MENTAL AND PHYSICAL ABILITY TO RESIST HIS OR HER CAPTOR.
FOR EXAMPLE, YOU'LL RECALL THAT OUR FIRST ACTION WAS TO REMOVE YOUR CLOTHES.
YOU SEEM TO BE A BRIGHT YOUNG LADY AND YOU'VE ATTENDED ONE OF YOUR MORE PRESTIGIOUS HIGHER LEARNING INSTITUTIONS, SO YOU'RE NO DOUBT ALREADY AWARE THAT THIS IS A VITAL FIRST STEP.
AMONG WESTERN CULTURES, FORCED NAKED-NESS IS SYNONYMOUS WITH A LOSS OF POWER AND CONTROL.
BASIC PSYCHOLOGY, RIGHT?

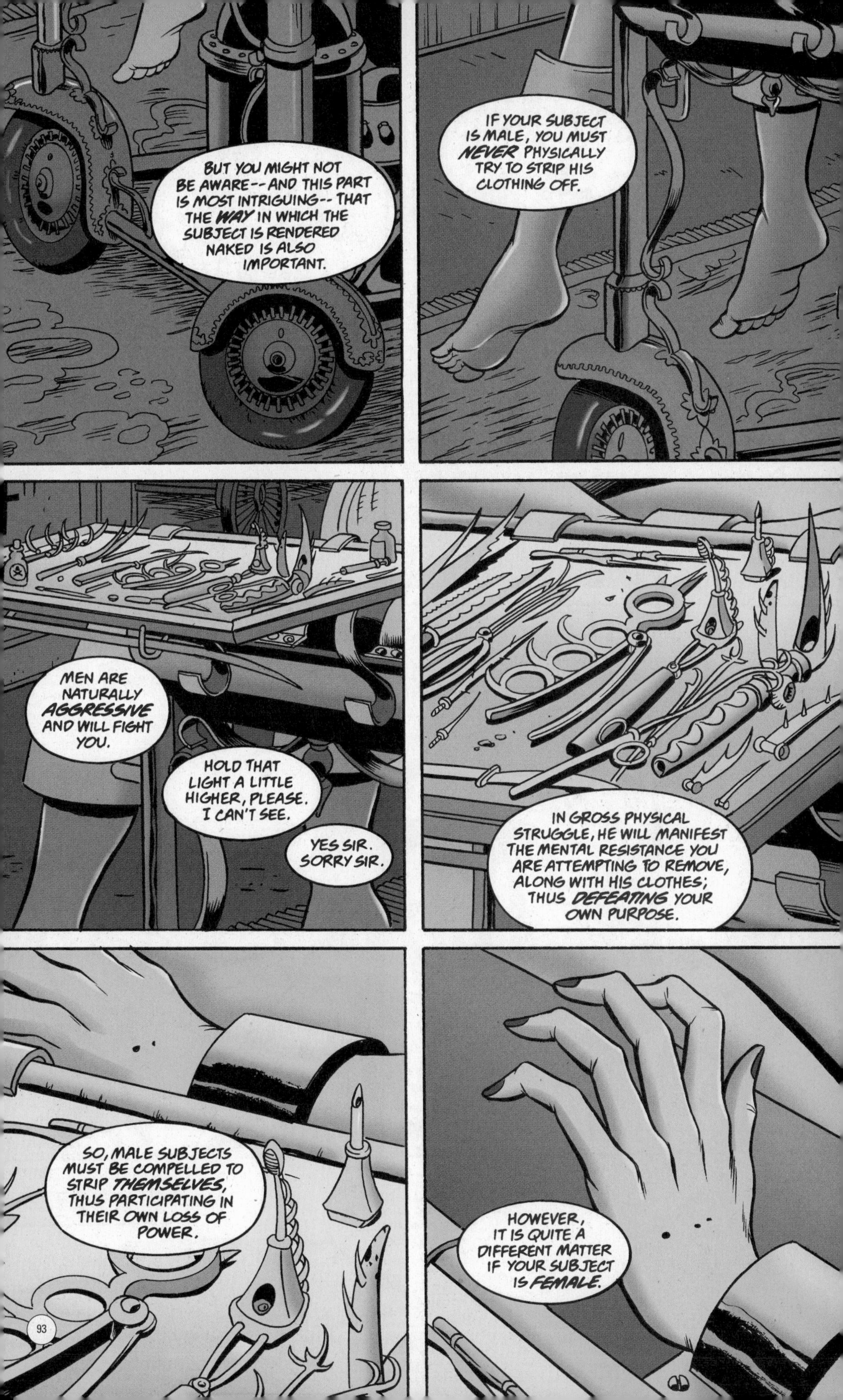
BUT YOU MIGHT NOT BE AWARE--AND THIS PART IS MOST INTRIGUING--THAT THE WAY IN WHICH THE SUBJECT IS RENDERED NAKED IS ALSO IMPORTANT.
IF YOUR SUBJECT IS MALE, YOU MUST NEVER PHYSICALLY TRY TO STRIP HIS CLOTHING OFF.
MEN ARE NATURALLY AGGRESSIVE AND WILL FIGHT YOU.
HOLD THAT LIGHT A LITTLE HIGHER, PLEASE. I CAN'T SEE.
YES SIR. SORRY SIR.
IN GROSS PHYSICAL STRUGGLE, HE WILL MANIFEST THE MENTAL RESISTANCE YOU ARE ATTEMPTING TO REMOVE, ALONG WITH HIS CLOTHES; THUS DEFEATING YOUR OWN PURPOSE.
SO, MALE SUBJECTS MUST BE COMPELLED TO STRIP THEMSELVES, THUS PARTICIPATING IN THEIR OWN LOSS OF POWER.
HOWEVER, IT IS QUITE A DIFFERENT MATTER IF YOUR SUBJECT IS FEMALE.

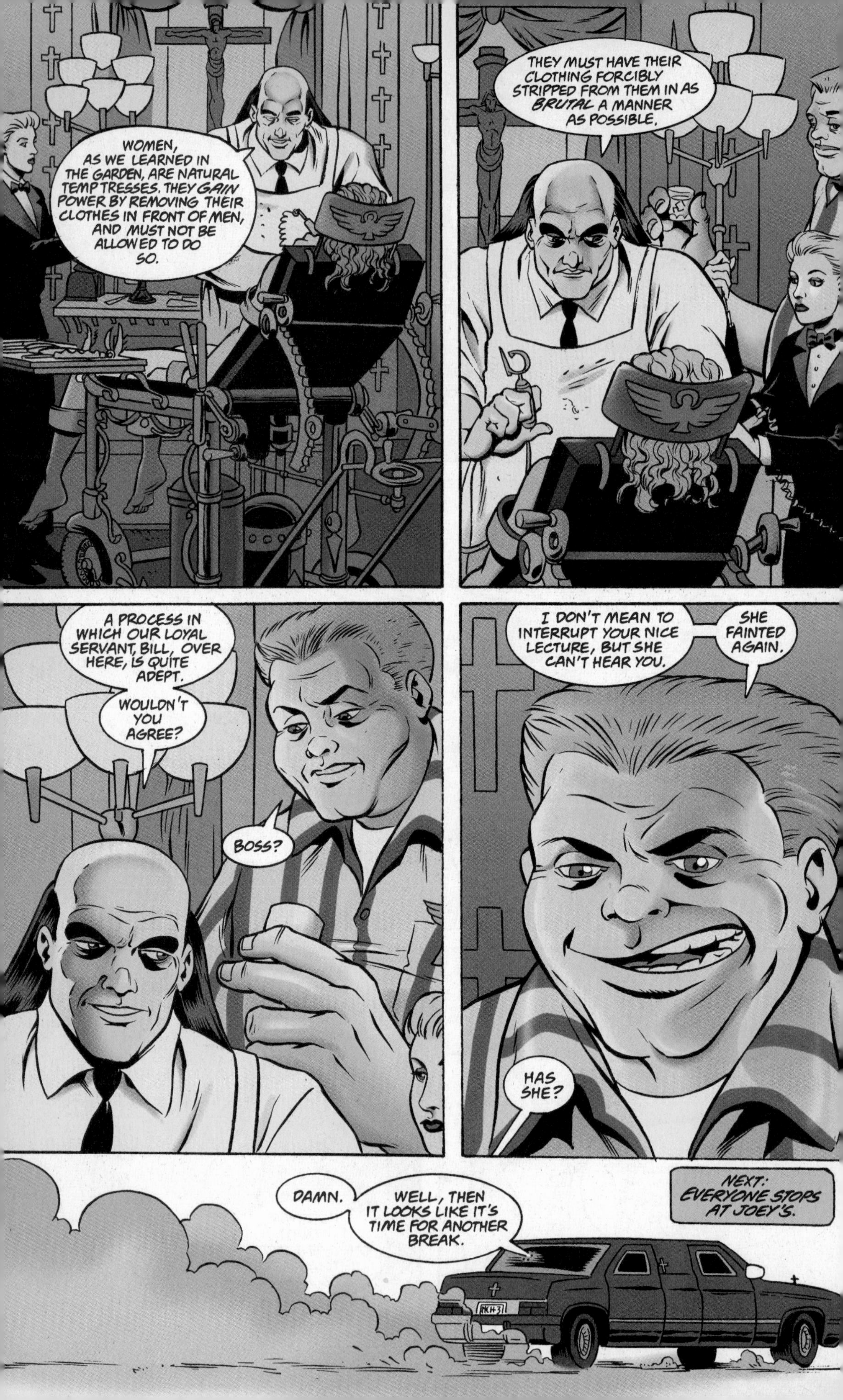
WOMEN, AS WE LEARNED IN THE GARDEN, ARE NATURAL TEMPTRESSES. THEY GAIN POWER BY REMOVING THEIR CLOTHES IN FRONT OF MEN, AND MUST NOT BE ALLOWED TO DO SO.
THEY MUST HAVE THEIR CLOTHING FORCIBLY STRIPPED FROM THEM IN AS BRUTAL A MANNER AS POSSIBLE.
A PROCESS IN WHICH OUR LOYAL SERVANT, BILL, OVER HERE, IS QUITE ADEPT.
WOULDN'T YOU AGREE?
BOSS?
I DON'T MEAN TO INTERRUPT YOUR NICE LECTURE, BUT SHE CAN'T HEAR YOU.
SHE FAINTED AGAIN.
HAS SHE?
DAMN.
WELL, THEN IT LOOKS LIKE IT'S TIME FOR ANOTHER BREAK.
NEXT: EVERYONE STOPS AT JOEY'S.

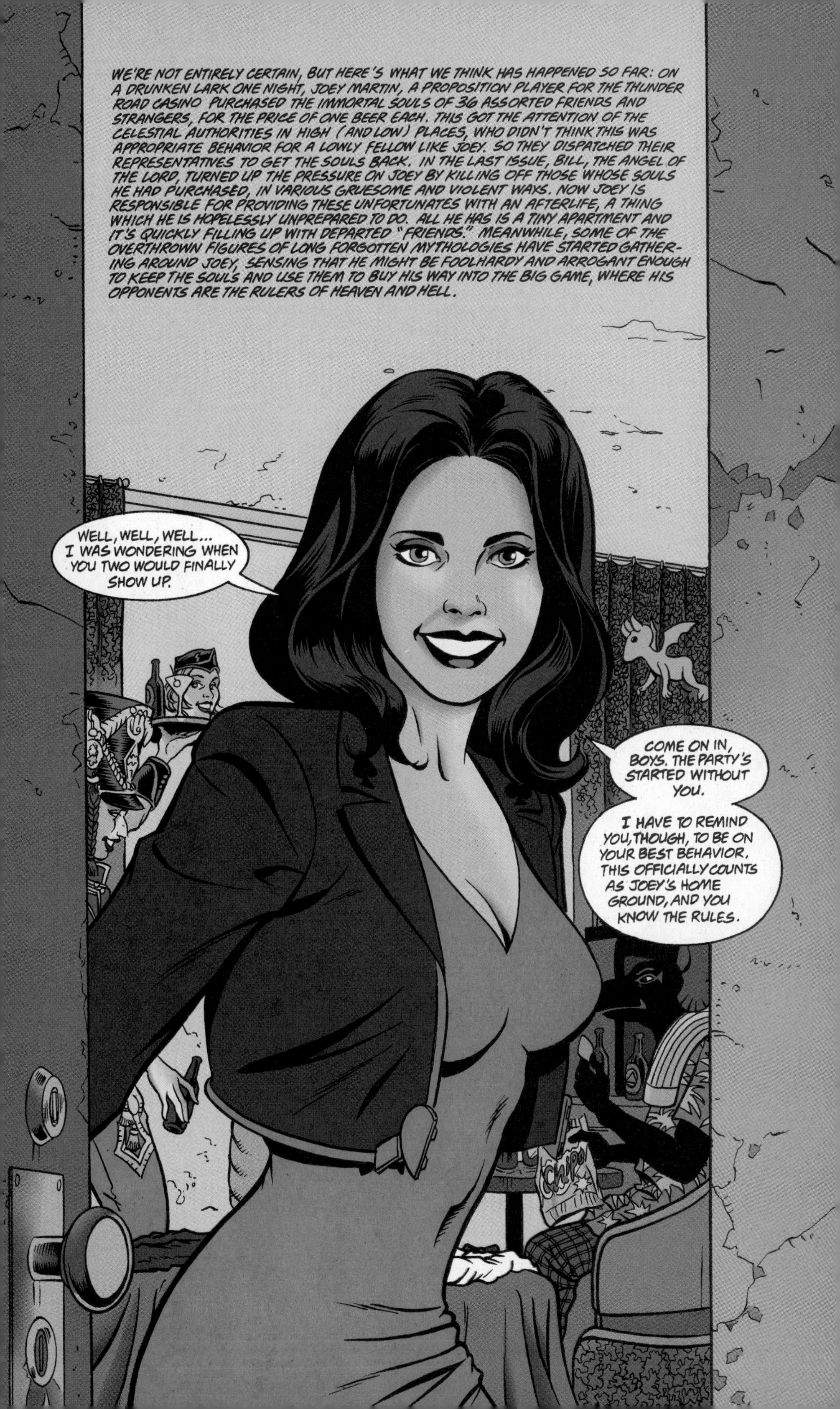
WE'RE NOT ENTIRELY CERTAIN, BUT HERE'S WHAT WE THINK HAS HAPPENED SO FAR: ON A DRUNKEN LARK ONE NIGHT, JOEY MARTIN, A PROPOSITION PLAYER FOR THE THUNDER ROAD CASINO PURCHASED THE IMMORTAL SOULS OF 36 ASSORTED FRIENDS AND STRANGERS, FOR THE PRICE OF ONE BEER EACH. THIS GOT THE ATTENTION OF THE CELESTIAL AUTHORITIES IN HIGH (AND LOW) PLACES, WHO DIDN'T THINK THIS WAS APPROPRIATE BEHAVIOR FOR A LOWLY FELLOW LIKE JOEY. SO THEY DISPATCHED THEIR REPRESENTATIVES TO GET THE SOULS BACK. IN THE LAST ISSUE, BILL, THE ANGEL OF THE LORD, TURNED UP THE PRESSURE ON JOEY BY KILLING OFF THOSE WHOSE SOULS HE HAD PURCHASED, IN VARIOUS GRUESOME AND VIOLENT WAYS. NOW JOEY IS RESPONSIBLE FOR PROVIDING THESE UNFORTUNATES WITH AN AFTERLIFE, A THING WHICH HE IS HOPELESSLY UNPREPARED TO DO. ALL HE HAS IS A TINY APARTMENT AND IT'S QUICKLY FILLING UP WITH DEPARTED "FRIENDS." MEANWHILE, SOME OF THE OVERTHROWN FIGURES OF LONG FORGOTTEN MYTHOLOGIES HAVE STARTED GATHERING AROUND JOEY, SENSING THAT HE MIGHT BE FOOLHARDY AND ARROGANT ENOUGH TO KEEP THE SOULS AND USE THEM TO BUY HIS WAY INTO THE BIG GAME, WHERE HIS OPPONENTS ARE THE RULERS OF HEAVEN AND HELL.
WELL, WELL, WELL... I WAS WONDERING WHEN YOU TWO WOULD FINALLY SHOW UP.
COME ON IN, BOYS. THE PARTY'S STARTED WITHOUT YOU.
I HAVE TO REMIND YOU, THOUGH, TO BE ON YOUR BEST BEHAVIOR. THIS OFFICIALLY COUNTS AS JOEY'S HOME GROUND, AND YOU KNOW THE RULES.
CHIPS

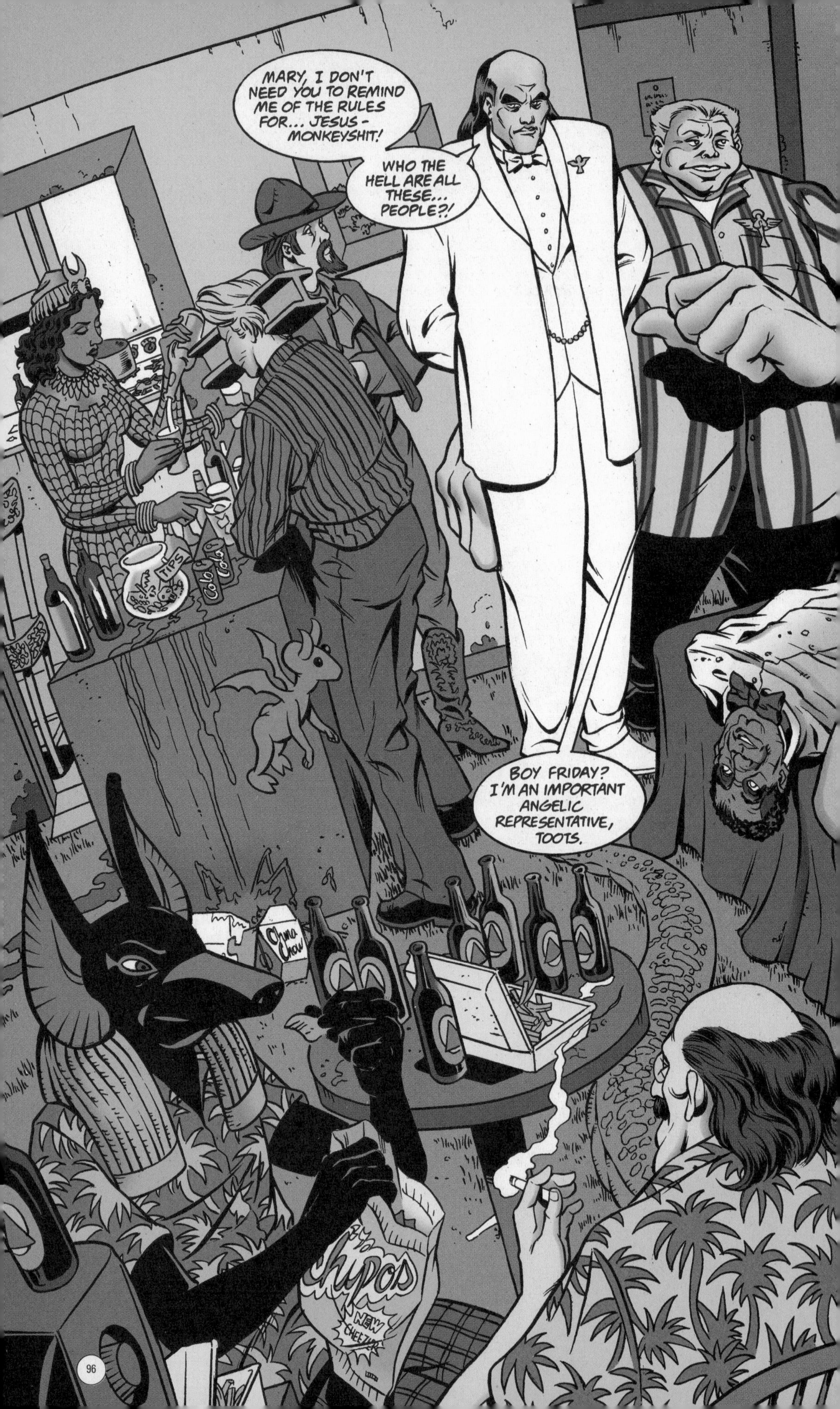
MARY, I DON'T NEED YOU TO REMIND ME OF THE RULES FOR... JESUS-MONKEYSHIT!
WHO THE HELL ARE ALL THESE... PEOPLE?!
BOY FRIDAY? I'M AN IMPORTANT ANGELIC REPRESENTATIVE, TOOTS.
TIPS
Cola
Cola
China Chow
Chipos
NEW CHEEZ!!

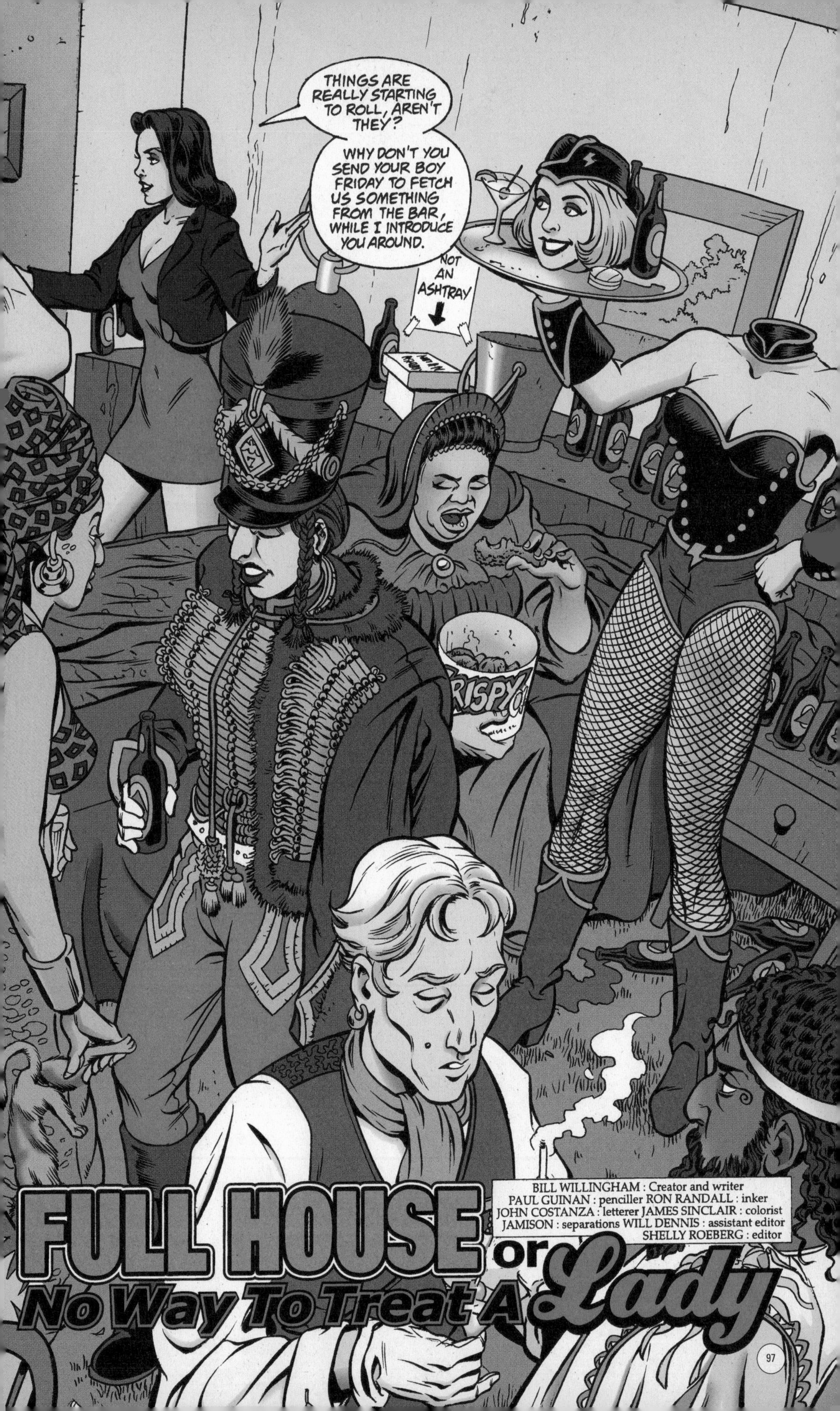

THINGS ARE REALLY STARTING TO ROLL, AREN'T THEY?
WHY DON'T YOU SEND YOUR BOY FRIDAY TO FETCH US SOMETHING FROM THE BAR, WHILE I INTRODUCE YOU AROUND.
NOT AN ASHTRAY
CRISPY
FULL HOUSE or No Way To Treat A Lady
BILL WILLINGHAM : Creator and writer
PAUL GUINAN : penciller RON RANDALL : inker
JOHN COSTANZA : letterer JAMES SINCLAIR : colorist
JAMISON : separations WILL DENNIS : assistant editor
SHELLY ROEBERG : editor

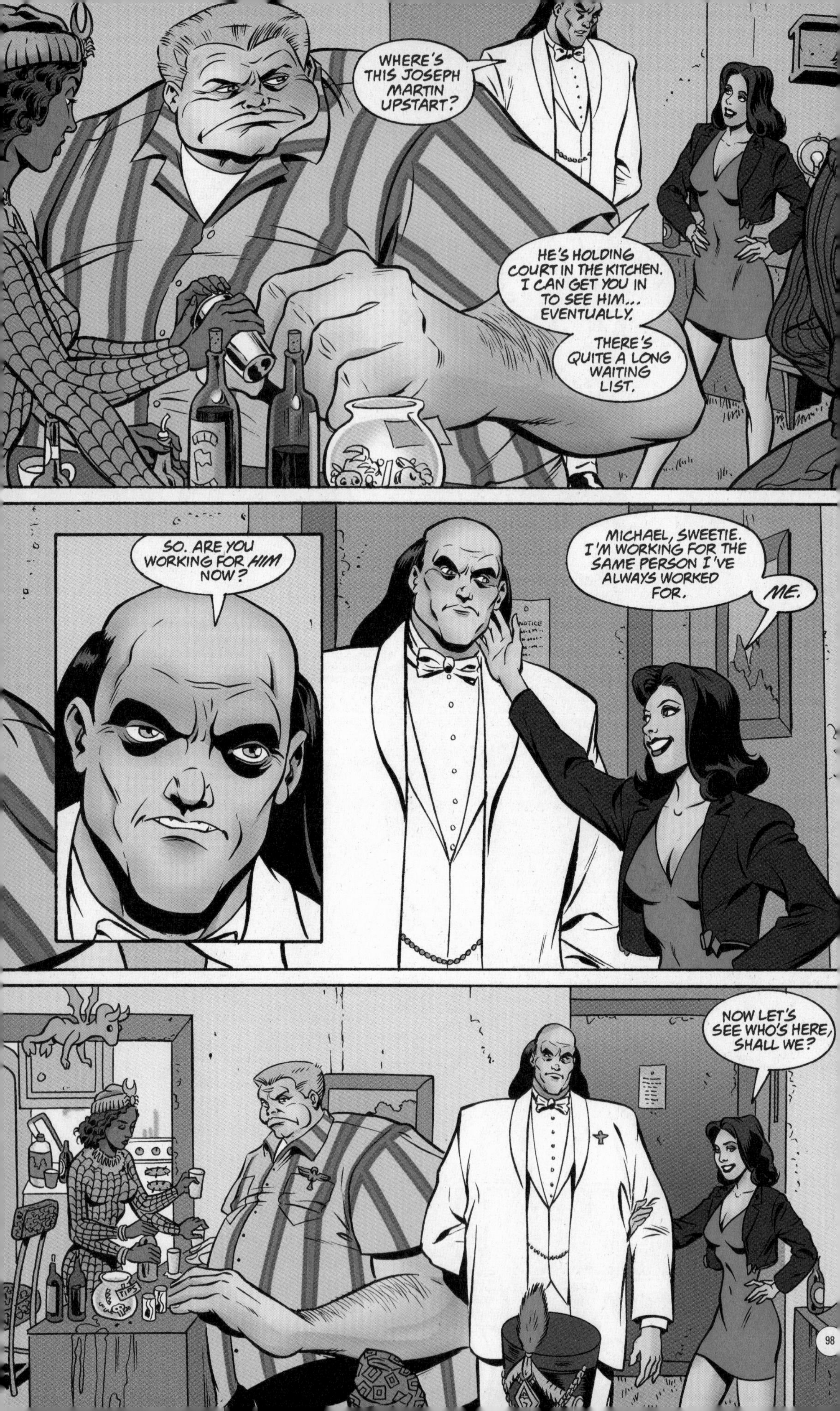
WHERE'S THIS JOSEPH MARTIN UPSTART?
HE'S HOLDING COURT IN THE KITCHEN. I CAN GET YOU IN TO SEE HIM... EVENTUALLY.
THERE'S QUITE A LONG WAITING LIST.
SO. ARE YOU WORKING FOR *HIM* NOW?
MICHAEL, SWEETIE. I'M WORKING FOR THE SAME PERSON I'VE ALWAYS WORKED FOR.
ME.
NOW LET'S SEE WHO'S HERE, SHALL WE?

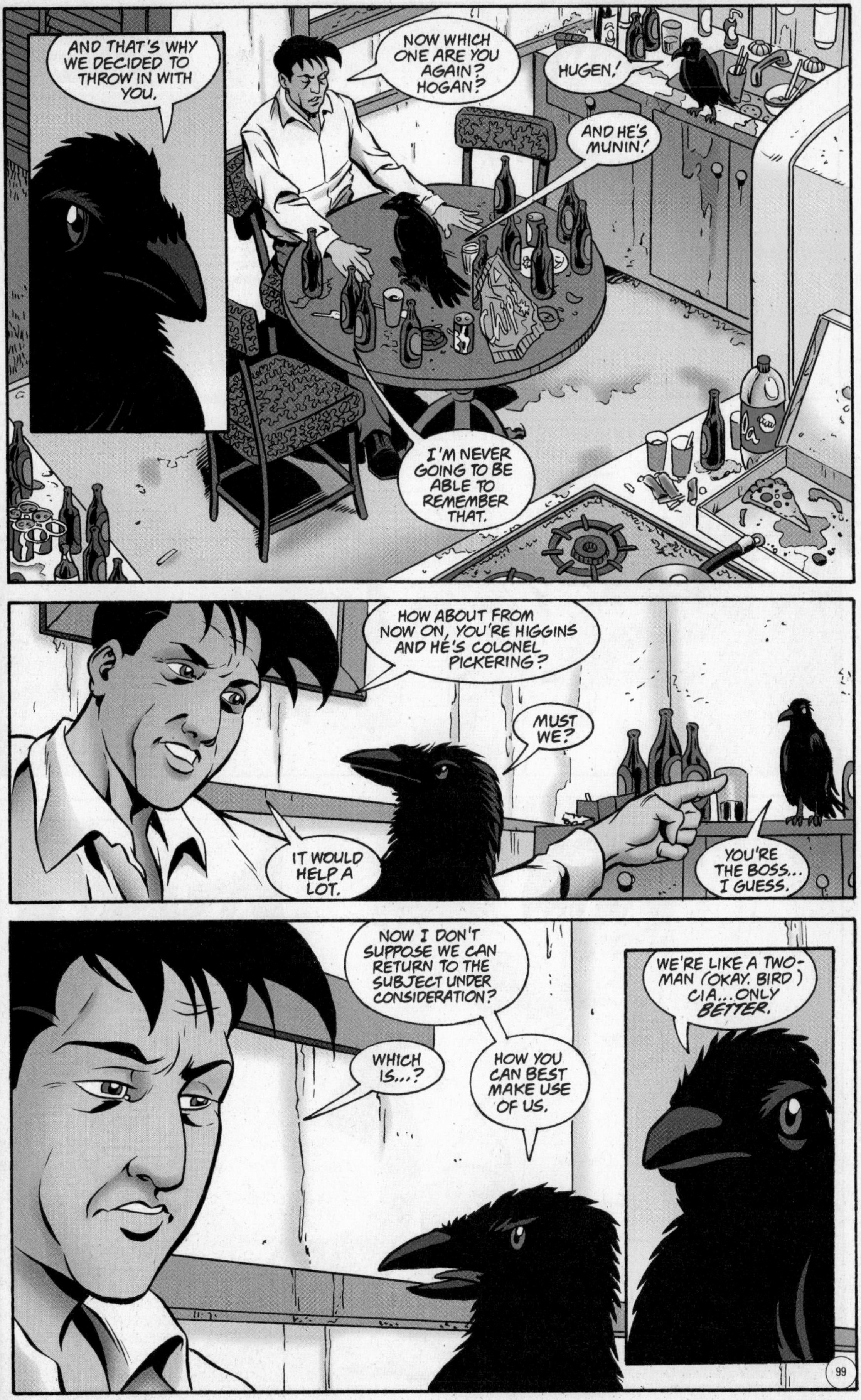
AND THAT'S WHY WE DECIDED TO THROW IN WITH YOU.
NOW WHICH ONE ARE YOU AGAIN? HOGAN?
HUGEN!
AND HE'S MUNIN!
I'M NEVER GOING TO BE ABLE TO REMEMBER THAT.
HOW ABOUT FROM NOW ON, YOU'RE HIGGINS AND HE'S COLONEL PICKERING?
MUST WE?
IT WOULD HELP A LOT.
YOU'RE THE BOSS... I GUESS.
NOW I DON'T SUPPOSE WE CAN RETURN TO THE SUBJECT UNDER CONSIDERATION?
WHICH IS...?
HOW YOU CAN BEST MAKE USE OF US.
WE'RE LIKE A TWO-MAN (OKAY. BIRD) CIA... ONLY *BETTER.*

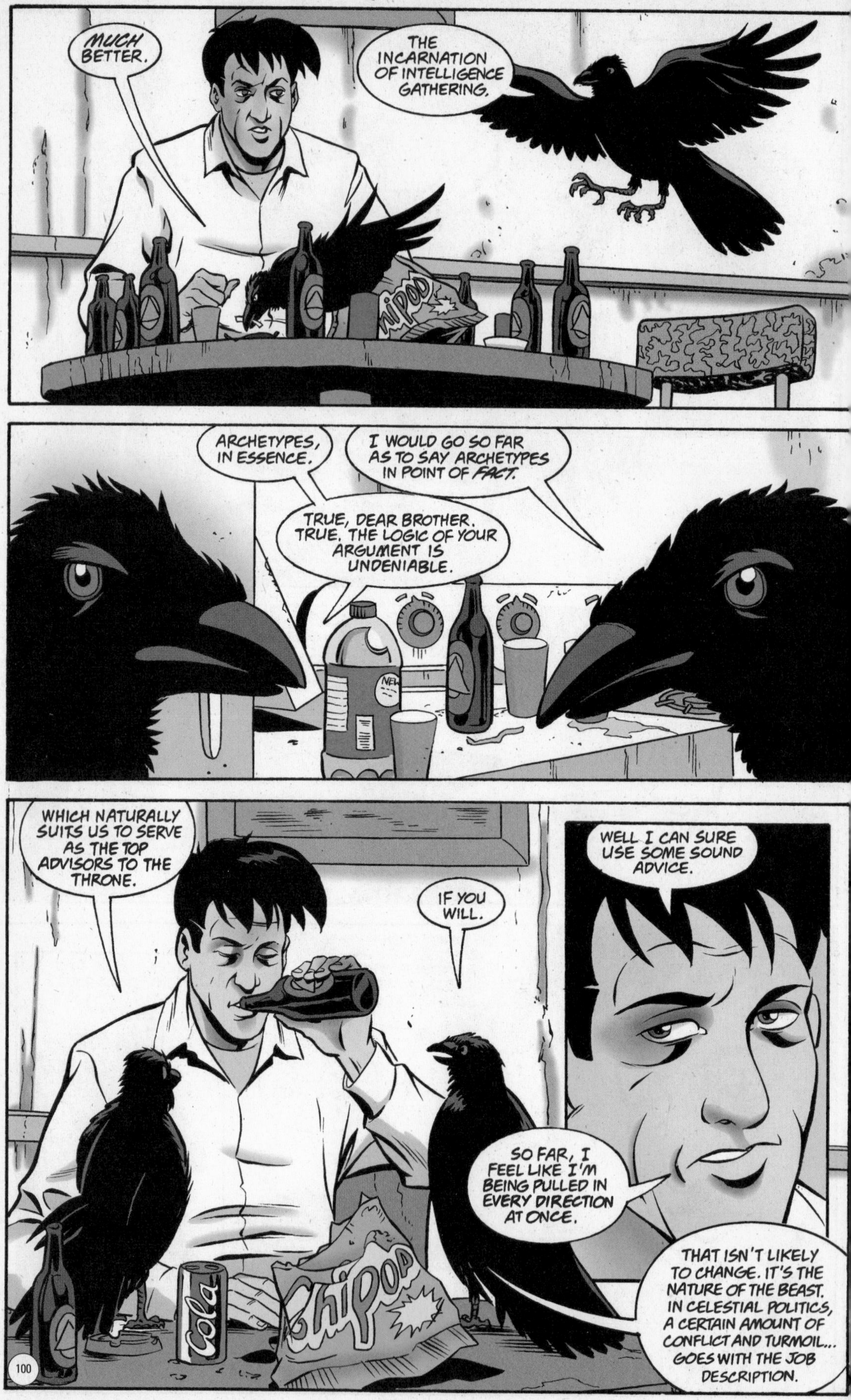
MUCH BETTER.
THE INCARNATION OF INTELLIGENCE GATHERING.
CHIPOP
ARCHETYPES, IN ESSENCE.
I WOULD GO SO FAR AS TO SAY ARCHETYPES IN POINT OF FACT.
TRUE, DEAR BROTHER. TRUE. THE LOGIC OF YOUR ARGUMENT IS UNDENIABLE.
NEW
WHICH NATURALLY SUITS US TO SERVE AS THE TOP ADVISORS TO THE THRONE.
IF YOU WILL.
WELL I CAN SURE USE SOME SOUND ADVICE.
SO FAR, I FEEL LIKE I'M BEING PULLED IN EVERY DIRECTION AT ONCE.
THAT ISN'T LIKELY TO CHANGE. IT'S THE NATURE OF THE BEAST. IN CELESTIAL POLITICS, A CERTAIN AMOUNT OF CONFLICT AND TURMOIL... GOES WITH THE JOB DESCRIPTION.
Cola
ChiPop

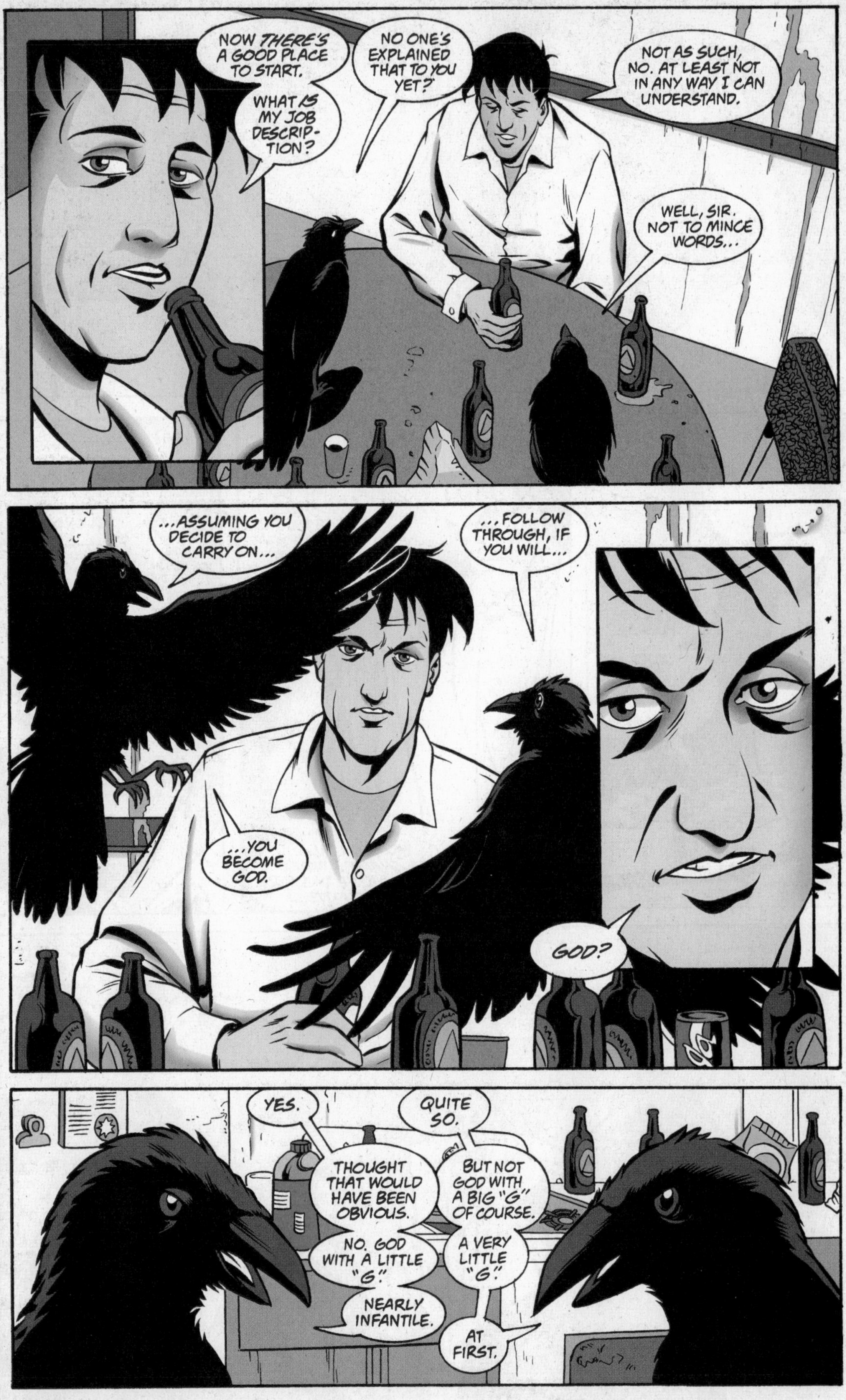
NOW *THERE'S* A GOOD PLACE TO START.
WHAT *IS* MY JOB DESCRIPTION?
NO ONE'S EXPLAINED THAT TO YOU YET?
NOT AS SUCH, NO. AT LEAST NOT IN ANY WAY I CAN UNDERSTAND.
WELL, SIR. NOT TO MINCE WORDS...
...ASSUMING YOU DECIDE TO CARRY ON...
...FOLLOW THROUGH, IF YOU WILL...
...YOU BECOME GOD.
GOD?
YES.
QUITE SO.
THOUGHT THAT WOULD HAVE BEEN OBVIOUS.
BUT NOT GOD WITH A BIG "G" OF COURSE.
NO. GOD WITH A LITTLE "G."
A VERY LITTLE "G."
NEARLY INFANTILE.
AT FIRST.

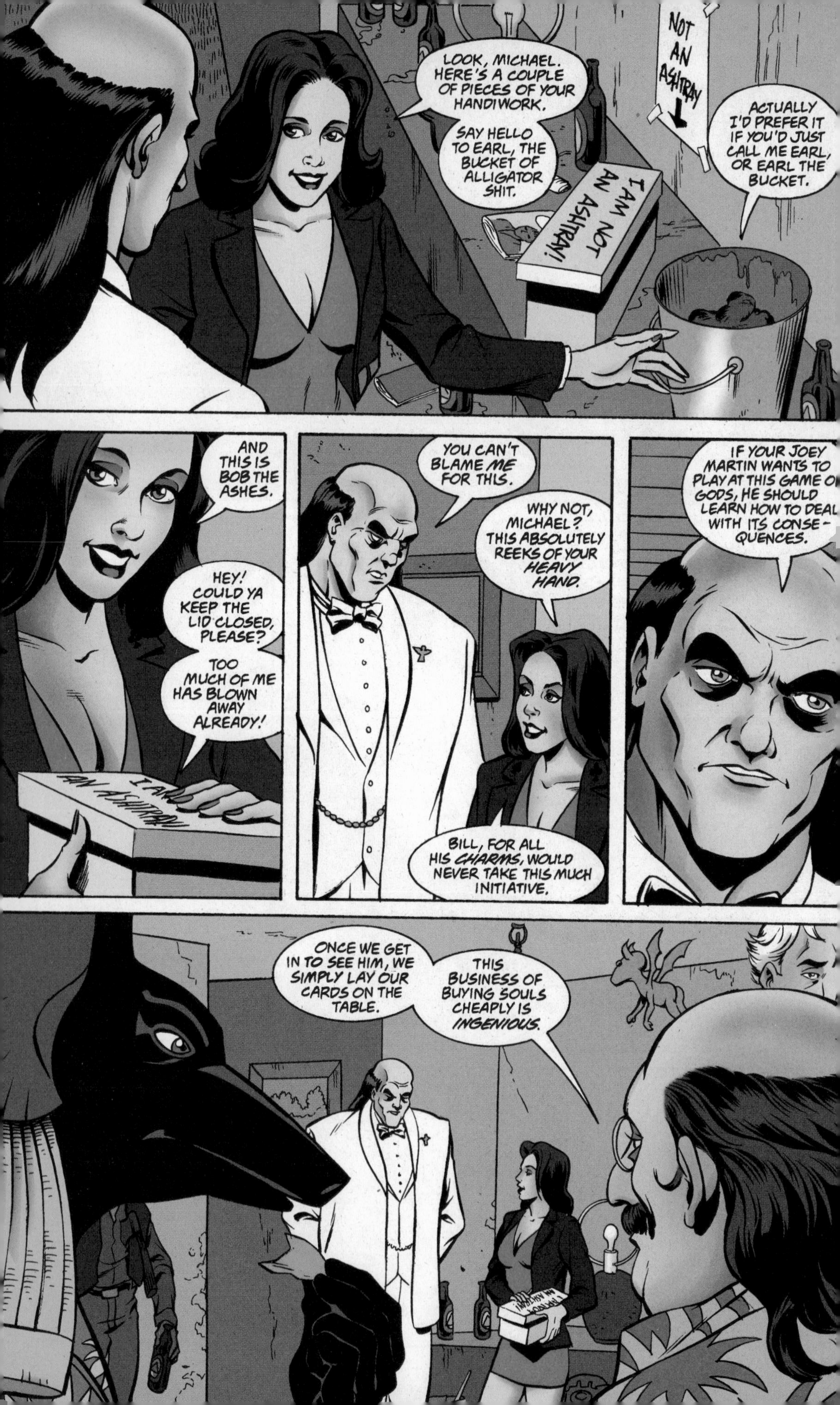
NOT AN ASHTRAY
LOOK, MICHAEL. HERE'S A COUPLE OF PIECES OF YOUR HANDIWORK.
SAY HELLO TO EARL, THE BUCKET OF ALLIGATOR SHIT.
I AM NOT AN ASHTRAY!
ACTUALLY I'D PREFER IT IF YOU'D JUST CALL ME EARL, OR EARL THE BUCKET.
AND THIS IS BOB THE ASHES.
HEY! COULD YA KEEP THE LID CLOSED, PLEASE?
TOO MUCH OF ME HAS BLOWN AWAY ALREADY!
YOU CAN'T BLAME *ME* FOR THIS.
WHY NOT, MICHAEL? THIS ABSOLUTELY REEKS OF YOUR *HEAVY HAND*.
BILL, FOR ALL HIS *CHARMS*, WOULD NEVER TAKE THIS MUCH INITIATIVE.
IF YOUR JOEY MARTIN WANTS TO PLAY AT THIS GAME OF GODS, HE SHOULD LEARN HOW TO DEAL WITH ITS CONSE-QUENCES.
ONCE WE GET IN TO SEE HIM, WE SIMPLY LAY OUR CARDS ON THE TABLE.
THIS BUSINESS OF BUYING SOULS CHEAPLY IS *INGENIOUS*.

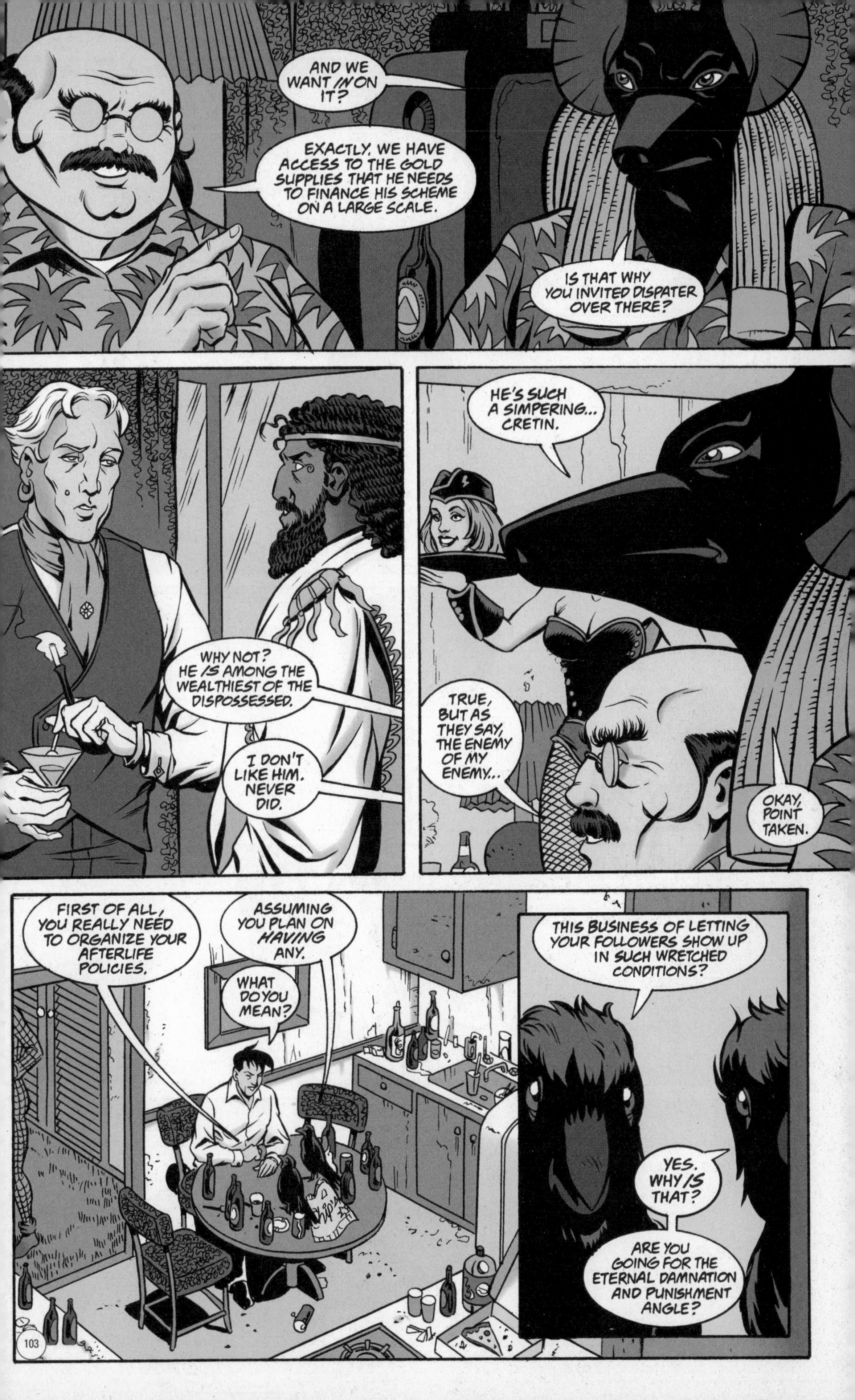
AND WE WANT IN ON IT?
EXACTLY. WE HAVE ACCESS TO THE GOLD SUPPLIES THAT HE NEEDS TO FINANCE HIS SCHEME ON A LARGE SCALE.
IS THAT WHY YOU INVITED DISPATER OVER THERE?
WHY NOT? HE IS AMONG THE WEALTHIEST OF THE DISPOSSESSED.
I DON'T LIKE HIM. NEVER DID.
HE'S SUCH A SIMPERING... CRETIN.
TRUE, BUT AS THEY SAY, THE ENEMY OF MY ENEMY...
OKAY, POINT TAKEN.
FIRST OF ALL, YOU REALLY NEED TO ORGANIZE YOUR AFTERLIFE POLICIES.
ASSUMING YOU PLAN ON HAVING ANY.
WHAT DO YOU MEAN?
THIS BUSINESS OF LETTING YOUR FOLLOWERS SHOW UP IN SUCH WRETCHED CONDITIONS?
YES. WHY IS THAT?
ARE YOU GOING FOR THE ETERNAL DAMNATION AND PUNISHMENT ANGLE?

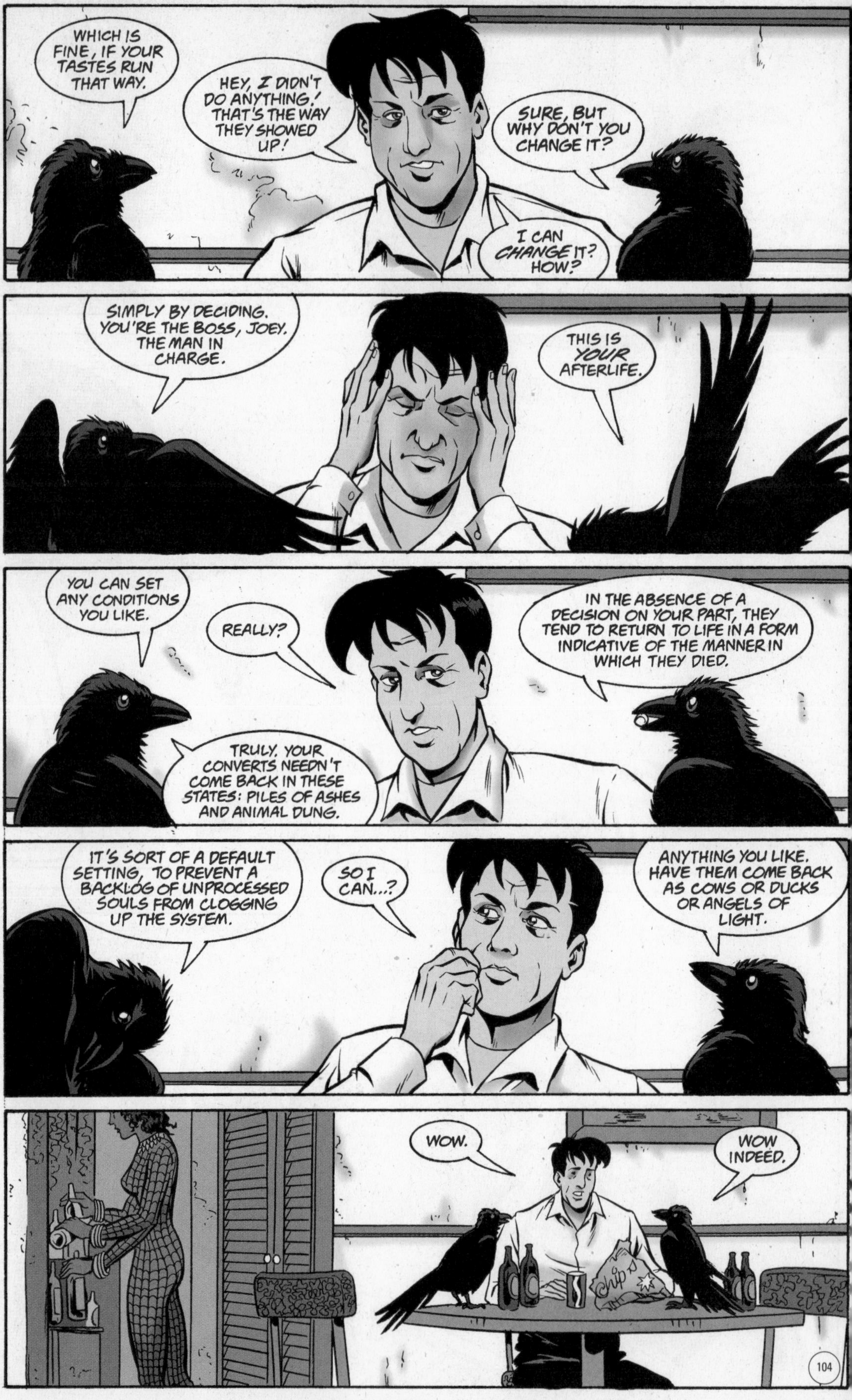
WHICH IS FINE, IF YOUR TASTES RUN THAT WAY.
HEY, I DIDN'T DO ANYTHING! THAT'S THE WAY THEY SHOWED UP!
SURE, BUT WHY DON'T YOU CHANGE IT?
I CAN CHANGE IT? HOW?
SIMPLY BY DECIDING. YOU'RE THE BOSS, JOEY. THE MAN IN CHARGE.
THIS IS YOUR AFTERLIFE.
YOU CAN SET ANY CONDITIONS YOU LIKE.
REALLY?
IN THE ABSENCE OF A DECISION ON YOUR PART, THEY TEND TO RETURN TO LIFE IN A FORM INDICATIVE OF THE MANNER IN WHICH THEY DIED.
TRULY. YOUR CONVERTS NEEDN'T COME BACK IN THESE STATES: PILES OF ASHES AND ANIMAL DUNG.
IT'S SORT OF A DEFAULT SETTING, TO PREVENT A BACKLOG OF UNPROCESSED SOULS FROM CLOGGING UP THE SYSTEM.
SO I CAN...?
ANYTHING YOU LIKE. HAVE THEM COME BACK AS COWS OR DUCKS OR ANGELS OF LIGHT.
WOW.
WOW INDEED.
Chips

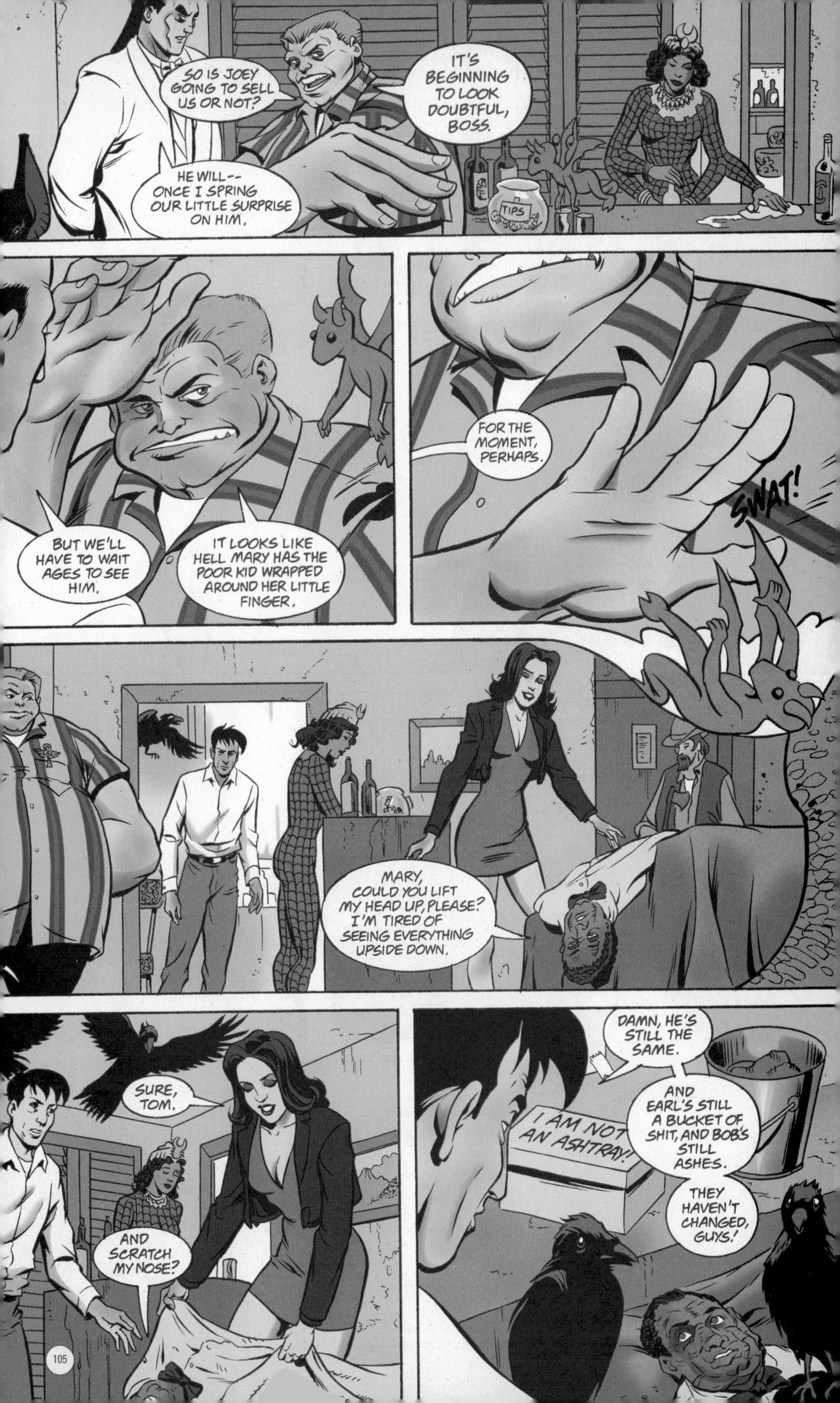

SO IS JOEY GOING TO SELL US OR NOT?
IT'S BEGINNING TO LOOK DOUBTFUL, BOSS.
HE WILL-- ONCE I SPRING OUR LITTLE SURPRISE ON HIM.
TIPS
BUT WE'LL HAVE TO WAIT AGES TO SEE HIM.
IT LOOKS LIKE HELL MARY HAS THE POOR KID WRAPPED AROUND HER LITTLE FINGER.
FOR THE MOMENT, PERHAPS.
SWAT!
MARY, COULD YOU LIFT MY HEAD UP, PLEASE? I'M TIRED OF SEEING EVERYTHING UPSIDE DOWN.
SURE, TOM.
AND SCRATCH MY NOSE?
DAMN, HE'S STILL THE SAME.
AND EARL'S STILL A BUCKET OF SHIT, AND BOB'S STILL ASHES.
THEY HAVEN'T CHANGED, GUYS!
I AM NOT AN ASHTRAY!

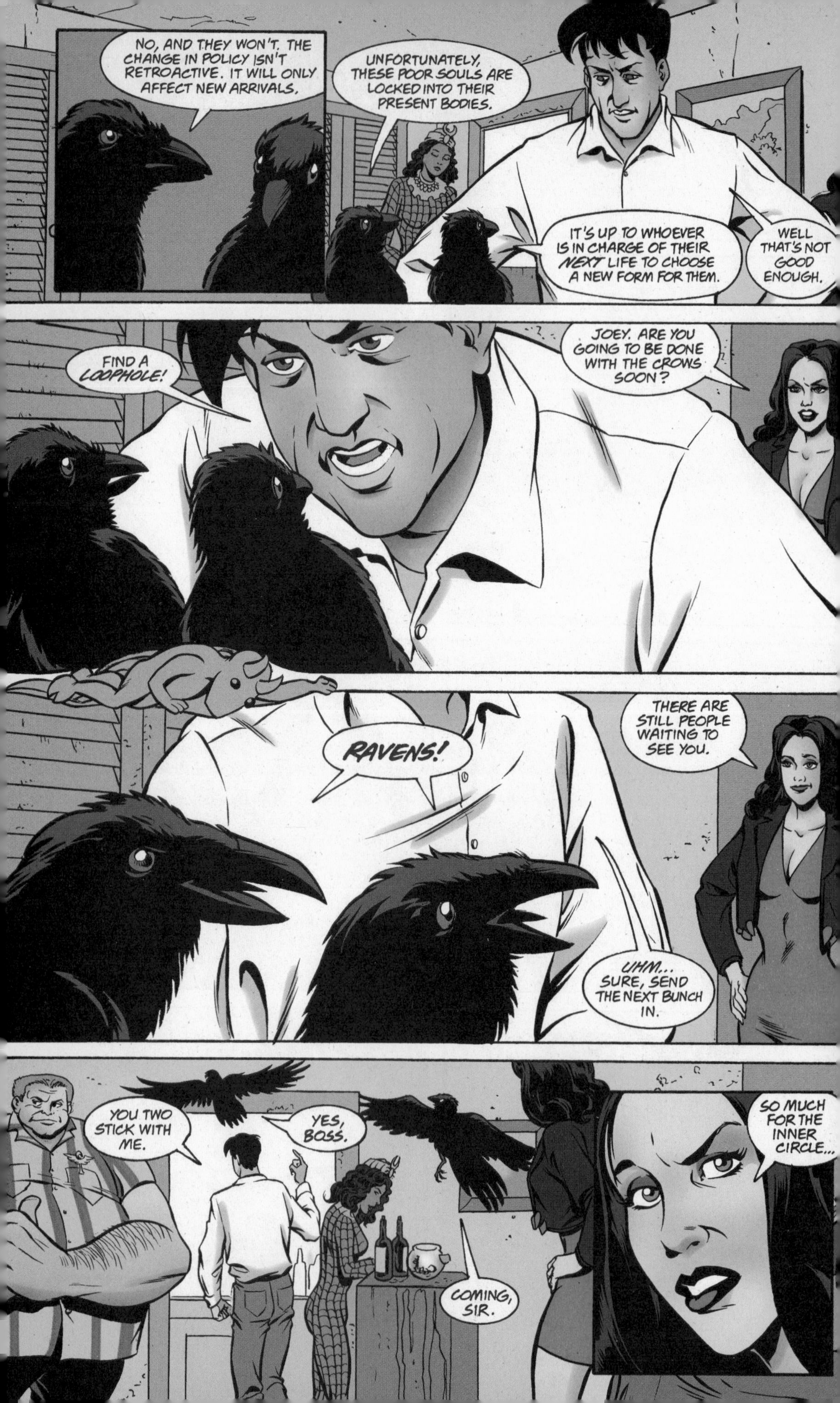

NO, AND THEY WON'T. THE CHANGE IN POLICY ISN'T RETROACTIVE. IT WILL ONLY AFFECT NEW ARRIVALS.
UNFORTUNATELY, THESE POOR SOULS ARE LOCKED INTO THEIR PRESENT BODIES.
IT'S UP TO WHOEVER IS IN CHARGE OF THEIR NEXT LIFE TO CHOOSE A NEW FORM FOR THEM.
WELL THAT'S NOT GOOD ENOUGH.
FIND A LOOPHOLE!
JOEY. ARE YOU GOING TO BE DONE WITH THE CROWS SOON?
RAVENS!
THERE ARE STILL PEOPLE WAITING TO SEE YOU.
UHM... SURE, SEND THE NEXT BUNCH IN.
YOU TWO STICK WITH ME.
YES, BOSS.
COMING, SIR.
SO MUCH FOR THE INNER CIRCLE...

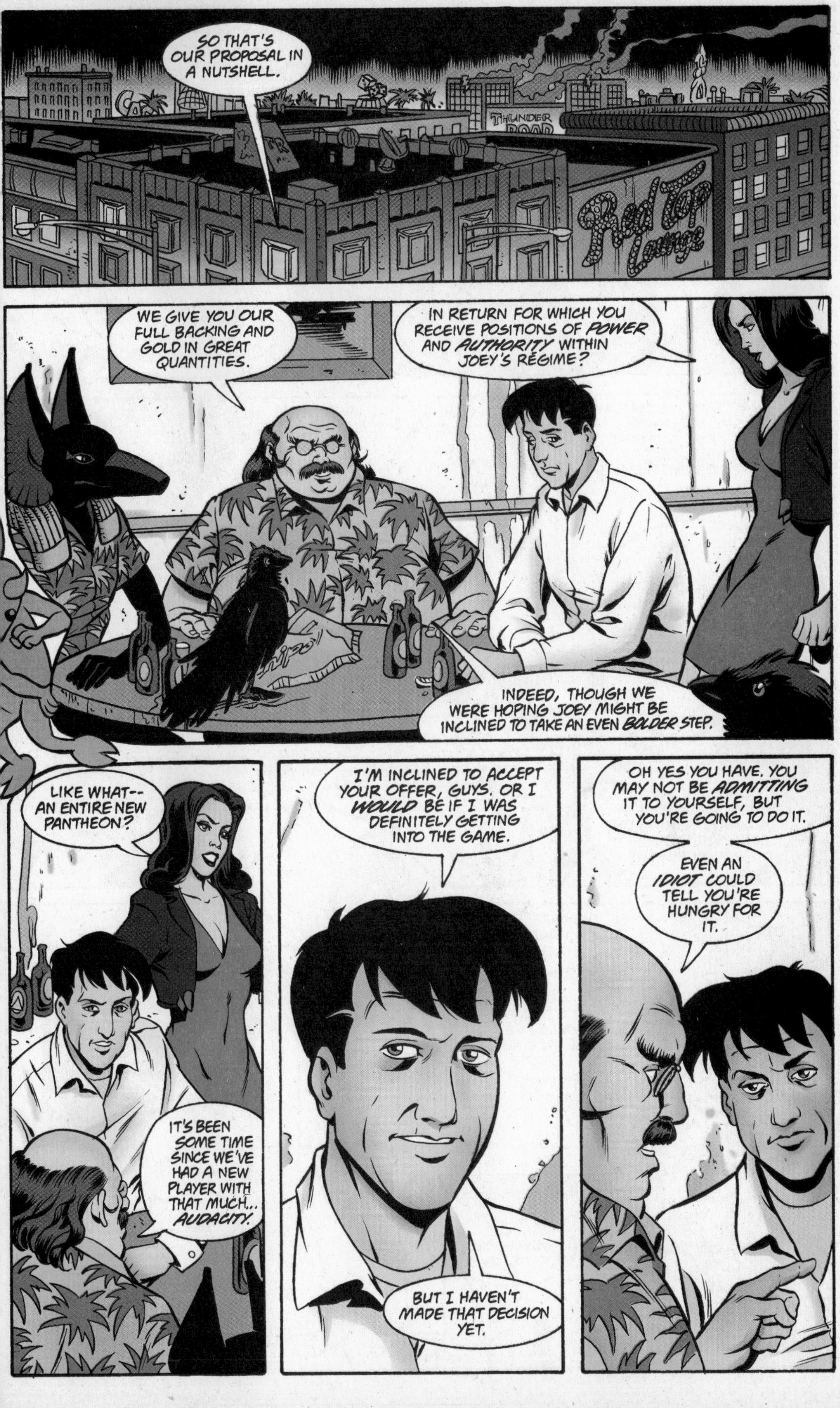
THUNDER ROAD
Red Top Lounge
SO THAT'S OUR PROPOSAL IN A NUTSHELL.
WE GIVE YOU OUR FULL BACKING AND GOLD IN GREAT QUANTITIES.
IN RETURN FOR WHICH YOU RECEIVE POSITIONS OF *POWER* AND *AUTHORITY* WITHIN JOEY'S RÉGIME?
INDEED, THOUGH WE WERE HOPING JOEY MIGHT BE INCLINED TO TAKE AN EVEN *BOLDER* STEP.
LIKE WHAT-- AN ENTIRE NEW PANTHEON?
IT'S BEEN SOME TIME SINCE WE'VE HAD A NEW PLAYER WITH THAT MUCH... *AUDACITY.*
I'M INCLINED TO ACCEPT YOUR OFFER, GUYS. OR I *WOULD* BE IF I WAS DEFINITELY GETTING INTO THE GAME.
BUT I HAVEN'T MADE THAT DECISION YET.
OH YES YOU HAVE. YOU MAY NOT BE *ADMITTING* IT TO YOURSELF, BUT YOU'RE GOING TO DO IT.
EVEN AN *IDIOT* COULD TELL YOU'RE HUNGRY FOR IT.

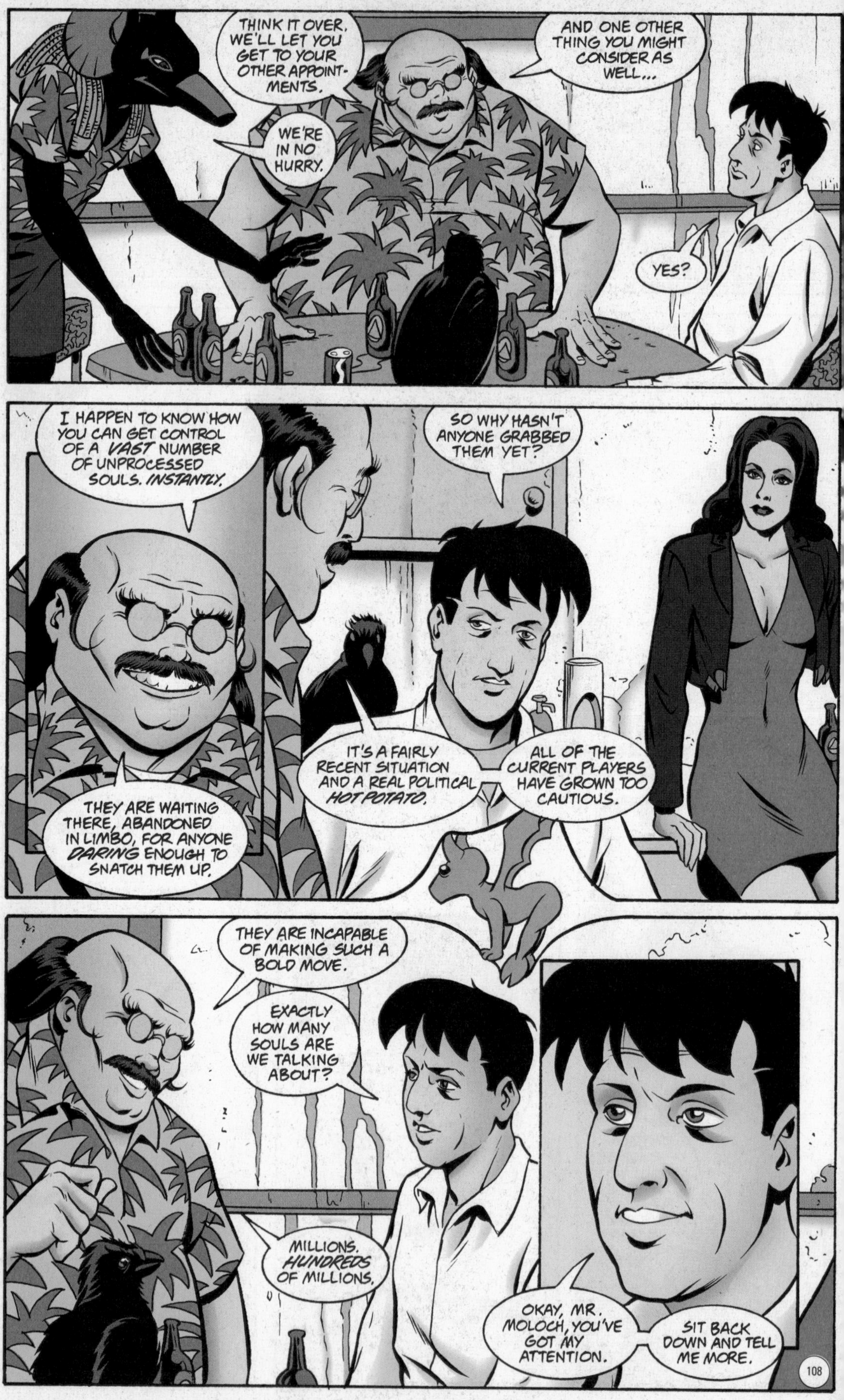
THINK IT OVER. WE'LL LET YOU GET TO YOUR OTHER APPOINTMENTS.
WE'RE IN NO HURRY.
AND ONE OTHER THING YOU MIGHT CONSIDER AS WELL...
YES?
I HAPPEN TO KNOW HOW YOU CAN GET CONTROL OF A *VAST* NUMBER OF UNPROCESSED SOULS. *INSTANTLY.*
SO WHY HASN'T ANYONE GRABBED THEM YET?
THEY ARE WAITING THERE, ABANDONED IN LIMBO, FOR ANYONE *DARING* ENOUGH TO SNATCH THEM UP.
IT'S A FAIRLY RECENT SITUATION AND A REAL POLITICAL *HOT POTATO.*
ALL OF THE CURRENT PLAYERS HAVE GROWN TOO CAUTIOUS.
THEY ARE INCAPABLE OF MAKING SUCH A BOLD MOVE.
EXACTLY HOW MANY SOULS ARE WE TALKING ABOUT?
MILLIONS. *HUNDREDS* OF MILLIONS.
OKAY, MR. MOLOCH, YOU'VE GOT MY ATTENTION.
SIT BACK DOWN AND TELL ME MORE.

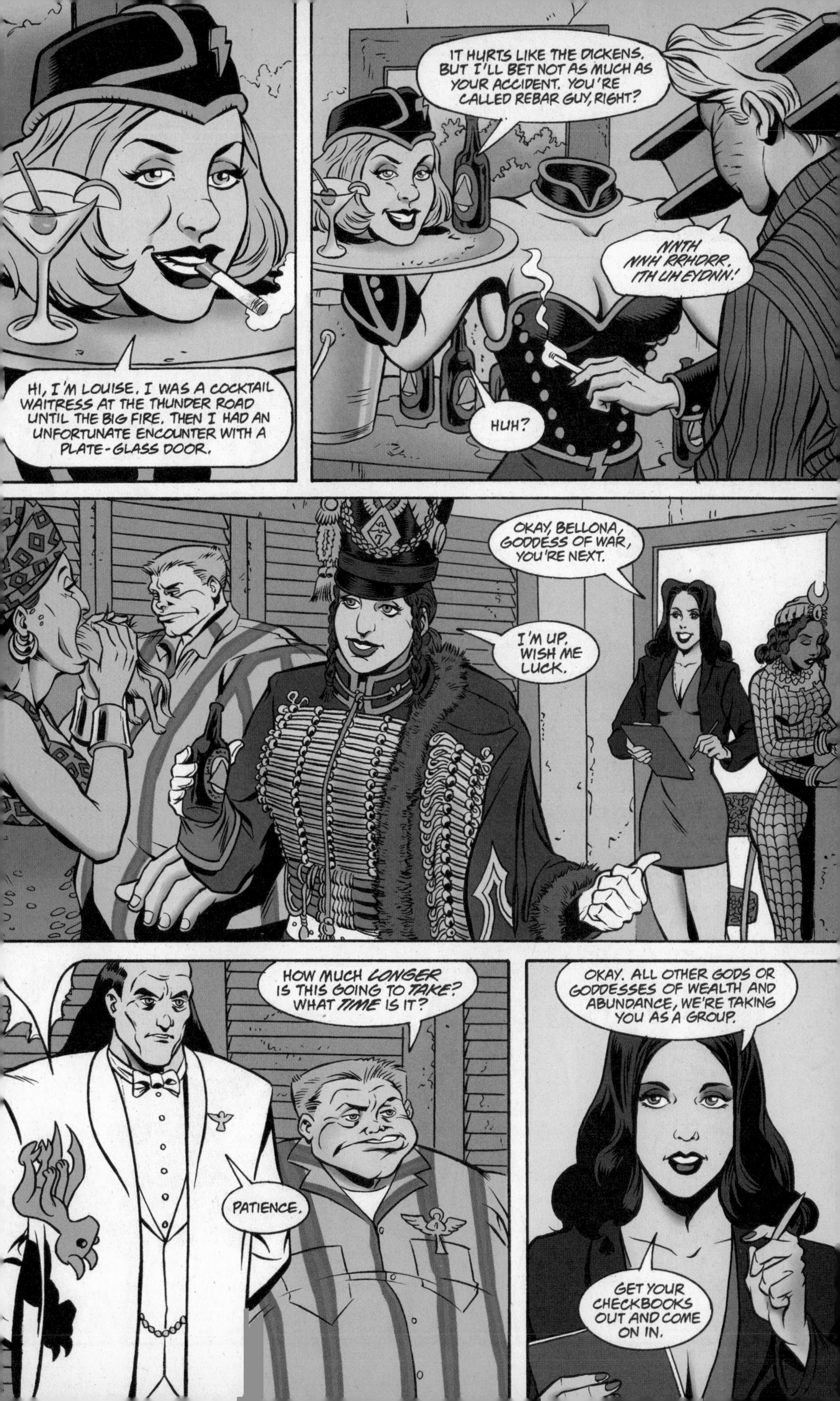
HI, I'M LOUISE. I WAS A COCKTAIL WAITRESS AT THE THUNDER ROAD UNTIL THE BIG FIRE. THEN I HAD AN UNFORTUNATE ENCOUNTER WITH A PLATE-GLASS DOOR.
IT HURTS LIKE THE DICKENS. BUT I'LL BET NOT AS MUCH AS YOUR ACCIDENT. YOU'RE CALLED REBAR GUY, RIGHT?
NNTH NNH RRHORR. ITH UH EYDNN!
HUH?
OKAY, BELLONA, GODDESS OF WAR, YOU'RE NEXT.
I'M UP. WISH ME LUCK.
HOW MUCH LONGER IS THIS GOING TO TAKE? WHAT TIME IS IT?
PATIENCE.
OKAY. ALL OTHER GODS OR GODDESSES OF WEALTH AND ABUNDANCE, WE'RE TAKING YOU AS A GROUP.
GET YOUR CHECKBOOKS OUT AND COME ON IN.

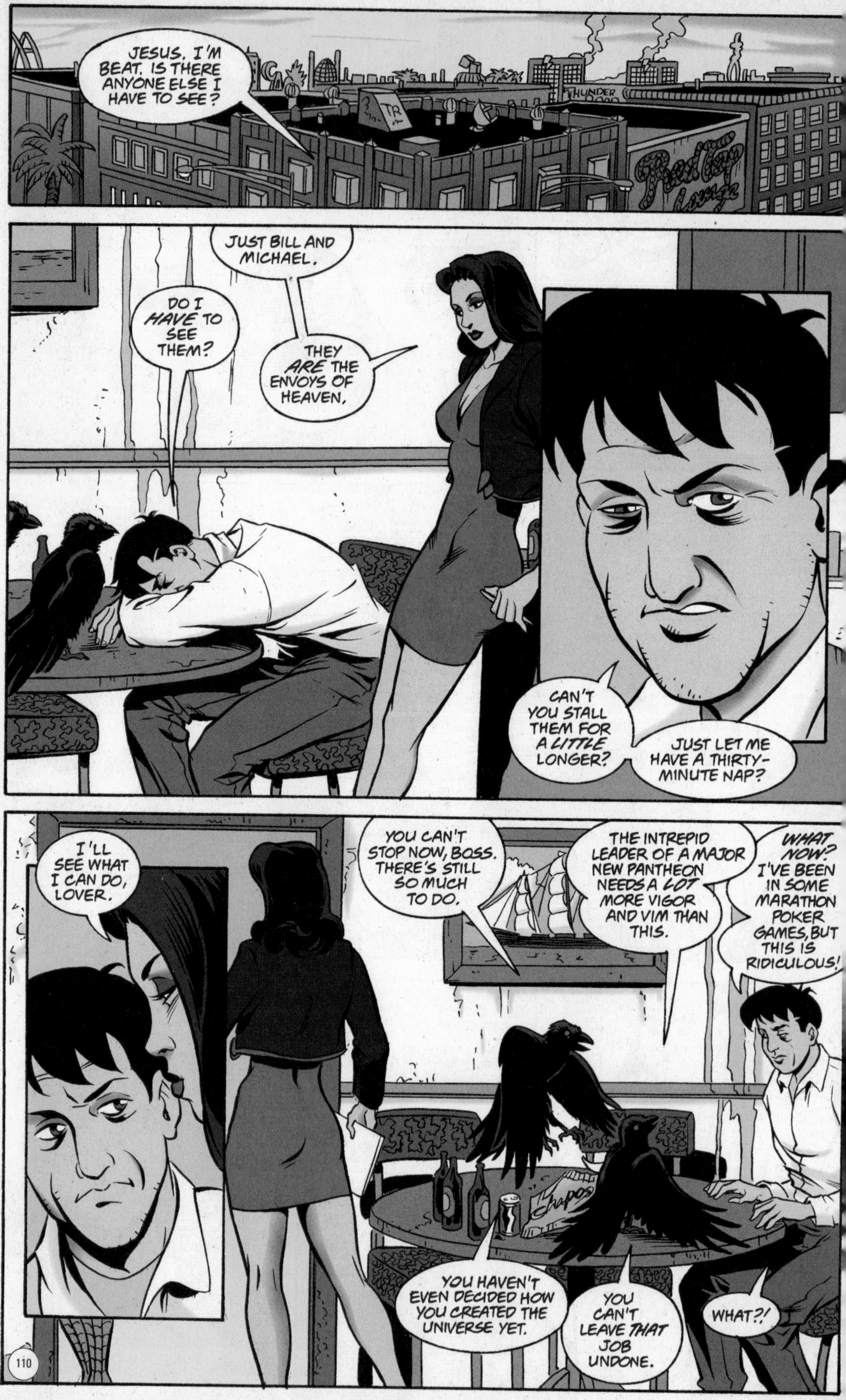

JESUS. I'M BEAT. IS THERE ANYONE ELSE I HAVE TO SEE?
JUST BILL AND MICHAEL.
DO I HAVE TO SEE THEM?
THEY ARE THE ENVOYS OF HEAVEN.
CAN'T YOU STALL THEM FOR A LITTLE LONGER?
JUST LET ME HAVE A THIRTY-MINUTE NAP?
I'LL SEE WHAT I CAN DO, LOVER.
YOU CAN'T STOP NOW, BOSS. THERE'S STILL SO MUCH TO DO.
THE INTREPID LEADER OF A MAJOR NEW PANTHEON NEEDS A LOT MORE VIGOR AND VIM THAN THIS.
WHAT NOW? I'VE BEEN IN SOME MARATHON POKER GAMES, BUT THIS IS RIDICULOUS!
YOU HAVEN'T EVEN DECIDED HOW YOU CREATED THE UNIVERSE YET.
YOU CAN'T LEAVE THAT JOB UNDONE.
WHAT?!

THAT'S BEEN *DONE.* I DIDN'T CREATE ANYTHING!

YOU DID IF YOU WANT TO BE ONE OF THE MAJOR PLAYERS.

JUST COME UP WITH SOMETHING.

YOU CAN'T POSSIBLY BE TOO FAR-FETCHED. AND YOU CAN'T GET IT *WRONG.*

THIS IS SILLY.

NAW, CREATING THE UNIVERSE BY HAVING A COSMIC COW LICK THE FIRST CREATURES OUT OF A BLOCK OF ICE WAS *SILLY.* BUT IT WORKED.

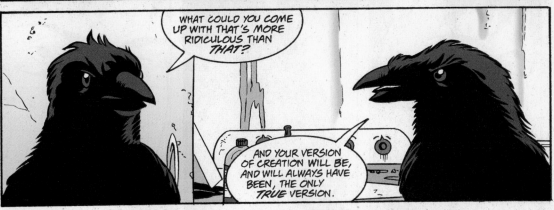

WHAT COULD YOU COME UP WITH THAT'S MORE RIDICULOUS THAN *THAT?*

AND YOUR VERSION OF CREATION WILL BE, AND WILL ALWAYS HAVE BEEN, THE ONLY *TRUE* VERSION.

OH, YEAH? THEN WHAT ABOUT THE OTHERS?

LIKE THE GARDEN OF EDEN, AND YOUR COW? AND SHIT LIKE THAT?

THEY ARE ALSO THE SINGULAR AND UNIVERSAL TRUTHS OF CREATION.

BUT THAT'S CONTRADICTORY! IT'S A PARADOX!

NOT AT ALL. THESE THINGS ARE APART FROM CON-TRADICTION AND PARADOX.

IT *TRANSCENDS* THEM. COOL, HUH?

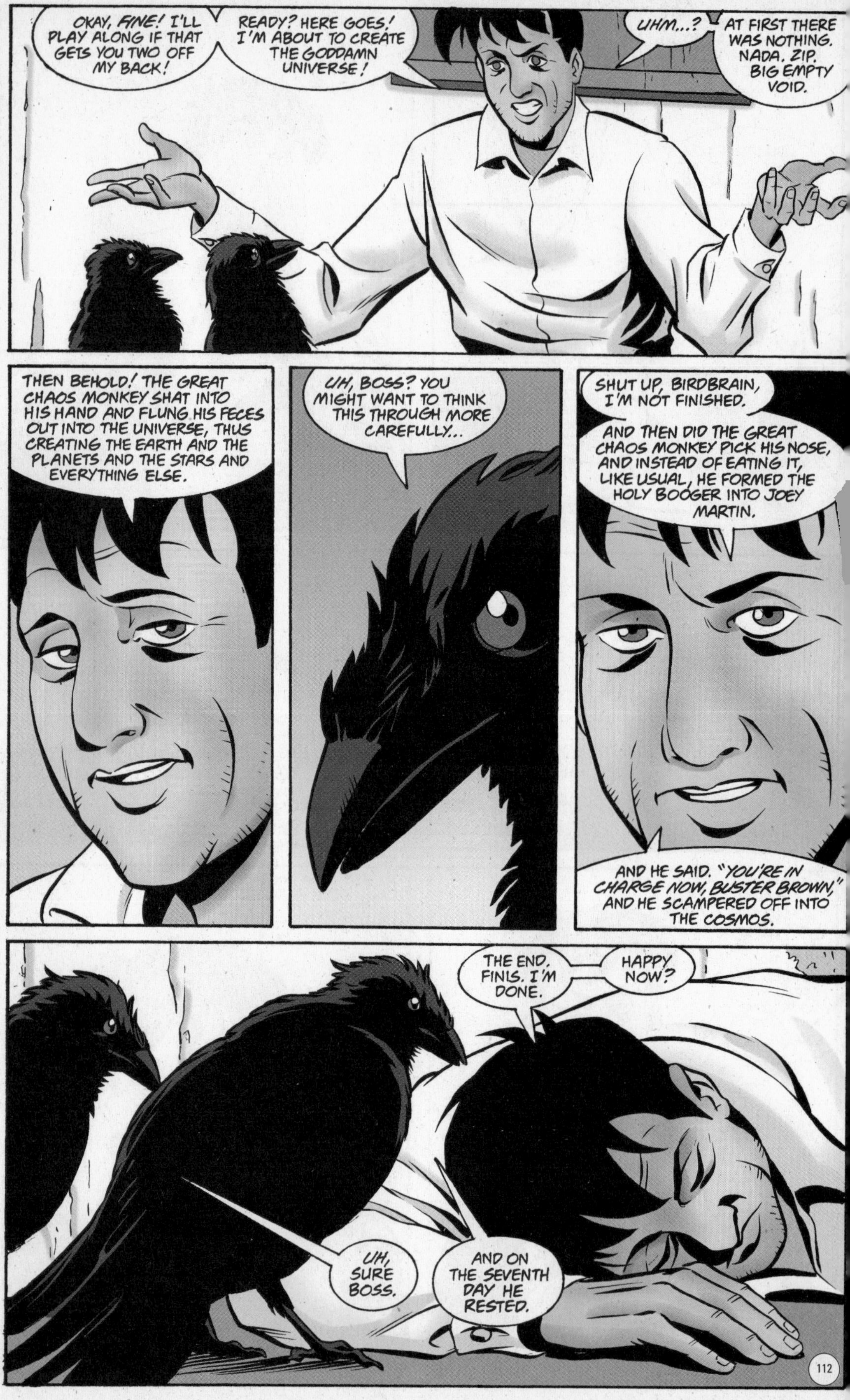
OKAY, FINE! I'LL PLAY ALONG IF THAT GETS YOU TWO OFF MY BACK!
READY? HERE GOES! I'M ABOUT TO CREATE THE GODDAMN UNIVERSE!
UHM...?
AT FIRST THERE WAS NOTHING. NADA. ZIP. BIG EMPTY VOID.
THEN BEHOLD! THE GREAT CHAOS MONKEY SHAT INTO HIS HAND AND FLUNG HIS FECES OUT INTO THE UNIVERSE, THUS CREATING THE EARTH AND THE PLANETS AND THE STARS AND EVERYTHING ELSE.
UH, BOSS? YOU MIGHT WANT TO THINK THIS THROUGH MORE CAREFULLY...
SHUT UP, BIRDBRAIN, I'M NOT FINISHED.
AND THEN DID THE GREAT CHAOS MONKEY PICK HIS NOSE, AND INSTEAD OF EATING IT, LIKE USUAL, HE FORMED THE HOLY BOOGER INTO JOEY MARTIN.
AND HE SAID. "YOU'RE IN CHARGE NOW, BUSTER BROWN," AND HE SCAMPERED OFF INTO THE COSMOS.
THE END. FINIS. I'M DONE.
HAPPY NOW?
UH, SURE BOSS.
AND ON THE SEVENTH DAY HE RESTED.

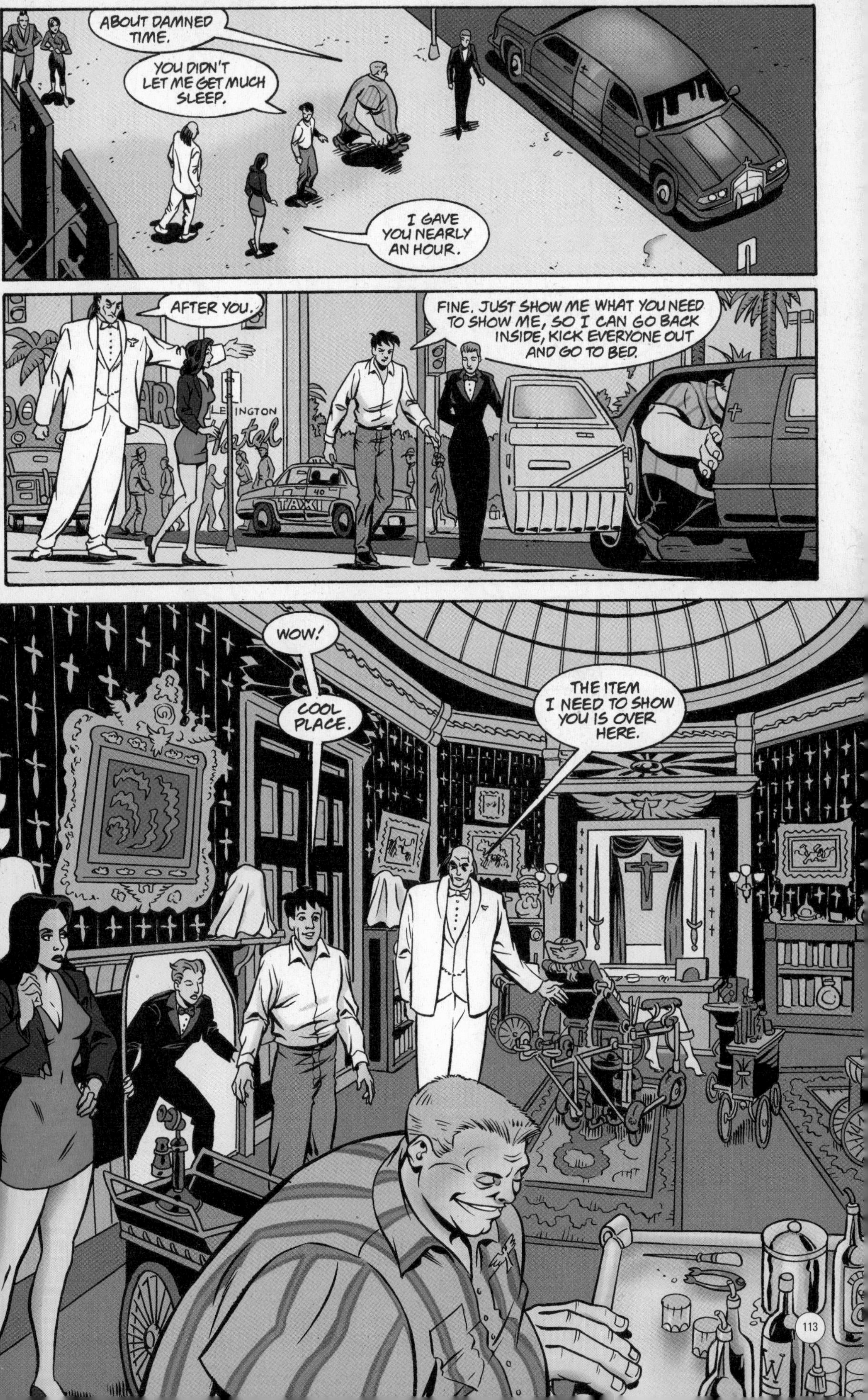
ABOUT DAMNED TIME.
YOU DIDN'T LET ME GET MUCH SLEEP.
I GAVE YOU NEARLY AN HOUR.
AFTER YOU.
FINE. JUST SHOW ME WHAT YOU NEED TO SHOW ME, SO I CAN GO BACK INSIDE, KICK EVERYONE OUT AND GO TO BED.
TAXI
WOW!
COOL PLACE.
THE ITEM I NEED TO SHOW YOU IS OVER HERE.

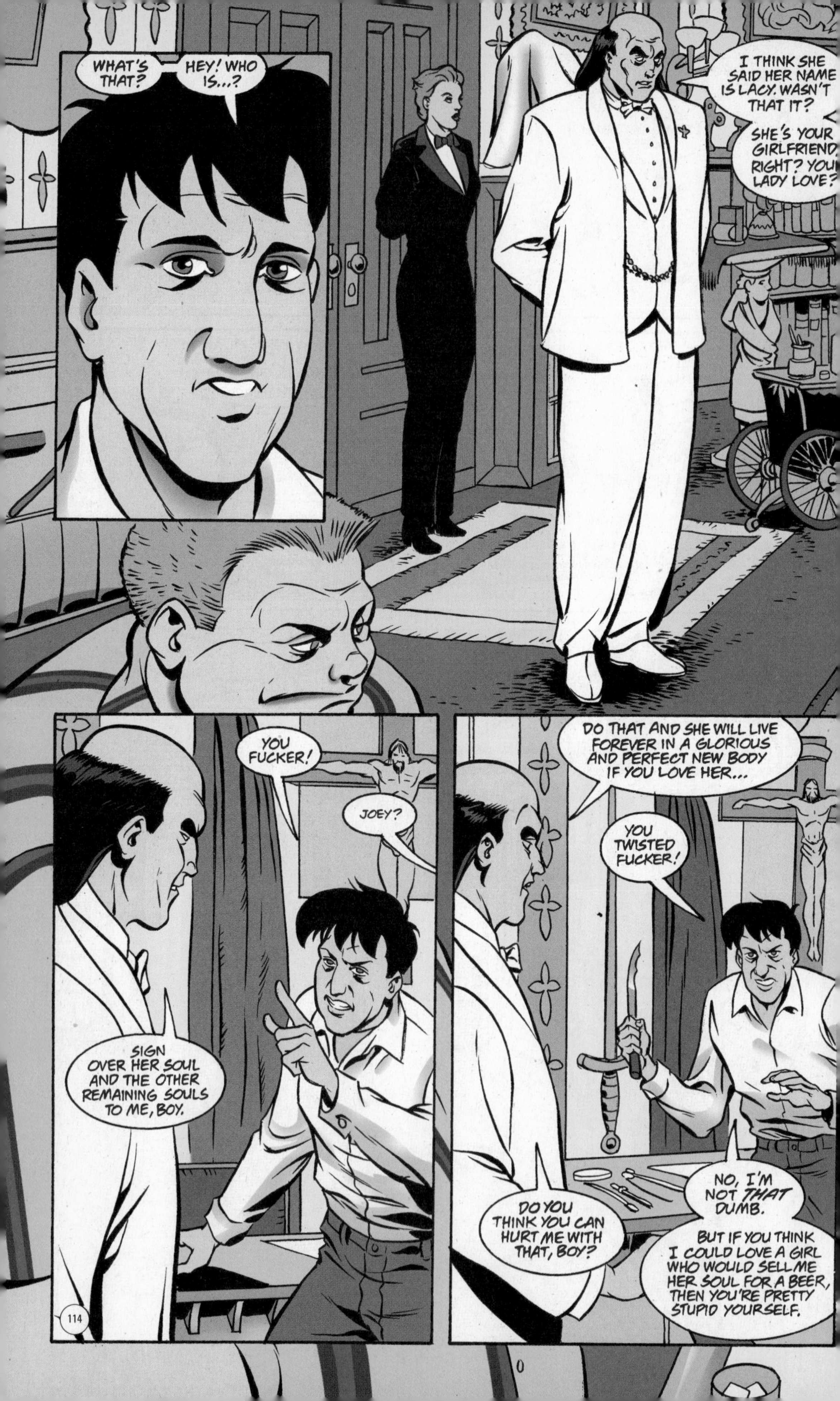
WHAT'S THAT?
HEY! WHO IS...?
I THINK SHE SAID HER NAME IS LACY. WASN'T THAT IT?
SHE'S YOUR GIRLFRIEND, RIGHT? YOU LADY LOVE?
YOU FUCKER!
JOEY?
SIGN OVER HER SOUL AND THE OTHER REMAINING SOULS TO ME, BOY.
DO THAT AND SHE WILL LIVE FOREVER IN A GLORIOUS AND PERFECT NEW BODY IF YOU LOVE HER...
YOU TWISTED FUCKER!
DO YOU THINK YOU CAN HURT ME WITH THAT, BOY?
NO, I'M NOT THAT DUMB.
BUT IF YOU THINK I COULD LOVE A GIRL WHO WOULD SELL ME HER SOUL FOR A BEER, THEN YOU'RE PRETTY STUPID YOURSELF.

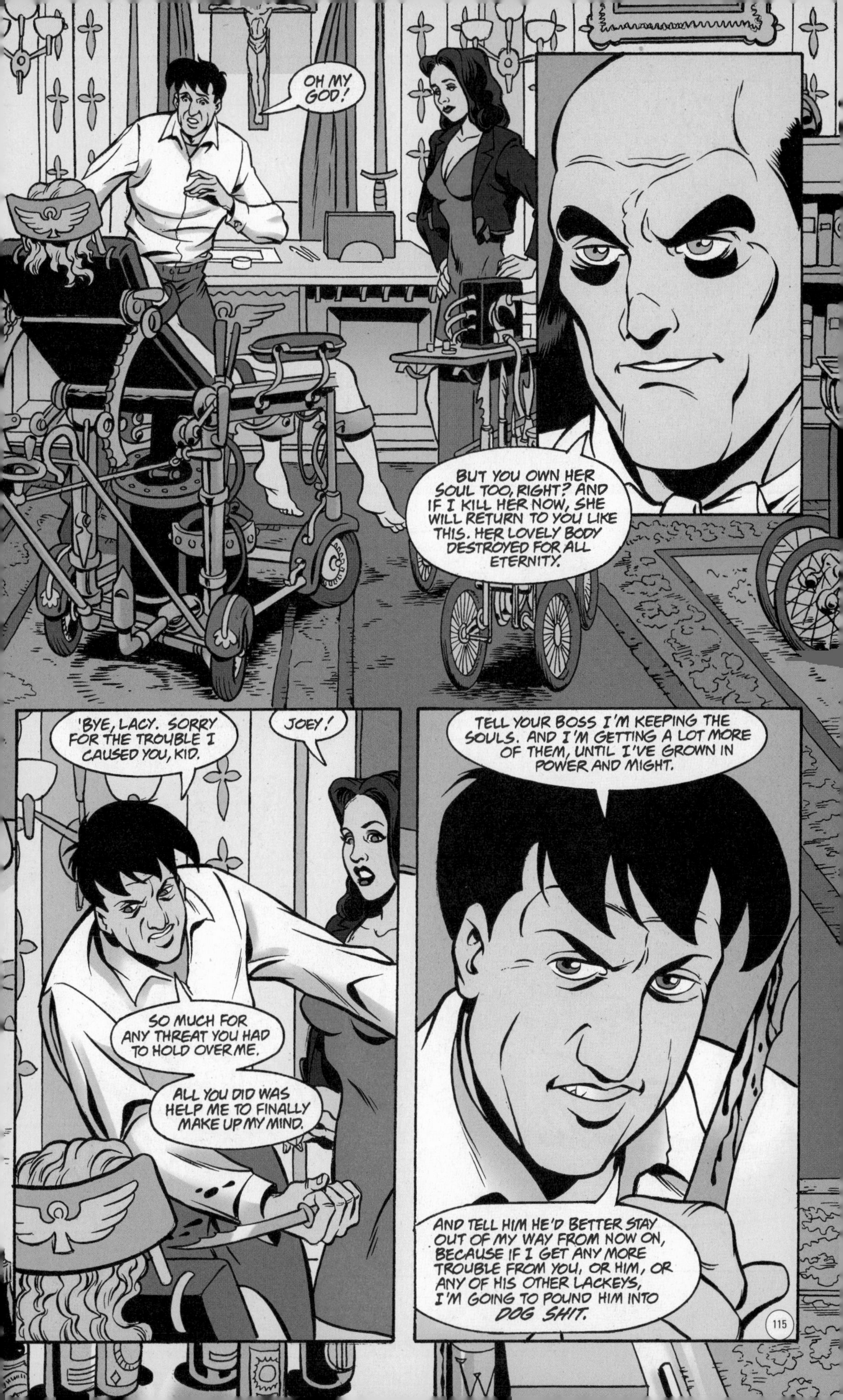
OH MY GOD!
BUT YOU OWN HER SOUL TOO, RIGHT? AND IF I KILL HER NOW, SHE WILL RETURN TO YOU LIKE THIS. HER LOVELY BODY DESTROYED FOR ALL ETERNITY.
'BYE, LACY. SORRY FOR THE TROUBLE I CAUSED YOU, KID.
JOEY!
SO MUCH FOR ANY THREAT YOU HAD TO HOLD OVER ME.
ALL YOU DID WAS HELP ME TO FINALLY MAKE UP MY MIND.
TELL YOUR BOSS I'M KEEPING THE SOULS. AND I'M GETTING A LOT MORE OF THEM, UNTIL I'VE GROWN IN POWER AND MIGHT.
AND TELL HIM HE'D BETTER STAY OUT OF MY WAY FROM NOW ON, BECAUSE IF I GET ANY MORE TROUBLE FROM YOU, OR HIM, OR ANY OF HIS OTHER LACKEYS, I'M GOING TO POUND HIM INTO DOG SHIT.

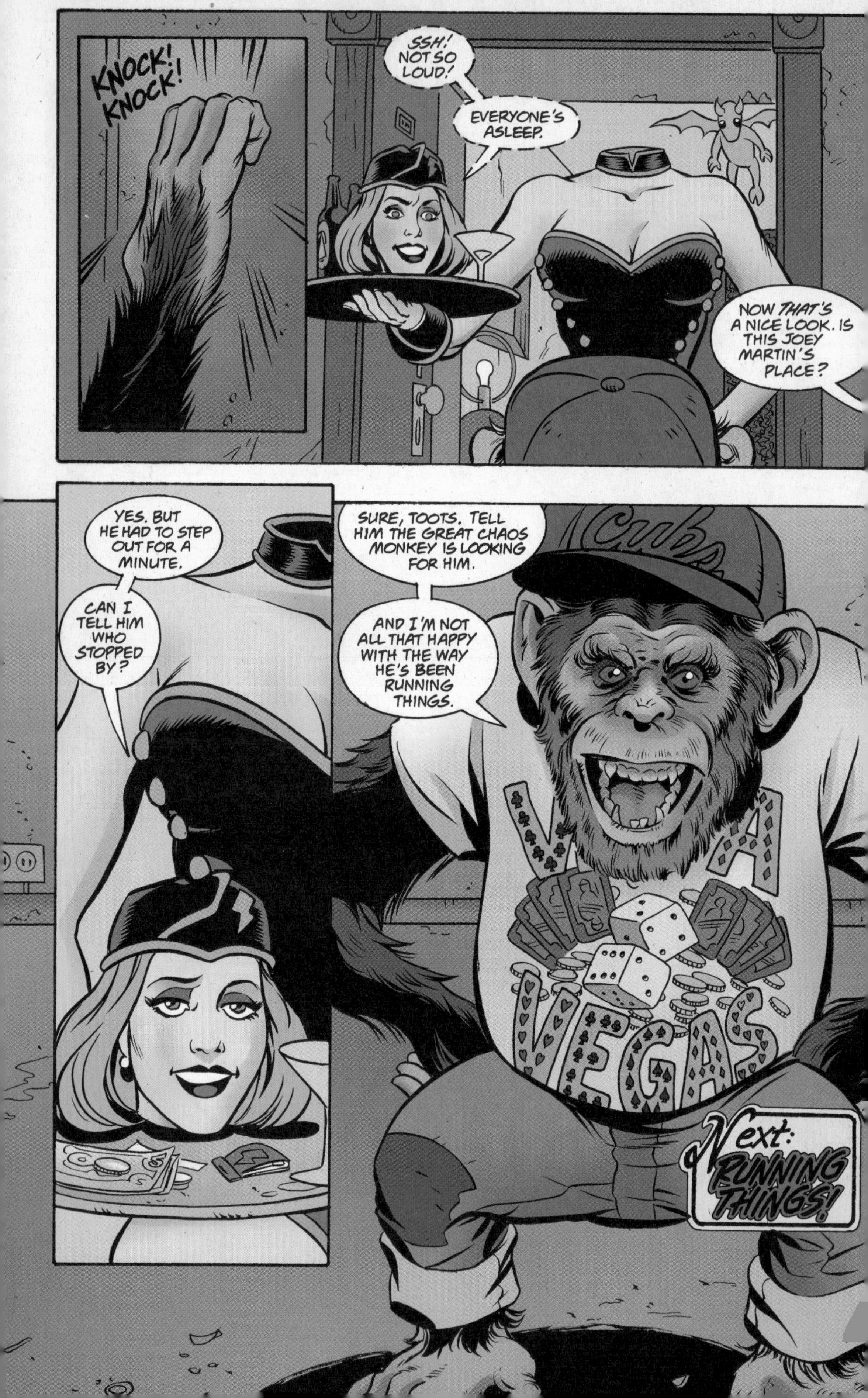
KNOCK! KNOCK!
SSH! NOT SO LOUD!
EVERYONE'S ASLEEP.
NOW THAT'S A NICE LOOK. IS THIS JOEY MARTIN'S PLACE?
YES. BUT HE HAD TO STEP OUT FOR A MINUTE.
CAN I TELL HIM WHO STOPPED BY?
SURE, TOOTS. TELL HIM THE GREAT CHAOS MONKEY IS LOOKING FOR HIM.
AND I'M NOT ALL THAT HAPPY WITH THE WAY HE'S BEEN RUNNING THINGS.
Cubs
VEGAS
Next: RUNNING THINGS!

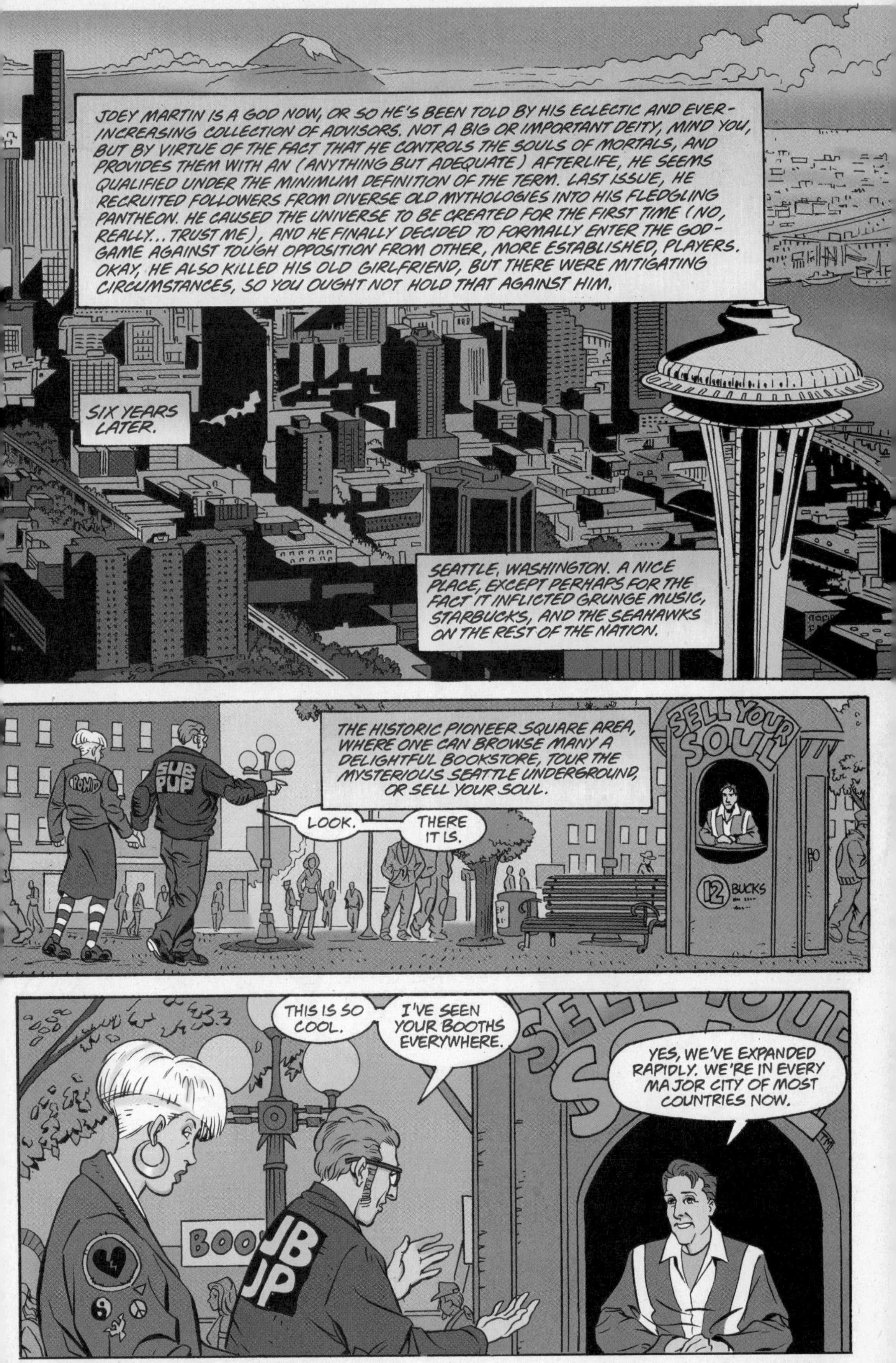
JOEY MARTIN IS A GOD NOW, OR SO HE'S BEEN TOLD BY HIS ECLECTIC AND EVER-INCREASING COLLECTION OF ADVISORS. NOT A BIG OR IMPORTANT DEITY, MIND YOU, BUT BY VIRTUE OF THE FACT THAT HE CONTROLS THE SOULS OF MORTALS, AND PROVIDES THEM WITH AN (ANYTHING BUT ADEQUATE) AFTERLIFE, HE SEEMS QUALIFIED UNDER THE MINIMUM DEFINITION OF THE TERM. LAST ISSUE, HE RECRUITED FOLLOWERS FROM DIVERSE OLD MYTHOLOGIES INTO HIS FLEDGLING PANTHEON. HE CAUSED THE UNIVERSE TO BE CREATED FOR THE FIRST TIME (NO, REALLY... TRUST ME), AND HE FINALLY DECIDED TO FORMALLY ENTER THE GOD-GAME AGAINST TOUGH OPPOSITION FROM OTHER, MORE ESTABLISHED, PLAYERS. OKAY, HE ALSO KILLED HIS OLD GIRLFRIEND, BUT THERE WERE MITIGATING CIRCUMSTANCES, SO YOU OUGHT NOT HOLD THAT AGAINST HIM.
SIX YEARS LATER.
SEATTLE, WASHINGTON. A NICE PLACE, EXCEPT PERHAPS FOR THE FACT IT INFLICTED GRUNGE MUSIC, STARBUCKS, AND THE SEAHAWKS ON THE REST OF THE NATION.
THE HISTORIC PIONEER SQUARE AREA, WHERE ONE CAN BROWSE MANY A DELIGHTFUL BOOKSTORE, TOUR THE MYSTERIOUS SEATTLE UNDERGROUND, OR SELL YOUR SOUL.
SELL YOUR SOUL
SUB PUP
LOOK.
THERE IT IS.
12 BUCKS
THIS IS SO COOL.
I'VE SEEN YOUR BOOTHS EVERYWHERE.
YES, WE'VE EXPANDED RAPIDLY. WE'RE IN EVERY MAJOR CITY OF MOST COUNTRIES NOW.

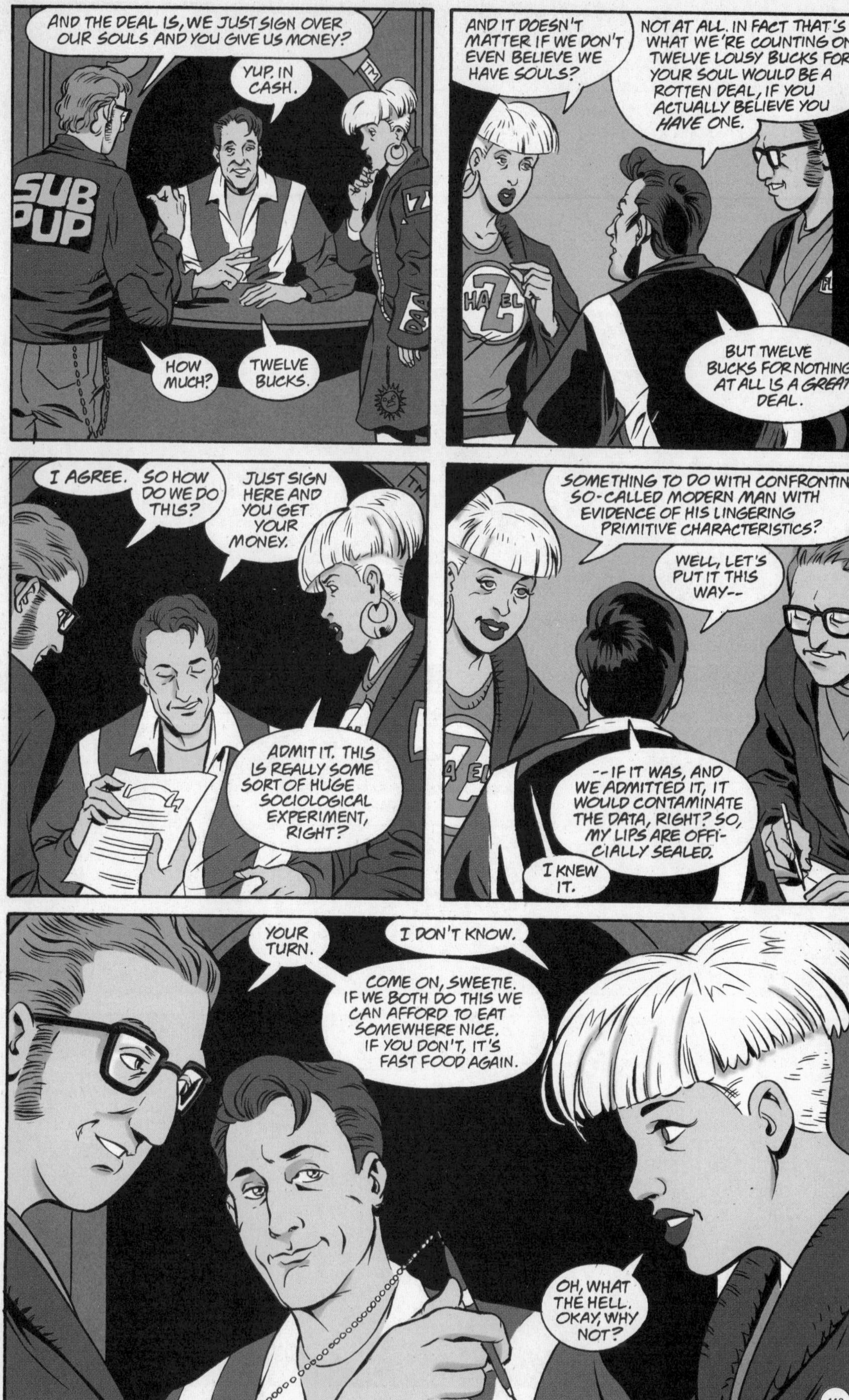
AND THE DEAL IS, WE JUST SIGN OVER OUR SOULS AND YOU GIVE US MONEY?
YUP. IN CASH.
SUB PUP
HOW MUCH?
TWELVE BUCKS.
AND IT DOESN'T MATTER IF WE DON'T EVEN BELIEVE WE HAVE SOULS?
NOT AT ALL. IN FACT THAT'S WHAT WE'RE COUNTING ON. TWELVE LOUSY BUCKS FOR YOUR SOUL WOULD BE A ROTTEN DEAL, IF YOU ACTUALLY BELIEVE YOU *HAVE* ONE.
HAZEL
BUT TWELVE BUCKS FOR NOTHING AT ALL IS A *GREAT* DEAL.
I AGREE.
SO HOW DO WE DO THIS?
JUST SIGN HERE AND YOU GET YOUR MONEY.
ADMIT IT. THIS IS REALLY SOME SORT OF HUGE SOCIOLOGICAL EXPERIMENT, RIGHT?
SOMETHING TO DO WITH CONFRONTING SO-CALLED MODERN MAN WITH EVIDENCE OF HIS LINGERING PRIMITIVE CHARACTERISTICS?
WELL, LET'S PUT IT THIS WAY--
--IF IT WAS, AND WE ADMITTED IT, IT WOULD CONTAMINATE THE DATA, RIGHT? SO, MY LIPS ARE OFFICIALLY SEALED.
I KNEW IT.
YOUR TURN.
I DON'T KNOW.
COME ON, SWEETIE. IF WE BOTH DO THIS WE CAN AFFORD TO EAT SOMEWHERE NICE. IF YOU DON'T, IT'S FAST FOOD AGAIN.
OH, WHAT THE HELL. OKAY, WHY NOT?

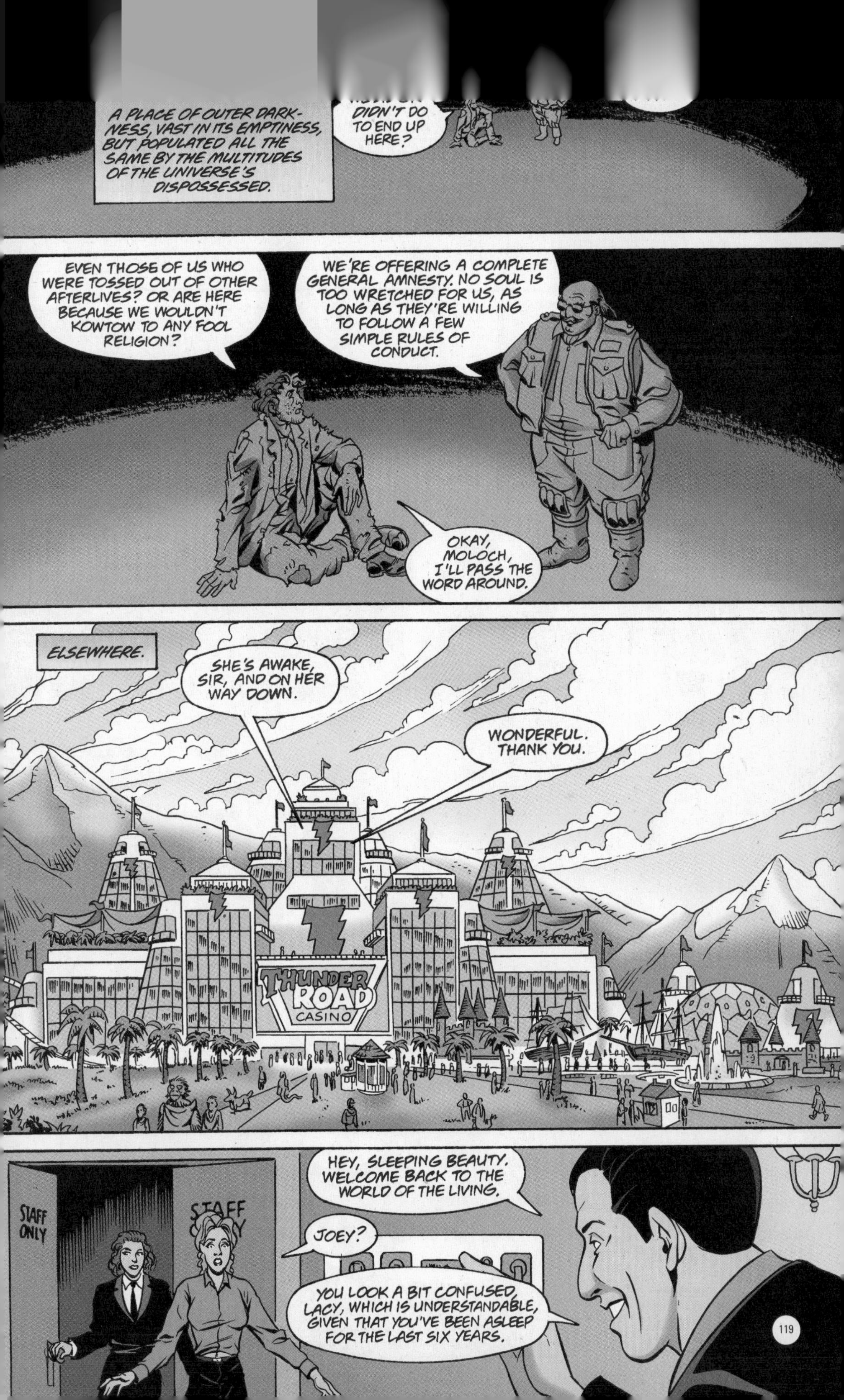
A PLACE OF OUTER DARKNESS, VAST IN ITS EMPTINESS, BUT POPULATED ALL THE SAME BY THE MULTITUDES OF THE UNIVERSE'S DISPOSSESSED.
DIDN'T DO TO END UP HERE?
EVEN THOSE OF US WHO WERE TOSSED OUT OF OTHER AFTERLIVES? OR ARE HERE BECAUSE WE WOULDN'T KOWTOW TO ANY FOOL RELIGION?
WE'RE OFFERING A COMPLETE GENERAL AMNESTY. NO SOUL IS TOO WRETCHED FOR US, AS LONG AS THEY'RE WILLING TO FOLLOW A FEW SIMPLE RULES OF CONDUCT.
OKAY, MOLOCH, I'LL PASS THE WORD AROUND.
ELSEWHERE.
SHE'S AWAKE, SIR, AND ON HER WAY DOWN.
WONDERFUL. THANK YOU.
THUNDER ROAD CASINO
HEY, SLEEPING BEAUTY. WELCOME BACK TO THE WORLD OF THE LIVING.
STAFF ONLY
JOEY?
YOU LOOK A BIT CONFUSED, LACY, WHICH IS UNDERSTANDABLE, GIVEN THAT YOU'VE BEEN ASLEEP FOR THE LAST SIX YEARS.

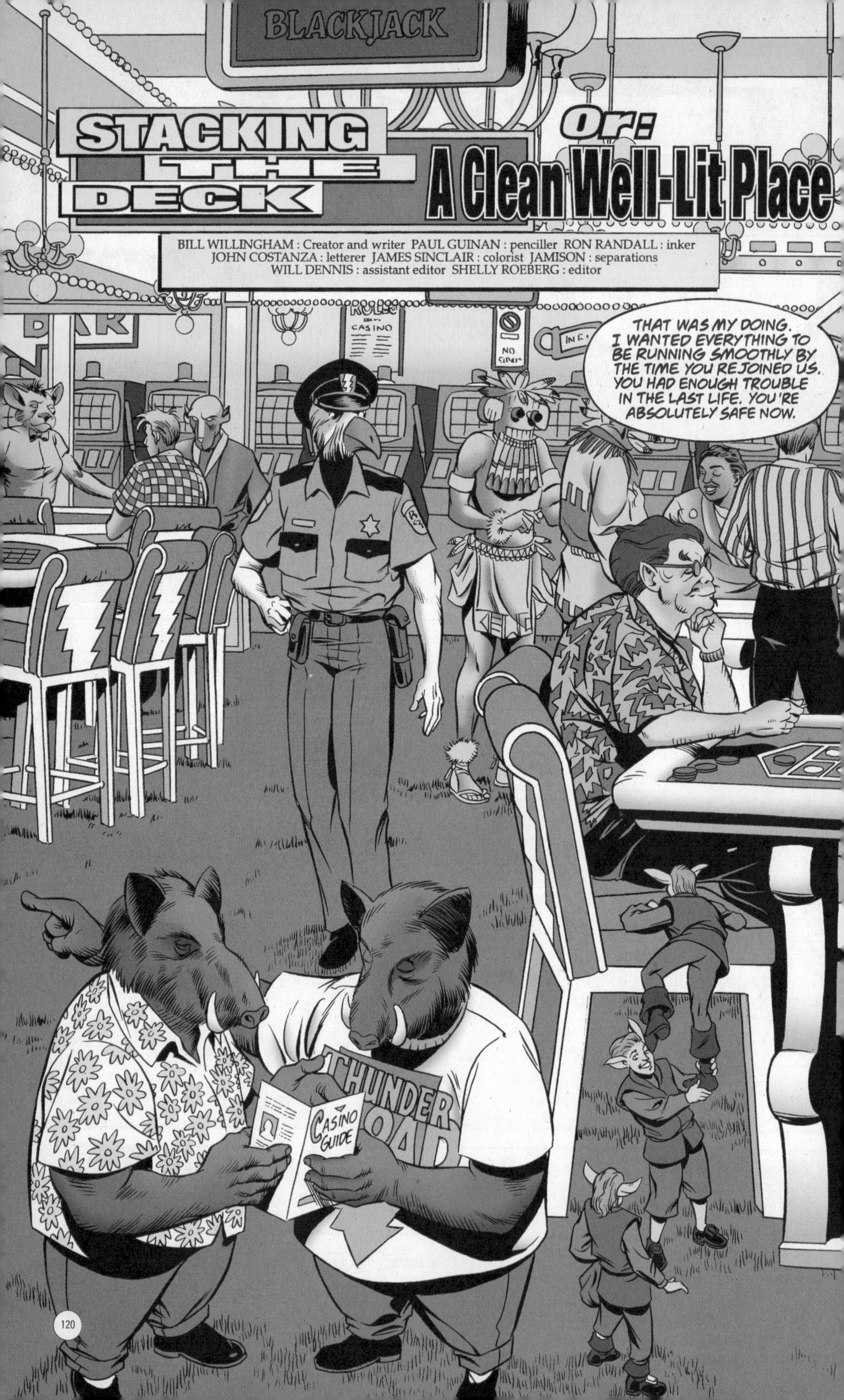
BLACKJACK
STACKING THE DECK
Or: A Clean Well-Lit Place
BILL WILLINGHAM : Creator and writer PAUL GUINAN : penciller RON RANDALL : inker
JOHN COSTANZA : letterer JAMES SINCLAIR : colorist JAMISON : separations
WILL DENNIS : assistant editor SHELLY ROEBERG : editor
CASINO
THAT WAS MY DOING. I WANTED EVERYTHING TO BE RUNNING SMOOTHLY BY THE TIME YOU REJOINED US. YOU HAD ENOUGH TROUBLE IN THE LAST LIFE. YOU'RE ABSOLUTELY SAFE NOW.
THUNDER
CASINO GUIDE

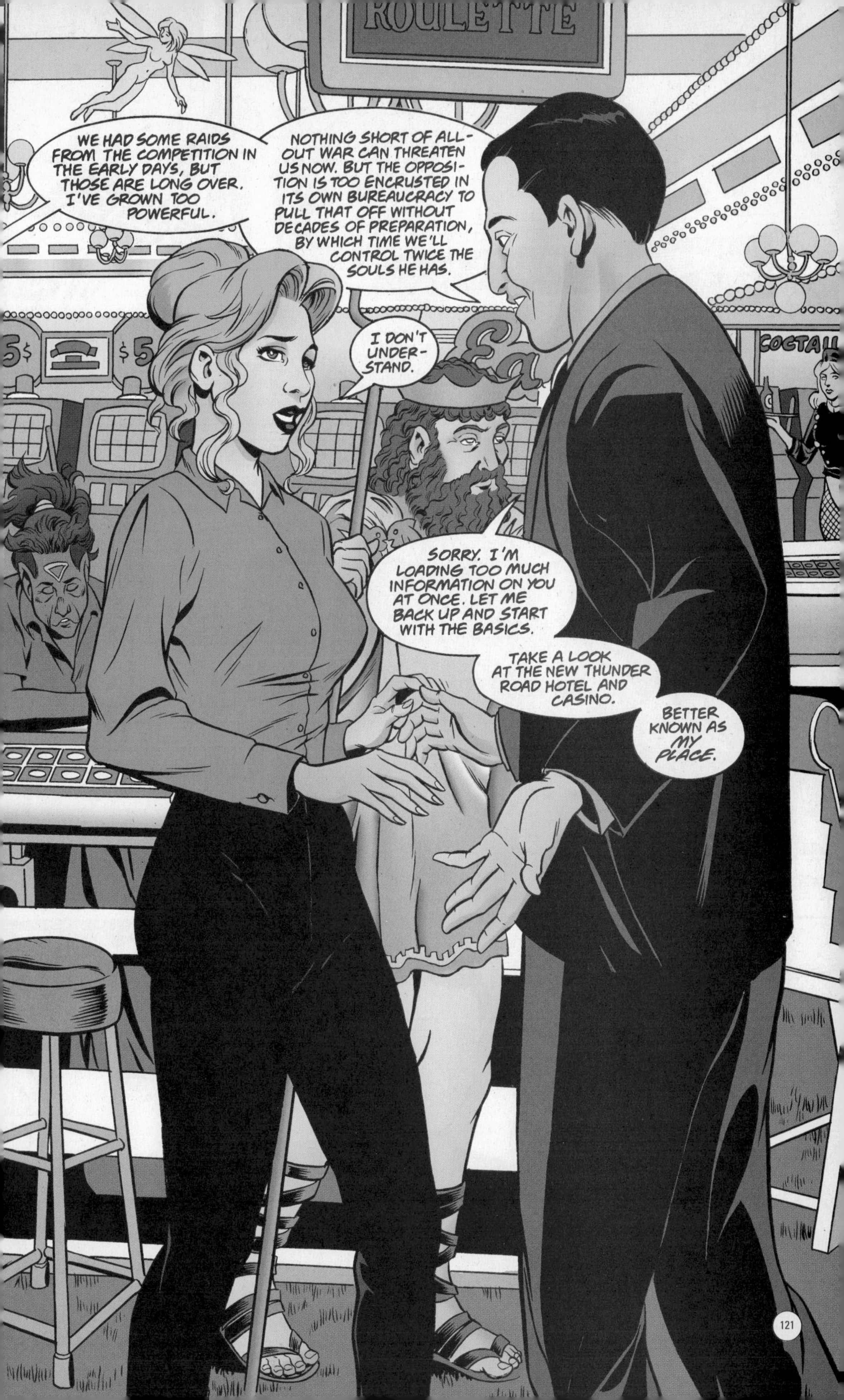
ROULETTE
WE HAD SOME RAIDS FROM THE COMPETITION IN THE EARLY DAYS, BUT THOSE ARE LONG OVER. I'VE GROWN TOO POWERFUL.
NOTHING SHORT OF ALL-OUT WAR CAN THREATEN US NOW. BUT THE OPPOSITION IS TOO ENCRUSTED IN ITS OWN BUREAUCRACY TO PULL THAT OFF WITHOUT DECADES OF PREPARATION, BY WHICH TIME WE'LL CONTROL TWICE THE SOULS HE HAS.
I DON'T UNDERSTAND.
SORRY. I'M LOADING TOO MUCH INFORMATION ON YOU AT ONCE. LET ME BACK UP AND START WITH THE BASICS.
TAKE A LOOK AT THE NEW THUNDER ROAD HOTEL AND CASINO.
BETTER KNOWN AS *MY PLACE*.

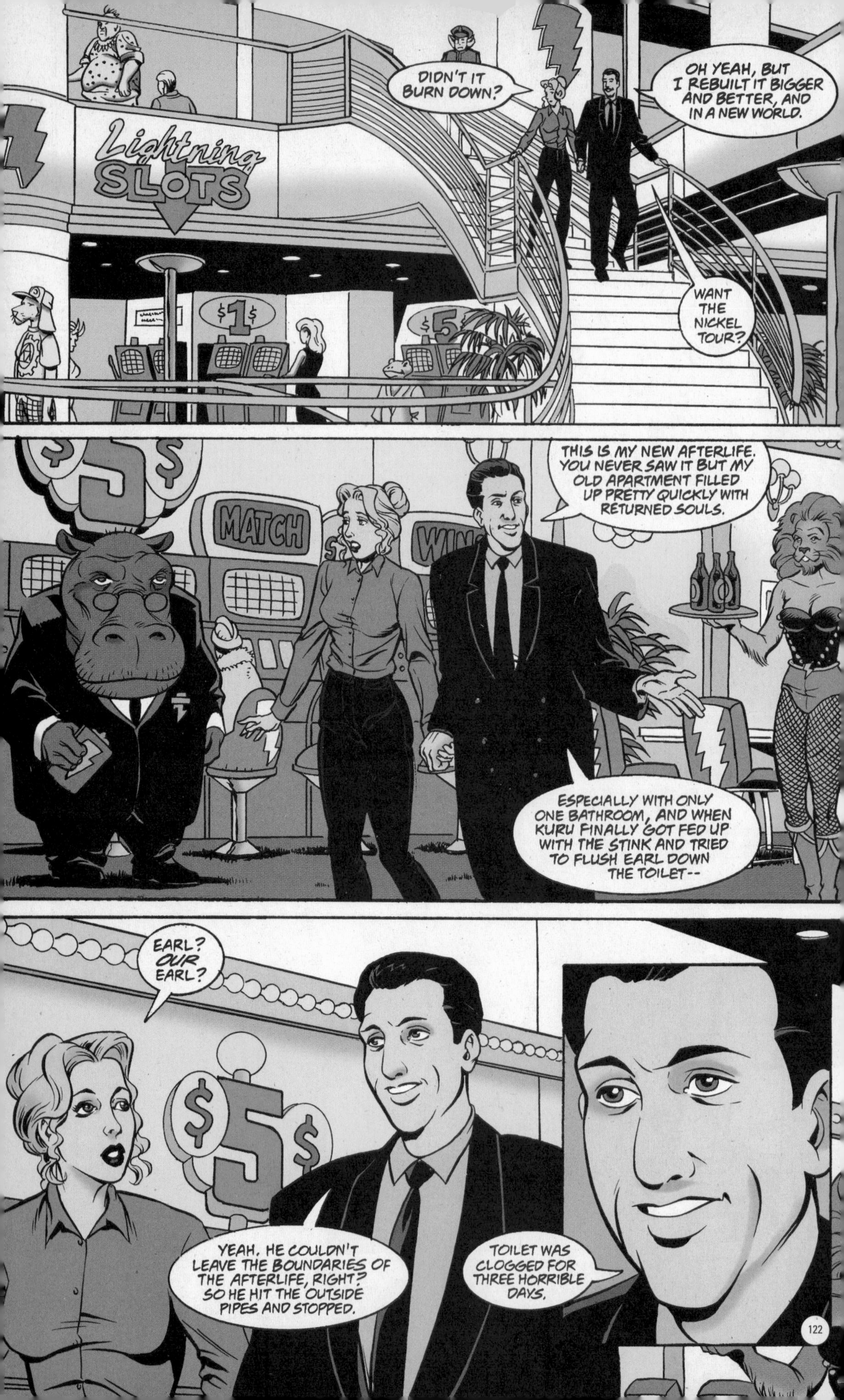
Lightning SLOTS
DIDN'T IT BURN DOWN?
OH YEAH, BUT I REBUILT IT BIGGER AND BETTER, AND IN A NEW WORLD.
WANT THE NICKEL TOUR?
THIS IS MY NEW AFTERLIFE. YOU NEVER SAW IT BUT MY OLD APARTMENT FILLED UP PRETTY QUICKLY WITH RETURNED SOULS.
MATCH
ESPECIALLY WITH ONLY ONE BATHROOM, AND WHEN KURU FINALLY GOT FED UP WITH THE STINK AND TRIED TO FLUSH EARL DOWN THE TOILET--
EARL? OUR EARL?
YEAH. HE COULDN'T LEAVE THE BOUNDARIES OF THE AFTERLIFE, RIGHT? SO HE HIT THE OUTSIDE PIPES AND STOPPED.
TOILET WAS CLOGGED FOR THREE HORRIBLE DAYS.

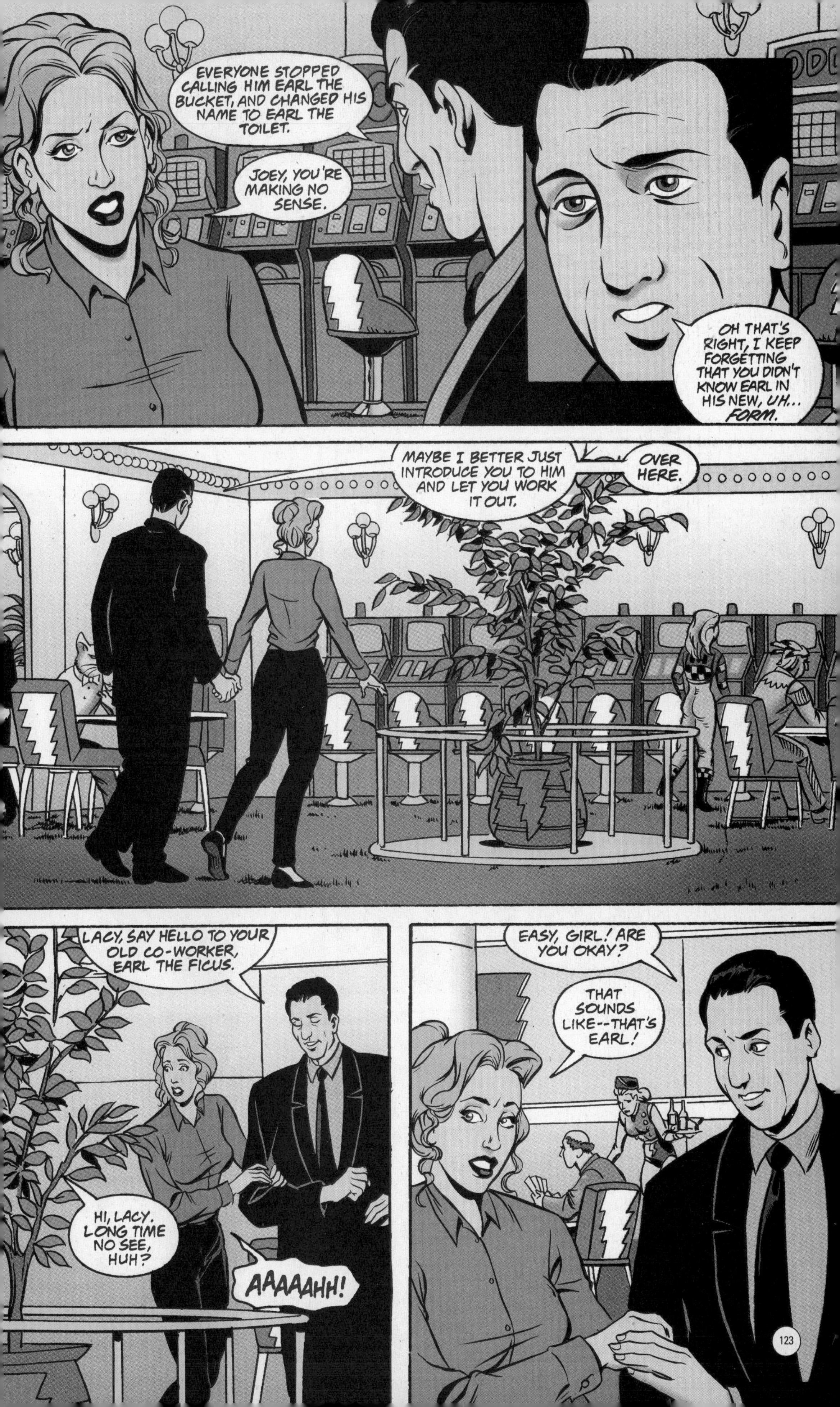
EVERYONE STOPPED CALLING HIM EARL THE BUCKET, AND CHANGED HIS NAME TO EARL THE TOILET.
JOEY, YOU'RE MAKING NO SENSE.
OH THAT'S RIGHT, I KEEP FORGETTING THAT YOU DIDN'T KNOW EARL IN HIS NEW, UH... FORM.
MAYBE I BETTER JUST INTRODUCE YOU TO HIM AND LET YOU WORK IT OUT.
OVER HERE.
LACY, SAY HELLO TO YOUR OLD CO-WORKER, EARL THE FICUS.
HI, LACY. LONG TIME NO SEE, HUH?
AAAAAHH!
EASY, GIRL! ARE YOU OKAY?
THAT SOUNDS LIKE--THAT'S EARL!

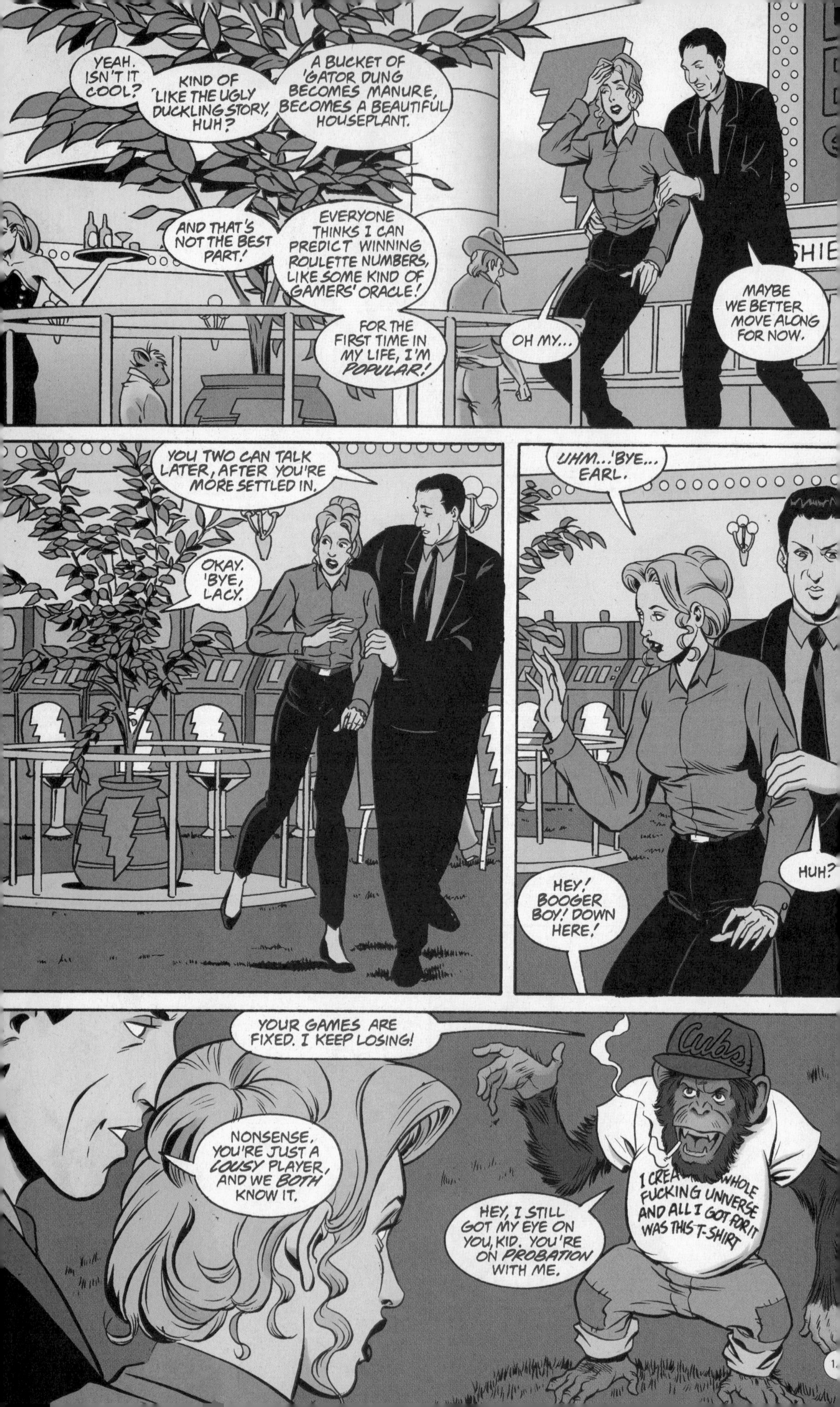
YEAH. ISN'T IT COOL?
KIND OF LIKE THE UGLY DUCKLING STORY, HUH?
A BUCKET OF 'GATOR DUNG BECOMES MANURE, BECOMES A BEAUTIFUL HOUSEPLANT.
AND THAT'S NOT THE BEST PART!
EVERYONE THINKS I CAN PREDICT WINNING ROULETTE NUMBERS, LIKE SOME KIND OF GAMERS' ORACLE!
FOR THE FIRST TIME IN MY LIFE, I'M POPULAR!
OH MY...
MAYBE WE BETTER MOVE ALONG FOR NOW.
SHIE
YOU TWO CAN TALK LATER, AFTER YOU'RE MORE SETTLED IN.
OKAY. 'BYE, LACY.
UHM... 'BYE... EARL.
HEY! BOOGER BOY! DOWN HERE!
HUH?
YOUR GAMES ARE FIXED. I KEEP LOSING!
NONSENSE. YOU'RE JUST A LOUSY PLAYER, AND WE BOTH KNOW IT.
HEY, I STILL GOT MY EYE ON YOU, KID. YOU'RE ON PROBATION WITH ME.
Cubs
I CREA WHOLE FUCKING UNIVERSE AND ALL I GOT FOR IT WAS THIS T-SHIRT

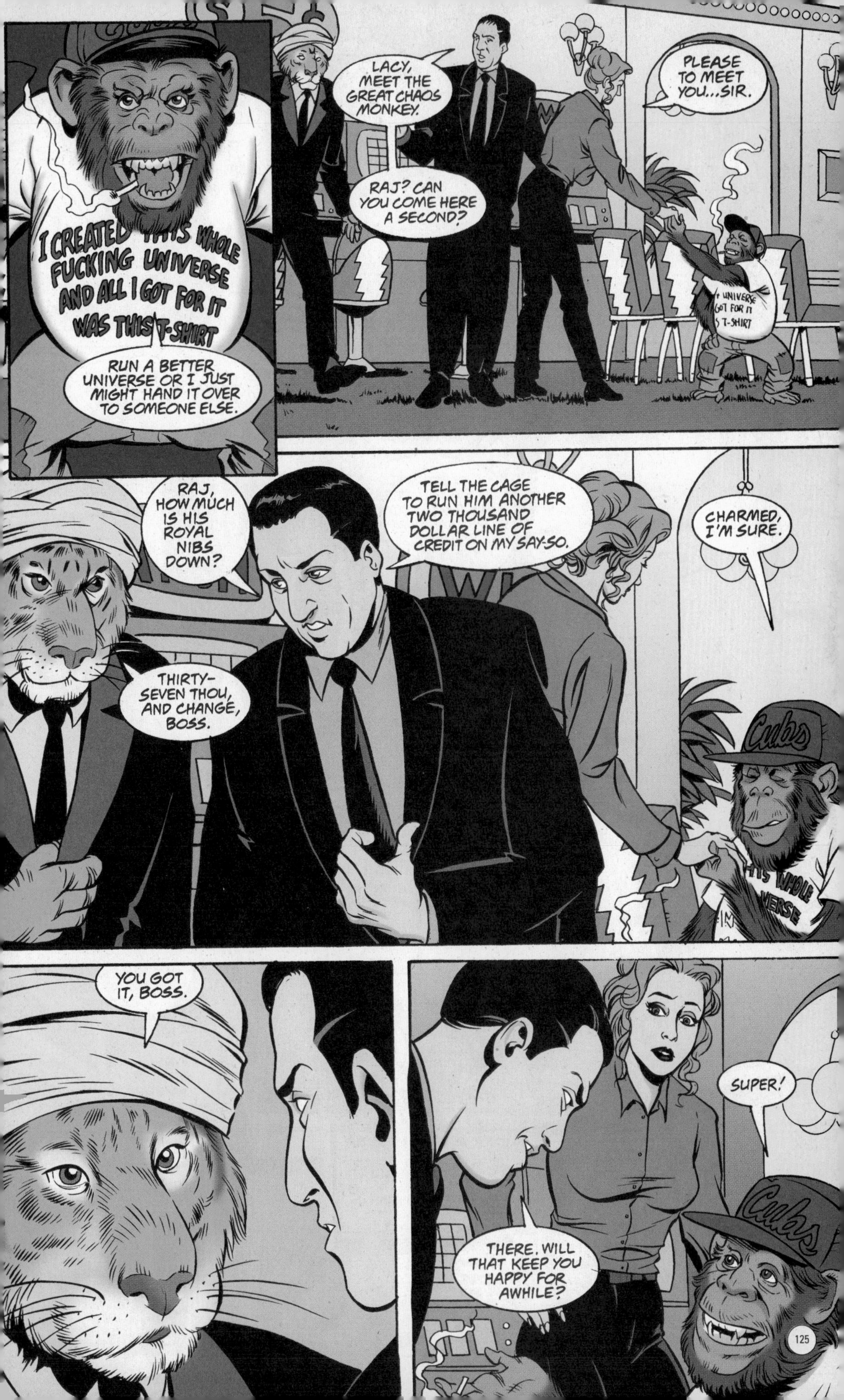
I CREATED THIS WHOLE FUCKING UNIVERSE AND ALL I GOT FOR IT WAS THIS T-SHIRT
RUN A BETTER UNIVERSE OR I JUST MIGHT HAND IT OVER TO SOMEONE ELSE.
LACY, MEET THE GREAT CHAOS MONKEY.
RAJ? CAN YOU COME HERE A SECOND?
PLEASE TO MEET YOU...SIR.
RAJ, HOW MUCH IS HIS ROYAL NIBS DOWN?
THIRTY-SEVEN THOU, AND CHANGE, BOSS.
TELL THE CAGE TO RUN HIM ANOTHER TWO THOUSAND DOLLAR LINE OF CREDIT ON MY SAY-SO.
CHARMED, I'M SURE.
Cubs
YOU GOT IT, BOSS.
SUPER!
THERE. WILL THAT KEEP YOU HAPPY FOR AWHILE?
Cubs

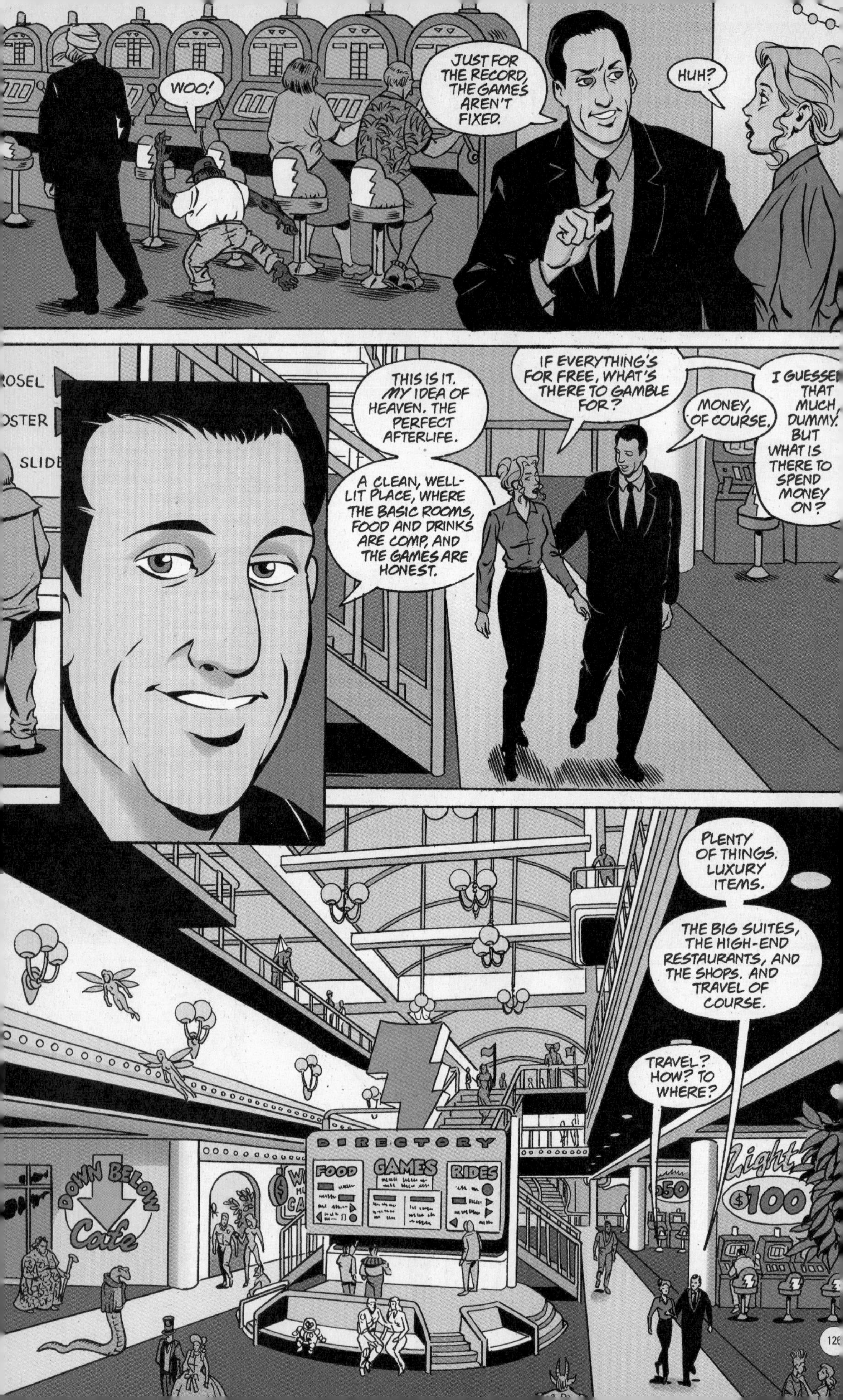
WOO!
JUST FOR THE RECORD, THE GAME'S AREN'T FIXED.
HUH?
ROSEL
OSTER
SLIDE
THIS IS IT. MY IDEA OF HEAVEN. THE PERFECT AFTERLIFE.
A CLEAN, WELL-LIT PLACE, WHERE THE BASIC ROOMS, FOOD AND DRINKS ARE COMP, AND THE GAMES ARE HONEST.
IF EVERYTHING'S FOR FREE, WHAT'S THERE TO GAMBLE FOR?
MONEY, OF COURSE.
I GUESSED THAT MUCH, DUMMY. BUT WHAT IS THERE TO SPEND MONEY ON?
PLENTY OF THINGS. LUXURY ITEMS.
THE BIG SUITES, THE HIGH-END RESTAURANTS, AND THE SHOPS. AND TRAVEL OF COURSE.
TRAVEL? HOW? TO WHERE?
DOWN BELOW
Cafe
DIRECTORY
FOOD
GAMES
RIDES
$100

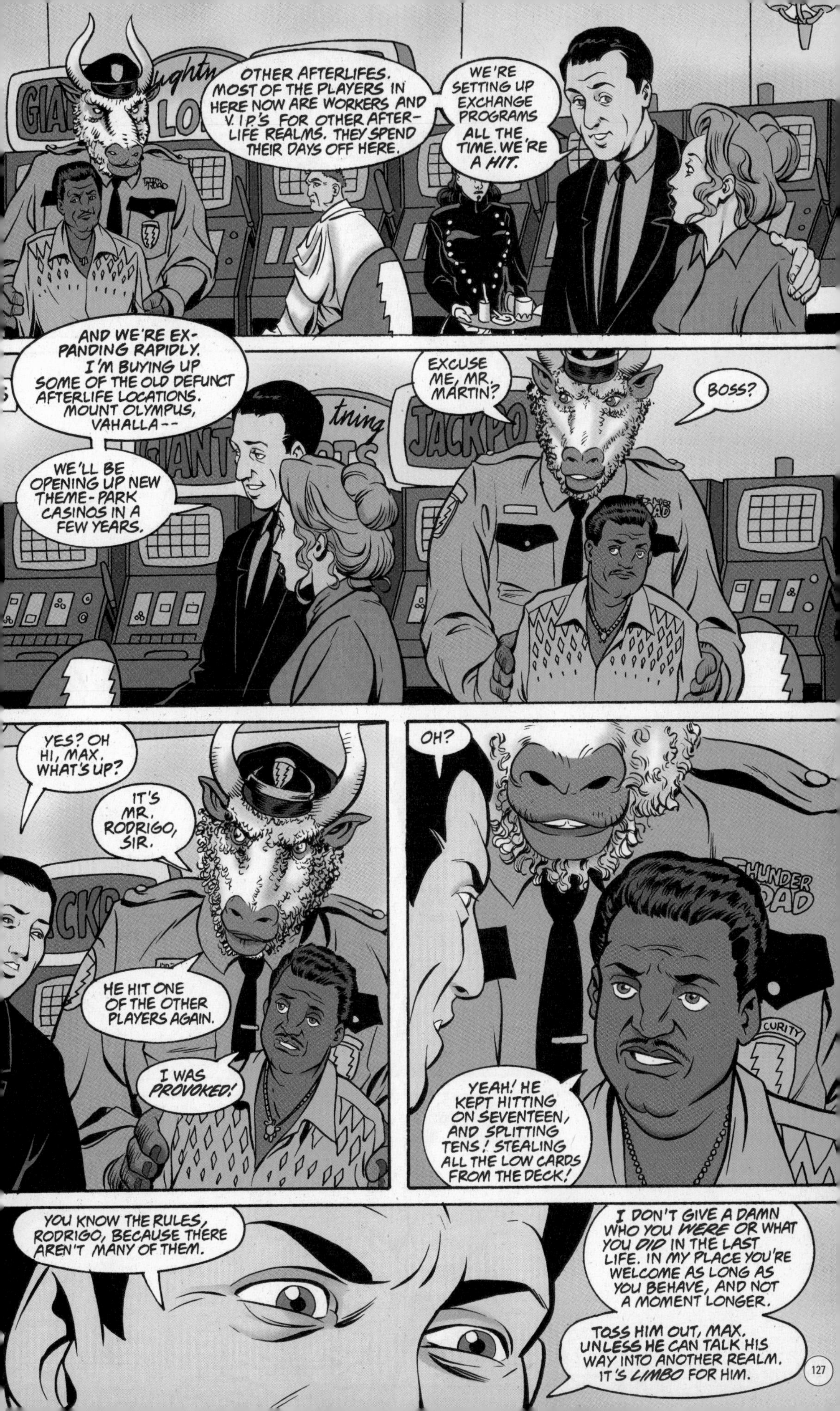
OTHER AFTERLIFES. MOST OF THE PLAYERS IN HERE NOW ARE WORKERS AND V.I.P.'S FOR OTHER AFTER-LIFE REALMS. THEY SPEND THEIR DAYS OFF HERE.
WE'RE SETTING UP EXCHANGE PROGRAMS ALL THE TIME. WE'RE A HIT.
AND WE'RE EX-PANDING RAPIDLY. I'M BUYING UP SOME OF THE OLD DEFUNCT AFTERLIFE LOCATIONS. MOUNT OLYMPUS, VAHALLA--
WE'LL BE OPENING UP NEW THEME-PARK CASINOS IN A FEW YEARS.
EXCUSE ME, MR. MARTIN?
BOSS?
YES? OH HI, MAX. WHAT'S UP?
IT'S MR. RODRIGO, SIR.
HE HIT ONE OF THE OTHER PLAYERS AGAIN.
I WAS PROVOKED!
OH?
YEAH! HE KEPT HITTING ON SEVENTEEN, AND SPLITTING TENS! STEALING ALL THE LOW CARDS FROM THE DECK!
YOU KNOW THE RULES, RODRIGO, BECAUSE THERE AREN'T MANY OF THEM.
I DON'T GIVE A DAMN WHO YOU WERE OR WHAT YOU DID IN THE LAST LIFE. IN MY PLACE YOU'RE WELCOME AS LONG AS YOU BEHAVE, AND NOT A MOMENT LONGER.
TOSS HIM OUT, MAX. UNLESS HE CAN TALK HIS WAY INTO ANOTHER REALM. IT'S LIMBO FOR HIM.
JACKPOT
THUNDER ROAD

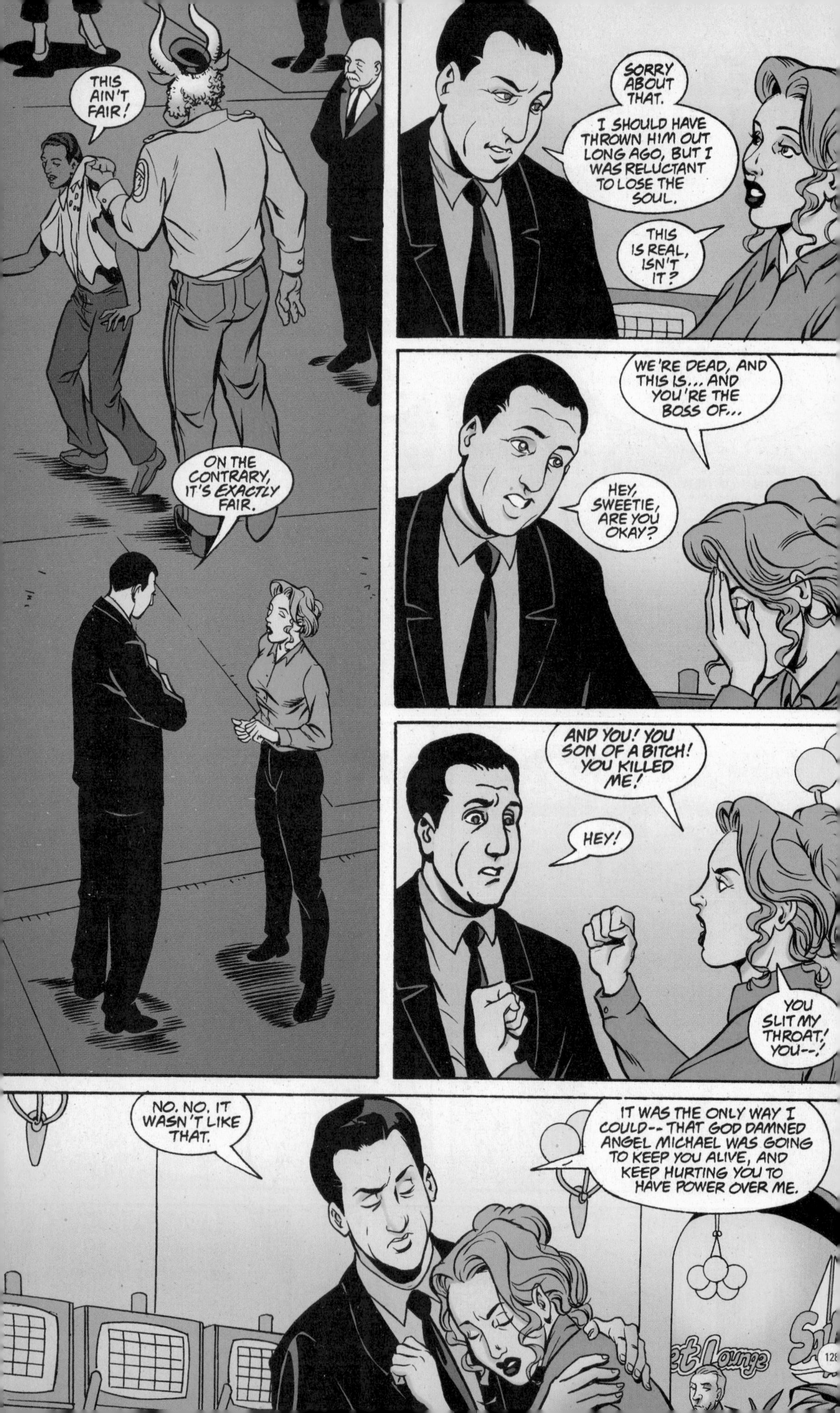
THIS AIN'T FAIR!
ON THE CONTRARY, IT'S EXACTLY FAIR.
SORRY ABOUT THAT.
I SHOULD HAVE THROWN HIM OUT LONG AGO, BUT I WAS RELUCTANT TO LOSE THE SOUL.
THIS IS REAL, ISN'T IT?
WE'RE DEAD, AND THIS IS... AND YOU'RE THE BOSS OF...
HEY, SWEETIE, ARE YOU OKAY?
AND YOU! YOU SON OF A BITCH! YOU KILLED ME!
HEY!
YOU SLIT MY THROAT! YOU--!
NO. NO. IT WASN'T LIKE THAT.
IT WAS THE ONLY WAY I COULD-- THAT GOD DAMNED ANGEL MICHAEL WAS GOING TO KEEP YOU ALIVE, AND KEEP HURTING YOU TO HAVE POWER OVER ME.
et Lounge

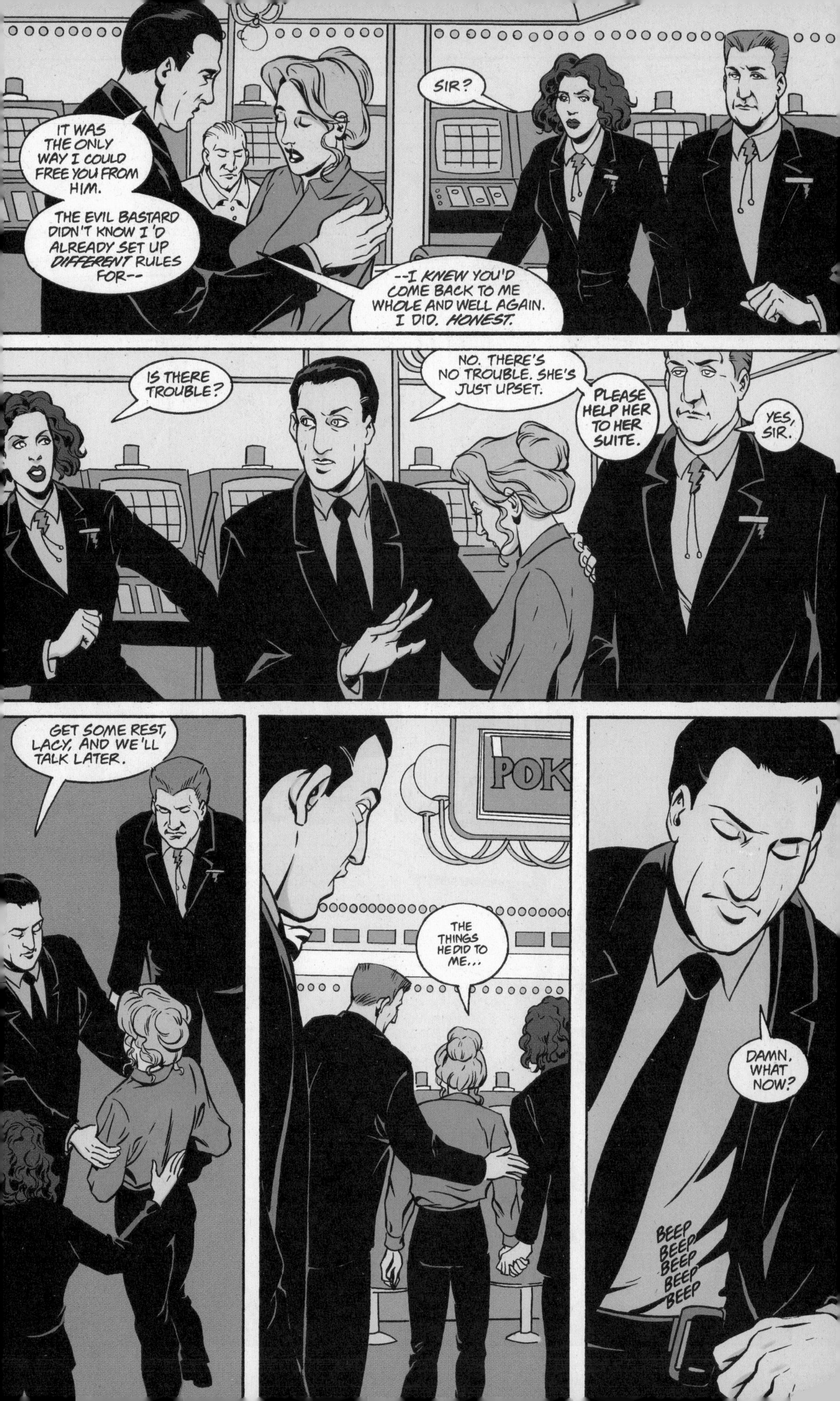
IT WAS THE ONLY WAY I COULD FREE YOU FROM HIM.
THE EVIL BASTARD DIDN'T KNOW I'D ALREADY SET UP *DIFFERENT* RULES FOR--
SIR?
--I *KNEW* YOU'D COME BACK TO ME WHOLE AND WELL AGAIN. I DID. *HONEST.*
IS THERE TROUBLE?
NO. THERE'S NO TROUBLE. SHE'S JUST UPSET.
PLEASE HELP HER TO HER SUITE.
YES, SIR.
GET SOME REST, LACY, AND WE'LL TALK LATER.
POK
THE THINGS HE DID TO ME...
DAMN. WHAT NOW?
BEEP BEEP BEEP BEEP BEEP

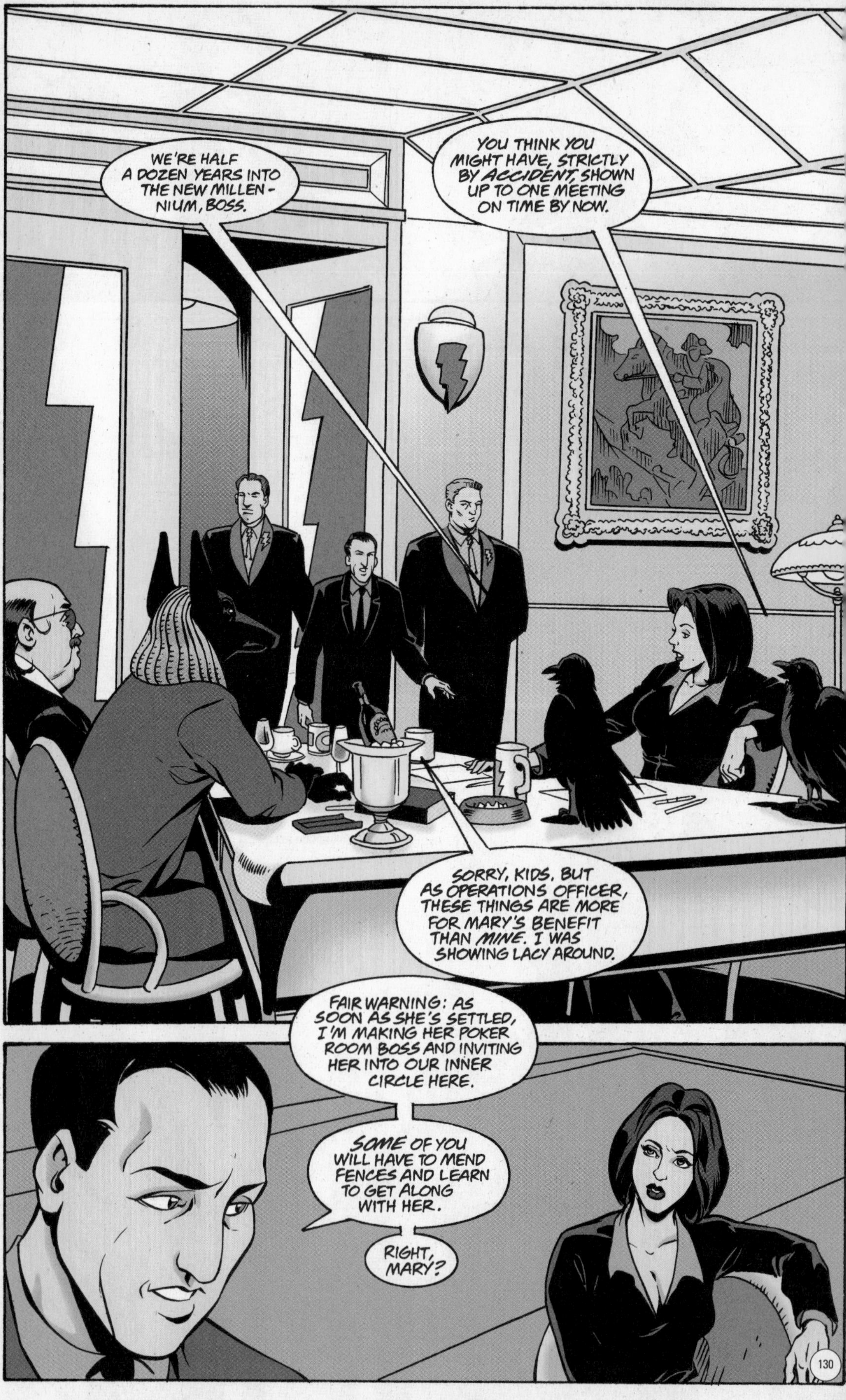

WE'RE HALF A DOZEN YEARS INTO THE NEW MILLEN-NIUM, BOSS.
YOU THINK YOU MIGHT HAVE, STRICTLY BY ACCIDENT, SHOWN UP TO ONE MEETING ON TIME BY NOW.
SORRY, KIDS. BUT AS OPERATIONS OFFICER, THESE THINGS ARE MORE FOR MARY'S BENEFIT THAN MINE. I WAS SHOWING LACY AROUND.
FAIR WARNING: AS SOON AS SHE'S SETTLED, I'M MAKING HER POKER ROOM BOSS AND INVITING HER INTO OUR INNER CIRCLE HERE.
SOME OF YOU WILL HAVE TO MEND FENCES AND LEARN TO GET ALONG WITH HER.
RIGHT, MARY?

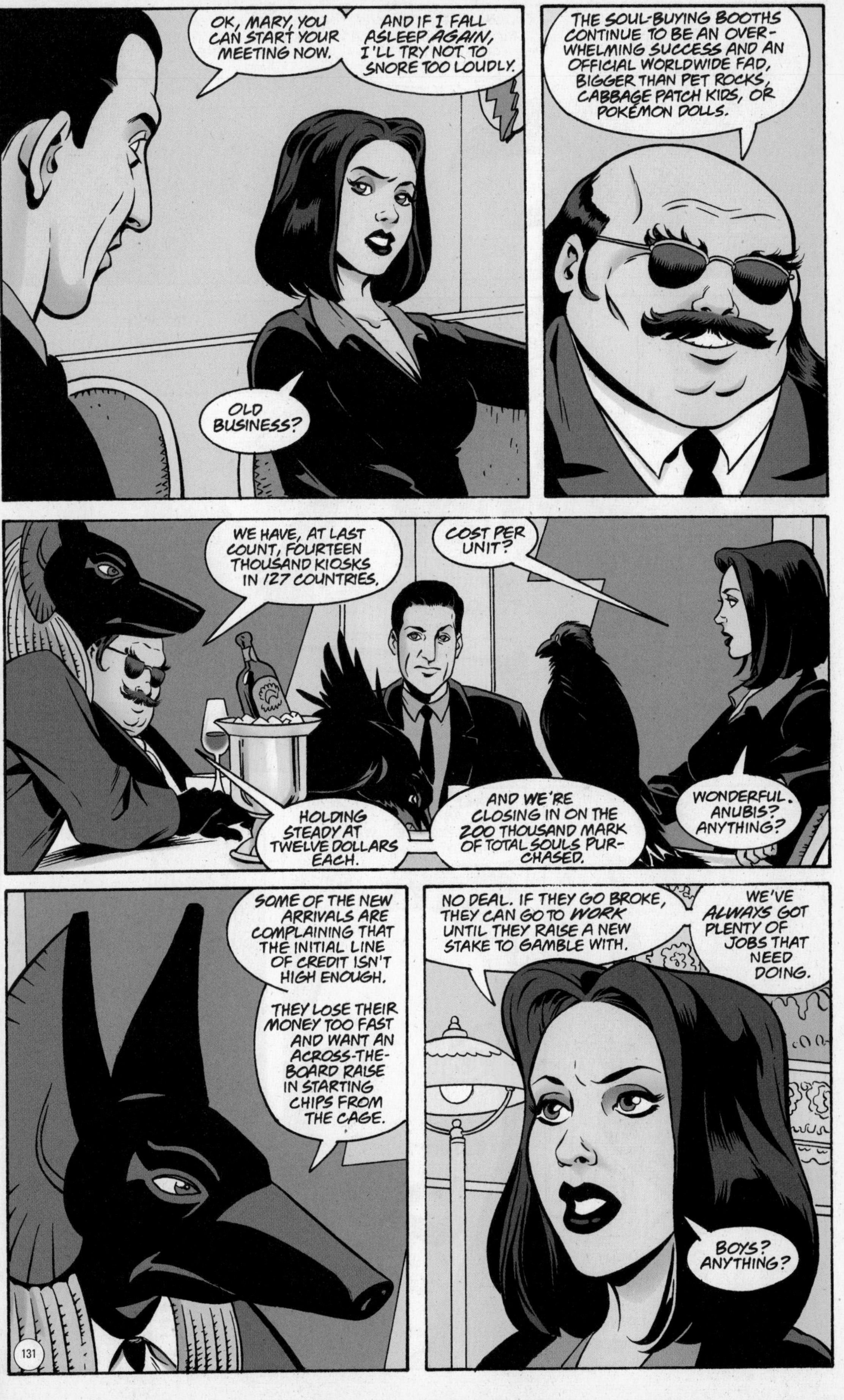
OK, MARY, YOU CAN START YOUR MEETING NOW.
AND IF I FALL ASLEEP *AGAIN*, I'LL TRY NOT TO SNORE TOO LOUDLY.
OLD BUSINESS?
THE SOUL-BUYING BOOTHS CONTINUE TO BE AN OVER-WHELMING SUCCESS AND AN OFFICIAL WORLDWIDE FAD, BIGGER THAN PET ROCKS, CABBAGE PATCH KIDS, OR POKÉMON DOLLS.
WE HAVE, AT LAST COUNT, FOURTEEN THOUSAND KIOSKS IN 127 COUNTRIES.
COST PER UNIT?
HOLDING STEADY AT TWELVE DOLLARS EACH.
AND WE'RE CLOSING IN ON THE 200 THOUSAND MARK OF TOTAL SOULS PUR-CHASED.
WONDERFUL. ANUBIS? ANYTHING?
SOME OF THE NEW ARRIVALS ARE COMPLAINING THAT THE INITIAL LINE OF CREDIT ISN'T HIGH ENOUGH.
THEY LOSE THEIR MONEY TOO FAST AND WANT AN ACROSS-THE-BOARD RAISE IN STARTING CHIPS FROM THE CAGE.
NO DEAL. IF THEY GO BROKE, THEY CAN GO TO *WORK* UNTIL THEY RAISE A NEW STAKE TO GAMBLE WITH.
WE'VE *ALWAYS* GOT PLENTY OF JOBS THAT NEED DOING.
BOYS? ANYTHING?

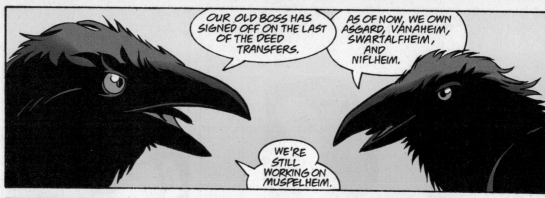

OUR OLD BOSS HAS SIGNED OFF ON THE LAST OF THE DEED TRANSFERS.

AS OF NOW, WE OWN ASGARD, VANAHEIM, SWARTALFHEIM, AND NIFLHEIM.

WE'RE STILL WORKING ON MUSPELHEIM.

GOOD, ANY OTHER OLD BUSINESS?

OKAY, ON TO NEW BUSINESS.

I'VE GOT SOMETHING.

I HAVE A REQUEST FROM THE THIRD FIGHTER WING OF THE FOURTEENTH ANGELIC HOST.

THEY WANT TO HOLD THEIR CONVENTION HERE, BUT IT'S SIX DAYS LONG.

I DON'T THINK WE CAN ACCOMMODATE THEM.

MONDAYS THROUGH WEDNESDAYS WE ALLOW TOURISTS FROM THE HEAVENLY HOSTS.

THURSDAYS THROUGH SATURDAYS ARE FOR THE INFERNAL ORDERS.

AND ON SUNDAYS WE REST.

WE'VE SEEN WHAT HAPPENS WHEN WE LET THE TWO REALMS OVERLAP THEIR VISITS. NEVER AGAIN.

132

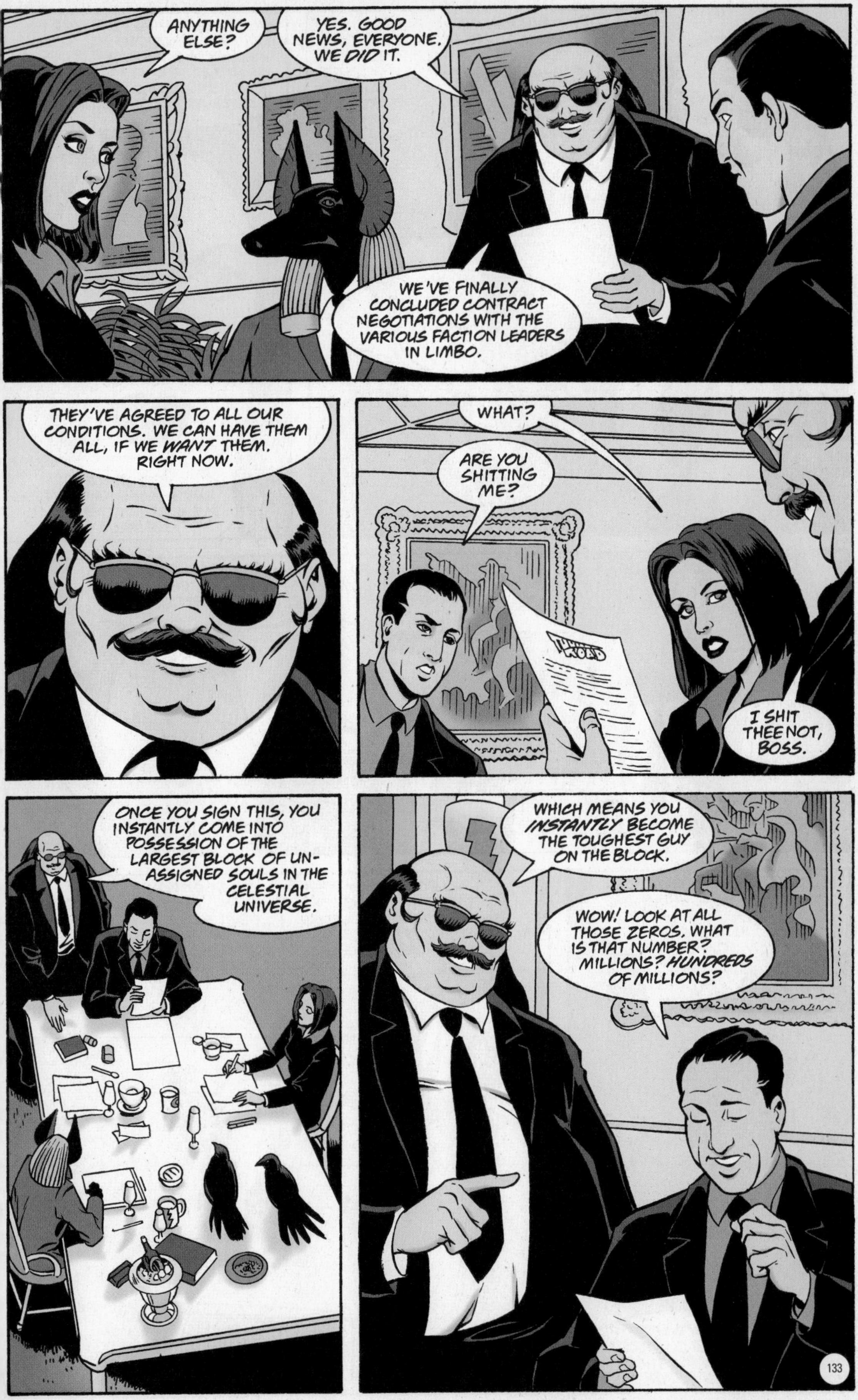

ANYTHING ELSE?
YES. GOOD NEWS, EVERYONE. WE *DID* IT.
WE'VE FINALLY CONCLUDED CONTRACT NEGOTIATIONS WITH THE VARIOUS FACTION LEADERS IN LIMBO.
THEY'VE AGREED TO ALL OUR CONDITIONS. WE CAN HAVE THEM ALL, IF WE *WANT* THEM. RIGHT NOW.
WHAT?
ARE YOU SHITTING ME?
I SHIT THEE NOT, BOSS.
ONCE YOU SIGN THIS, YOU INSTANTLY COME INTO POSSESSION OF THE LARGEST BLOCK OF UN-ASSIGNED SOULS IN THE CELESTIAL UNIVERSE.
WHICH MEANS YOU *INSTANTLY* BECOME THE TOUGHEST GUY ON THE BLOCK.
WOW! LOOK AT ALL THOSE ZEROS. WHAT IS THAT NUMBER? MILLIONS? *HUNDREDS* OF MILLIONS?

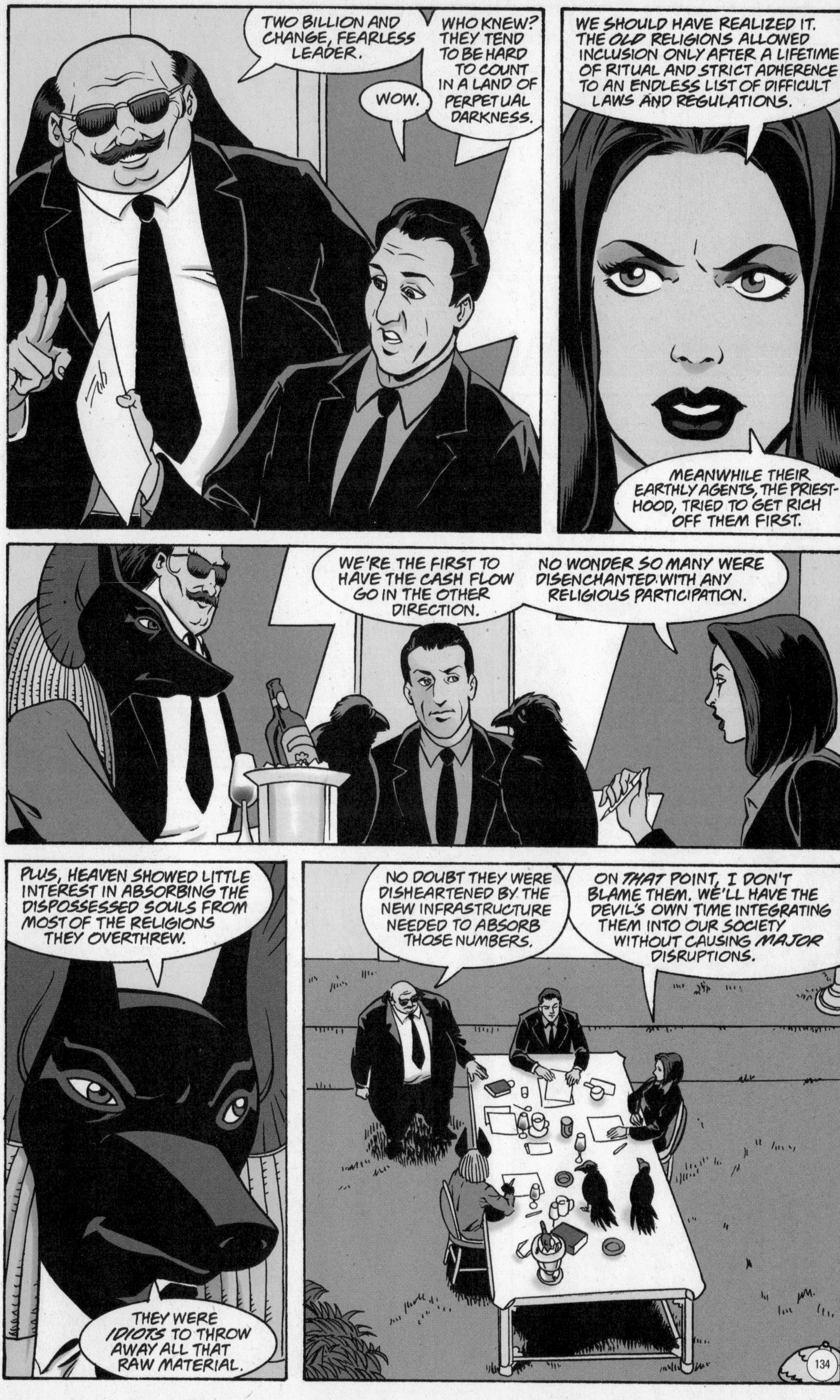
TWO BILLION AND CHANGE, FEARLESS LEADER.
WOW.
WHO KNEW? THEY TEND TO BE HARD TO COUNT IN A LAND OF PERPETUAL DARKNESS.
WE SHOULD HAVE REALIZED IT. THE OLD RELIGIONS ALLOWED INCLUSION ONLY AFTER A LIFETIME OF RITUAL AND STRICT ADHERENCE TO AN ENDLESS LIST OF DIFFICULT LAWS AND REGULATIONS.
MEANWHILE THEIR EARTHLY AGENTS, THE PRIESTHOOD, TRIED TO GET RICH OFF THEM FIRST.
WE'RE THE FIRST TO HAVE THE CASH FLOW GO IN THE OTHER DIRECTION.
NO WONDER SO MANY WERE DISENCHANTED WITH ANY RELIGIOUS PARTICIPATION.
PLUS, HEAVEN SHOWED LITTLE INTEREST IN ABSORBING THE DISPOSSESSED SOULS FROM MOST OF THE RELIGIONS THEY OVERTHREW.
THEY WERE IDIOTS TO THROW AWAY ALL THAT RAW MATERIAL.
NO DOUBT THEY WERE DISHEARTENED BY THE NEW INFRASTRUCTURE NEEDED TO ABSORB THOSE NUMBERS.
ON THAT POINT, I DON'T BLAME THEM. WE'LL HAVE THE DEVIL'S OWN TIME INTEGRATING THEM INTO OUR SOCIETY WITHOUT CAUSING MAJOR DISRUPTIONS.

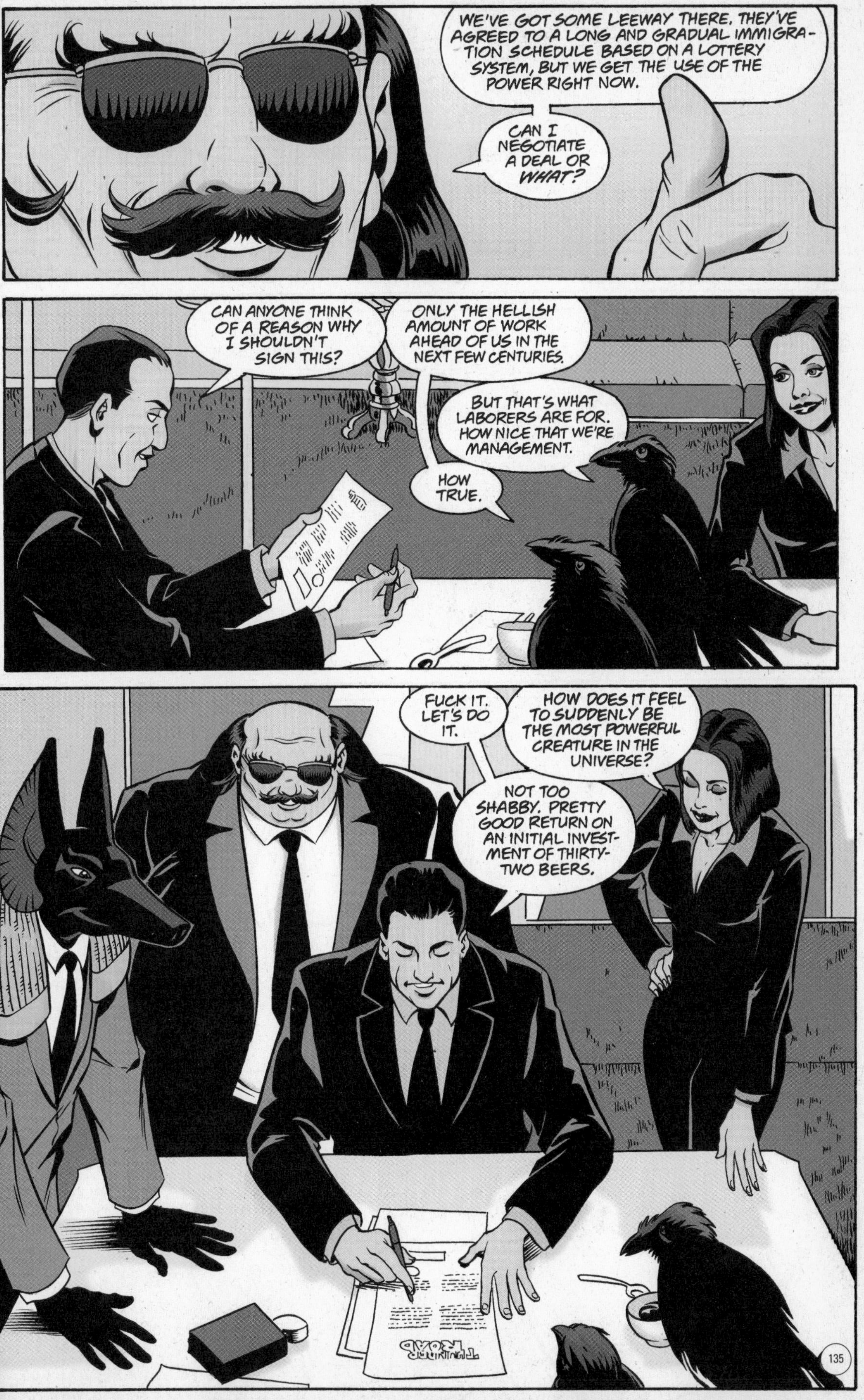
WE'VE GOT SOME LEEWAY THERE. THEY'VE AGREED TO A LONG AND GRADUAL IMMIGRA-TION SCHEDULE BASED ON A LOTTERY SYSTEM, BUT WE GET THE USE OF THE POWER RIGHT NOW.
CAN I NEGOTIATE A DEAL OR WHAT?
CAN ANYONE THINK OF A REASON WHY I SHOULDN'T SIGN THIS?
ONLY THE HELLISH AMOUNT OF WORK AHEAD OF US IN THE NEXT FEW CENTURIES.
BUT THAT'S WHAT LABORERS ARE FOR. HOW NICE THAT WE'RE MANAGEMENT.
HOW TRUE.
FUCK IT. LET'S DO IT.
HOW DOES IT FEEL TO SUDDENLY BE THE MOST POWERFUL CREATURE IN THE UNIVERSE?
NOT TOO SHABBY. PRETTY GOOD RETURN ON AN INITIAL INVEST-MENT OF THIRTY-TWO BEERS.

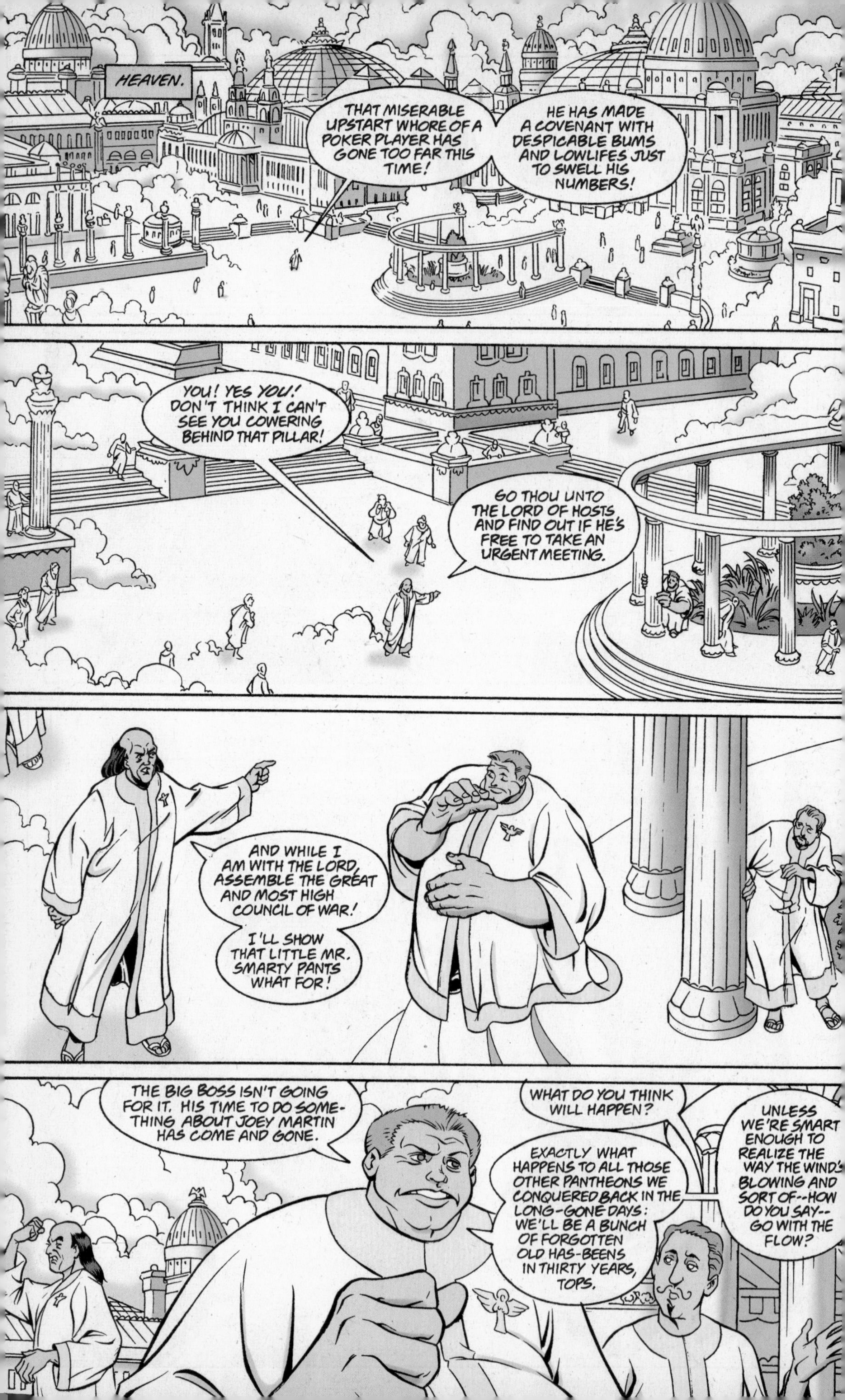
HEAVEN.
THAT MISERABLE UPSTART WHORE OF A POKER PLAYER HAS GONE TOO FAR THIS TIME!
HE HAS MADE A COVENANT WITH DESPICABLE BUMS AND LOWLIFES JUST TO SWELL HIS NUMBERS!
YOU! YES YOU! DON'T THINK I CAN'T SEE YOU COWERING BEHIND THAT PILLAR!
GO THOU UNTO THE LORD OF HOSTS AND FIND OUT IF HE'S FREE TO TAKE AN URGENT MEETING.
AND WHILE I AM WITH THE LORD, ASSEMBLE THE GREAT AND MOST HIGH COUNCIL OF WAR!
I'LL SHOW THAT LITTLE MR. SMARTY PANTS WHAT FOR!
THE BIG BOSS ISN'T GOING FOR IT. HIS TIME TO DO SOMETHING ABOUT JOEY MARTIN HAS COME AND GONE.
WHAT DO YOU THINK WILL HAPPEN?
EXACTLY WHAT HAPPENS TO ALL THOSE OTHER PANTHEONS WE CONQUERED BACK IN THE LONG-GONE DAYS: WE'LL BE A BUNCH OF FORGOTTEN OLD HAS-BEENS IN THIRTY YEARS, TOPS.
UNLESS WE'RE SMART ENOUGH TO REALIZE THE WAY THE WIND'S BLOWING AND SORT OF--HOW DO YOU SAY--GO WITH THE FLOW?

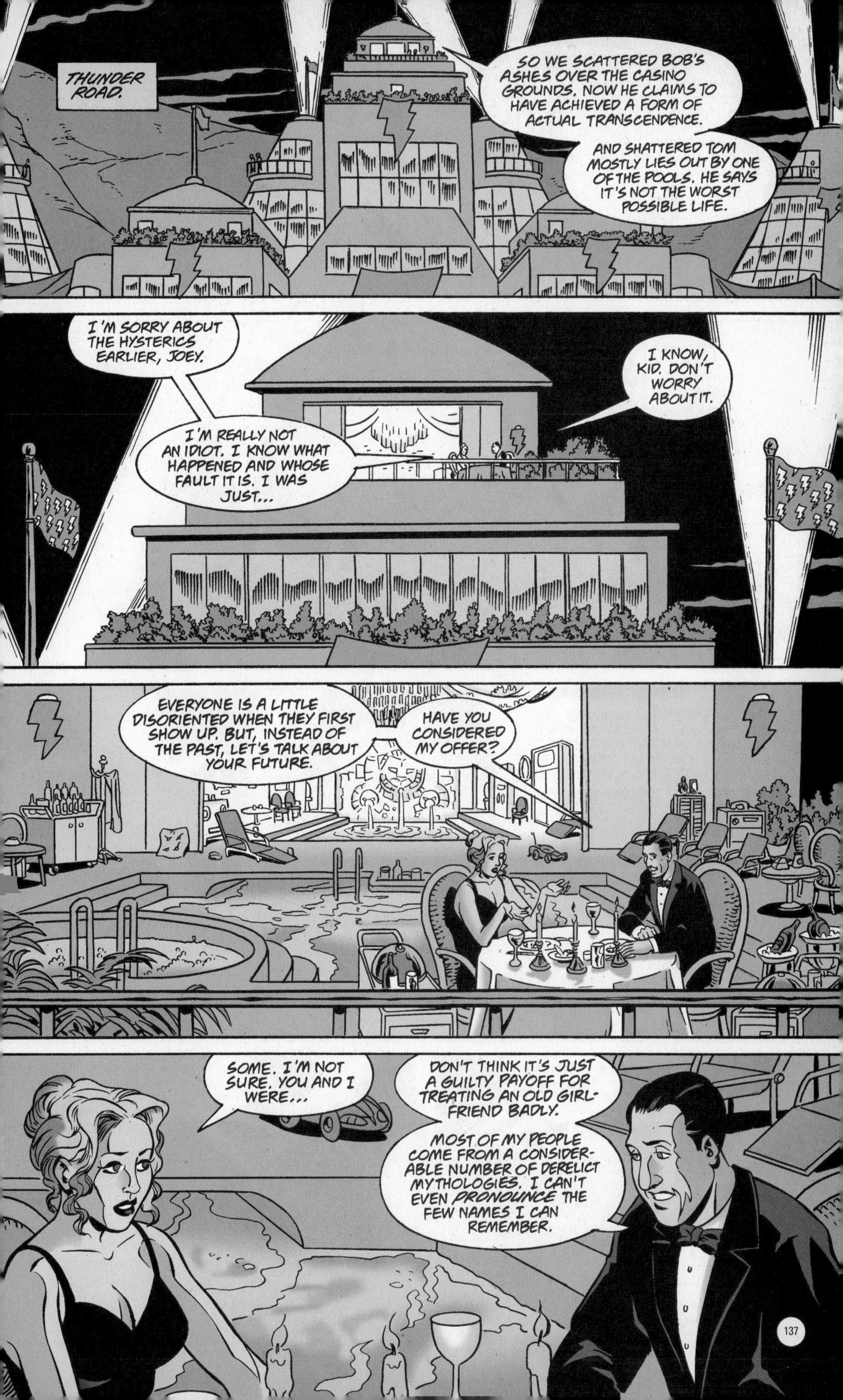

THUNDER ROAD.
SO WE SCATTERED BOB'S ASHES OVER THE CASINO GROUNDS. NOW HE CLAIMS TO HAVE ACHIEVED A FORM OF ACTUAL TRANSCENDENCE.
AND SHATTERED TOM MOSTLY LIES OUT BY ONE OF THE POOLS. HE SAYS IT'S NOT THE WORST POSSIBLE LIFE.
I'M SORRY ABOUT THE HYSTERICS EARLIER, JOEY.
I'M REALLY NOT AN IDIOT. I KNOW WHAT HAPPENED AND WHOSE FAULT IT IS. I WAS JUST...
I KNOW, KID. DON'T WORRY ABOUT IT.
EVERYONE IS A LITTLE DISORIENTED WHEN THEY FIRST SHOW UP. BUT, INSTEAD OF THE PAST, LET'S TALK ABOUT YOUR FUTURE.
HAVE YOU CONSIDERED MY OFFER?
SOME. I'M NOT SURE. YOU AND I WERE...
DON'T THINK IT'S JUST A GUILTY PAYOFF FOR TREATING AN OLD GIRL-FRIEND BADLY.
MOST OF MY PEOPLE COME FROM A CONSIDER-ABLE NUMBER OF DERELICT MYTHOLOGIES. I CAN'T EVEN *PRONOUNCE* THE FEW NAMES I CAN REMEMBER.

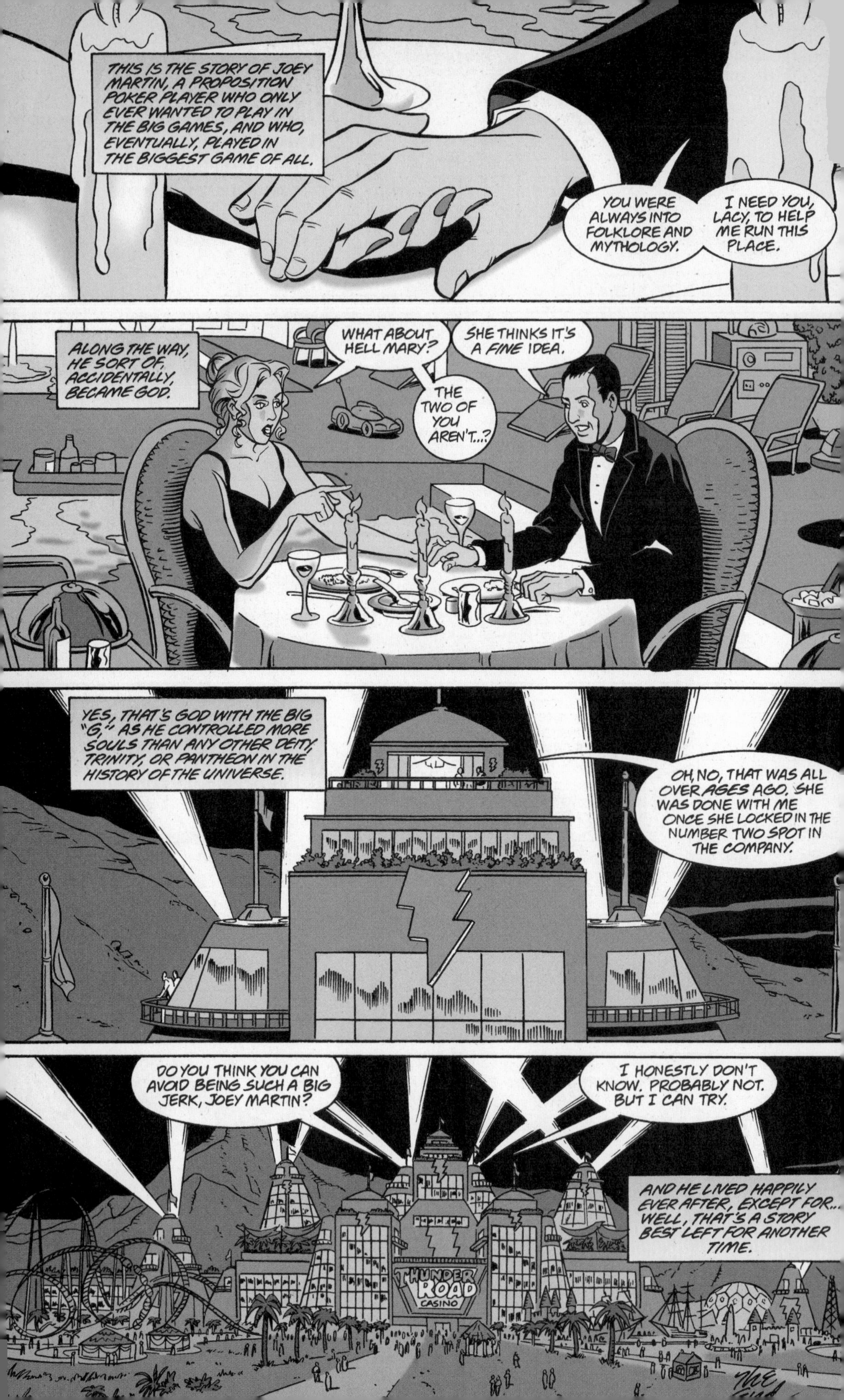
THIS IS THE STORY OF JOEY MARTIN, A PROPOSITION POKER PLAYER WHO ONLY EVER WANTED TO PLAY IN THE BIG GAMES, AND WHO, EVENTUALLY, PLAYED IN THE BIGGEST GAME OF ALL.
YOU WERE ALWAYS INTO FOLKLORE AND MYTHOLOGY.
I NEED YOU, LACY, TO HELP ME RUN THIS PLACE.
ALONG THE WAY, HE SORT OF, ACCIDENTALLY, BECAME GOD.
WHAT ABOUT HELL MARY?
SHE THINKS IT'S A FINE IDEA.
THE TWO OF YOU AREN'T...?
YES, THAT'S GOD WITH THE BIG "G," AS HE CONTROLLED MORE SOULS THAN ANY OTHER DEITY, TRINITY, OR PANTHEON IN THE HISTORY OF THE UNIVERSE.
OH, NO, THAT WAS ALL OVER AGES AGO. SHE WAS DONE WITH ME ONCE SHE LOCKED IN THE NUMBER TWO SPOT IN THE COMPANY.
DO YOU THINK YOU CAN AVOID BEING SUCH A BIG JERK, JOEY MARTIN?
I HONESTLY DON'T KNOW. PROBABLY NOT. BUT I CAN TRY.
AND HE LIVED HAPPILY EVER AFTER, EXCEPT FOR... WELL, THAT'S A STORY BEST LEFT FOR ANOTHER TIME.
THUNDER ROAD CASINO

PROPOSITION PLAYER #1 cover art by John Bolton

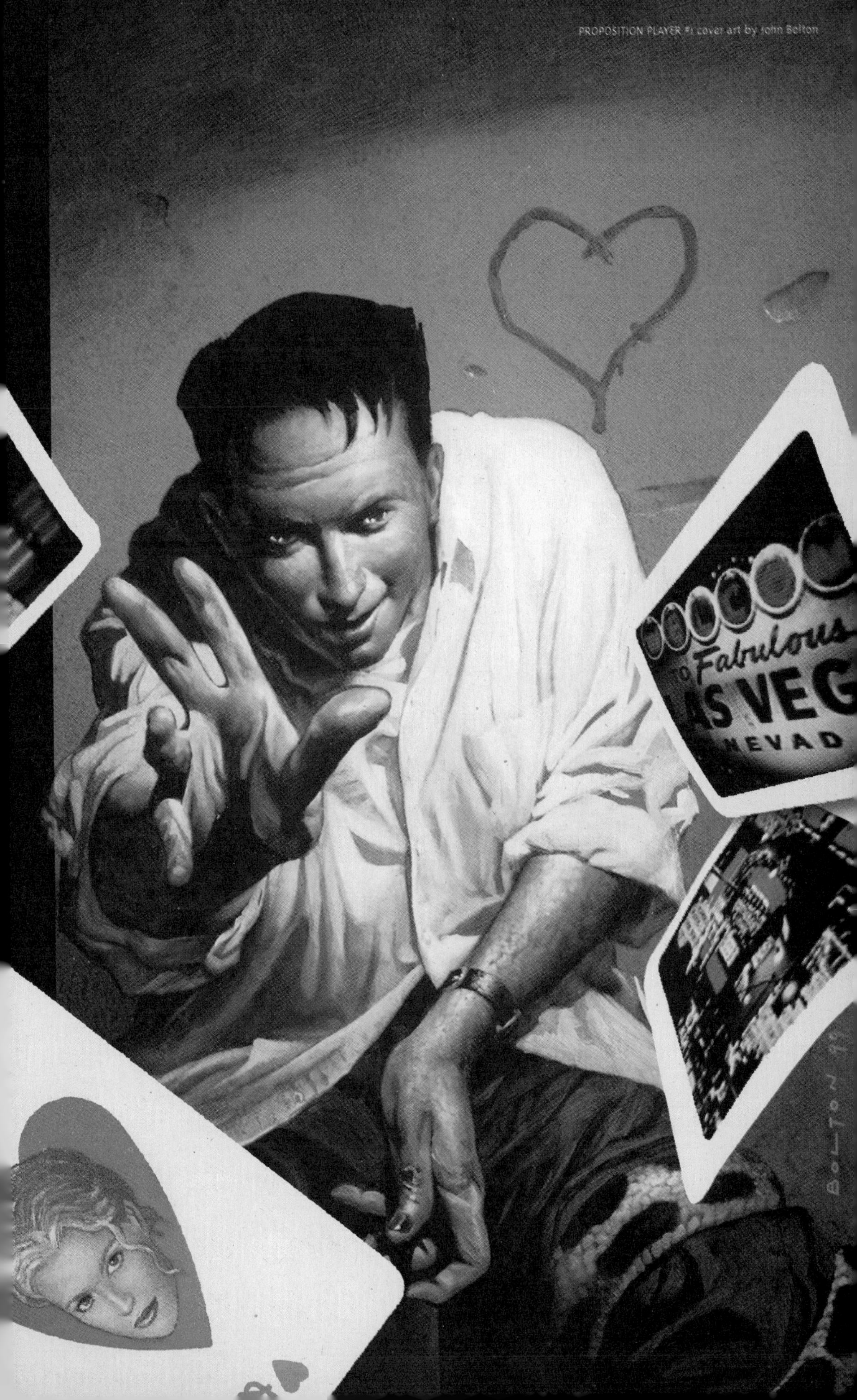

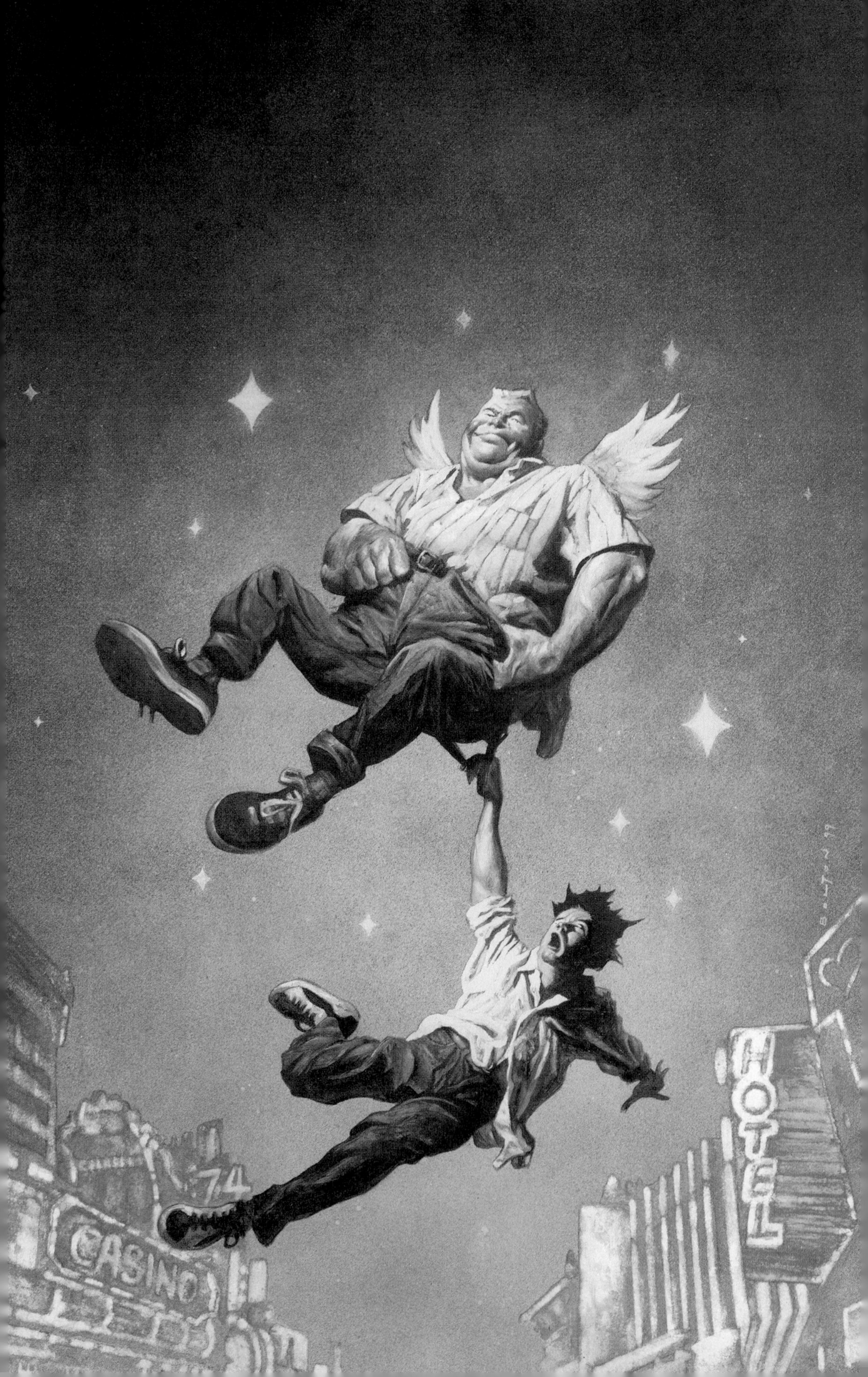
74
CASINO
HOTEL

PROPOSITION PLAYER #2 cover art by John Bolton

PROPOSITION PLAYER #3 cover art by John Bolton

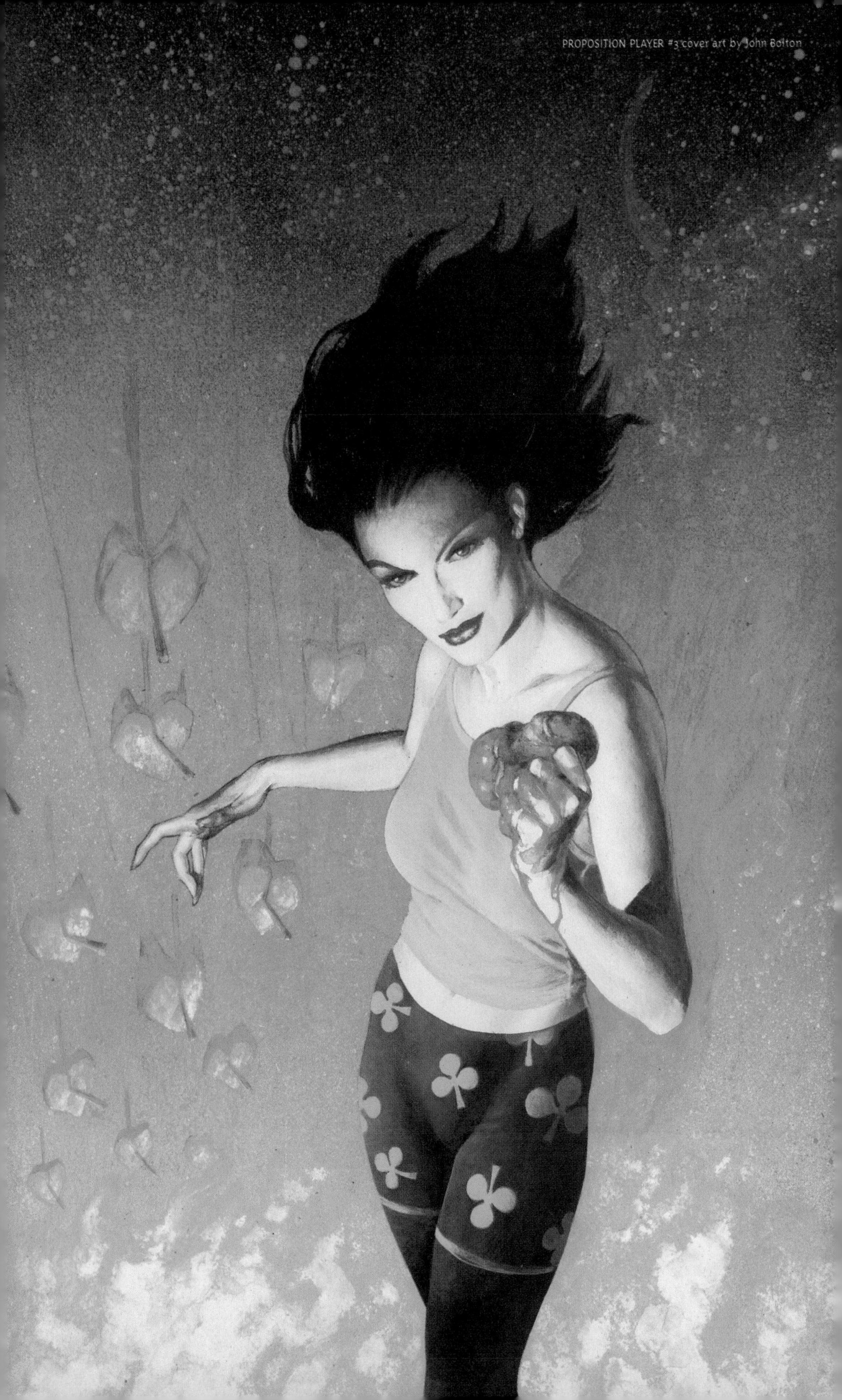

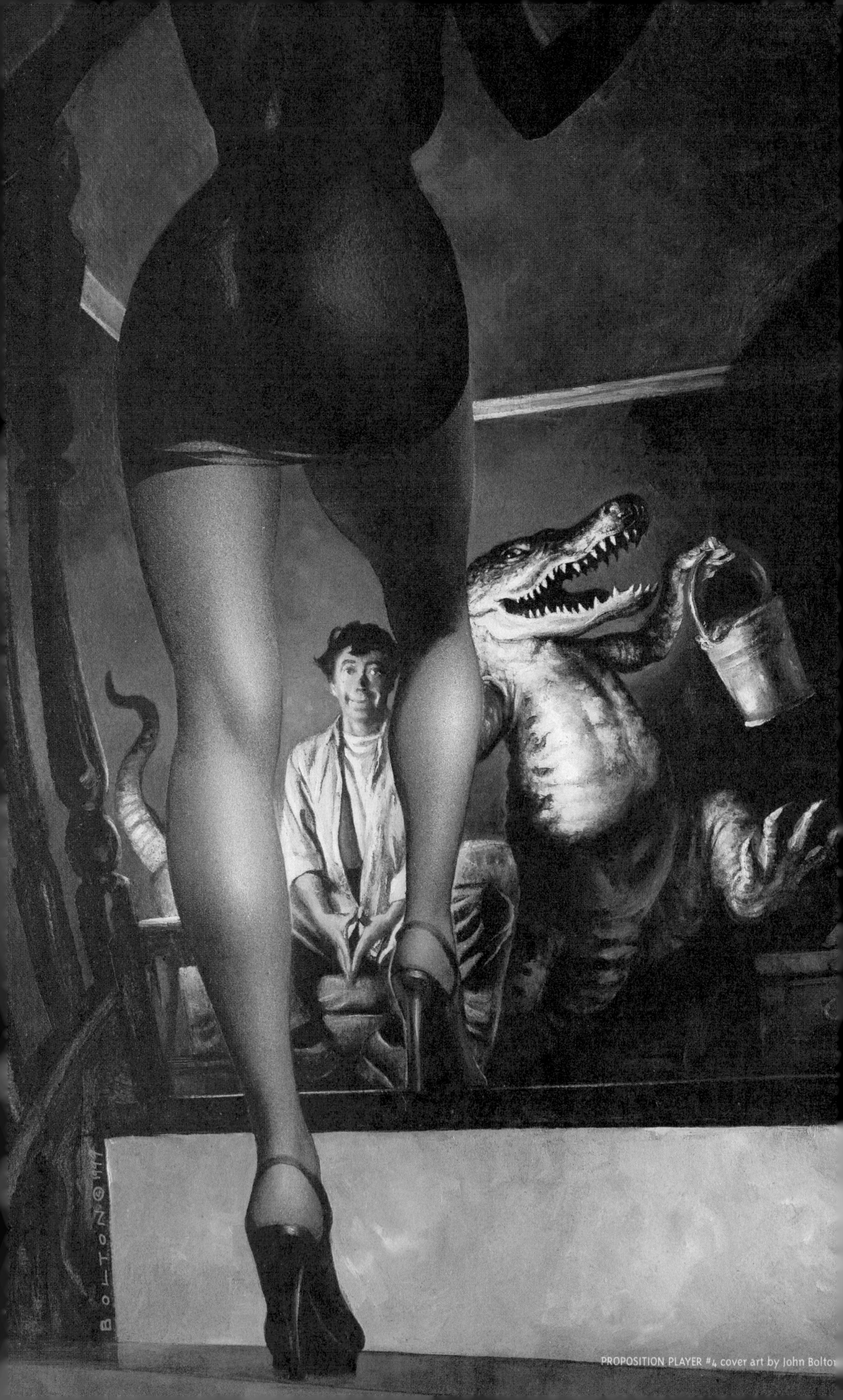

PROPOSITION PLAYER #4 cover art by John Bolton

PROPOSITION PLAYER #5 cover art by John Bolton

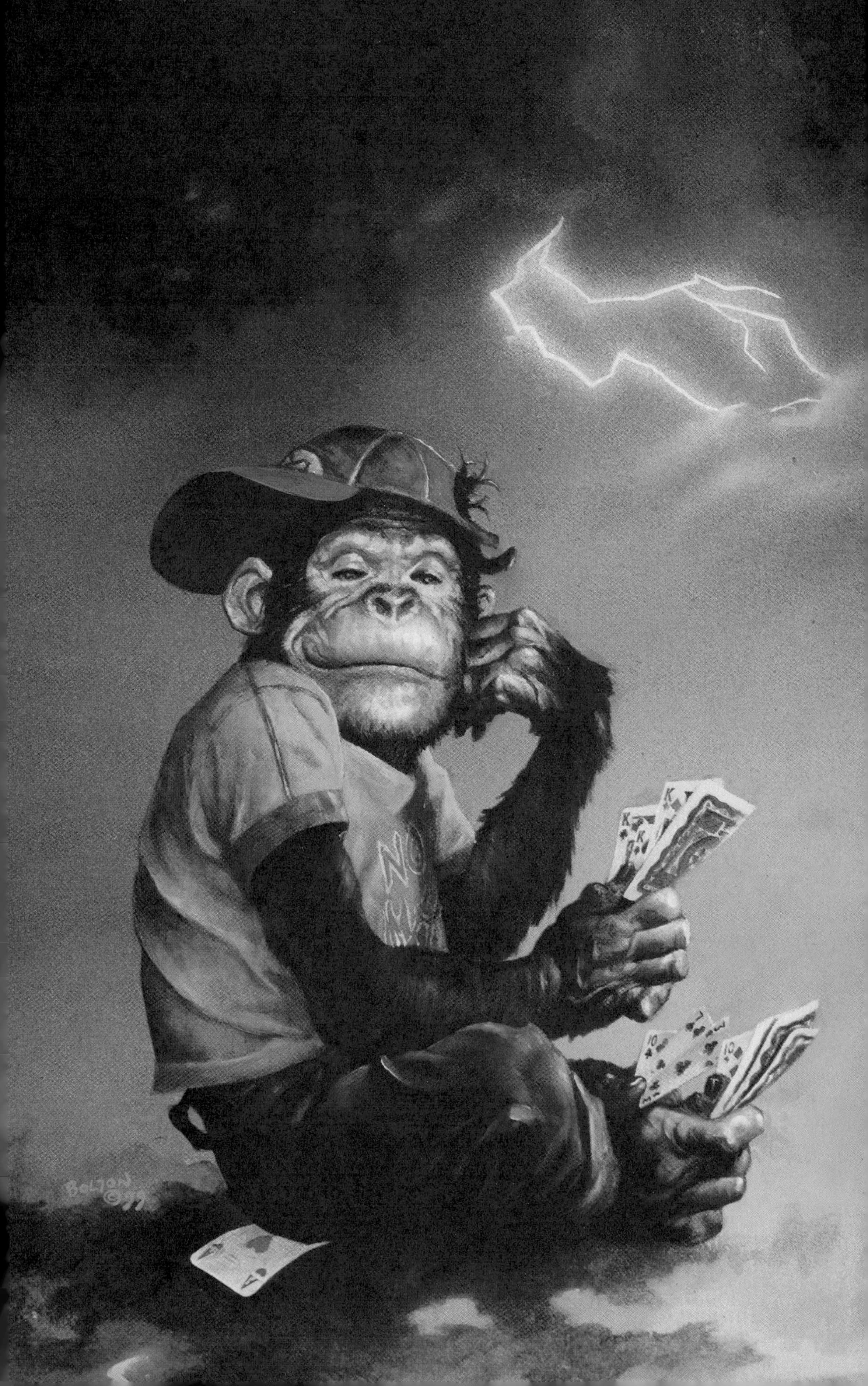
BOLTON
©99

PROPOSITION PLAYER #6 cover art by John Bolton

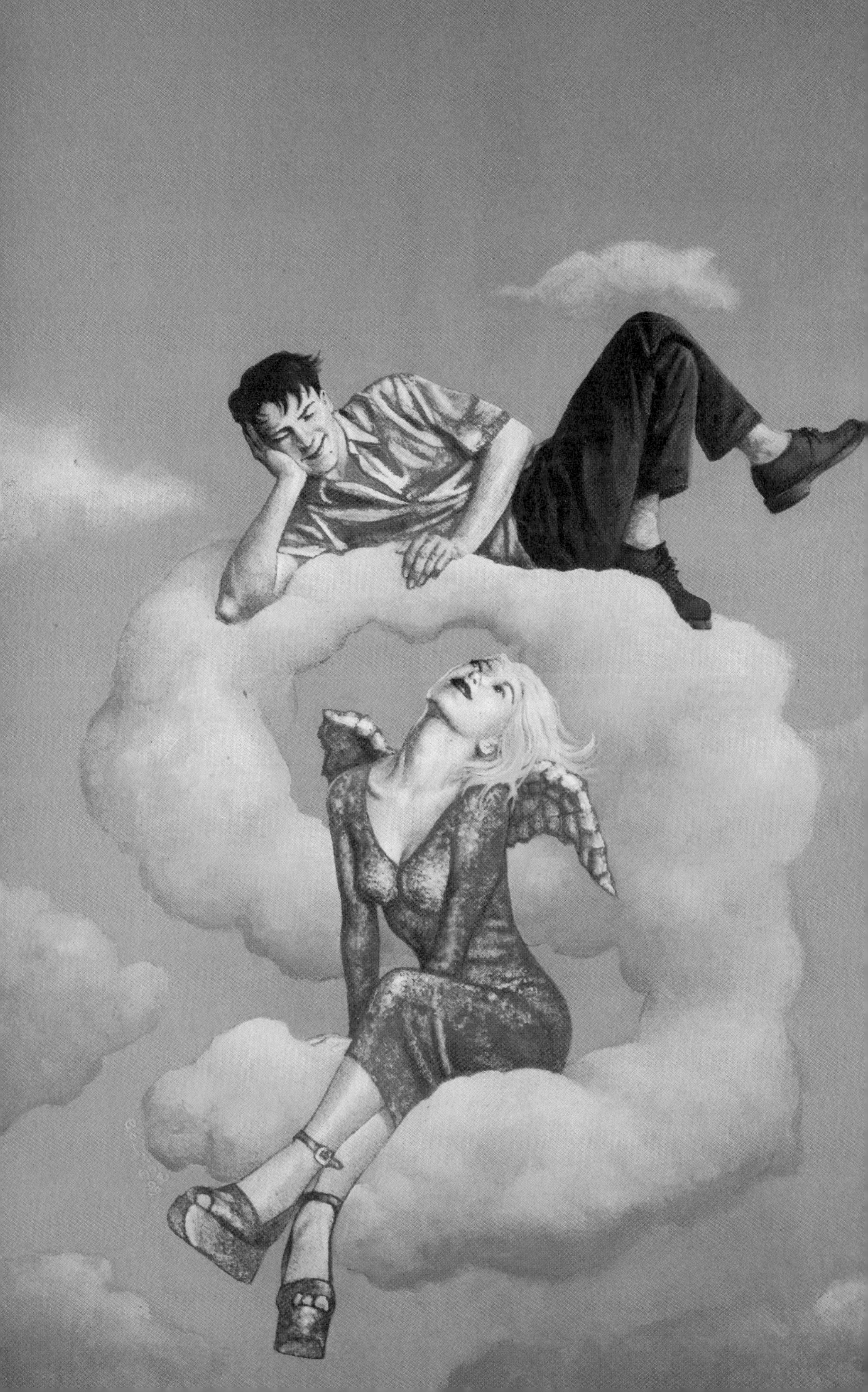